Library of Congress Cataloging in Publication Data

Nelson, Harold D.
   Area handbook for Senegal.

   ,"DA Pam 550-70."
   "One of a series of handbooks prepared by Foreign Area Studies (FAS) of the American University."
   Edition of 1963 prepared by the Foreign Area Studies Division of American University.
   Bibliography: pp. 353-383
   1. Senegal. I. American University, Washington, D.C. Foreign Area Studies. II. American University, Washington, D.C. Foreign Area Studies Division. Area handbook for Senegal. III. Title.
            DT549.N4 1974   **916.6′3′035**   **72-600061**

For sale by the Superintendent of Documents, U.S. Government Printing Office
Washington, D.C. 20402—Price $6.10

FOREWORD

This volume is one of a series of handbooks prepared by Foreign Area Studies (FAS) of The American University, designed to be useful to military and other personnel who need a convenient compilation of basic facts about the social, economic, political, and military institutions and practices of various countries. The emphasis is on objective description of the nation's present society and the kinds of possible or probable changes that might be expected in the future. The handbook seeks to present as full and as balanced an integrated exposition as limitations on space and research time permit. It was compiled from information available in openly published material. An extensive bibliography is provided to permit recourse to other published sources for more detailed information. There has been no attempt to express any specific point of view or to make policy recommendations. The contents of the handbook represent the work of the authors and FAS and do not represent the official view of the United States government.

An effort has been made to make the handbook as comprehensive as possible. It can be expected, however, that the material, interpretations, and conclusions are subject to modification in the light of new information and developments. Such corrections, additions, and suggestions for factual, interpretive, or other change as readers may have will be welcomed for use in future revisions. Comments may be addressed to:

The Director
Foreign Area Studies
The American University
5010 Wisconsin Avenue, N.W.
Washington, D.C. 20016

PREFACE

Senegal, an African republic that gained full independence only in 1960, owes its existence more to political action than to cultural and social forces. Foreign colonial power—that of France—brought Senegal's various peoples together as a territorial group under Western influence. In little more than a decade of sovereignty, the Senegalese government has moved with some progress toward its goal of creating a modern unified nation from the colonial past.

When the first edition of the *Area Handbook for Senegal* was written in 1963, the continuous process of interaction between the new and the old within the young republic was only beginning to form a coherent national pattern out of the people's differing attitudes, values, and institutions. Although Senegalese development has been gradual, much of the specific information in the earlier handbook has been modified by subsequent events. Moreover, the later publication of the results of research by a number of social scientists permits a more recent picture of the country and its people.

The first edition of the handbook was prepared by a research team composed of Irving Kaplan, Barbara Lent, Dennis H. Morrissey, Charles Townsend, and Neda Franges Walpole under the chairmanship of T. D. Roberts. The revised edition, in a shorter and somewhat different form, seeks—like the earlier work—to provide a compact and objective exposition of the dominant social, political, and economic aspects of Senegalese society. It is designed to give the reader an understanding of the forces operating within the society. There remain, however, a number of gaps in information to which attention has been called.

The spelling of Senegalese terms, proper names, and Arabic words conforms to current usage in the country. An exception is made in the case of words of Arabic origin that appear in *Webster's New Collegiate Dictionary* (abridged). Such words appearing in this handbook retain their anglicized spelling. Unless otherwise noted, the metric system has been used for tonnages. Currency conversion factors appear in the Glossary, which is included as an appendix for the reader's convenience.

COUNTRY SUMMARY

1. COUNTRY: Formal name, Republic of Senegal; short form, Senegal; former member of Mali Federation, which negotiated independence from France on April 4, 1960; federation broke up on August 20, 1960, when Senegal seceded and proclaimed itself a republic; April 4 is celebrated as independence day. National capital, Dakar.

2. SIZE: 76,000 square miles; maximum north-south width, 285 miles; east-west length, 360 miles.

3. TOPOGRAPHY: A flat savanna plain extending inland from westernmost point of Africa; elevations more than 300 feet above sea level only in southeast; long coastline on Atlantic Ocean marked by three major estuaries and Cap Vert peninsula. Major rivers are sluggish; shallow estuaries extend deep inland.

4. CLIMATE: Tropical subdesert regime with distinct wet (summer) and dry (winter) seasons; rainfall varies from moderately heavy in south to light and erratic in north. Temperatures range from warm to hot throughout year; temperatures along northwest coast slightly reduced by cool winds from Atlantic Ocean.

5. POPULATION: Estimated at 4 million in 1973; annual growth rate 1.93 percent. Rural densities much greater in western one-quarter of country; most major towns also located in this area; very low densities in subdesert eastern and northeastern areas. Fifteen percent of population lives in Dakar. Six African ethnic groups constitute 90 percent of population; most share many similar cultural values. Europeans, mostly French, form slightly more than 1 percent of population; most live in Dakar.

6. LANGUAGES: Major languages are Wolof, Serer, Pulaar (language of the Peul), Manding, Diola, and Sarakolé. Official language is French, which is dominant in government, commerce, and mass media. Wolof is widely understood.

7. RELIGION: Estimated that more than 80 percent of all Senegalese are Muslims; approximately 6 percent are Christians; remainder adhere to indigenous religious beliefs and practices.

8. EDUCATION: In 1973 about 40 percent of school-age population attended school; roughly 25 percent of all elementary students and 13 percent of all secondary students attended private schools. Educational advancement limited by shortage of qualified teachers, especially in vocational training. Educational reforms of secondary and higher

educational systems underway. Number of students graduating from University of Dakar increasing. In 1970 literacy rate estimated at between 5 and 10 percent for population aged fourteen years and over; lowest rates in rural areas.

9. HEALTH: Most major epidemic diseases with high death rates, such as smallpox and yellow fever, suppressed by preventive medicine programs, but sporadic outbreaks occur. High incidence of nutritional and infectious diseases in 1973 reflected inadequate diets, insufficient modern medical care, contaminated water supplies, and lack of knowledge of hygiene and sanitation. Malaria, tuberculosis, schistosomiasis, gastroenteric infections, and influenza particularly prevalent; other diseases included encephalomyelitis, hepatitis, venereal infections, tetanus, and leprosy. Mass preventive medicine programs being increased in 1973.

10. GOVERNMENT: Constitution of 1963 transformed government into presidential system in which almost all power is in national administration. In 1973 President Léopold-Sédar Senghor directed the government, assisted by prime minister and cabinet; both selected by president. Legislature consisted of 100-member unicameral National Assembly, elected by universal adult suffrage at same time as president. For administrative purposes country divided into seven regions, each headed by a governor appointed by and responsible to the national executive. Governing political party founded in 1948 and led by President Senghor; political skills of leadership and lack of significant opposition have resulted in a de facto one-party state.

11. JUSTICE: Independent judiciary and considerable protection of civil rights provided by constitution. Legal system has French origins but considerably modified; law based on codes, as in French system. Highest court is Supreme Court, whose judges are presidentially appointed; responsible for rulings on constitutionality of laws and international agreements; three separate sections, one of which serves as court of final appeal in civil and criminal matters. Below Supreme Court, judicial system has three levels of courts.

12. ECONOMY: Relatively well developed but largely stagnant during 1960s as recurrent droughts interrupted growth; manufacturing recovered from initial loss of markets and expanded rapidly, as did fishing. Small-scale peasant cultivation predominates, mainly groundnuts (peanuts) for export and food grains for subsistence. Dependence on France declining since mid-1960s, but French ownership still predominant in private business.

13. PRINCIPAL EXPORTS: Groundnut oil and feed cakes; phosphates and phosphate fertilizers; canned fish.

14. PRINCIPAL IMPORTS: Rice, sugar, other foodstuffs; machinery and transport equipment; intermediate materials for industry.

15. CURRENCY: African Financial Community franc (Communauté

Financière Africaine franc—CFAF) tied to French franc (CFAF50 equal 1 French franc). Exchange rates determined by relative values of French franc and United States dollar. Exchange rates per United States dollar were: from 1958 through 1968, CFAF246.8; from August 10, 1969 through November 1971, CFAF277.8; from December 1971 through January 1973, CFAF255.79; after February 1973, CFAF230.2.

16. COMMUNICATIONS: Postal service and domestic telephone and telegraph service provided by central government; international telecommunications service by mixed government-private firm. Telecommunications network being modernized in 1973. Overseas connections via France and telecommunications satellite. Government-owned and -operated radio was most effective of modern mass media. Government-owned television in Dakar; one daily newspaper, various weekly publications and professional periodicals.

17. RAILROADS: 640-mile meter-gauge railroad system handles most freight traffic, including trade from abroad to neighboring Mali and Mauritania. Rail network well developed in western half of country; single line through sparsely populated east.

18. INLAND WATERWAYS: Limited barge traffic along border on Sénégal River, only seasonally navigable.

19. PORTS: Well-developed international port at Dakar handles much transit traffic as well as more than 90 percent of country's own foreign trade. International Bank for Reconstruction and Development (IBRD—also known as the World Bank) credit for supertanker drydock at Dakar approved mid-1973.

20. ROADS: About 1,400 miles of paved roads and 2,100 miles of intermittently maintained gravel and dirt roads. Most roads old and poorly maintained. Network basically sound in west; provides main links to other regions. Rural feeder roads inadequate.

21. CIVIL AVIATION: Yoff International Airport at Dakar can accommodate long-range jets, is important stop for international flights between Europe and South America; seventeen international air carriers use it regularly; runway may be extended. Sixteen other minor airfields take domestic passenger flights.

22. INTERNATIONAL MEMBERSHIPS AND AGREEMENTS: Member of United Nations (UN) and its specialized agencies, including Economic Commission for Africa (ECA). Within Africa, member of Organization of African Unity (OAU) and its African Liberation Committee; African, Malagasy, and Mauritius Common Organization (Organisation Commune Àfricaine, Malgache, et Mauricienne— OCAM); West African Economic Community (Communauté Economique de l'Afrique de l'Ouest—CEAO); West African Monetary Union (Union Monétaire Ouest-Africaine—UMOA); and majority of specialized inter-African technical bodies. Member of franc area (see Glossary), having monetary and other cooperation agreements with

France. In 1973 member of eighteen-nation group of African and Malagasy Associates (Etats Africains et Malgaches Associés—EAMA)
of European Economic Community (EEC, known as the Common Market). New and expanded version of EAMA was under negotiation.

23. SECURITY FORCES: In 1973 military forces numbered about
6,000 men, mostly ground troops, plus 200-man air force and 150-man
navy. Training based on French philosophies. France provided equipment and technical support, but military aid had been reduced after
1970. Paramilitary forces included 1,600-man National Gendarmerie
and about 3,600 civil police.

SENEGAL

TABLE OF CONTENTS

LIST OF ILLUSTRATIONS

LIST OF TABLES

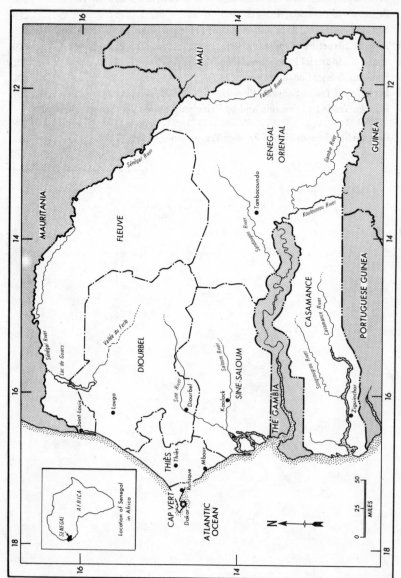

Figure 1. The Republic of Senegal

SECTION I. SOCIAL

CHAPTER 1

GENERAL CHARACTER OF THE SOCIETY

The Republic of Senegal is one of the recently emergent African states that became political entities for the first time as a result of colonial partitions of the continent during the eighteenth and nineteenth centuries and that ultimately gained independence when France relinquished most of its holdings south of the Sahara in the early 1960s (see ch. 2). It was the first French colony in Africa and for many years was the base for French penetration and development in West Africa. When it emerged as a sovereign state in 1960, the country was one of the world's leading producers of groundnuts (peanuts) and had a more advanced economy than any of its immediate neighbors. Its sophisticated leadership, trained for several generations in French schools and political institutions, maintained friendly ties with France. At that time Dakar, the national capital, was the intellectual center for most of French-speaking Africa.

Geographically, the country occupies the westernmost tip of Africa, where the continent bulges outward into the Atlantic Ocean (see fig. 1). Its 260 miles of coastline extend roughly north and south, and the land boundaries converge like the sides of a broad wedge to a point some 360 miles inland, covering an area of about 76,000 square miles. The continuity of the southern half is broken by the independent country of The Gambia. Formerly a British colony, the narrow enclave extends eastward from the coast more than halfway across the enveloping Senegalese republic. In addition to The Gambia, Senegal shares borders with Mauritania, Mali, Guinea, and Portuguese Guinea (see ch. 3).

Dakar, at the tip of Cap Vert peninsula, is a large modern city with a fine seaport, a first-class international airport, and adjoining industrial and residential developments that have extended throughout much of Cap Vert Region. The capital is linked to a rather barren hinterland by a rail system and highways that reach the few main towns but serve little of the eastern half of the country (see ch. 15).

Urbanization is proceeding rapidly, but most of the towns of importance are in the west, within 100 miles of the coast. This is also the area where the rural population is most dense. In contrast, some regions far inland are almost uninhabited. Except near Dakar and the larger

1

towns, most of the people live in small scattered villages or agricultural settlements and, like their ancestors, gain a livelihood from the land.

Ethnic diversity characterizes the population, which approximated 4 million inhabitants in 1973. The Senegalese people are divided into a dozen or so African ethnic groups, each of which has its own customs and language (see ch. 4). The largest single group is that of the Wolof, who constitute over one-third of the population. Their language has come into rather general use and is more or less understood by two-thirds of the Senegalese. Although there is general recognition of ethnic affiliation, the differences cause no serious friction. The different groups have lived together peaceably for several generations and have intermingled to some extent. The greater part of the non-African residents are Europeans—primarily French—and Lebanese, most of whom live in Dakar and other urban centers, where they are engaged in business or the professions.

Islam is professed by more than 80 percent of the population, including practically all the Wolof, and is widely diffused among many of the other peoples, especially in the northern half of the country. The Muslim faithful are divided into a number of brotherhoods that are based not only on sectarian differences but also, at least partly, on ethnic lines. Some of the brotherhoods have a good deal of economic and political power. Approximately 6 percent of the people are Christians, mostly Roman Catholics, but they are heavily represented among the educated elite. The remainder of the Senegalese adhere to indigenous religious beliefs and practices. Although Senegal is predominantly Muslim, it is a secular state and is tolerant of all faiths. The constitution guarantees freedom of religion and provides for separation of church and government. Nevertheless, political leaders take careful account of the interests of religious institutions and groups when formulating policies and programs (see ch. 7; ch. 10).

The long history of French rule set in motion forces that brought about many changes in the country's economic and social life within the span of a few generations. The changes continued, and traditional and modern elements act on each other constantly to form new situations and create new social pressures. Few people have not been affected—directly or indirectly—by economic development, modern innovations, or Western education. Social and cultural change has weakened the traditional views and moral sanctions and has developed new ones. Therefore, there is some clash of values between persons of separate generations or of different backgrounds. Many of the younger generation who have had some education have come to question their status and to doubt the authority of age and custom. The most urgent challenge has come from university students who oppose the continued French influence in the fields of education and the national economy. The family remains a fairly stable element in the rural areas, but many have abandoned the traditional setting in answer to the challenge of life in the cities. New social and political groups are developing in response to the strains engendered by the process of modernization (see ch. 5).

Those most affected by change are the educated elite of government and the professions—a group substantially influenced by European culture—and a growing number of workers who have made their homes in the urban areas. The mass of the people still respond mostly to traditional values and follow much the same life as did their forefathers. Thus, a wide gap has developed between the world view and mode of life of the small urbanized elite and those of the vast majority of the people, a situation that hinders the emergence of a cohesive nation-state.

The traditional social structure based on kinship and on a rigid stratification remains important but is being modified by the spread of education and by increased economic opportunity, the population movement toward the urban and industrial centers, and the extension of the cash economy to remote regions. In the rural areas the bonds of kinship and the sanctions and security of communal living centered in villages remain fairly effective. In the fast-growing urban centers, however, the scope of kinship rights and obligations has been narrowed, and the body of kin included has been reduced. Status distinctions based on occupation and education have emerged, but these factors have not completely superseded the older system of status ranking, nor have they resulted in a system of social classes. On the other hand, kinship and other traditional ties often are converted to use in newer groups that compete for status and power.

In 1973 the country's political life was dominated by President Léopold-Sédar Senghor, who had remained in power as chief executive during the entire thirteen years of Senegalese independence. A statesman of great personal popularity, educated in French universities, and a poet and an intellectual of international stature, he had become a leading political figure south of the Sahara by 1948 and guided his country to sovereignty. Senghor's executive authority was underscored by strong powers bestowed by constitutional provisions. Much of his public appeal, however, lay in his mastery of the tactics of political coalition and in his ability to balance and reconcile the traditional interests and modern forces that swayed the country's society. Although his appeal did not extend to all Senegalese—particularly the young intellectuals at the University of Dakar—it was a reliable commodity among the masses, who faithfully responded to the efforts of local ethnic and religious leaders at election time to keep him in office. In 1973, for example, he was continued in power for a third five-year term by over 97 percent of the country's registered voters (see ch. 10).

Although opposition political parties were not illegal, the republic was, in effect, a one-party state. The president had the power to ban opposition political organizations, but he has usually found it more effective to persuade opposition members to join his party. Thus the Senegalese Progressive Union (Union Progressiste Sénégalaise—UPS) has long been the party of government, a legacy that has persisted over the years after its founding by Senghor. The structures and practices of government were based on French models, and the country had several bilateral assistance and other agreements with France. It employed French technical experts and advisers in the government service and in private industry, although a policy of their ultimate replacement by Senegalese nationals was receiving priority attention in the early 1970s.

The UPS is a moderate party that advocates a form of socialism based on traditional African communal institutions. In practice, however, the government leaves considerable scope to private enterprise, including foreign investment in commerce and light industry. Political opposition has come more frequently in recent years from students at the country's single university. A student strike in 1968, accompanied by rioting in Dakar and a general strike called by the national labor union, was followed by military occupation of the university (see ch. 10; ch. 16). The university was reopened later, but a less violent repeat performance occurred in 1969, leading to reforms in the educational system; improvements in the conditions of urban labor; and the placing of younger men in party and government jobs. Although the government's concessions to students and labor diminished the more active forms of political opposition somewhat, the students remained a source of potential unrest in 1973.

Political strife has seldom threatened the stability of the Senegalese government. Late in 1962, however, President Senghor successfully coped with a serious intraparty crisis that culminated in an attempt by his longtime political associate, Prime Minister Mamadou Dia, to take control of the National Assembly by armed force. The crisis arose from differences between those in the government who wanted to hasten economic development and modernization at any social cost and Senghor's faction, who did not want to risk alienating the more conservative traditional elements in the society and who thought it best to seek the goals more gradually. The power play by Dia was defeated, and actions to consolidate the president's executive powers were instituted. A decade later, however, the basic differences between these two factions remained a fundamental political and social issue.

Senegal's foreign policy, like other aspects of its political and economic life, bear the unmistakable stamp of President Senghor's personality and political philosophy. Basic to his government's relations with other countries are the principle of nonalignment; the belief that international problems should be resolved through peaceful means; and a conviction that Senegal should cooperate with all countries, regardless of political persuasions. Having long been exposed to French

4

cultural life and values, Senghor has remained a loyal supporter of France, although in the early 1970s he was not entirely uncritical of some of that country's policies (see ch. 11).

Senegal gained independence from France in an atmosphere of general goodwill and cooperation. Throughout the 1960s a prime objective of Senegalese foreign policy was the maintenance of close cultural, economic, and personal ties with France. The new government regarded France as an equal partner in a relationship that was mutually beneficial to both countries but that did not preclude bilateral arrangements with other powers and friendly relations with all.

Despite the failure of an earlier political federation with Mali, the ideal of African unity remains alive in Senegal (see ch. 2). Senghor and his UPS party regard unity as an ultimate goal, but one to be reached by first perfecting less ambitious arrangements for close economic and technical cooperation among states sharing common backgrounds and interests. As a result, over the years Senegal has led or joined a number of regional groups, such as the African, Malagasy, and Mauritius Common Organization (Organisation Commune Africaine, Malgache, et Mauricienne—OCAM), the Organization for Development of the Sénégal River (Organisation pour la Mise en Valeur du Fleuve Sénégal—OMVS), and the West African Monetary Union (Union Monétaire Ouest-Africaine—UMOA). On an even broader scale the Senegalese take an active part in the Organization of African Unity (OAU) and the United Nations and most of its specialized agencies.

By the early 1970s there were indications that Senghor was interested in lessening to some degree his country's ties with France in favor of reliance on a more diversified range of bilateral and multilateral sources of trade and aid. He was also seeking to strengthen the existing political and economic links with West African neighbors through gradually extended regional cooperation. The nucleus of the expanding region he foresees is the West African Economic Community (Communauté Economique de l'Afrique de l'Ouest—CEAO), scheduled to begin operating in January 1974. The CEAO, which counts as members the countries of former French West Africa (Afrique Occidentale Française—AOF) and Togo, aims at restoring some measure of the economic integration that had existed during the area's colonial era. Balanced economic development throughout the region through mutual assistance is the ultimate goal.

Concern for equitable solutions to the problems created by their strange geographic juxtaposition has long underlain relations between Senegal and The Gambia. Both the Senegalese and Gambian leaders have often expressed a favorable attitude toward ultimate unification, but they have been able to agree only on a limited course in this direction. Throughout the early 1970s relations between the two countries remained largely static.

During its short period of independence, Senegal has persistently voiced strong opposition toward the white minority regimes in Portuguese African provinces, in Rhodesia, and in South Africa. Relations with its southern neighbor, Portuguese Guinea, had been affected adversely by frequent incursions upon Senegalese territory by Portuguese troops engaged in retaliatory action against insurgent forces of Portuguese Guinea who sought refuge in southern Senegal (see ch. 11; ch. 16).

In 1973 the Senegalese government was more concerned with the economy than with political affairs. The country has a growing processing industry, and commercial fishing is expanding rapidly; the economy, however, is founded basically on agriculture (see ch. 13). Over three-fourths of the people live off the land, and agricultural products not only account for most of the export trade but also form the basis for a substantial part of the country's industrial strength and domestic commerce. Groundnuts are by far the main cash crop, and most of the production is for export. For some years groundnuts and their associated products enjoyed a guaranteed market in France at artificially high prices. When this arrangement ended in the late 1960s, prices became uncertain, and fluctuating output resulted in serious effects on the country's foreign exchange position and individual farm incomes. Efforts at crop diversification in the early 1970s had yet to affect more than about 5 percent of the country's farmers (see ch. 14).

Raising staples for the primary purpose of feeding the producing family unit has always been an important means of livelihood for the majority of the people, but most produce at least one cash crop, usually groundnuts. In 1973 pockets of exclusive subsistence production were disappearing. As urbanization increased in the 1960s and early 1970s, the surplus food grain production of traditional cultivators was increasingly inadequate to meet the growing demand. Domestic food production failed to meet the country's needs, and staple foodstuffs had to be imported in large quantities.

Senegal depends on importing most of the manufactured goods it requires. Except for construction and service enterprises, the country's industrial sector is mainly involved in processing or extracting primary products for export. Many of the enterprises that manufacture for domestic consumption and for the nearby West African markets have to import most of their raw materials. Indications point to continued industrial growth, but the rate is dependent on success in expanding regional markets.

The close financial and commercial relations with France that existed before 1960 were not materially changed when Senegal became independent. Because of membership in a monetary union of former AOF territories in association with France, the Senegalese currency is tied to and supported by the French franc, with guarantees of convertibility. Public and private funds from France continue to supply a large part of the investment capital needed to develop the country. The Senegalese government, however, is seeking to broaden its trade relations and sources of investment capital (see ch. 15).

Since independence Senegal has experienced difficulty in achieving an adequate rate of economic growth to support national development (see ch. 13). Ever-increasing economic pressures have arisen from over-population and soil depletion in the most productive agricultural areas, and increasing urbanization has resulted in high rates of unemployment and underemployment. The effects of heavy dependence on a single crop—groundnuts—during the 1960s also contributed to retarded economic growth. Moreover, the country was suffering from increasing chronic balance-of-payments problems.

In 1972 economic reforms had produced a dramatic improvement in agricultural production, and there was an accelerated rate of growth in the fishing and manufacturing sectors. Despite this favorable trend, however, continued success of the government's economic policy has been challenged by the devastating effects of the worst drought in sixty years, which has permeated the Sahel and Sudan ecological zones of Africa (see ch. 3; ch. 14). Although Senegal has not suffered as severely as have the other five African countries affected by this widespread natural catastrophe, the drought will have long-term cumulative consequences in terms of water supplies, permanent loss of natural vegetation for livestock grazing, and a continuing influx of rural inhabitants to the urban centers in search of relief.

CHAPTER 2

HISTORICAL SETTING

Although the history of Senegal as a political entity dates from 1920, when the colony and the protectorate of Senegal were joined under a single, uniform administration, the area possessed a well-established history of structured political interaction. Included in such a tradition were the tribute systems of a series of empires, the first of which can be traced back to the fourth century A.D., and a variety of lesser kingdoms and other sociopolitical organizations.

European penetration of the area began in the fifteenth century under the Portuguese, but contact was largely restricted to the coastal area until the nineteenth century. The French, who later dominated the area, penetrated interior river valleys, but their focus was on trade rather than on administration. It was not until the last half of the nineteenth century that the French turned their full attention to the area.

The French administrative concept of assimilation proposed the substitution of French social, political, and economic institutions for indigenous ones as the first stage of a process leading to the eventual integration of colonial peoples into the French nation. The application of this concept over the years and from one area to another was affected by changes in the colonial administration and by practical considerations. A high degree of assimilation was achieved in certain coastal enclaves. French schools were in operation in these areas well before the end of the nineteenth century, and a core of urban intellectuals evolved. Senegal became the only French African colony in which elected government councils were established before World War II.

During the last half of the nineteenth century both the French and the local political systems had expansionist ambitions. Indigenous political structures had known a cyclic tradition of consolidation and disintegration, and competition with European institutions proved disruptive to local stability. Many turned to one of the various Islamic brotherhoods as an alternate mechanism offering both political and personal security in a time of increasing social and political upheaval. The most influential of these was the Muridiya brotherhood of the Wolof, which along with other Muslim orders has played an important role in postindependence politics (see ch. 7; ch. 10).

Before Senegalese independence in 1960 membership in a federation to be composed of four former French African colonies was proposed. Membership in this ill-fated Mali Federation was opposed by both conservative Islamic leaders and various left-wing elements in the country. The initial government policy following the dissolution of the federation advocated administrative decentralization. It was hoped that such a policy would increase the satisfaction of local groups with their roles in the decisionmaking process. A period of parliamentary dissension, civil unrest, and constitutional modification followed. By 1964 the government had revised its position on decentralization, and within two years—in a move designed to increase central control of national development—it had created a single national party. The supervision of political development and national security came to rest in the hands of President Léopold-Sédar Senghor.

THE PRE-EUROPEAN PERIOD

Although a few archaeological discoveries have been made since World War II, much remains to be ascertained about the prehistory of the area that is present-day Senegal. Samples of paleolithic and neolithic tools, of pottery, and of wall paintings have been found in the area of the Cap Vert peninsula and in the middle valley of the Sénégal River. Megaliths, ranging from three to six feet in height and set in a circular pattern, have been found in the Sine-Saloum area. Metal artifacts, dating from more recent but pre-Islamic periods, have also been found. The most common objects of metal are rings, swords, and jewelry; the most spectacular is a collar made of gold found at Rao near Saint-Louis. The traditions of present-day Senegalese give no indication of prehistoric cultures that might have produced these objects, and the origin of the items has yet to be clarified.

The first written accounts of the area are in the chronicles of Arab traders who crossed the Sahara from North Africa in the ninth and tenth centuries A.D. Their writings and those of the early Portuguese traders indicate that the ancestors of the Wolof, Serer, and Toucouleur were once in an area considerably north of their present-day location. They reached their modern-day position between the tenth and fifteenth centuries, having been pushed gradually southward, particularly by groups fleeing forceful Islamization in North Africa. From about the tenth century onward, the peoples of Senegal had regular contact with the peoples of North Africa through both trade and periodic invasions by Arabs and Berbers. These relations left a permanent imprint in the form of Islam, which first came to Senegal in the eleventh century with the conversion of the Toucouleur but which was not firmly implanted in the rest of the country until the nineteenth century (see ch. 7).

Between the fourth and sixteenth centuries a number of empires and lesser kingdoms evolved in the sub-Saharan area (see fig. 2). Although centered to the east of the present-day eastern border of Senegal, their influence extended into and in several cases incorporated major portions of the country. Most grew around the major terminals

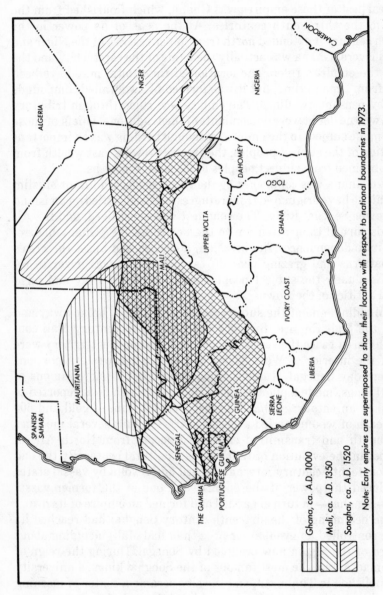

Note: Early empires are superimposed to show their location with respect to national boundaries in 1973.

	Ghana, ca. A.D. 1000
	Mali, ca. A.D. 1350
	Songhai, ca. A.D. 1520

Source: Adapted from Roland Oliver and J. D. Fage, *A Short History of Africa*, (Penguin African Library, AP2). Baltimore, 1962, p. 87.

Figure 2. Early West African Empires

11

of the trans-Saharan trade in slaves, gold, and a variety of commodities. Through their control of trade, assisted by a strong military arm and a tribute system, these empires were able to dominate an extensive area that included numerous ethnic groups and smaller organized states.

The earliest of these empires was Ghana, which flourished from the fourth to the thirteenth centuries. At the peak of its power in the eleventh century it extended north from upper reaches of the Niger and Sénégal rivers. Ghana was actually the name of the capital city and the title of the empire's ruler. The location of the capital may have been moved from time to time, but it was formed by two walled compounds joined by peasant dwellings. The empire was ruled through tributary princes who no doubt were descendants of the traditional chiefs of those groups made subject to the empire. Although herding was an important occupation of the subject peoples, the empire drew its vast wealth from gold it obtained from subject peoples in the southern areas.

In 1076 Ghana was conquered by the Almoravids, a militant Muslim group said to have originated from refugees who had settled on an island in the lower Sénégal River. The conquest was short lived, and the Almoravids turned their attention to the north; by 1087 Ghana had regained its independence. The invasion, however, had upset the area's trade patterns and grazing procedures, and Ghana was never to recover. Gradually the subject peoples began to break away and form political entities of their own.

The Manding, one of the subject peoples of Ghana, broke away and formed the Mali Empire. By the early fourteenth century Mali controlled an area twice the size of Ghana; included in this territory were most of the interior of West Africa and all but the western portions of present-day Senegal. Kankan Musa (1312-37), the most famous of the Mali kings, made a pilgrimage to Mecca on which he is reported to have taken an entourage that included a camel train of gold and 500 slaves, each of whom carried a golden staff. He built several mosques in Timbuktu and transmitted cultural concepts from North Africa, which began the evolution of that city as a cultural center. By the end of the fourteenth century internal discord and revolts by vassal states had reduced the power of the empire, and one of the former vassal states—Songhai—in turn expanded and formed an empire of its own.

By the beginning of the sixteenth century Songhai had reached its peak. It controlled an even larger area than had Mali, including about one-third of the region now occupied by Senegal. During the reign of Muhammad Askia, the most famous of the Songhai kings, a university was established in Timbuktu, and the city became a center of learning respected throughout the Islamic world. By the end of the century the empire was challenged by northern groups, and in 1591 Timbuktu was seized by Moroccan troops. Being unable to defend itself from external military threats and internal factionalism, the empire disintegrated, never again to be re-formed.

Although the influence held by the interior empires over the area now contained within the borders of Senegal varied, until the early sixteenth-century tribute and trade networks touched at least portions of the eastern half of the country. As the last of the empires disintegrated, the local lesser empires and kingdoms sought to assert their independence or to expand positions they already held. Contemporary knowledge of the histories of these political systems is fragmented and comes largely from genealogies and oral literature. Although sometimes disrupted by wars and local disputes, communication between the local peoples includes the exchange of both commodities and ideas. There was also a considerable degree of social and political mobility. Political stability was not long lived, and most states possessed histories characterized by conquest, rebellion, and usurpation. The major examples were the Toucouleur kingdom of Tekrur, the Wolof Empire, and the Manding Kingdom.

In the north of the country along the Sénégal River valley, there was a succession of states built one upon the other. The first was the kingdom of Tekrur, established in the eleventh century by ancestors of the Toucouleur. Various peoples in search of fertile lands, including the Peul, Wolof, and Sarakolé came to settle in the river valley area (see ch. 4). They soon competed with the Toucouleur for political power and established their dynasties over the Islamized Toucouleur masses. Most of these dynasties were not Islamic.

During the fourteenth century the area was absorbed by the Mali Empire. Ruled by a Manding dynasty as the kingdom of Fouta Toro, the political system was more a federation of principalities than a unified kingdom. During the sixteenth century the Saltigi dynasty of the Peul was established, and the central administration was strengthened. Dissension over the political structure, religious issues, and land uses increased, and the restive Toucouleur sought to overthrow the Peul dynasty. Efforts at land reform failed, a revolution was initiated in 1769, and the dynasty fell in 1775.

The Toucouleur subsequently reestablished themselves and instituted their own dynasty. The upper stratum of the Toucouleur had maintained its faith, using Maure clerics to educate its sons. They led the increasingly Islamized masses in the formation of an Islamic state, which was a federation of *clans* (figuratively, cliques) headed by an *almany* (head of state) elected by a council of *clan* chiefs. The *almany* quickly became a figurehead, and power resided in the hands of the seven *clan* chiefs who formed the state council.

In the mid-1850s Al Haj Omar, a member of the Toucouleur ruling class who had made a pilgrimage to Mecca and had become a member of the Islamic Tidjaniya brotherhood, embarked on a religious war against the ruler of upper Senegal and against the French, who were expanding into the area. He attacked the Toucouleur rulers for alleged religious laxity and attempted an appeal to the masses on the basis of ethnic pride, the promise of a return to stability, and expulsion of the French. Having signed a peace treaty with the French after military defeat in 1860 and faced by continued resistance from clans to the south of the Sénégal River, Omar—and his followers after his death—expanded to the east into present-day Mali. Violence was endemic to the new empire, and the followers of Omar found administration more difficult than conquest. The disturbances created by the civil war and subsequent disputes within the ranks of the bellicose factions offered an opportunity to the French to extend their influence by military action.

Although first mentioned in the mid-fifteenth century, the Wolof Empire is believed to have come into existence during the last half of the thirteenth century when the Mali Empire was concentrating its attention on expanding eastward into the interior of West Africa. The Wolof occupied an area running inland from Dakar about 200 miles between the basins of the Sénégal River and the Gambie (the Gambia River) (see ch. 3). The empire was formed as a result of the conquest of five Wolof states—Cayor, Baol, Oualo, Sine, and Saloum—by the state of Djolof. The Wolof were known mainly for their military rivalries and showed little interest in stable agricultural pursuits.

In the course of Wolof history other people were in constant contact with them. Serer in Sine and Saloum were subject to Wolof rulers. Toucouleur and Peul were sometimes dominated by, and sometimes in direct and successful conflict with, Wolof states. Wolof relations with the Manding were often hostile. The Maures in earlier times sought to conquer and convert the Wolof to Islam; later they just tried to convert them. The Diola were raided for slaves, many of whom were absorbed into Wolof society.

The empire lasted until the sixteenth century, when first Cayor and then other states revolted and attained independence. The states quarreled and fought with each other until the nineteenth century, when the French intervened in order to protect their trade and placed the states under French protection.

A major migration of Manding into the already populated basin of the Gambie occurred around the beginning of the fourteenth century with the general expansion of the Mali Empire. The first wave of warriors was followed by more permanent settlers and traders. The Manding organized a commercial network along both banks of the river and established fourteen small states in defense of their interests. Although these kingdoms were vassals initially of the Mali Empire, the strongest ties with the central administration of the empire were commercial rather than political. By the end of the century the Mali Empire had entered a state of decline.

Each state was organized along lines similar to social patterns on the local level and was headed by a king and a state council. The kings of the states in the coastal areas are reported to have had greater power in decisionmaking than did those farther upriver, and all were jealous of one another's ambitions. During the eighteenth century and the beginning of the nineteenth century they were frequently at war with one another and were unable to overcome factionalism in the face of increasing Wolof advances.

By the middle of the nineteenth century the individual state political systems, long dominated by a stagnant elite, came to experience stress. The profits from the slave trade, growing groundnut (peanut) trade, and trade with Europeans were for a time used to benefit the whole of society. By the 1850s, however, increasing dissatisfaction was being expressed by groups excluded from the privileges of the ruling class. Although still a minority, various revivalist Islamic groups joined the other dissidents, and in 1862 Maba Diakhou, a Peul cleric, led a revolt. As a result the ruling elite was removed, and a restructuring of society was begun. This disruption further weakened the Manding kingdoms, and pacification by the colonial powers was effected by the end of the century.

ADVENT OF THE EUROPEANS

Trade and First Settlement

The first modern European navigators to explore the shores of West Africa were the Portuguese under the sponsorship of Prince Henry the Navigator, whose curiosity, interest in trade, and missionary zeal motivated a systematic program of exploration and discovery. In 1444 Portuguese seamen rounded Cap Vert, and the following year they explored the mouth of the Sénégal River. By 1460 they had explored the entire coast of Senegal and established a profitable trade in slaves, gold, and other items from a base in the Cape Verde Islands.

Until about the mid-sixteenth century Portugal enjoyed a monopoly, granted by the pope, of trade along the coast of West Africa. Its merchants settled among the natives and through intermarriage created an influential *métis* (mixed European and African ancestry) society. From the beginning of the sixteenth century, however, merchants from England, France, and Holland began to intrude on the Portuguese and gradually undermined their monopoly. The Dutch, in particular, established trading posts along the whole West African coast, and by the middle of the seventeenth century they virtually dominated all trade. In 1617 they established a settlement on the island of Gorée, just off Cap Vert.

The French established their influence along the Sénégal River by exploring it as far inland as Podor. In 1626 a group of Rouen merchants formed an association for the commercial exploitation of the Sénégal and Gambie rivers, and in 1633 they obtained exclusive trade rights for ten years. The first French settlement was established in 1638 on an island at the mouth of the Sénégal River, and in 1659 it was named

Saint-Louis. For the next century and a half Saint-Louis was the center of French activity in West Africa. Gorée was captured from the Dutch in 1677 and was made into a naval base.

The main item of trade was gum arabic, which was in great demand in Europe at the time. Slaves were traded in Gorée, but the European slave trade in Senegal never reached the intensity it had along the Gulf of Guinea coast. The commerce in gum arabic extended far up the Sénégal River, and in time permanent posts were established to protect traders.

Despite the active trade, however, the early years of French commercial activity in Senegal saw one trading company after another collapse because of poor management, inefficiency, and corruption of its agents. Living conditions in Saint-Louis and Gorée were extremely bad, and the traders engaged in a variety of illegal activities as compensation. Many of them abandoned their posts and went into business for themselves. Like the Portuguese before them, they intermarried with the local women and enlarged the group of *métis*.

Only during the years from about 1690 to 1720, when the Senegal outposts were managed by André Bruce, did they know any real prosperity. Bruce undertook a program of development and exploration, established a French monopoly over the gum arabic trade, and set out to exploit the goldfields of Bambouk, in present-day Mali. Soon after he left, however, the old problems returned, and the British had no difficulty in capturing all the French outposts in 1758.

While the French were establishing themselves on the Sénégal River, the British did the same on the Gambie, and a fierce rivalry developed. Between the beginning of the Seven Years' War (1756) and the end of the Napoleonic Wars (1815), the French settlements along the coast of Senegal repeatedly changed hands between the French and the British and finally were restored in their entirety to the French at the Congress of Vienna in 1815.

Rather than rebuild their trade after 1815 the French decided to experiment with the planting of cotton and tropical crops on the banks of the Sénégal River. They had lost virtually all of their colonies during the recent wars, and the similarity between Senegal and the West Indies, including the abundance of cheap black labor, offered promise of success. Africans, however, were not willing to cede the required land, and the French treasury could not support military conquest. The scheme was abandoned in 1829, and the French again turned to trade.

The Early Colony

Until the mid-nineteenth century the French settlements in Senegal were administered as temporary commercial outposts while attention was focused on the permanent colonies in America and Asia. During the wars of the late eighteenth century, France had lost most of these colonies to the British, and its only hope for remaining a colonial power was to expand in Africa. By the time of the July Monarchy (1830-48), the country had sufficiently recovered from the wars and upheavals that followed the French Revolution to attempt to establish itself firmly in Senegal. In 1840 an ordinance established Senegal as a permanent French possession with a government—including a judiciary and representative councils—whose jurisdiction extended over all settlements then effectively under French control and over those territories likely to be annexed to them.

French colonial policy was guided in principle by the theory of assimilation, based on the doctrine of the equality of man but at the same time assuming the superiority of French civilization over all others. The ultimate goal was the complete cultural and political integration of the colonial peoples into the French nation. Application of this theory required direct rule and the complete destruction of the traditional government apparatus, which—if permitted to continue—would perpetuate the traditional culture and hinder assimilation. In practice, however, application of the assimilation theory encountered several obstacles, and throughout colonial history, particularly after France acquired its vast African possessions in the late nineteenth century, it remained more a theoretical goal than an actual policy.

Direct rule was difficult to impose because the French at first lacked the military forces necessary to pacify the indigenous peoples and because later they lacked sufficient numbers of administrators to govern the vast areas in their possession. Leadership in the traditional social systems was based on the fullfillment of a variety of sociopolitical functions not easily transferred either to the French or to the indigenous officials they appointed. Thus out of necessity the French utilized the traditional governmental structure as an instrument of government until they were able fully to assert their authority.

Another serious limitation on the full application of assimilation, however, was opposition to the policy among influential persons in France. Much of the opposition was based on the practical problems involved, but many political theorists opposed it because they did not accept the egalitarian principle on which it was based. For many years after the French Revolution, France was a battleground for proponents of the liberal revolutionary principles and adherents of the old authoritarian regime, and the conflict was reflected in a vacillation between republican and monarchical governments at home and in alternating colonial policies abroad. Virtually no protests were raised, however, about the elimination of existing African cultures.

Senegal was the only French African colony where the policy of assimilation was applied to a relatively large segment of the population, and the effect on the social, political, and economic structure of the country was profound. The first step in the assimilation process was education, and Senegal was the only African colony in which the French made a real, sustained effort to educate the indigenous population.

The first Western school had been opened in 1816 by a Roman Catholic priest in Saint-Louis, and another, shortly afterward, opened in Gorée. A mission school had been started at about the same time by the Sisters of Saint-Joseph of Cluny about ninety miles north of Dakar. In 1841 the French government asked the Brothers of Ploermel, a Roman Catholic teaching order, to open schools at the trading settlements of Dagana, Podor, Bakel, and Sédhiou. These schools taught the French language and manual skills. Within two years there were two schools in both Saint-Louis and Gorée with a total enrollment of about 600 students in all four schools. A secondary school was opened shortly afterward at Saint-Louis but was forced to close in 1849 because of financial and administrative problems.

The major step toward assimilation, and one that was to have profound influence on Senegal from then on, was taken in 1848 during the Second French Republic. Inspired by the egalitarian ideals of the revolution, the French government once and for all abolished all forms of slavery (trade in slaves had already been abolished in 1818) and granted all persons born in a French colony, both black and white alike, the civil rights of a French citizen. The four communes were given the right to elect a deputy to the National Assembly in Paris. In 1852, however, the Second French Republic was overthrown, and Louis Napoleon established the authoritarian Second Empire. In Africa he revoked Senegal's right to send a deputy to the National Assembly and embarked on a policy of forcible expansion.

Indigenous Social Revolution

The French effort at expansion in the mid-nineteenth century coincided with widespread social upheaval in traditional political systems and with the expansion of Islam. The displacement of traditional elites had been effected in both the north and south of the country; internecine strife was common among both the Manding kingdoms and the remains of the political system of Fouta Toro; and revivalist Islamic leaders were attempting to restructure traditional society. These developments represented responses to internal pressures within traditional society and were not the result of European intrusion, which at that point was still marginal. Although reformist groups increasingly became anti-French, they also allied themselves with the French against indigenous rivals. Thus both the reformists and the French sought to use one another in furthering their respective goals of expansion.

Islam as a social force had not significantly affected the area that later became Senegal until the eleventh century, when the ruler of Tekrur and his family converted to Islam. During the fifteenth century the Maures, an ethnic group inhabiting what is now Mauritania, became the leading purveyors of Islam to the Senegalese. Maure marabouts—Islamic teachers and clerics—traveled to the courts of the Wolof rulers, where they served as advisers or were called upon to work their reputed magic powers. The attachment of these rulers to Islam was not profound, and they or their successors usually returned to the traditional religious beliefs of their locality. Occasionally a Wolof state sought Maure or Toucouleur aid in its struggles with other Wolof states. In return for their support, these Islamic groups sometimes tried—often unsuccessfully—to impose Islam by force. Although segments of the lower classes were sometimes converted, they represented a marginal portion of the total population. In the middle 1800s after centuries of effort by Maures, the Wolof had been only slightly touched by Islam.

Within a little over half a century, however, virtually all of the Wolof had been converted to Islam. Although previous efforts had laid the groundwork, this sudden growth of Islam among the Wolof represented a search for security in the midst of increasing sociopolitical instability within traditional society. Islam represented a universal religion that seemed to offer a better rationale for social organization than did local religious beliefs. To an initially lesser but later increasing degree, it was also regarded as a better foundation for encounter with the French.

As the French gained control over increasing amounts of Wolof territory, the ability of Islamic clerics to move freely in the Wolof countryside increased. The French, accustomed to Islam by virtue of their North African experience, tended to show more respect for Islam than for local practices. The *tiedo*, a military class, deprived of their customary way of life, turned from their previously strong resistance to Islam and embraced it. Increasingly, Islamic leaders rather than chiefs became the focus of Senegalese loyalties.

As the French began to expand into the interior, the traditional chiefs and militant marabouts were locked in a struggle for power. French policy was consistent only in that it represented a divide-and-rule policy, but they usually gave support to the chiefs, who were more readily assimilated into the colonial administrative system that was evolving. The selection of traditional chiefs for local administrative positions, however, tended to accelerate the transfer of loyalty to Islamic leaders rather than to elevate the status of the chiefs. For the first time in Senegalese history, Islamic brotherhoods became influential.

The Islamic brotherhoods began as mystical, ascetic movements with decentralized organizational structures (see ch. 7). The two principal orders brought by the Maures to Senegal were the Tidjaniya and the Qadiriya. At the end of the nineteenth century a third brotherhood, the Muridiya, was founded as an offshoot of the Qadiriya order by Amadou Bamba. There are no deep doctrinal differences among the three groups, and they are distinguished from one another mainly by ritual observances and, to a lesser extent, by rules of conduct. The Muridiya played a significant role in agriculture and later moved into urban politics (see ch. 7).

Until the last quarter of the nineteenth century, urban social protest largely concerned the establishment of local political institutions. The *métis*, who had associated with the French elite since the late eighteenth century, led the urban movement. The increase of stable French business interests in the colony, however, brought competition from local French residents, and after the turn of the century assimilated Africans also sought political roles in competition with the *métis*.

Although the Roman Catholic clergy—first Portuguese, then French—touched the shores of Senegal in the fifteenth century, organized mission effort began only in the eighteenth century. Until the middle of the nineteenth century the missionaries were handicapped by small numbers, by conflicts with local administrators, by lack of knowledge of the indigenous languages, and by demands on their time for service to the European community. Although they were to administer the state school system until 1901, the religious orders did not represent a social force of significance among the local peoples.

Inland Expansion

The French could not see an end to the internecine warfare of the African kingdoms during the mid-nineteenth century. The resulting instability generated by such conflicts interfered with French commercial interests, and the French adopted a policy of forced pacification of the belligerent factions. The aggressive policy of the Second Empire had the full backing of local merchants, who requested the appointment of General Louis Faidherbe as governor to carry it out. Faidherbe had already distinguished himself in skirmishes against Al Haj Omar and by his studies of Senegalese ethnic groups. In 1854 he took command of a colony consisting of Saint-Louis and the banks of the Sénégal River up to Bakel. Gorée and a piece of land on the Cap Vert peninsula were administered separately by the commander of the Gorée naval station. From Saint-Louis, Faidherbe undertook a series of campaigns to pacify first the people of the Sénégal River valley and then those of the area between Saint-Louis and the Cap Vert peninsula, on which Dakar had been founded in 1857. To conduct these campaigns, he organized the Senegalese Riflemen (Tirailleurs Sénégalais), an army of African volunteers under French commanders, which later achieved worldwide fame.

Faidherbe's goal was to establish a sufficiently large colony with an efficient government to allow peaceful economic development. His aim was to extend French influence eastward as far as Médina, in Mali, but he encountered serious opposition from Omar, who was in the process of expanding his Toucouleur empire on the upper Sénégal River. After several military encounters, Omar signed a peace treaty in 1860 and directed his expansion eastward, away from the river. In the meantime, Faidherbe's troops subjugated Sine and Saloum and began penetrating into Casamance. Upper Casamance was brought under control in 1861, but the Diola in lower Casamance refused to submit to the French until after World War I. Greatest resistance was offered by Cayor, east of the Cap Vert peninsula. In 1862 the people revolted against their French-supported ruler and replaced him with Lat-Dior, who initiated a war against the French. In 1865 a precarious peace was signed, and Cayor was annexed to the colony of Senegal; complete peace, however, was not achieved until 1895, when Lat-Dior was killed during an uprising.

Military conquest, however, was only a means to achieving Faidherbe's goal. During his ten years of governorship, he established the administrative, economic, and social institutions that allowed Senegal to develop into a prosperous colony. The territory was divided into three districts, governed from Saint-Louis, Bakel, and Gorée. These were in turn divided into smaller districts (*cercles*), each at first administered by a French-appointed African chief. An official newspaper, *Moniteur du Sénégal*, was established in 1855. In the economic sphere Faidherbe founded the Bank of Senegal, started building the port of Dakar, and promoted the export of groundnuts. On the social level his greatest accomplishment was the establishment of a state school system. A number of schools, conducted by Christian missionaries, were already operating in Saint-Louis, but the people of Senegal were by then mostly Muslim and would not send their children to mission schools. The state schools established by Faidherbe and the scholarships that his administration offered for advanced study in France provided the beginnings of an educated African elite in Senegal.

By about 1880 the French controlled a wide strip along the entire coast of Senegal and both sides of the Sénégal River as far as Kayes. The settlements—Saint-Louis, Gorée, Rufisque, and Dakar—were under direct French administration and constituted the colony. The rest of the area was a protectorate under military administration. The colony's right to elect a deputy to the French Parliament had been restored in 1871 at the same time that the representative General Council was created. Representation in the council, however, was limited to citizens of the colony, including *métis* and Africans born in the towns.

From this base, in the early 1880s, an intensive drive was begun east across the sub-Saharan area and south into the forest regions of the Gulf of Guinea coast. At first the drive was motivated by curiosity and a desire to expand French commercial activity in Africa. Ever since a number of German, French, and English explorers in the eighteenth century described the prosperous cities and market towns south of the Sahara, Europeans had been interested in this area. The

French plan was to establish a series of outposts connecting the Sénégal and Niger rivers and eventually to construct a railroad from Saint-
Louis into the interior. After the Berlin Conference of 1885 these
commercial interests gave way to a politically motivated race for
power and influence among the various European countries interested
in Africa.

When the second Berlin agreement, signed in 1890, decreed that only
effective occupation by a colonial power would be recognized as valid,
the French conceived the so-called Grand Design, which was to take
the French flag across West Africa to the Nile River and then to unite
this area with the French possessions in North Africa and along the
Congo River. During the next nine years several military missions
were dispatched from Senegal and from various points in North Africa
and on the Gulf of Guinea coast to come together at Lake Chad and
plant the French flag along the way. By 1899 the Grand Design was
fulfilled, and the French emerged as the dominant power in western
and central Africa.

In the course of expansion Senegal's boundaries became defined.
In 1886 an agreement with Portugal settled the boundary with Portuguese Guinea; in 1889 French Guinea became a separate administrative entity, and agreements in the same year with Great Britain
established the border with The Gambia, the British enclave following
the banks of the Gambie, which was declared a British protectorate
five years later. Beginning in 1895 Senegal, which at that time included
most of the territory of Mali and Mauritania, was administered by a
civil governor who was also appointed governor general for the newly
constituted federation of French West Africa (Afrique Occidentale
Française—AOF), which grouped together all French West African
colonies. In 1904 the territory south and east of the Sénégal and Falémé
rivers was separated from Senegal to form the French Sudan, and in
1920 the territory north of the Sénégal River became Mauritania (see
ch. 3).

THE FEDERATION OF FRENCH WEST AFRICA

Colonial Administration

Pacification of local peoples by the French occurred rapidly during
the last decades of the nineteenth century. A series of decrees promulgated between 1895 and 1904 consolidated eight territories (of which
Senegal was one) in the federation of French West Africa. Although
the federation underwent several major changes after World War II,
it served as an administrative structure until 1958. At the head of the
federation was a governor general resident in Dakar, capital of the
federation; Saint-Louis served as the capital of Senegal during the
federation. The governor general was responsible to the minister for

the colonies and ultimately to the French Parliament. He was assisted by the consultative Council of Government (Conseil de Gouvernement) and various administrative departments and councils. The powers of the governor general were never clearly defined by law and therefore were gradually expanded. Each of the territories constituting the federation had its own governor and budget. In theory each was to have a great deal of independence of action, but in practice the federal government intervened in practically every sphere of activity.

The territories were divided into districts (*cercles*), each governed by a district commandant (*commandant du cercle*). Because poor communication facilities greatly limited the extent of central control over the commandants, they had an exceptional degree of freedom in the execution of their responsibilities. Within a district the commandant ruled through a hierarchy of chiefs who were chosen and appointed by him and could be dismissed at will. He was advised by a council of notables (*conseil des notables*) consisting of these chiefs and of other traditional leaders appointed by him.

The power of the chiefs derived solely from the French administration, and an understanding of French was a requirement for appointment. If the chief's performance did not meet French approval, he was dismissed and replaced by someone more acceptable, whether he had any traditional claim to the title or not. The authority of chiefs was confirmed in principle, but chiefs who refused to submit to French directives were deposed and replaced with more cooperative ones. With the consolidation of French power in West Africa, French officials assumed more and more direct administrative powers, and indigenous chiefs were reduced to the level of low-ranking local officials. A career service of colonial administrators with specialized functions gradually developed under the Ministry for the Colonies.

Municipal government was based on a system of communes with various degrees of self-government depending on the importance of the municipality and the supposed political maturity of its inhabitants. Saint-Louis and Gorée became self-governing communes (*communes de plein exercice*) in 1872, Rufisque in 1880, and Dakar in 1887. Until after World War II they were the only four municipalities in French West Africa to achieve this status.

Within this general framework of administration, Senegal occupied a unique position. It was the only territory in the federation of French West Africa in which some of the inhabitants enjoyed the rights of French citizenship and exercised a voice in their own government by electing representatives to municipal councils, to the General Council for the colony, and to the French Parliament. As the oldest French African colony it was also distinguished by a relatively large group of educated, westernized Africans whose participation in representative government gave them early training in modern politics. Although the councils had no legislative powers, they were able to exercise considerable influence through their right to vote on the budget and to levy taxes.

The rights of citizenship and the franchise, however, were limited to persons born in the four self-governing communes, and a sharp difference developed between these assimilated, urbanized *originaires* (see Glossary) and the rest of the Senegalese, who were treated as colonial subjects. In 1920 the General Council was expanded to include representatives of subjects as well as of citizens, but the subjects' representatives were appointed by the administration rather than elected. Nevertheless, until after World War II it remained the only popularly elected, multiracial legislative body in Africa elected on a single-college system. In the 1920s it had eight white and thirty-two black members.

The distinction between citizens and subjects concerned not only political but also civil matters. Citizens were liable to French law administered in French courts, although *originaires* were allowed to retain their own *statut personnel* (private or customary law) in matters concerning marriage, divorce, inheritance, and civil disputes. Subjects were responsible to customary or Muslim law administered by indigenous courts presided over by French administrative officers who had discretionary powers to enforce *indigénat* (minor disciplinary law). These courts handled a variety of offenses, including insults to the dignity of French officials, and the *indigénat* was one of the more detested institutions of the colonial period.

African citizens had the right of assembly and were eligible to hold positions in the civil service under the same conditions as Frenchmen; subjects were not. On the other hand, subjects were liable to the *prestation* system, under which they could be drafted for work on plantations and public projects as part of their tax responsibility, but citizens were not. Although the rights of citizens were not always honored by the French administration, their existence on paper was resented by the subjects.

Subjects could qualify for citizenship if they surrendered their rights under customary law, were literate in French, and had either served in the French army or been employed by the French for at least ten years. Although these requirements could be met by many Africans, few were willing to surrender their *statut personnel* for the privileges of citizenship, particularly since the *originaires* enjoyed both.

The privileges of the *originaires* were also resented by the French, who made several attempts to nullify them. The governor found himself repeatedly at odds with the elected General Council and was anxious to eliminate its power. Most of the resentment, however, was aimed at the *statut personnel*, which was seen as allowing African citizens to escape from the obligations of French citizenship while enjoying all its privileges. A new citizenship law, passed in 1916 in exchange for the efforts of the recently elected African deputy from Senegal, Blaise Diagne, in recruiting large numbers of Senegalese to fight in World War I, confirmed the rights of the *originaires* and even extended the rights to their descendants.

Economic Development and Social Change

Having acquired a large expanse of territory at considerable expense during the last decades of the nineteenth century, France was anxious to divest itself as soon as possible of the burden of maintaining this territory by making it economically self-supporting. In 1900 the French treasury initiated a policy of economic self-sufficiency for the colonies, whereby each colony was responsible for raising the funds required for its administration and defense and France would offer assistance only when needed. Senegal and other coastal colonies that already had a flourishing trade with Europe had little difficulty in complying with this policy, but the interior colonies with little trade found it extremely difficult to meet even part of their expenses. A prime reason for the creation of the federation, therefore, was an attempt to pool the resources of all French West African colonies and make the richer ones help support the poorer.

France had embarked on the conquest of interior West Africa partly because of a desire to open it to trade and exploitation from Senegal. The plan called for using the Sénégal and Niger rivers as the main routes of communication by linking their navigable stretches by railroad. Construction of a railroad from Kayes to Bamako was begun in 1882, but before it was completed in 1906 the whole plan was found to be impractical because the Sénégal was navigable only three months of the year and Saint-Louis, at its mouth, was unsuitable for a modern port. In 1885, therefore, construction was begun on a railroad from Saint-Louis to Dakar, which was being transformed into a deepwater port. Another railroad linking Kayes with the port of Dakar was begun in 1907, and after its completion in 1923 Dakar became the most important port in West Africa.

Until the 1920s great rivalry existed between Dakar and Saint-Louis and between Dakar and Rufisque. Saint-Louis had long enjoyed dominance as a commercial center because of its location at the mouth of the Sénégal River. Dakar, however, had a better port and, after the rail link with Saint-Louis was established, gradually took over most of its trade.

The rivalry between Dakar and Rufisque was based on the groundnut trade. Although not native to Africa, groundnuts were already being used as a local food in the early years of French activity in Senegal. By 1840 they had become an important item of trade, and the French began to encourage their cultivation as a cash crop in the western parts of Diourbel and Sine-Saloum. The local market at Rufisque was the center for the groundnut trade until the railroad took over transportation of the crop from the interior to Dakar (see ch. 14).

The public works programs undertaken by the colonial government as a foundation for economic development required a great deal of manpower. The French therefore imposed the system of *prestation* under which each adult African man and woman who was not a French citizen was required to work for ten days each year without compensation on an economically useful project as part of his obligation to the state. The system was subject to extreme misuse by both French administrations and African chiefs, who were responsible for recruitment among their own people, and it was a hated aspect of colonial rule.

In addition to political and economic changes, the French also introduced social institutions that brought about fundamental changes in the way of life. In the mid-nineteenth century, Faidherbe had established a basic system of health services and a school system that could prepare students for French universities. Until the turn of the century these services were limited to the four communes but, once French West Africa was federated and Senegal received a unified administration, they were gradually extended to the rest of the country.

In response to the degree of self-government granted Senegal, the French made an effort to educate the electorate. The real basis of Western education had been laid by Governor Faidherbe in the late 1850s. During his administration parochial secondary schools were established for children of Europeans and *métis*, and the School for the Sons of Chiefs and Interpreters was established at Saint-Louis to train children of African chiefs and notables as colonial administrators. All existing schools were then organized into a state school system but were left under the administration of various Roman Catholic orders. The system was secularized in 1901, and in 1903 it was integrated into the expanded system of the federation of French West Africa.

The primary schools in most parts of the country sent their best students to several secondary schools at Dakar and Saint-Louis and, although only a small percentage of the school-age population actually attended school, Senegal had an impressively large educated African elite on the eve of World War II. The education provided was completely French and was neither relevant nor adapted to the realities of the African environment and historical traditions of the local peoples. Thus, the *évolués* (educated elite) became, culturally, Frenchmen who knew more about the history of France than of their own peoples.

While French schools were producing a new elite, the traditional elite was being gradually destroyed by reducing the chiefs to junior civil servants and by indiscriminately appointing as chiefs persons with no legitimate claim to the title. In areas where traditional leaders retained their position and power, strong rivalry often developed between them and the *évolués*, who tried to usurp that leadership on

the grounds that the education and modern outlook of the é̵
better suited them for the position. In 1898 the chiefs were pla͏
fixed salaries. Although the French administration advocate
selection of canton chiefs from the dominant ethnic group ͏ᴏᵣ ͏ᴛ͏ᴴᴱ
area, by World War I the chiefs above the village level had become professional bureaucrats trained in French schools.

The role of the Muridiya brotherhood during this period was both
expanded and modified. The major organizational innovation was the
adaptation of the *daara* (community of disciples), where the young
came for religious education, into a collective farm. Although some
daara continued to fulfill educational functions and required only inci-
dental acts of labor, the new agricultural *daara* were composed of
older youths who willingly worked under arduous conditions for religious merit. Some sought membership in a *daara* as an escape from
military conscription, and some viewed the stamina necessary for such
labor as a symbol of manhood.

The Muridiya had been cool to the French initially—in contrast to
the Tidjaniya, who cooperated with the French—but their cooperation
increased both during and after World War I. As relations improved,
they came to provide most of the agricultural settlements established
for groundnut cultivation in the Terres Nueves (New Lands) near the
rail line (see ch. 3). Although Muridiya political activity existed during
this period, it remained sporadic and marginal. After 1927 and the
death of Amadou Bamba, there was no unified Muridiya political
interest. Rivalries of marabouts became involved with the disputes
of urban politicians, who in turn found it increasingly advantageous
to utilize the jealousies and conflicts within the brotherhood for their
own causes.

World War II and Postwar Reforms

World War II had a profound effect on the future of all French West
Africa. After the fall of France and the creation of the Vichy government, the French colonies were faced with the problem of declaring
their loyalty to Marshal Philippe Pétain, who headed the Vichy regime,
or to the French forces in exile under General Charles de Gaulle, whose
headquarters were in London. Although Pierre Boisson, governor general of French West Africa, and all of his subordinate governors remained personally loyal to Pétain, many Senegalese supported de
Gaulle. Some who were in France, such as Senghor, fought with the
underground.

Under the Vichy regime Senegalese representative institutions were
suppressed, and the country was subjected to heavy economic exploitation. The concept of racial superiority officially applied against Black
Africans resulted in political, economic, and social discrimination.
The recruitment of forced labor was intensified as was the drafting of
men into the armed forces. Farmers were assigned production quotas

27

for exportable foodstuffs that often could be met only at the expense of the local residents, whose standard of living had already been greatly lowered by the cutting off of imports from France.

After the Allied landings in North Africa in November 1942, Governor General Boisson, on the orders of Admiral Jean Darlan, came over to the Allied side. On November 25 he declared the allegiance of French West Africa to de Gaulle's French Provisional Government in Algiers.

In early 1944 René Pleven, commissioner of colonies in the provisional government, called a conference of governors of French Black Africa in Brazzaville. Events of the war and the help the Africans had given the French made the French realize that it was time to revise radically their formal relationship. Inspired also by the ideals of the Atlantic Charter and the right of self-determination, the conference recommended far-reaching political, social, and economic reforms. In effect, the recommendations were a compromise between the points of view of assimilationists such as Pleven and of federalists such as Félix Eboué, the African governor of Chad, and were intended to extend the privileges enjoyed by Senegal to the other African colonies of France.

It was considered indispensable that the colonies send delegates to the constituent assembly that was to draw up a new French constitution after the war and that all be granted political representation in whatever parliamentary body the constitution provided. The colonies themselves were to be given greater autonomy in administration and a legislative assembly elected on a double slate by both Europeans and Africans. A program for economic development was also proposed. The most striking recommendations, however, were in the social field and were inspired by Eboué: local customs were to be respected and safeguarded; the *indigénat* was to be abolished and a new penal code adopted; *prestation* was to be ended; and health and education facilities were to be improved. In addition, positions in the colonial administration were to be opened to all Africans.

The Brazzaville Conference signaled the beginning of a new era in colonial policy, but its only immediate effect was the passage of a law in August 1944 granting all labor in French Black Africa the right to organize. When the constituent assembly met in Paris at the end of 1945, sixty-three of the 600 delegates represented the African colonies. The African delegates, among them Lamine Guèye and Senghor from Senegal, played an active role in the deliberations. The assembly offered them an opportunity to air publicly the grievances and aspirations of their fellow Africans; their demands received strong support from the Socialists and the Communists, who were powerful at that time. Out of the debates of the assembly came a reevaluation of colonial policy and a draft plan for the union of France and its colonies.

In the meantime, a number of important reforms concerning Africans had been achieved by decree. The hated *indigénat* and *prestation* were abolished; residents of the colonies were granted freedom of speech, of association, and of assembly; the Monnet Plan for economic reconstruction in France was extended to the West African colonies; and funds were provided for economic and social development. In Senegal, Senghor was given credit for having achieved the abolition of *prestation* and as a consequence achieved great popularity. The French penal code was made applicable to all of French West Africa in April 1946, and in May the Law Lamine Guèye (so called after the deputy from Senegal) extended French citizenship to all the inhabitants of French colonies without prejudicing their *statut personnel*.

The first constitution drafted by the constituent assembly included whole passages of the Brazzaville recommendations. It proved too liberal for the French electorate, which rejected it in a referendum in May 1946. When a second constituent assembly convened in June, pressure from conservative elements in France and in the colonies was strong, and sharp differences of opinion developed among the delegates. The advocates of colonial autonomy, including all the colonial deputies and the French political left wing, favored political autonomy within the framework of metropolitan France in a strong revival of assimilationist ideas. The extremists among them, including deputies from North Africa and Madagascar, demanded political independence, but the deputies from Black Africa, including Guèye and Senghor, supported the idea of local self-government and political equality of Frenchmen and the colonial peoples.

Colonial interests, on the other hand, and the French political Right and Center inclined toward a nominally federalist system, within which France would preserve its dominant position. A compromise was finally reached, and the plan for the French Union was written into a new draft constitution, which was adopted by the assembly on September 28, 1946. All the deputies from Black Africa voted for it, and it was approved as the constitution of the Fourth French Republic in a referendum held throughout France and the overseas possessions on October 13, 1946.

The French Union, established by the constitution in 1946, consisted of metropolitan France and its overseas possessions, which were classified as overseas departments, overseas territories, associated territories, protectorates, and associated states. The West African colonies were designated overseas territories, which together with the overseas departments and metropolitan France constituted the French Republic. The federal structure of French West Africa remained unchanged, but each territory was given an elected general council and these in turn sent representatives to a federal council. Legislation for the territories remained the exclusive province of the French Parliament, in which, however, all the African territories were now represented.

The constitutional position of Senegal changed little under the

French Union. In fact, the 1946 reforms were intended primarily to extend to the rest of French Black Africa the political system that had existed in Senegal for some time. The Senegalese did benefit, however, from the elimination of the distinction between citizens and subjects, and they were granted a special concession in being allowed to retain a single-college electorate while all other territories had separate electorates for Africans and Europeans.

In the early 1950s the French government granted additional reforms that were to a large extent the work of the African deputies in the National Assembly. In 1950 the Second Law Lamine Guèye admitted all Africans to high civil service positions on equal terms with Europeans, and in 1952 a new labor code, patterned on the code in force in metropolitan France, was promulgated for all French colonies. The most significant reform, however, was the passage in June 1956 of the so-called *loi-cadre* (enabling act), which granted universal suffrage and a single electoral college in all territories, thus eliminating the last remaining difference between Senegal and the other territories. In addition, the *loi-cadre* gave broad legislative powers to territorial assemblies, while enumerating the powers reserved to the French government, and provided for an African cabinet to assist the territorial governors. No change was made in the federal structure of French West Africa, but with the new powers of the territorial governments the federal government lost almost all significance, a feature that Senghor strongly opposed.

While at last implementing fully the egalitarian features of assimilation, the *loi-cadre* in effect adopted association as the basis of future relations between France and its possessions. This reorientation of philosophy opened the way for independence within four years.

THE MOVE TOWARD INDEPENDENCE

Political Development

Although the citizens of the four communes had organized themselves to elect representatives, political parties did not come into their own until about World War II. The quasi-political organizations dating from the first half of the century focused on the distribution of patronage within the communes on the basis of personal following and alignments rather than over issues. They were elitist and were organized of and for the citizens of the commune, virtually ignoring the mass of subjects who were the majority of the population; it was not until after World War II that urban politicians began to court the nonurban majority of the population.

Guèye was the first Senegalese to recognize fully the importance of political organization. By the early 1930s he had increased his personal following by establishing the Senegalese Socialist Party (Parti Socialiste Sénégalaise—PPS). In 1938 Guèye expanded his position by affiliating the PSS with the French Socialist Party (Section Française de l'Internationale Ouvrière—SFIO).

Until World War II the policy of assimilation that France applied in Senegal had the complete approval of those Africans who had publicly addressed themselves to the matter. In fact, the only criticism leveled against it was that it did not go far enough in changing Africans to Frenchmen. Blaise Diagne, the first African to sit in the French National Assembly, was elected in 1914 for advocating complete assimilation, and his lifelong popularity was based largely on his continued struggle for this ideal. The man who succeeded him in Paris, Guèye, also saw the issue of equal rights for Africans as the major political issue. Independence, even in the distant future was not contemplated. The desired goal of politically conscious Senegalese was complete integration into a French multiracial community.

The racist policies of Vichy France, so completely out of keeping with what the Senegalese had come to expect from France, came as a rude shock. When the 1946 reforms failed to live up to Senegalese expectations for a resurgence of assimilationist policy, their disappointment was great. The sincerity of the French with respect to assimilation had already come under question among some of the younger educated elite, and the inadequacy of the postwar reforms and the slowness with which they were put into practice confirmed these suspicions. In addition, a number of intellectuals—among them Senghor—began to question the basic tenet of assimilation, which placed French culture above all others and denied the value of African traditions.

In 1948, dissatisfied with party response to his bid the previous year for increased representation of nonurban interests in party councils, Senghor broke away from the local section of the SFIO and formed his own party, the Senegalese Democratic Bloc (Bloc Démocratique Sénégalais—BDS). A party newspaper called *La Condition Humaine* was established shortly afterward, and Senghor began to build the base of his popular support through coalition politics.

Although the BDS did not affiliate itself with external political groups, there was some discussion about affiliation with the regional African Democratic Assembly (Rassemblement Démocratique Africain—RDA). Senghor decided against such affiliation because of RDA connections with the French Communist Party and the possibility of increased alliance with the Soviet Union. He did, however, maintain personal membership in the Overseas Independents (Independants d'Outre-Mer—IOM), created by several overseas representatives in Paris.

Senghor's main support came from the mass of Senegalese peasants who had long resented the privileges offered by assimilation to the urban *originaires* and, having gained the franchise in 1946, were eager to give expression to their resentment. In 1951 Guèye, the champion of assimilation, was defeated at the polls by Senghor who, with his political philosophy of *négritude* and the new Africa, was to dominate the Senegalese scene (see ch. 10). Guèye soon sought BDS membership in order to assure himself a future political role. Despite his emphasis on African self-assertion, however, Senghor did not yet seek independence from France but advocated African autonomy within a French federation.

Although the backbone of the BDS was the Senegalese peasant, the principal and most vocal reaction to assimilation came from the educated elite—the intellectuals who had been most strongly subjected to assimilation. It is a telling illustration of the extent of their "Frenchness" that their revolt did not result in a demand for political independence but rather in an attempt to find cultural emancipation. They did not resent the lack of self-government so much as they resented the assertion that Africans were a primitive, barbarous people until France brought its civilization to them. A major aspect of the revolt against assimilation, therefore, was a search into the past of their own and other African histories.

Support from the local Muslim brotherhoods had become increasingly important, and shortly after its inception the BDS entered into a period of bitter competition with the SFIO for the Muslim vote. Both parties advocated policies designed to appeal to Muslim leaders. The SFIO attempted to exploit the fact that Senghor was a Roman Catholic, and he in turn emphasized that there was no division between Christian and Muslim Senegalese but rather between religious and nonreligious men. After the BDS won the territorial elections in 1952, the religious issue was largely dropped.

In the January 1956 elections for the French Parliament, four parties offered slates of candidates. The BDS supported Senghor and Mamadou Dia, and the local section of the SFIO presented Guèye and Assane Seck. Other candidates were supported by the Senegalese Popular Movement (Mouvement Populaire Sénégalaise—MPS), a moderate section of the RDA, and the Senegalese Democratic Union (Union Démocratique Sénégalaise—UDS), an extreme left-wing RDA dissident party. After the elections the BDS called for unity, but only the UDS responded. Together the BDS and UDS formed the Senegalese Popular Bloc (Bloc Populaire Sénégalaise—BPS). The local SFIO section did not join but re-formed itself as the African Socialist Movement (Mouvement Socialiste Africain—MSA). Other small opposition parties such as the communist-oriented African Party of Independence (Parti Africain d'Indépendance—PAI) organized and sought to gain popular support through platforms calling for complete independence.

In 1959 the BPS and MSA merged with some smaller groups and formed the Senegalese Progressive Union (Union Progressiste Sénégalaise—UPS). The UPS under Senghor's leadership considered itself the government party. It advocated a platform of national socialism, which was defined as the adapting of socialist concepts to the realities of the African environment. The UPS also established a parallel organization called the Youth Movement of the Senegalese Progressive Union (Mouvement de la Jeunesse de l'Union Progressiste Sénégalaise—MJUPS).

The African Community and the Mali Federation

The dissolution of the Fourth French Republic in 1958 after de Gaulle came to power offered an opportunity to write a revised relationship between France and its colonies into the constitution for the new Fifth French Republic. This change would reflect not only de Gaulle's own ideas but also the economic and political changes that had occurred since 1946.

Constitutional reforms since 1946, culminating in the *loi-cadre*, had progressively weakened the centralized structure of administration and had given more authority to local bodies. At the same time, the formation of political parties and the piecemeal extension of the franchise to various groups of literate and semiliterate Africans and eventually to the whole population had steadily increased the number of Africans participating in their own government.

The Constitution of 1958, creating the Fifth French Republic, provided for the free association of autonomous republics within the French Community, where France was envisaged as the senior partner. The community had jurisdiction over foreign policy, defense, currency, common economic and financial policy, policy on strategic raw materials, and—unless specifically excluded by agreement—over higher education, internal and external communications, and supervision of the courts. The community's executive was presided over by an elected president, who was also the president of the French Republic, and consisted of the Executive Council (composed of the president, the prime ministers of the member states, and the French ministers concerned with community affairs) and the Senate (composed of members elected indirectly by each member state in proportion to its population). The community also had a common high court of arbitration. Each member state was to have its own government established by a separate constitution.

The new constitution was submitted to the electorate of the French Union in a referendum on September 28, 1958. The choice was either to accept the constitution and consequent membership in the community or to reject it, resulting in immediate severance of ties with France. No provision was made in the constitution for eventual independence for members within the community.

Senegal voted overwhelmingly in favor of the constitution but not without reluctance. Although it provided for the Franco-African community that Senghor has been advocating for almost a decade, the structure of the proposed community was not to Senghor's liking. He disapproved of what he called the balkanization of Africa, which split

French West Africa into over half a dozen separate states, and argued in favor of retaining a federation with a strong executive. Senghor believed that only through union could Africans contribute effectively to the Franco-African—and ultimately to the world—community. He was also not oblivious of the fact that much of Senegal's wealth and influence derived from its position as the commercial and administrative center of French West Africa and the lifeline to the vast hinterland.

Senghor's advocacy of federation was vehemently opposed by Félix Houphouët-Boigny of Ivory Coast, who was not only jealous of Senegal's dominant position in French West Africa but also resented having to share his country's wealth under a federal arrangement in which he had no effective voice in the distribution of that wealth. Houphouët-Boigny wanted a direct relationship between France and the African territories without the interference of a federal intermediary and, backed by the political power of the RDA, of which he was the head, was able to secure the victory of his ideas over those of Senghor. He did this first with the terms of the *loi-cadre*, which Senghor had opposed, and then with the French Community.

Despite his dislike for the structure of the community, Senghor was not ready to break away from France—not only because such a break would do great economic harm to Senegal but also because the historic and psychological ties of assimilation between Senegal and France were too strong. He therefore secured an affirmative vote for the 1958 Constitution and enrolled Senegal as a member of the community.

Establishment of the community, however, did not put an end to Senghor's efforts at federation in West Africa. In December 1958 delegates from Senegal, French Sudan, Upper Volta, and Dahomey met to discuss the creation of a new federation, and in January 1959 a federal constitution was promulgated. When the Mali Federation came into being in April 1959, however, it consisted of only Senegal and the French Sudan because Dahomey and Upper Volta withdrew at the last minute under pressure from Houphouët-Boigny and from France, both of whom opposed the federation. Within Senegal, also, the Mali Federation encountered opposition from a number of conservative Muslim leaders, two minor left-wing political parties, and even some important members of Senghor's own party—all of whom joined to campaign against the adoption of the federal constitution. Senghor, however, received overwhelmingly popular support, and the constitution was adopted.

From the beginning the Mali Federation had difficulties in its relations with France, which for several months refused to recognize its existence. Before the end of 1959 the leaders of the federation decided to seek independence from France but requested to be allowed to remain within the community. After prolonged negotiations France agreed to grant independence to the Mali Federation within the community in April 1960 and amended the 1958 Constitution to make this possible. Independence, declared on June 19, 1960, and signed on June 22, marked the beginning of the end of the French Community. In less than a year all of French Africa had achieved independence, and the community had virtually ceased to function.

INDEPENDENCE

Dissolution of the Mali Federation

Although the ability of the Mali Federation to have served the interests of the four territories originally scheduled for membership would seem to have been improbable, the viability of the federation without the participation of Upper Volta and Dahomey was even more marginal. The economies of French Sudan—later to be renamed Mali—and Senegal had not been developed equally and were in no respect complementary. The hastily drawn-up constitution was vague and open to divergent interpretation by leaders of the two states, whose political views and approaches were dissimilar. Fundamental disagreements existed over the role of political parties in the federal government and over policies regarding regional African and international affairs.

The rupture came during preparations for the August 27, 1960, elections and concerned the very structure of the federal government as well as the candidates for office. The UPS had advanced the candidacy of Senghor for the office of federal president. The Sudanese advocated a stronger central government that that proposed by Senghor and, upset over the selection of the Senegalese colonel as chief of staff by Dia, who was serving as federal minister of defense, they vowed not to vote for the UPS candidate. The Sudanese official who was the federal prime minister panicked when he heard that great numbers of UPS militants were reported on their way to Dakar, the new federal capital, and called a special session of the federal cabinet. Only one of the Senegalese federal cabinet members appeared. The cabinet proceeded to proclaim a state of emergency, withdrew Dia as defense minister of the federation, and called upon federal military forces to safeguard the security of the federal capital.

The French colonel commanding the federal forces decided to obey the local Senegalese. The Sudanese leaders were subsequently placed under house arrest, and troops loyal to Senegal were deployed throughout the capital. The Senegalese cabinet met, declared the independence of Senegal, and withdrew the state from the Mali Federation. A cabinet reshuffle followed, providing for the incorporation of three federal ministers in the national cabinet. The Sudanese leaders were then escorted under guard on a train back to French Sudan. Constitutional modification was effected on August 25, 1960. Senghor was unanimously voted president the following September, and Dia became prime minister of the new state.

As a result of previous political activity—which included having served as a member of the French Senate during the 1950s—Dia was the second ranking politician in the country. He was not as widely known as Senghor and drew most of his support from the urban middle class. Socialist in orientation, he was one of the best informed economists among African leaders. He was deputy secretary general of the UPS, and the control of party organization and administration rested largely in his hands. His role in internal politics was strengthened by the fact that in addition to serving as prime minister he held the key position of national defense minister and also supervised the High Commission for Planning.

Conflict between Senghor and Dia became apparent from the start. Dia surrounded himself with a group of Socialists calling for a more radical leadership than that offered by Senghor, and he sought to usurp political leadership. Faced on December 17, 1962, with the likelihood of a parliamentary vote of no-confidence and loss of his position as prime minister, Dia called out the national police in an effort to prevent the vote from being cast. The military threw its support to Senghor and, after a few days of uncertainty, Dia and his supporters were arrested. A few months later they were condemned to long terms of imprisonment (see ch. 16).

Following the attempted coup d'etat by Dia, new constitutional provisions were drafted and adopted by a referendum on March 3, 1963. Under the new provisions a presidential system with power concentrated in the hands of the president was substituted for the parliamentary system. New parliamentary and presidential elections were then scheduled for December 1963. Shortly before the elections, however, continued dissension between the supporters of Dia and those of Senghor erupted in violent riots in Dakar. Military intervention was again required (see ch. 16).

The major opposition party in 1963 was the African Realignment Party of Senegal (Parti du Regroupement Africain-Sénégal—PRA-Sénégal), which considered itself more revolutionary in its approach to socialism than the UPS. Censorship and limitations on public meetings had hindered PRA-Sénégal organizational efforts, and some of its leaders had been arrested for implication in an alleged ring dealing in illegal arms traffic. The Bloc of Senegalese Masses (Bloc des Masses Sénégalaises—BMS), formed in 1961, was the only other major opposition party. Its platform was little different from that of the UPS. The PAI had been formally dissolved in 1960 but continued to operate underground. After the 1963 elections, opposition groups began to lose their strength relative to the UPS. The BMS was abolished in 1964. In June 1966 the UPS formed a coalition government with three PRA-Sénégal leaders and became the sole official political party in the country. Political opposition shifted to the protests of students and organized labor (see ch. 10).

Social and Economic Integration and Development

One of the major tasks faced by the Senegalese government in the postindependence years has been the coordination of social and economic integration and development in ways that reinforce the government's interest in modernization and the development of national unity. Senegalese society at the time of independence was polarized between a politicized urban minority and the large mass of rural agriculturalists who represented about 80 per cent of the total population but who only marginally participated in the urban-based national political culture. Government efforts at mobilizing the rural population through development schemes were restricted by the dependence of the economy on the cultivation of a single crop—groundnuts—and the large degree of agricultural production carried out on the landholdings of traditionally oriented Islamic brotherhoods (see ch. 14).

Government efforts to stimulate national development have relied on the formation of national development plans, the first of which was a four-year plan inaugurated in 1961. Central government agencies and institutions were created to supervise regional planning centers and to facilitate coordination. Central control over development planning was strengthened in 1962 when overall planning functions were transferred to a secretary of state for planning and development, who was attached to the office of the president and aided by a national planning commission (see ch. 13).

The major focus of economic planning was on the agricultural sector, and government policy in regard to industrial development was that such expenditures as did occur should support agricultural development. Over half of the overall expenditures in the early 1960s were for improvement of the transportation and communication system with heavy emphasis on the road network—clearly envisioned as an aid to agricultural marketing (see ch. 15). The majority of government funds for development came from the French, primarily through the Investment Fund for Economic and Social Development of the Overseas Territories (Fonds d'Investissement pour le Développement Economique et Social—FIDES) and its successor, the Aid and Cooperation Fund (Fonds d'Aide et Coopération—FAC).

One of the prime institutions utilized to promote rural integration and development was the agricultural cooperative. The government established a major role for itself, moreover, in controlling the marketing of agricultural produce. In many cases, however, local production continued to be overseen by representatives of traditional religious groups or other elites. It was difficult to determine the long-range effect that initial government efforts had had.

The majority of social programs developed by the government were largely restricted to urban centers. Structural unemployment, delinquency, and problems related to the disintegration of traditional society were on an increase in the postindependence years. Although government efforts to train social workers had been initiated and the reorganization of medical education programs had been effected, the majority of the limited government funds for social problems attacked the more tangible urban problems such as the need for modern, low-cost private dwellings. Although some recreational facilities were planned, emphasis was on the provision of basic services, such as pure water supplies, sewers, and paved streets and marketplaces. Meeting a variety of urban social pressures, including those advanced by students and organized labor, placed increased demands upon the resources the government had to allocate (see ch. 8; ch. 5).

CHAPTER 3

GEOGRAPHY AND POPULATION

Senegal extends inland from a 300-mile coastline on the Atlantic Ocean, which is marked near its center by the Cap Vert peninsula—the westernmost point in Africa. Most of its land area, covering nearly 76,000 square miles, is a flat plain—a western segment of the broad savanna that extends across the continent at the southern edge of the Sahara.

Contiguous neighboring nations are Mauritania, Mali, Guinea, Portuguese Guinea, and The Gambia (see fig. 1). The Gambia is an elongated enclave, surrounded by Senegal except for its coastline on the Atlantic Ocean.

As all of Senegal lies south of 17°N latitude—well within the tropics—temperatures are high throughout the year. Annual rainfall is almost entirely limited to the summer wet season, which lasts up to six months in the south and decreases to three months in the north. The level of rainfall—moderate in most of the nation in the best of years—was significantly lower than average during most of the 1968-73 period. By 1973 the drought had become the worst in sixty years. Cumulative shortages of groundwater, forage, and subsistence foods had become a disaster affecting Senegal, particularly the northern area; the neighboring nations of Mauritania and Mali; and other Sahelian nations farther east (see ch. 14).

Even in years of normal rainfall, vegetation in most of northern Senegal is limited to fibrous grasses and thorn scrub, shading into open grasslands marked by shrubs and scattered trees near the center of the country. Southward more trees encroach upon the grassy, open areas, and mixed subtropical forests prevail in the extreme south, particularly between the lower reaches of the Casamance River and the border with Portuguese Guinea.

Most of the country, including northeastern Senegal—more than 200 miles from the Atlantic coast—is less than 300 feet above sea level. The predominant landscape is a flat expanse of sparse grasses and woody shrubs, remarkable only for the near-total absence of natural landmarks or major changes in elevation. Broken terrain and steep slopes are found only in the extreme southeast, where a few ridges stand above 1,300 feet. Because gradients are so shallow, all the largest rivers—the Sénégal, Sine, Saloum, and Casamance—are sluggish, marsh-lined streams emptying into ill-defined estuaries along the Atlantic Ocean.

Extensive riverine areas have been converted to farmland, especially in the Sine and Saloum River basins lying east and southeast of the Cap Vert peninsula. Beyond these areas, however, most of the land has little potential except as pasturage.

Population densities are highest in the agricultural areas and in the industrial complexes in Cap Vert and Thiès, the westernmost of Senegal's seven administrative regions. Of an estimated national total of slightly less than 4 million people in mid-1973, nearly one-third lived in these two regions on less than 4 percent of the nation's total land area. In general, population densities decreased in direct ratio to the distance from the Atlantic coast. Most of the land in the easternmost regions—Fleuve and Sénégal Oriental—supported fewer than ten persons per square mile.

About 70 percent of the people were rural dwellers, more or less directly dependent upon agriculture for a livelihood. Through internal growth combined with a continuing influx of migrants from rural areas, the larger towns—already holding about 30 percent of the population—were growing at rates of at least 4 percent per year, as compared with an overall national growth rate officially estimated in 1971 at about 1.9 percent.

Over a period of several decades many of these rural migrants—and considerable numbers of migrants from nations bordering on Senegal—have made their way to Dakar. As the nation's capital, major port, and center of industry, commerce, and culture, the city continued its previously established pattern of rapid growth into the 1970s. By 1973 the Dakar urban complex had an estimated population of more than 600,000 people, six times as large as that of any other urban center in the country.

Railroads and a few all-weather highways, supplemented by feeder roads, served the more densely populated and developed areas in western Senegal, and a railroad extended from Dakar eastward across Senegal and into neighboring Mali. This was the only railroad that extended into the eastern half of the nation, which also lacked all but a bare minimum of improved roads (see ch. 15).

BORDERS AND ADMINISTRATIVE DIVISIONS

Most of Senegal's peripheral borders follow lines that originally marked internal administrative units of former French West Africa. Borders follow physical features in some segments, but other sections are arbitrary lines across open terrain. The borders with Portuguese Guinea and The Gambia—the latter an enclave enclosed by Senegal except for its coastline on the Atlantic—are the result of bargaining between colonial powers. Although many of the ethnic groups living in border areas are closely related to their neighbors in the adjoining states, the borders have been generally accepted, partially because they can be easily crossed in most areas by nomads and migrants. Border frictions or disputes were not a major problem in 1973.

In the north, Senegal's boundary with Mauritania extends inland from a survey point north of Saint-Louis, bends northeastward to the main channel of the Sénégal River, and then follows the river's northern and northeastern bank for about 500 miles to its confluence with the Falémé River. The line was first established de facto by the French in the 1850s as a military measure to protect river traffic and the people on the south side from marauders living farther north. It was later confirmed by treaties with several Mauritanian emirs.

In southeastern Senegal the border with Mali extends from the junction of the Sénégal and Falémé rivers upstream along the main channel of the Falémé for about thirty miles. It then curves in an irregular line some fifteen miles east of the watercourse for about sixty miles before again joining the river for another 130 miles, where it reaches the meeting point of the states of Senegal, Mali, and Guinea. From here, the border with Guinea swings irregularly westward across the northern spurs of the Fouta Djallon highlands for 150 miles to the northeastern corner of Portuguese Guinea and has little or no relation to natural features.

After a long series of disputes, the boundary with Portuguese Guinea was settled by a Franco-Portuguese treaty in 1886. The line extends due west from the corner of Guinea for 100 miles, then swings southwestward and westward for about the same distance to the sea. This latter section of the boundary follows the watershed ridge line between the Casamance River, which is about twenty miles to the north, and the Cacheu River, about the same distance southward in Portuguese Guinea.

Senegal has extensive borders with The Gambia, a separate nation along the Gambia River (central segments of this major river are in Senegal, where it is called the Gambie). From a short coastline on the Atlantic Ocean at the mouth of the Gambie, Gambian territory extends 200 miles inland along the river. Senegal surrounds this enclave, except for its coastline, and The Gambia's elongated wedge of land partially separates Senegal's southernmost region (Casamance) from the central and northern regions.

The westernmost segments of the Senegal-Gambia borders are artificially drawn straight lines, except for a small section near the coast on the Casamance side of The Gambia. Farther east the borders are winding lines conforming to the course of the river, encompassing lowlands five to ten miles wide on each side of the main channel.

Internal administrative boundaries were redrawn in 1960 to establish seven regions replacing the former circles (*cercles*) (see ch. 9). Many of the new internal boundary lines were artificially drawn; only a few segments follow identifiable terrain features. Nevertheless, they appear to have been based on a consideration of demographic factors.

One of the announced purposes of the territorial reorganization into regions was to create homogeneous economic units in order to facilitate economic planning.

The westernmost regions, Cap Vert and Thiès, are the two smallest in Senegal. They are the sites of the country's main urban and industrial developments and support more than a quarter of its inhabitants. Fleuve Region consists of the well-populated and fertile valley of the Sénégal River and an extensive area of sparsely inhabited semidesert that includes most of the Ferlo (see Major Geographic Areas, this ch.).

The regions of Casamance and Sénégal Oriental coincide with poorly defined but recognizable geographic units. The relatively wet lowlands of Casamance are separated from the moderately elevated area of Sénégal Oriental by an internal boundary that follows the Koulountou and Gambie rivers. Both regions are remote from the nation's most important political and economic centers.

MAJOR GEOGRAPHIC AREAS

Most of Senegal is an ancient sedimentary basin. Most ridges or other highly visible physiographic features have long since been smoothed into a gently undulating plain by erosion, and ancient valleys or depressions have been filled with alluvium and windblown sand. Volcanic action created the Cap Vert peninsula and the nearby islets. Metamorphic and igneous rock formations appear only in southern Sénégal Oriental Region, in the southeastern part of the country. Except for several minor hills near Thiès, a few miles inland from the Cap Vert peninsula, the southeast is the only area with elevations of more than 300 feet above sea level; even there, only a few ridges exceed 1,300 feet.

Contrasts between geographic regions are primarily functions of climate and the availability of surface and subsurface water supplies. The lower river basins in the west are only a few dozen feet above sea level. Above their floodplains, variation in elevation is so minor that it has little influence on the zonal differences in climate and vegetation. In most inland areas the absence of distinctive terrain features makes it difficult to establish regional or zonal borders except in a most general way (see fig. 3). The few minor exceptions include a narrow zone along the coast, which is marked by dunes separating small pools and estuaries.

Coastal Belt

Much of the coastal belt north of the Cap Vert peninsula is covered by small swamps or pools separated by very old dunes that were originally built up by wave and wind action. The belt is still known as the Cayor, a name retained since the sixteenth century, when kings of the Wolof ethnic group dominated this area. This northern half of Senegal's shoreline sweeps in a smooth, uninterrupted curve southwestward from the estuary of the Sénégal River to the westernmost point of land

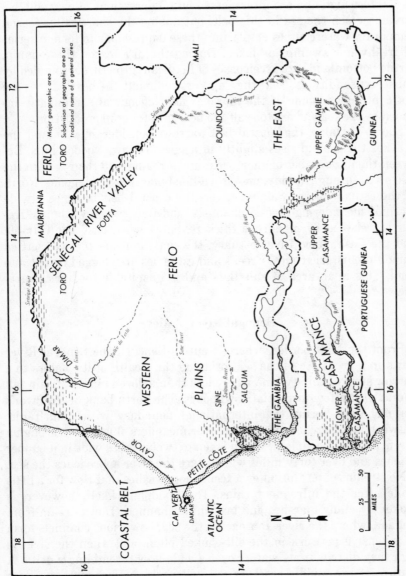

Figure 3. Major Geographic Areas of Senegal

FERLO   Major geographic area
TORO   Subdivision of geographic area or
        traditional name of a general area

MAURITANIA

MALI

SENEGAL RIVER VALLEY

FOÛTA

TORO

Senegal River

Senegal River

Falémé River

BOUNDOU

THE EAST

UPPER GAMBIE

Gambie River

GUINEA

Koulountou River

FERLO

UPPER CASAMANCE

DIMAR

Lac de Guiers

Vallée du Ferlo

WESTERN

Sine River

PLAINS

SINE

Saloum River

SALOUM

Songrougou River

THE GAMBIA

LOWER CASAMANCE

Casamance River

CASAMANCE

PORTUGUESE GUINEA

COASTAL BELT

CAYOR

PETITE CÔTE

CAP VERT

DAKAR

ATLANTIC OCEAN

N

0   25   50
MILES

43

on the peninsula, northwest of Dakar. The associated coastal belt of dunes and swampy areas extends inland as much as fifteen miles. The combined influence of the Canary Current, which moves southwestward along the coast, the northeast trade winds, and heavy surf have formed a wide, sandy beach backed by dunes. Some dunes are as much as 100 feet high and are interspersed with depressions of clay soil. No streams reach the sea in this belt, but during the short rainy season temporary watercourses empty into these depressions to form a series of freshwater swamps or lakes. During the dry season these damp, fertile bottomlands are green oases of luxuriant growth, surrounded by subdesert conditions. Near the Cap Vert peninsula the beach dunes are not continuous; some of the marshes and lagoons are frequently invaded by the sea and are too salty to be useful for crop production.

South of Dakar the coastal belt narrows considerably. Behind the beaches the ground rises slightly in a series of low, wooded hills. Between them a number of short, seasonal streams find their way to the sea, often through muddy, mangrove-lined marshes and lagoons. North of the estuary of the Saloum River, the coastal belt becomes a wide maze of meandering creeks, channels, and flat, swampy islands, frequently choked by mangrove thickets. Southward, past The Gambia and the Casamance River estuary, the coast appears to have settled during prehistoric times. Creeks and estuaries are clogged by silt and sand. This is an area of salt flats and is unsuitable for agricultural use.

Sénégal River Valley

From the Mali border, where it enters Senegal, the Sénégal River flows in a great arc to the sea, bringing the wealth of its waters to a narrow strip of thirsty land where less than a dozen inches of rain fall annually in a few torrential downpours. The north bank of the river's main channel forms the international boundary with Mauritania. Between low, parched ridges, the river meanders sluggishly through a green, alluvial floodplain, which is ten to twelve miles wide in its upper reaches and over forty miles wide where the river approaches the sea.

No streams enter the valley, except short washes that flow for a little while after the infrequent rains. The floodplain itself, however, is broken by many marshes and branching channels. Downstream from Dagana, where the river approaches the sea, its various channels form an extensive network in the silt-choked plain, and when the river is high they distribute its waters over a wide area resembling a delta. A feature of the middle reach of the valley above Dagana is the Ile à Morfil—a narrow island several hundred miles long between the river's main channel and the sluggish Doué channel on the opposite side.

Human life in this region is governed by the river's annual flood. Rising water spreads through the whole system of channels, sloughs, and adjacent lowlands until most of the valley is a sheet of water from which the tops of trees appear as green patches; villages stand out as isolated islands. Crops are sown as the flood recedes. Soon after, as the long dry season sets in, the region offers the contrast of a green ribbon winding through a countryside burned brown by the harmattan, a persistent wind from the Sahara.

Western Plains

Except for the dunes in the coastal belt, the only noteworthy elevation in the western plains is a small group of hills that rise to about 200 feet above sea level northwest of the town of Thiès (see fig. 1). The lowlands extending southeastward from Thiès to Kaolack have developed into an important agricultural area, producing groundnuts (peanuts) and other food crops (see ch. 14). Soils are loose and sandy and are easily depleted. The original vegetative cover has been almost completely cleared. During the dry season the land in this area is almost barren except in a few depressions where groundwater is close to the surface. Where the earth is not altogether bare, it is covered with dry grass, dead stubble, stunted bushes, and scattered trees. Shortly after the first rains in June, however, the land comes to life. New grass sprouts, and fields of groundnuts, interspersed with millet and other food crops, form a green landscape.

The Ferlo

An inland continuation of the western plains, the Ferlo is a generally featureless expanse of savanna covering most of the area between the Sénégal River, along the border with Mauritania, and The Gambia. The annual rainfall is so scanty and the thin, sandy soil so porous that water can be obtained during the dry season only from wells located along the few shallow depressions that cross the flat landscape. Nomads move through the area during the short rainy season, when sparse forage is available for their animals. They leave as the rainy season ends. Dried tufts of sun-yellowed grass, scrub, and thorn trees dominate the scene during the rest of the year.

Casamance

Casamance is partially separated from most of Senegal by The Gambia and is slightly different in terms of relief, rainfall, and vegetation. The valleys inland from the coastal belt are flat and subject to flooding each year, but they are separated by areas high enough to escape annual inundations. In the southeastern corner of the region a divide that rises south of the Casamance and Gambie river basins reaches a 200-foot elevation. The Casamance River is tidal and salty as far as seventy-five miles inland. As a consequence, low areas along the tidal reaches of the river and along its lower tributaries are often infertile and can support only a limited variety of vegetation unless protected by dikes. Rainfall is heavier, and the rainy season is longer than in the region north of The Gambia. The town of Ziguinchor, for example, usually has three times as much rain as Dakar. Thus, although terrain differences are minimal, vegetation in the coastal area of Casamance is quite different from that in the majority of Senegal's land area and includes mangrove, thick forest, and oil palms. This vegetation shades into wooded or open savanna in the central and eastern parts of the region, where soils are poor and the population is sparse.

The East

A poorly defined plain extends southeastward from the Ferlo to the borders of Mali and Guinea. It straddles a low, poorly defined north-south divide separating the watershed of the Gambie on the west from the narrower Falémé River basin on the east. West of the Falémé confluence with the Sénégal River, ill-defined high ground extends westward to form another minor divide between the Ferlo and the northern half of the Gambie basin. Except for the Falémé River and a few short tributaries, the only perennial watercourses in this area are tributaries of the Gambie. Rainfall and other climatic conditions are about the same as in the Ferlo, except that the annual rainfall increases substantially toward the southern end of the plain, and temperature ranges are wider. Most of the region is poor, seasonal pastureland, dotted with acacia and scrub growth. There are many areas of infertile laterite. The region is thinly populated and, except for the Ferlo, is the latest developed part of Senegal.

DRAINAGE

The Sénégal River, which marks the northern border of the country for a considerable distance, carries water from wetter areas farther south into the subarid fringe of the Sahara and eventually to the Atlantic Ocean near Saint-Louis. Over 2,500 miles long, the Sénégal rises in neighboring Guinea, where sixty to eighty inches of rain fall each year. Its main upper tributary is known as the Bafing River until it is joined in eastern Mali by the Bakoy River, forming the Sénégal River. As it enters Senegal, it is joined from the south by the Falémé River, which also rises in Guinea. Downstream there are no falls or rapids, and the average gradient is only a few inches per mile.

The river's annual floods are fed mainly by the heavy seasonal rains that begin in April in the mountains of Guinea, but flood crests do not arrive in Senegal until mid-September and thereafter take about six weeks to reach the sea. Annual maximums average about forty-five feet above minimums at the Senegal-Mali border, decreasing to well under twelve feet when the crest is within 100 miles of the mouth of the river. There, heavy stream deposition and reduced gradient cause the floodwaters to break into a network of distributaries, drawing off so much volume that crests are scarcely perceptible in the river's estuary at Saint-Louis.

During normal low water, ocean tides range nearly 300 miles upstream; the river is salty for half that distance, and the system of distributaries becomes a maze of brackish swamps and backwaters. For a month or so during the higher stages of the flood, however, the salty water is forced seaward, and the system is filled with fresh water. In recent years this ebb and flow has been checked at some points by dikes that are opened to admit the fresh water and are later closed to impound it for use during the dry season and to exclude any advancing salt water. The most important arrangement of this kind includes a dam and a gate on the Taoué channel, a hundred miles inland, not far from Dagana, which control a shallow lake, extending southward about fifty miles and averaging about eight miles in width, known as the Lac de Guiers. At highest level the lake waters reach another forty to fifty miles southeastward into the Ferlo valley, replenishing the water table in an otherwise parched area.

Above Saint-Louis the river forms an estuary that is divided southward by a long sandbar. Known as the Langue de Barbarie, this barrier is not more than half a mile wide and is so low that waves wash across it in some places during rough seas. Throughout the last century its length has varied between ten and twenty miles. At its extremity, where the river meets the open sea, there is a dangerous shifting bar that sometimes prevents the passage of ships for several weeks at a time.

The Saloum River and its major affluent, the Sine River, are sluggish streams feeding into an extensive tidal swamp just north of The Gambia. Only the lower reaches carry water all year, and these are brackish, as the tides penetrate far up the various channels through the swamp.

The middle reaches of the Gambie are within Senegal. Rising in the Fouta Djallon, a highlands area in Guinea, the Gambie enters the southeastern corner of Senegal, swings northwestward, and winds for about 200 miles to the border with The Gambia. In addition to a few intermittent tributaries on its northern flank, the river receives the flow of a perennial river, the Koulountou, which runs north from Guinea to join it near the Gambian border.

The Casamance River in southern Senegal drains a narrow basin, less than twenty miles wide, between The Gambia and the border with Portuguese Guinea. It is sluggish and swampy for most of its 200-mile length. Its main tributary is the Songrougrou River, which joins it from the north about sixty-five miles from the sea. Downstream from this point, the river is a broad estuary, six miles wide at the mouth, and there are several smaller outlets separated by flat islands. Tides penetrate about 100 miles inland.

CLIMATE

The outstanding characteristics of the climate are relatively high daytime temperatures throughout the year and a long annual dry season. As the country lies between 12°N and 17°N latitude, well south of the Tropic of Cancer, days vary less in length, and solar radiation is more intense and persistent than in temperate latitudes.

Rainfall is generated in a broad contact zone, or intertropical front, when warm, humid equatorial and maritime air masses shift northward during the first half of the year in response to the changing angle—or apparent northward migration—of the sun. Moisture from equatorial land and sea areas rides northward on warm winds from the south and southwest.

Meanwhile, a cooler, drier continental air mass prevails in temperate zones, including northern Africa. In Senegal the prevailing wind for much of the year is from the northeast—the dry, dusty harmattan from the central Sahara.

Interaction between these two air masses produces a broad belt of instability and rain, which shifts northward to cover all the country in late summer and then retreats southward in late summer or early autumn, along with the apparent return of the sun to equatorial areas. The thirsty harmattan again prevails, desiccating vegetation and evaporating any remaining accumulations of surface water.

Rainfall may vary greatly from week to week or from year to year, causing floods or droughts. Average annual percipitation in most of the Casamance Region of southern Senegal is between fifty and sixty inches and is spread over a six-month period from May through October; in central Senegal, including the densely populated areas between Dakar and Diourbel, it is twenty-five to thirty inches and falls during the four months from mid-June to mid-October; the north receives less than twenty inches, almost all of it limited to the three months of July, August, and September (see fig. 4).

Droughts seriously affected Senegal and other nations along the southern edge of the Sahara during the late 1960s and early 1970s. The cumulative effects, compounded by a continuation of the drought, made 1973 a disaster year for most of these nations. A large percentage of the livestock in northern Senegal died. In mid-1973 much of the human population of this area was either seriously short of food or actually starving. The United Nations Food and Agriculture Organization (FAO), other international bodies, and various individual nations provided emergency aid, including airlifts of food for people and animals. Whether or not the droughts would continue in future years, great damage had already been done to the natural vegetative cover as well as to human and animal populations.

Temperatures in coastal areas rarely fall below 60°F, and daily, monthly, and annual ranges are limited. Inland, away from the moderating influence of the ocean, seasonal daily maxima are often above 100°F. The difference between the mean monthly maxima and minima may be 35°F, and the daily range can be more than 40°F.

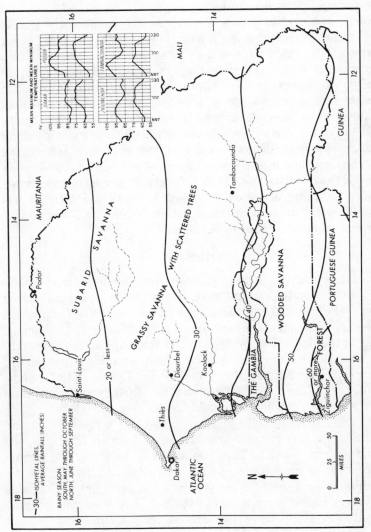

Source: Adapted from Senegal, Ministère du Plan et du Développement, *Cartes pour servir à l'aménagement du territoire*, Dakar, October 1965.

Figure 4. Climate of Senegal

49

Within these limits the climate is relatively homogeneous throughout the country, except in a narrow strip along the northwestern coast between Cap Vert and the border with Mauritania. This area is influenced by trade winds from the Atlantic Ocean and by the cool water of the Canary Current flowing from the north. Temperatures are somewhat lower and more uniform than those recorded in the interior, and the rainy season is a few weeks shorter.

Ordinarily the surface winds throughout the country are gentle; annual averages at most stations are two to four miles per hour. Along the northwestern coast, however, the average speed is nearer ten miles per hour when trade winds prevail. Once the seasonal winds are established, nights are generally calm, but the wind comes up at dawn and is strongest by late afternoon. Along the coast, land and sea breezes may modify the pattern. Winds of gale strength occur chiefly at the beginning and end of the rainy season in connection with line storms along the intertropical front. Known locally as *tornades*, they are not the same as the tornadoes of the United States. Apt to occur anywhere in the country, the *tornades* move rapidly from east to west, accompanied by thunder, lightning, and squalls of wind that may exceed fifty miles per hour. They are of short duration but are usually followed by torrential rain that lasts for one or two hours.

SOILS

The various types of soils in the country are distributed in zones extending approximately east and west, which can be loosely correlated with the level of rainfall and the density of the vegetation from which the necessary components of soil are derived. Most soils are acidic, especially in the south. The red-brown soils extending across the northernmost area of the country have a fairly good organic content but are likely to become very hard during the dry season. The soil of the Sénégal River valley in the northern border area is benefited by annual deposits of alluvium borne in during the annual flood.

The savanna types of soil lying in a broad belt across central and southern Senegal vary considerably, but all of them are thin soils, low in organic content. North of The Gambia the soil is sandy and permeable, except for accumulations of clay in swamps and floodplains. Although this soil is suitable for the production of groundnuts, the fields in many areas in the western part of the belt have been exhausted by bad farming practices. Along the tidal reaches of all the estuaries, salt water invades the land during the dry season and, unless controlled by dikes, causes sterile salt flats unsuitable for cultivation.

Across Casamance Region and the southern area of Sénégal Oriental, the soil is strongly acid and heavily leached, contains much free iron, and tends to laterize. Impermeable and very weak laterites are common in southeastern Senegal, where high temperatures prevent the accumulation of humus by encouraging the decomposition of plant fibers soon after the plant dies. Heavy rains wash away the partially decomposed plant materials before they can become part of the soil. They also penetrate subsurface soil layers, where they leach out all kinds of nutrients and organic compounds and carry them to levels below the reach of root systems. As a result, the soil lacks plant nutrients and contains a high proportion of iron, aluminum oxides, and hydroxides. Such lateritic soil becomes acidic, tends to harden, and is difficult to work. At its worst it can form a barren, hard crust several feet deep.

VEGETATION

The distribution of the common types of vegetation is determined by the amount of annual rainfall and its seasonal distribution. Temperatures throughout the year favor plant growth if water and plant nutrients are available. Because annual rainfall decreases from south to north, vegetation zones tend to be ill-defined belts extending from east to west across the country, ranging from dense cover in the southern swamps to scattered trees and scrub in the northern plains. The most convenient description covers three main belts and a narrow subzone along the Atlantic coast.

Subarid savanna vegetation covers much of the northern part of the country between the Sénégal River and the latitude of Dakar and the Cap Vert peninsula, excluding the immediate coastal region. This is an area of scrub and sparse grasses, all of which can survive and reproduce under seasonally dry conditions. Woody species are not numerous, rarely occur in groves, and do not grow to great heights. Most prominent, and important as sources of gum arabic and cattle feed, are gum trees and other varieties of acacia. Some characteristic trees are the desert date, several kinds of jujube, and the African myrrh. Most of the trees and shrubs are thorny and bear only very small leaves, which are dropped as the dry season advances. Several types of grasses grow in tufts, interspersed with low herbaceous cover during the short season of rains. They wither when the harmattan brings hot, dry weather. Except for groundnuts and rice grown in floodplain areas, few foreign species of plants have been successfully introduced here.

A belt of grassy savanna interspersed with trees and shrubs stretches across the country between the subarid northern savanna, or Sahelian zone, and The Gambia. In this belt plant life is more varied than that of the north, but the natural vegetation has been largely destroyed or modified in the well-populated western part of the belt. Here, however, there are a great many introduced species that are valuable for food or for commercial or aesthetic purposes. The natural vegetation of the zone consists of a mixture of trees and grasslands. The most characteristic trees are from twenty to fifty feet high and are more frequently individually spaced than standing in groves. Where groves occur, they are usually dominatd by a local variety of mimosa. Among the larger trees are the shea tree, a dry-zone mahogany, the baobab, and members of the bombax family. Several species of combretum grow in the eastern part of the zone in areas of laterized soil. Fairly tall grasses are common in uncultivated areas. They make poor forage but are not dense enough to impede travel. Grasses die or become dormant during the dry season, and most of the trees lose their leaves for at least a short time.

A narrow belt of coastland extending northward from Dakar is influenced by air masses from the ocean and is generally classified as the Senegal coastal, or subcanarian, vegetation zone. This is a region of sand dunes and brackish swamps, where greater humidity and water resources encourage a vegetation mix similar to that in humid areas farther south, but the soil may be saline from the nearby ocean and may support only the most salt-resistant plant life. Oil palms reach north into this subzone and are found in groves around the fertile swamps, which are also sites for market gardens. In less favored locations there are salt cedars, a few varieties of acacia, and clumps of coarse grass. Ironwoods have been planted over extensive areas to control soil erosion and serve as windbreaks; some of them are also cut as Christmas trees. Around Saint-Louis a variety of mimosa is commonly used to form protective hedgerows.

The southernmost of Senegal's vegetation zones, the Casamance woodlands, extends across all of Casamance Region and into the upper Gambie area in Sénégal Oriental Region. Because of a transition from rather heavy forest in the west to more open woodland in the east, some authorities classify the eastern half as a separate zone.

Western Casamance Region, which has a comparatively heavy rainfall and a high water table, supports a vegetative cover similar to that of Portuguese Guinea and other humid areas nearer the equator. The Casamance River and coastal channels, up to tidal limits, are bordered with mangrove trees mixed on the landward side with saltbush, screw pine, raffia, and rattan palms. Many areas have been cleared for the production of rice and are protected by elaborate artificial embankments and ditches. Government plans call for the continuing development of the rice-growing potential of areas extending for fifty miles along the central reaches of the Casamance River and along its major tributary, the Songrougrou River (see ch. 14). On higher ground are many groves of oil palms and fairly heavy stands of forest festooned with parasitic plants, vines, and woody creepers. Among the larger trees are mahogany, African teak, and several varieties of bombax. In recent years Asiatic teak has been planted in quantity. East of the middle of this zone the trees thin out, and there are patches of thick, low brush. Some of the more prominent trees in this area are the bombax and a number of varieties of palm.

MINERALS

The country's mineral resources had not been fully explored in 1973.

The only minerals being actively exploited were aluminum and calcium phosphates for fertilizers, salt, and such construction materials as marble and limestone. The aluminum and calcium phosphate beds being worked were located near Thiès and Taiba. Other phosphates in a broad area along the northern border, near Podor, were being studied. Salt was extracted from deposits located inland along the Saloum River, near Kaolack. Marly limestone, which is not common in West Africa, furnished raw material for a portland cement plant near Rufisque on the Cap Vert peninsula, which also had deposits of brick clay. Deposits of ilmenite and rutile, which contained titanium and iron compounds, and zircon were found in ores at the mouth of the Saloum River estuary and were exploited for a time in the 1960s by a French-owned firm, but exploitation was suspended in 1965 because of declining profits and reserves. Iron ore was available near the Falémé River in the southeastern corner of the country, but further study was considered necessary before a decision could be made on its economic potential.

Random prospecting has indicated that there may be other useful minerals in Sénégal Oriental Region, including columbite-tantalite, copper, tin, graphite, and diamonds. A small crew from the Soviet Union was prospecting, reportedly for gold, in eastern Senegal during 1972. Gold was extracted from alluvial sands hundreds of years ago in what is now eastern Senegal, and the purpose of the earliest French penetration of the Falémé River areas was to search for gold-bearing ores. These deposits proved to be disappointing and have not been thought to be worth exploiting with modern equipment.

Technicians from Western nations were testing for petroleum in offshore waters along the coast of Casamance Region, but a deposit of about 100 million tons located in early 1973 was of such viscous quality that reportedly it could be commercially exploited only if world petroleum prices should rise to exceptional heights.

WILDLIFE

Some species of wildlife are still common despite encroachment by the growing human population. Very few large mammals survive, however, except in the southern part of Sénégal Oriental Region. In this area, along the middle reaches of the Gambie, the government has established the Niokolo Koba National Park, a game preserve covering about 675 square miles. Elephants and hippopotamuses are found here, and grazing animals, such as waterbuck, cobs, elands, and gazelles, are numerous. Large and small members of the cat family, including a kind of lion that has no mane, roam this area, as do chimpanzees, monkeys, hyenas, jackals, and wild pigs.

There are fewer varieties in most other areas of the country and hardly any large mammals. Nevertheless, there are types of gazelle and antelope, wild pigs, and such animals as small members of the cat

53

family, monkeys, squirrels, hare, and rats of varying sizes.

Bird life is abundant and includes both local species and winter migrants from colder climes. Many waterfowl, such as cormorants, herons, egrets, ducks, terns, and pelicans, live in the estuaries of the major rivers and in the swamplands extending upstream. Grainfields in nearby agricultural areas are plagued by great flocks of queleas (sparrowlike members of the weaverbird family) and by other grain-eating birds. Drier areas support other birds, including the secretary bird, bustard, and ostrich. Quail, partridge, bush fowl, parakeets, hornbills, vultures, and kites are also found in Senegal.

Reptiles include crocodiles in the Sénégal River and the upper Gambie. Snakes are most numerous in southern Senegal (in Casamance Region), where the list of species includes the exceptionally dangerous green mamba, several kinds of vipers, cobras, and pythons.

Freshwater fish are plentiful only in the Sénégal River and its tributaries, where they are an important source of food. One of the most important species is the large Nile perch. Marine life, including oysters and prawns as well as fish, is more abundant in the estuaries of the major rivers. Saltwater fish go far upstream and are common in offshore waters. Commerical fishermen take tuna and a number of other edible varieties, and sportsmen hook sailfish, amberjack, and dolphin.

Insects are active all year. Grasshoppers, plant lice, termites, and other varieties are common enough to be serious pests. Various ants, flies, gnats, and chiggers are present in all seasons. Mosquitoes, which may be carrying malaria, yellow fever, or dengue, are common in most areas. The tsetse fly, which may transmit the parasite resulting in sleeping sickness in horses and cattle and trypanosomiasis in humans, is present in some of the more humid, wooded areas in southern Senegal.

SETTLEMENT PATTERNS

The level of rainfall and the availability—or absence—of drinking water during the dry season have probably been the primary determinants of patterns of settlement. In most inland areas groundwater is quickly evaporated, or it seeps away to underground channels, out of the reach of plant roots, soon after the end of the rainy season. The Ferlo in northeastern Senegal is the most readily identifiable area of this kind, but adjacent areas, including nonriverine areas near the west coast, are subject to similar problems. Herdsmen move about with their flocks in these seasonal pastures during the short rainy season. Neither forage nor water for their animals is available during the dry season except at scattered waterholes or wells. Considerable areas have no permanent residents.

On the other hand, the lower reaches of the river basins in western Senegal are flooded every year, and the subsoil retains some of the moisture well into the dry season. These areas fostered local sedentary farm cultures many centuries ago. Commercial farming expanded during the colonial period, the Thiès area and the Sine-Saloum river basin emerging as the most productive. Soils and climate especially favored the groundnut, which became the primary commercial and subsistence crop.

Other food crops also grew fairly well, encouraging settlement in the lower reaches of several river basins. The lower Sénégal River floodplain has had a dense population for hundreds of years. Swamplands among old coastal dunes along the northwest coast also supported a heavier population than that of drier inland areas. But in the nineteenth century and the first half of the twentieth century the groundnut culture flourished in the Sine-Saloum basin, and it became the area of greatest population growth. By the time of independence, however, the more productive lands in the Sine-Saloum area had been settled and exploited.

In 1973 the great majority of the population lived within 100 miles of the Atlantic coast, either on the land or in the towns. The urban centers—including the capital city of Dakar—owed much of their existence to a century of growth of subsistence and commerical agriculture in the lower reaches of the river basins.

Cities and Towns

The French, who shifted their interest from the Sénégal River area to west-central Senegal during the mid-1800s, began to develop Dakar in 1857, originally as a naval base, on a site that had previously held only a fishing village. Saint-Louis at the mouth of the Sénégal River was then the headquarters for French holdings in sub-Saharan Africa, but the administrative center was shifted to Dakar after 1900. By then Dakar was becoming an important commercial deepwater port.

Meanwhile, railroads and roads were under construction in the areas east of the Cap Vert peninsula and by 1923 had been developed into a network serving a semicircular arc of land extending inland beyond Louga, Diourbel, and Kaolack. River ports much smaller than Dakar had also been developed, but much of the commercially grown groundnut crop was hauled to Dakar for shipment to world markets. More land was developed for commercial crop production during the period from 1900 to World War II, and the population increased. Small towns appeared along railroads, at crossroads, or at river ports in the farm areas where previously only villages had stood. The towns remained relatively small until 1946, when they entered a period of rapid growth that continued in 1973. Migration from rural areas and from other nations was responsible for most of the increase in urban populations.

The capital city of Dakar is a complex mixture of administrative, commercial, and cultural activities, noteworthy for its importance to the nation and its rapid growth, which is attributed to its attraction for migrants. More than 15 percent of the nation's people lived in the Dakar complex in 1973. The great majority had been born elsewhere in Senegal or in other countries. Dakar was the nation's only truly urban center and the site of one of the great seaports and industrial complexes of West Africa. As a crossroads city it reflects European, Mediterranean, and African influences.

When the federation of French West Africa was formed in the late nineteenth century, Dakar became the seat of the federal government (see ch. 2). Despite the dissolution of the federation and the achievement of independence by the nations formed from the territory of the defunct federation, Dakar continued to be the major commercial and cultural center of the area formerly included in French West Africa.

The city proper occupies the southern end of the Cap Vert peninsula. Here on a plateau about 100 feet above the sea on either side are the tall, modern buildings, handsome residences, and tree-lined avenues of the business and administrative district. The architecture clearly shows its French origins. The harbor and port facilities are on the eastern side, sheltered from the open sea by the southward bend of the peninsula and by extensive sea walls. A crowded quarter adjoins the business district on the north. Known as the Médina, it is a mixture of shacks, cottages, and apartment buildings. Beyond, on the north, are residential districts and suburbs, including Grand Dakar, Colobane, Baobab, Pointe E, Liberté, and Pikine. Some are of haphazard growth; others are planned arrays of comfortable houses, surrounded by trees and gardens.

The industrial area is on the eastern side of the peninsula, along the railroad to Rufisque and the interior. On the western side beyond the Médina and facing the open sea are the buildings of the University of Dakar and the fashionable suburb of Fann. Yoff International Airport is about ten miles northwest of the center of Dakar, not far from the Pointe des Almadies, the westernmost tip of African continent.

Almost all of the other large urban centers are within 100 miles of the coast, and most are in the west-central agricultural area. The most noteworthy exception is Tambacounda, the capital of Sénégal Oriental Region, located some 250 miles inland along the Dakar-Mali railroad. The town and smaller agricultural settlements along the railroad in central Senegal reflect a modest exception to the primary migratory movements from inland to coastal areas and from rural areas to the towns. The increase in population along the central segments of the cross-country railroad consisted partly of migrants from the heavily populated farming areas in the west.

In the agricultural areas nearer the coast Kaolack and Diourbel, two of the largest agricultural towns, thrived on the production, processing, and transportation of groundnuts (see ch. 14). Thiès benefited directly from the same factors and was also the site of the main railroad division point and repair facilities (see ch. 15).

In 1973 Ziguinchor, in southern Senegal, was prospering as the commercial and administrative center of Casamance Region. In a more recent repetition of the history of land development and commercial food production in the Sine-Saloum valley and the adjoining farm areas near the central coast, land was being developed in the Ziguinchor hinterland for the production of food crops (see ch. 14). Rainfall was heavier there than in the central coastal area.

Saint-Louis, secondary port and capital of the northern region of Fleuve, had stagnated during the first few decades of the twentieth century after the administrative headquarters for French West Africa were transferred to Dakar. It retained administrative control of the Senegal portion of these French holdings until 1958, when this authority was also moved to Dakar. Despite such problems and the natural limitations on its port, it was growing at approximately the same rate as most other towns during the preindependence period. The hinterland served by the minor port and commercial interests at Saint-Louis extends deep inland. It includes an area of moderately heavy population density in the floodplains along the river and a few marshy tributaries, where sedentary agriculture is possible. The nonriverine areas in the town's natural trade territory contain very few people.

Seven of the ten largest towns, excluding Louga, Rufisque, and Mbour, are the capitals of their regions. All except Ziguinchor and Mbour are served by railroads. In the early 1970s industrial development was limited in almost all towns, as most of Senegal's industries were in or near Dakar (see ch. 14).

Some areas in Saint-Louis retained vestiges of the urban amenities and visual characteristics of its earlier history as a capital, but more recent growth has been haphazard. Since 1970 urban leaders in Thiès have been developing plans for improving some areas of the town and for controlling future growth.

Most sections in these or other large towns are little different from the smaller towns. Many neighborhoods were built up during the rapid growth period between 1946 and 1973 without local government guidance or assistance.

Smaller towns in most cases are expanded villages or agricultural settlements that have grown into formless agglomerations with a nominal status as towns, usually along the railroad lines or at crossroads. Most of them are minor service centers for local farms and collection centers for commercial crops. Like Dakar, all other towns have their unplanned squatter settlements of improvised huts and other shelters.

Villages

Despite the rapidity of the shift to the towns, most Senegalese still live in villages. Projections for the late 1970s and the early 1980s indicate that the majority of the population will continue to live in rural settings, removed for the most part from whatever amenities may become available in the larger towns.

Most villages are clusters of huts built from clay, fibrous plants, or rough timber. In some areas the clusters of dwellings and storage buildings belonging to a family group are built around a central courtyard, and the entire complex is screened by reed fences. These compounds and other dwelling units may be scattered on all sides of a centrally located village market.

In the past, the year-round water source was usually a stream or pool. The site selected for a village was usually near a water supply that could be depended upon during the last months of the annual dry season, even though the water might be stagnant and contaminated. Villagers usually select sites on slightly elevated ground in or near these wet areas, preferably close to a year-round water supply and to the land they are farming. Wells have become more common in recent years and undoubtedly have affected selection of some new village sites.

Nationwide, villages average about 200 people each. They usually have fewer than 200 residents in Sine-Saloum Region and adjacent parts of the main groundnut production area, and they were also small in eastern Casamance Region. They range from 200 to 500 or more people in central Casamance, where soil conditions in some river bottoms are more favorable than in other parts of the region.

Still larger villages, ranging up to 1,000 or more people, exist on high ground in or near the floodplain of the Sénégal River. Flood-borne silt from far upstream enriches the soil in the bottomlands every year. The subdesert areas a few miles away, beyond the reach of floods or irrigation projects, are visited by nomadic herdsmen but support only a few scattered small villages.

POPULATION

Population data available in 1973 were based for the most part on an official preliminary analysis of data collected by a demographic inquiry carried out by the Senegalese government in 1970 and 1971 with assistance from the United Nations. A previous inquiry had been carried out in 1960 and 1961, providing a basis for analysis of population trends, but no complete census has ever been carried out. Although limited to a small sample of the population, the inquiries appear to have been reasonably accurate, and they provide a basis for general conclusions and further study. They showed, for example, that the Wolof and Serer ethnic groups constituted more than half the population, but a dozen other groups were well represented (see ch. 4).

The pre-1960 population figures were based on estimates made by local administrators, which were reported regularly to the colonial administration. These crude estimates indicated a population of 1.5 million in Senegal in 1930 and 2 million in 1950. The 1960-61 inquiry, based on a sampling survey among selected sectors of the population, indicated a total of approximately 3 million people.

Analysis of the data collected in the 1960-61 and 1970-71 surveys indicated an average annual population growth rate during the 1961-71 period of 1.93 percent. This was somewhat lower than the previously reported rate of about 2.2 percent, which had been used as the basis for various estimates during the 1960s. This preliminary estimate was subject to further review, and some internationally respected observers continued in 1972 and 1973 to base their analyses of Senegalese population changes on the 2.2 percent rate.

Whichever was most accurate, growth at approximately the same general rate—roughly 2 percent annually—was likely for the near future; existing evidence did not suggest major reversals of the growth and migration trends of the early 1970s. Growth at about 2 percent per year, based on an estimated population of about 4 million in mid-1973, would result in a total of approximately 5.25 million by 1985.

If the Dakar-Cap Vert urban complex should continue to grow at the 6-percent-per-year rate observed during the 1965-73 period (some observers have suggested that the rate was probably nearer 8 percent), it would have more than 1.4 million residents by 1985. This would be about one-fourth of the total population projected for that time. Other towns were also expected to continue to grow, reflecting both the continuing coastward movement and rapid urbanization.

In 1973 the estimated population density for the entire nation, projected from data in the 1970-71 official demographic inquiry, was fifty-three persons per square mile (see table 1). By region, densities were highest, at 3,400 per square mile, in the small western region of Cap Vert, which is regarded by some observers as essentially urban in character. The adjacent, somewhat larger region of Thiès had about 220 persons per square mile, but small areas within the region, and a few farm areas elsewhere in the country, ranged upward to 250 per square mile. Between 1960 and 1970 the highest regional growth rate— 4.1 percent annually—had been in the remote inland region of Sénégal Oriental. Nevertheless, this large region was estimated to contain only about 256,000 people in mid-1973. Average density was approximately eleven per square mile. The Ferlo and adjacent areas east of 15°30'W longitude, approximately represented by a line from Dagana in the north to Sédhiou in the south, were inhabited by very few people, mostly nomadic or seminomadic herdsmen. Large areas of Fleuve Region averaged fewer than eleven persons per square mile.

Population Dynamics

The potential for continuing overall population growth was indicated by the youthfulness of the population, traditional attitudes that encouraged all women to marry, and an almost universal desire for many children. About 52 percent of the population was under twenty years of age in 1973. Women of this age were entering their most prolific years, from age twenty to twenty-four.

Table 1. Estimated Population by Region, Senegal, 1960, 1970, and 1973

| Region | Total Area (square miles) | Estimated Population[1] | | | | People per Square Mile |
		July 1960[2]	July 1970[2]	Percentage Annual Increase 1960–70[2]	July 1973[3]	
Sine-Saloum	9,243	727	772	0.6	786	85
Cap Vert	212	444	649	3.9	728	3,434
Diourbel	12,949	503	607	2.0	644	50
Casamance	10,943	530	601	1.3	628	57
Thiès	2,548	410	527	2.5	568	223
Fleuve	17,033	345	372	0.8	381	22
Sénégal Oriental	23,006	151	227	4.1	256	11
National Totals	75,934	3,110	3,754[4]	1.93	3,991[5]	53

[1]In thousands.
[2]From government of Senegal demographic enquiries.
[3]Projected, based on 1960–70 growth rate.
[4]Does not total because of rounding.
[5]Some published estimates indicate up to 4.2 million.

Source: Adapted from Senegal, Ministère des Finances et d'Affaires Economiques, *Enquête Démographique Nationale, 1970–71; Résultats Provisoires du 1er Passage*, Dakar, 1971.

Although men usually marry at a somewhat later age, most women marry by the age of nineteen. Single women of marriageable age are rare, particularly single women over twenty-five years. The 1970-71 survey data indicated the probability of six births for the average woman during her childbearing years (nominally fifteen to forty-five years of age).

Except among a tiny minority of westernized families, very few people had any knowledge of or interest in modern family planning. No government policy for such programs had been promulgated. Review of popular attitudes suggests that efforts to persuade parents to limit the size of their families would be resisted or disregarded.

Estimates of the number of children born to the average mother were in accord with other statistical data. These included a reported fertility rate of 174 per 1,000 and an estimated national birthrate of forty-three live births per 1,000 people per year.

As in most developing countries, the potential for rapid growth suggested by these factors was limited by high mortality rates affecting all age-groups. Because of inadequate diets, disease, and lack of medical care there are many stillbirths, and the infant mortality rate was approximately ninety-three per 1,000 or nearly 10 percent of all live births. Infant mortality in rural areas was about 181 per 1,000, dropping to about eighty-three per 1,000 in the larger towns. Most of the country's doctors and medical facilities were in Dakar and a few other towns, and the availability of medical care was undoubtedly a major factor in the rural-urban differential (see ch. 6).

Ages one to five remained hazardous for children who survived their first year. In some groups traditional taboos and customs increased rather than alleviated problems of diet and disease that affected the younger children. An average of 40 percent of the infant population died before reaching the age of five years.

Death rates were also high in older groups. The mortality rate for the entire population was about seventeen per 1,000 persons per year in the early 1970s. In the largest towns the rate was reportedly similar to rates of about ten per 1,000 recorded in a number of industrialized nations, but the estimated rate among the rural majority was nearly nineteen per 1,000. Life expectancy at birth, according to estimates based on the government's demographic surveys, increased from less than thirty-eight years in 1960 to about forty-two years in 1970.

Migration Patterns

Migration had already been a factor in the growth of the commercial food production area during the nineteenth century before rail and road construction programs were increased. Transportation improvements, including the completion of most of the railroads by 1923, encouraged more travel. In many cases migrants came from inland areas of Senegal or from neighboring countries for seasonal work on farms.

The majority of the seasonal workers from outside Senegal came from Mali and Guinea. Migrants also came from The Gambia, Upper Volta, and Portuguese Guinea.

Some of the migrants returned home after a season. Others moved to the towns during the dry season and then returned to the farms for another work season or more before returning to their homelands. Still others became permanent residents in Senegal. Some, who could properly be regarded as urban residents, were in the towns for only half the year, spending the agricultural work season on farms in a more or less permanent pattern of seasonal migrations. The patterns of migration from other countries, internal seasonal migration, and urbanization had become too interrelated and complex to separate.

The annual trek from various areas into the farming sectors has been important for many decades. Total numbers involved have varied greatly, ranging from 10,000 in some years to more than 50,000 in others. It continued into the 1970s, but the number of seasonal workers participating reportedly had declined after 1960. The droughts of the late 1960s and early 1970s, which in 1973 had become a disaster in countries all along the southern fringe of the Sahara, brought a resurgence of the trek from subdesert inland areas, but no data were available in mid-1973 on the numbers involved.

War in Portuguese Guinea and political and economic problems in Guinea have also led to migration into Senegal (see ch. 11). Sporadic reports indicated that by 1965 about 35,000 people had crossed into Senegal from Portuguese Guinea, and news reports indicated that this figure had risen to 82,000 by 1973.

In 1971 the president of Senegal referred to the presence of 800,000 non-Senegalese people in the country. In the absence of complete records on migrations and related data, officials apparently estimated that about 20 percent of the people were immigrants.

Information available in 1973 indicated that the total number of emigrants from Senegal was much smaller than the number of immigrants, although no specific official figures were available for either. Most native-born Senegalese who have left to live elsewhere have gone to France. It was estimated that 21,000 Senegalese were in Paris in May 1973; probably many others lived elsewhere in France and a few in other countries, but statistics were not available.

Urban Growth

No other population change has approached, in scope or significance, the movement from rural villages to the towns. The urban migration was the primary change of the post-World War II period, and it apparently accelerated after independence. Only Dakar and a few other towns had populations of more than 10,000 people in 1946. By 1973 about twenty-five towns exceeded that figure, and more than 1.2 million people, 30 percent of the nation's population, were tabulated as urban residents. More than half of them were in Dakar, and most of the remainder were in the nine next largest towns (see table 2).

Almost all towns were growing at rates of at least 4 percent per year; approximately half this rate was attributed to migration. Most of the large towns were located within 100 miles of the Atlantic coast and had grown primarily on an economic basis of commercial agriculture and closely related activities. The town of Tambacounda was an important exception, as it was located some 250 miles inland along the Dakar-Mali railroad line. Like the western towns, it grew along with the increases in cultivated land and rural population in the surrounding area. Lesser towns in central Senegal, served by the railroad and the highway that followed essentially the same route, were also growing.

Nearer the coast, Kaolack and Diourbel were among the largest towns where growth was based almost entirely on activities related to agriculture. Thiès benefited directly from the same activities and was growing more rapidly (5 percent per year) than any other large town except Dakar.

Table 2. Ten Largest Urban Centers, Senegal, 1973

Town	Geographic Location	Estimated 1973 Population	Percent Annual Growth Rate
Dakar.............	West-central coast.......	600,000	6+
Kaolack	West-central...........	113,500	4
Thiès..............	....do	105,000	5
Saint-Louis	Northern border	99,000	4
Ziguinchor........	Southern	57,500	4
Rufisque	West-central coast.......	54,000	4
Diourbel..........	West-central...........	43,500	4
Louga............	Northwest.............	40,000	4
Mbour............	West-central coast.......	30,000	4
Tambacounda.....	Inland, southeast........	24,500	4

Source: Adapted from Senegal, Ministère des Finances et des Affaires Economiques, Direction de la Statistique, *Situations Economique du Sénégal, 1971*, Dakar, 1972; and Senegal, *Enquête Démographique Nationale, 1970–71; Resultats Provisoires du 1er Passage*, Dakar, 1971.

Other Internal Migratory Movements

Against the background of generally westward or southward movements during previous centuries and the exodus from rural areas to the towns, another migration trend involved a relatively small number of people. Following a pattern of resettlement that was begun in the early twentieth century by Muslim pioneers, rural Senegalese had been shifting from the densely populated west-central regions to set up new homes and farms in the Terres Neuves (New Lands) of central Senegal (see ch. 14). Some were settling in the Sandougou River valley around the town of Tambacounda, capital of Sénégal Oriental Region. Other small numbers of migrants were moving south to the river basins in Casamance Region.

Nomadic or seminomadic peoples were also a part of a national pattern of historic and present-day migration. Seasonal movements into grazing lands in northern and central areas involved thousands of families of herdsmen. Some moved northward with the summer rains from a broad area of mixed grazing and farmlands in the west-central area and returned months later; others who had wintered in the marshy areas near Saint-Louis and the Sénégal River estuary moved eastward or southwestward for the forage that was available after the short rainy season had begun. Other groups followed traditional routes northward or westward from Sénégal Oriental Region, returning late in the year to winter ranges in the southeast.

CHAPTER 4

ETHNIC GROUPS AND LANGUAGES

Ethnic diversity characterizes Senegal as it does other African states. Reliable statistics regarding the strength of ethnic groups were not available in 1973. Six major groups constituted nearly 90 percent of the population, according to 1971 estimates. They were the Wolof—who alone accounted for more than one-third of the total—the Serer, Peul, Toucouleur, Diola, and Manding (see table 3).

Table 3. Estimated Population of Ethnic Groups in Senegal, 1971

Group	Number	Percentage
Wolof (Ouolof)	1,375,000	36.2
Serer (Sérère)	722,000	19.0
Peul (Fulbé, Fulani) Toucouleur (Tokolor, Tukolor) }	817,000[1]	21.5
Diola (Djola, Jola)	266,000	7.0
Manding (Malinké, Mandingo, Mandinka, Maninka) } Bambara (Bamana)	243,000[1]	6.4[1]
Sarakolé (Soninké) Diankhanké }	79,800[1]	2.1[1]
Lebou (Lebu)	68,400	1.8
Bassari, Balanté, Mandjaque, Mancagne, and others	83,000	2.2
Maures	57,000	1.5
Cape Verde Islanders	30,000	0.8
Europeans (chiefly French)	40,000[2]	1.0
Lebanese	18,000	0.5
TOTAL	3,800,000[3]	100.0

[1] Groups in braces speak same or related languages and are occasionally intermixed; individual numerical size of these groups has been combined to accommodate variations reflected in available source materials.
[2] French estimates show Senegal's 1970 French population as only 29,000 (27,500 in Dakar alone); Senegalese estimates are higher.
[3] Figures do not total because of rounding.

Few Wolof, Serer, or Diola live outside Senegal. The Toucouleur do but are most heavily represented within the country. The Peul, Manding, Bambara, and some of the small ethnic groups that make up the remaining 10 percent are found primarily in neighboring countries.

In spite of the diversity there is no sharp interethnic strife. Ethnic membership and local allegiances are important, but they are counterbalanced by many relationships and associations that cut across ethnic lines. Moreover, there is a long history of interpenetration and mutual adaptation. For hundreds of years before the colonial era the peoples of Senegal and adjacent areas were in contact—sometimes hostile, sometimes amicable—with each other. In the colonial and postcolonial periods the frequency of interaction among members of different ethnic groups increased, mainly because of urbanization, modern education, and economic development.

The extent to which ethnic groups participate in modern political and economic life is not altogether consistent with their numerical importance in the total population. The differences do not seem to be the result of extraordinary ethnic solidarity in political and economic matters or of the oppression of particular groups but rather the degree of urbanization and of geographic location (see fig. 5). These factors have favored the Wolof and the Serer and, to some degree, the Lebou. The Peul and the Toucouleur are more lightly represented in the modern sector in proportion to their numbers. The people of Casamance Region, such as the Manding, the Diola, and others, have on the whole tended to participate less in modern development than groups north of The Gambia. In some areas the uneven involvement in economic development has sharpened awareness of local interests.

The majority of Senegalese societies, including most of the larger groups, are characterized by marked and relatively rigid systems of stratification. Although changing, these systems were still conspicuous in the early 1970s. For some of the traditional upper strata, differences of caste and class rather than ethnic affiliation continue to be more important barriers to social and marital relations. Some of the lower strata, on the other hand, are more concerned with eliminating status disadvantages than with ethnic differences (see ch. 5).

A few people, chiefly the well educated and the urban, see themselves primarily as Senegalese nationals. For most, however, full-fledged identification with the nation-state is yet to come. On the other hand, no group seeks autonomy on ethnic grounds. National leaders— in and out of power—may on occasion cater to local or ethnic interests, but all publicly express the necessity and desirability of developing a national consciousness and of eliminating ethnic affiliation as an important basis for public and private relations.

A number of factors are conducive to these efforts. Culturally the Senegalese are fairly homogeneous, including similar patterns of dress and diet (see ch. 6). Nearly three-fourths of the population has close historical and ethnic connections, and most groups resemble each other in their social and political organization. More than 90 percent of the people adhere to Islam (see ch. 7). Senegalese Islam, however, is split into several brotherhoods that partly coincide with ethnic divisions. To some degree this is offset by ethnic groups (the Wolof, for example) belonging to different brotherhoods.

A major unifying influence is the widespread use of Wolof as a

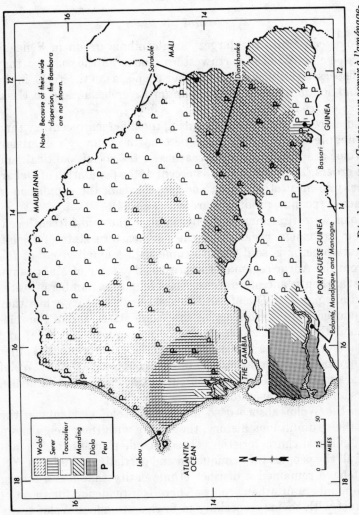

Source: Adapted from Senegal, Ministère du Plan et du Développement, *Cartes pour servir à l'aménagement du territoire,* Dakar, October 1965, p. 11; and Souleymane Diarra, "La Population du Sénégal," *Bulletin de l'Institut Fondamental d'Afrique Noire* (Series B) [Dakar], XXXIII, No. 3, 1971, p. 645.   *Figure 5. Distribution of Ethnic Groups in Senegal, 1971*

lingua franca. It is commonly used in public situations, and national leaders use it on ceremonial occasions to address crowds, often after an initial formal statement in French. Wolof is strictly a Senegalese language and is not spoken outside the country. The growing consciousness of the existence of a Senegalese nation owes a great deal to the extension of the Wolof language.

MAJOR ETHNIC GROUPS

Wolof

The Wolof constitute the largest single ethnic group in Senegal. Concentrated chiefly in the northwestern quarter of the country, they are also dispersed elsewhere among other people, as in the Ferlo, in the eastern and southern areas of the Saloum River basin, and in Casamance Region (see fig. 1).

Touched more deeply by change during the nineteenth century than other Senegalese, the Wolof have become the country's dominant group. Wolof are found in all the reaches of the social, political, and economic orders. They represent 43 percent of the population of Dakar, the majority in most other cities, and two-thirds of the population in the groundnut (peanut) producing areas (see ch. 14).

The Wolof were first mentioned by name in the mid-fifteenth century. Their expansion began from the northeastern state of Djolof, whose first emperor is said to have come with a small group of followers from the Adrar region of the present-day state of Mauritania. These first authentic ancestors of the Wolof founded a number of states that owed allegiance to Djolof until the sixteenth century when they became independent. The history of the Wolof states and of the relations among them were characterized by conquest, rebellion, and usurpation (see ch. 2). As the Wolof conquered and assimilated other groups, they became increasingly heterogeneous so that many Wolof families acknowledge Serer, Toucouleur, Peul, Sarakolé, Bambara, and others among their ancestors.

Because the Wolof absorbed so many non-Wolof elements in the course of their tumultuous history, they share with their neighbors a variety of cultural characteristics. These include elements of the languages of all the peoples they conquered and partially assimilated. Yet the Wolof have remained a distinct ethnic entity that has a strong appeal to members of other groups. There is a tendency for those in close contact with them—especially in towns—to adopt Wolof traits and to declare themselves Wolof when there is only a very slight claim to Wolof ancestry. The capacity to influence the ways of others, to adapt to changing situations, and yet to maintain a distinctive culture has remained characteristic of the Wolof.

Serer

In no other area of Senegal, with the exception of Casamance Region in the south, has an ethnic group occupied the same area as long as the Serer have in the Sine-Saloum and Thiès regions. Little is known of their earlier history, but their oral traditions and their present-day relations with the Peul and Toucouleur indicate that all formerly lived together in the Sénégal River valley and perhaps north of it. The Serer left that region during the eleventh and twelfth centuries because they refused, in contrast to the Toucouleur, to accept Islam. Perhaps they were also driven away by the political upheavals caused by the Almoravids and the demise of the Ghana Empire (see ch. 2). The Serer moved in family groups to settle farther south. When the Wolof established their kingdoms in these areas in the fifteenth and sixteenth centuries, those Serer who refused to become integrated in the Wolof political structures moved again to settle permanently in the forest-covered regions south and east of Cap Vert. The tradition of their passing through historical Wolof territory is preserved.

Thus the Serer in their present-day location are the descendants of those who first refused to accept Islam and later rejected assimilation by the Wolof. In the course of their relations with the Toucouleur and the Wolof, the Serer may have contributed to the formation of these other groups while absorbing non-Serer elements themselves.

Customarily the Serer are divided into two groups, the Serer-Sine and the Serer-Non. The former—and by far the larger—group is located in Sine-Saloum Region; the latter, in the Lac Tamma area in Thiès Region. The Niominka, a coastal group, seem to be Serer, distinguished from the others by their reliance on fishing rather than farming as a way of life. Another group sometimes classified as Serer is the Ndout of the areas around and between Thiès and Mont Rolland. The groups other than the Serer-Sine constitute well under 10 percent of the total Serer population. Linguistic research suggests that some of the dialects usually called Serer are not and that some of the people commonly included among the Serer are unrelated or only peripherally related to them. One linguist classifies Ndout, Non, and several apparently related languages spoken in a few villages around Thiès as Cangin. The common identification by outsiders may have contributed to a self-conception of these people as Serer, but the extent to which they so identify themselves is not clear.

Most Serer are cultivators. Their remarkable farming skills have made dense settlements possible. In fact, the population density in Serer areas—often as many as 250 people per square mile—is the highest in Senegal except for some parts of Casamance Region where rice is cultivated. The Serer combined the cultivation of millet with stockraising and concentrated on these activities even when they adopted groundnuts as a cash crop. In the early 1970s, however, their agricultural productivity could often no longer keep pace with a rapidly increasing population, accentuating a move begun in the previous decade to settle on new lands in eastern Sine-Saloum Region. During the dry season their young men and women often go to work temporarily in the towns to help earn money for the family. Comparatively few Serer have gone to live permanently in the cities, and those who have soon tend to designate themselves as Wolof.

Many Serer adhere to local traditional religious beliefs and have been slower than the Wolof and some other ethnic groups to accept modernizing trends. They do, however, participate in the modern economy through market crop cultivation, wage labor, and petty trading. Some have recently become Muslims, and about 15 percent are Christians. It is chiefly among the latter that educated Serer are found. President Léopold-Sédar Senghor is a Roman Catholic Serer.

Peul

The Peul belong to a large ethnic group spread through much of West Africa from Senegal to northern Cameroon. Their language is spoken by about 7 million people. They call themselves Fulbé (sing., Pullo) or some variant of that name. Outsiders usually refer to them as Peul in French-speaking countries and as Fulani in English-speaking areas.

Although their ultimate point of origin is still at issue, their nomadic ancestors are thought to have come from the area north of the Sénégal River and to have moved gradually southward and eastward during the last 400 or 500 years. During these migrations many became sedentary or semisedentary and mixed with local groups.

The Senegalese Peul are mostly stockraisers. About one-fifth are estimated to be still nomadic. Two large concentrations of sedentary and semisedentary Peul are found in the middle valley of the Sénégal River, in the zone immediately south of it, and in upper Casamance Region. In the river area they live mixed with Toucouleur, constituting fairly often their noble families and sharing the same language.

The nomadic or nearly nomadic Peul live chiefly in the arid and semi-arid Ferlo area in eastern Senegal. They can hardly be said to participate in the national life. They live in small groups headed by family chiefs who are, rather tenuously, under the authority of a lineage chief (ardo). In the late 1960s and early 1970s more and more nomads were becoming sedentary. Less mobile and more closely interdependent with sedentary peoples are the Peul who live among the Wolof, with whom they exchange cattle products for agricultural produce while maintaining their social autonomy. The sedentary Peul are among the most fervent Muslims in Black Africa. They are inclined to consider the nomadic Peul, who are usually either indifferent Muslims or adherents of traditional religious beliefs, as pagans.

The Peul maintain their ethnic identity, but they do not constitute a unified group because of their dispersion, varying historical experience, and—in the case of the nomads—their migrations. In the early 1970s a few Peul, chiefly from sedentary communities, migrated to the cities.

Toucouleur

The Toucouleur probably derive their name from the ancient kingdom of Tekrur, which was first mentioned by Arab writers in the eleventh century (see ch. 2). The Toucouleur may be the result of ancient mixing between Serer and Peul. This theory is supported by the fact that they frequently intermarry with the Peul, speak their language, and have a special "joking" relationship with the Serer (see Interethnic Relations, this ch.). Their traditional domain is the Fouta Toro, the part of the valley that the Sénégal River inundates from east of Dagana to about twenty miles north of Bakel. Some 50,000 Toucouleur are on the Mauritanian side of the river, many of them closely related to those in Senegal. Additional Toucouleur live in Mali, Guinea, and other West African countries.

The riverine Toucouleur are cultivators. In the last two decades their community has been subject to many stresses and strains. The poverty of their homeland, caused partly by a considerable increase in population, coupled with a decreasing income from marketable crops, has forced many of them to go elsewhere in order to find work. According to a survey made in the mid-1960s more than 25 percent of the Toucouleur lived outside their traditional homeland, many of them in urban centers. An estimated 100,000 Toucouleur lived in Dakar in the early 1970s. Others live in middle Casamance Region, southern Sine-Saloum Region, and Sénégal Oriental Region. It has been estimated that 25 percent of all men above the age of fourteen are regularly absent for varying lengths of time. Despite the poverty of their homeland, the vast majority of Toucouleur consider the valley their home and hope to return to it sooner or later.

The Toucouleur, led by their ruling dynasty, accepted Islam in the eleventh century and thus were among the earliest converts south of the Sahara. They were largely instrumental in spreading the Muslim faith. Their rigid system of social stratification is akin in some respects to that of the neighboring Wolof and of the sedentary Peul. Toucouleur ethnic consciousness, including pride in their ancient Islamization and in their language—which they share with the Peul and which is considered a language of culture and civilization—led them to form special political and social groups before independence (see ch. 2).

Diola

The Diola, Senegal's most isolated large group, are rice cultivators who have developed remarkably intensive methods using irrigation, transplanting, and fertilization. Their domain is the fertile, well-watered area of the lower Casamance River. They grow rice for consumption; groundnuts, introduced some forty years ago, are grown as a cash crop.

Diola history is uncertain. They may be remotely related to some of the country's major ethnic groups. According to one tradition they descended from the same ancestors as the Serer and like them may have moved in the past from a point farther north to their present-day location. The Diola, however, already were living in the Casamance area as ricegrowers when the Portuguese arrived in the fifteenth century. They consider themselves and are regarded by others as the region's original inhabitants. All the others—the Manding, Mancagne, Wolof, and Peul—are said to be strangers who came later.

The Diola are divided into a number of subgroups who speak several mutually understandable dialects. The most recent classification of groups mentions the Floup, Diamat, Dyiwat, Her, the Diola of Pointe Saint-Georges, the Diola of Brin-Seleky, and the Bayot. This classification also includes the distantly related Bainuk (Banyun), reputed to be the oldest group in southern Casamance Region. All are south of the Casamance River, and a few extend into Portuguese Guinea. North of the river are the Bliss-Karone and Fogny. These different groups had no common name until the middle of the twentieth century. In the early 1970s people in lower Casamance Region referred to themselves as Diola, and they demonstrated a certain solidarity when facing outsiders or immigrants, such as the Manding, who had begun penetrating their region.

The Diola differ markedly from other Senegalese in that they did not develop central political structures or social hierarchies (see ch. 5). Their traditional beliefs encompass a complicated cosmology, but a number of Diola have adopted either Christianity or Islam. Like others, the Diola have begun to go to the towns, most of them seasonally but a few permanently. Their regional isolation is gradually breaking down, but they still see themselves as people of the Casamance area rather than as Senegalese.

Manding

More than 1 million Manding are distributed among several West African countries in an arc of some 800 miles from the mouth of the Gambie (Gambia River) in the northwest to the interior of Ivory Coast in the southeast. Aside from those in Senegal, about 500,000 live in Guinea, several hundred thousand each in Ivory Coast and Mali, and smaller numbers in Portuguese Guinea and The Gambia. Although neither homogeneous nor monolithic, all Manding are linguistically and culturally related, and their ancestors were once united in the great Mali Empire (see ch. 2). Its successive capitals were located in the traditional heartland called Mande, or Mandin, on the Upper Niger River.

The Manding came into Senegal in two waves. The first occurred in the course of the expansion of the Mali Empire in the early fourteenth century. Sometimes referred to as the Socé (Sosse), they penetrated into the areas of Casamance, Sine-Saloum, and The Gambia as far as the Atlantic Ocean. Some imposed their rule on the Serer but were assimilated and became Serer, although their descendants recognize their Manding origin. These early Manding came into hostile contact with Wolof, Peul, and Toucouleur who were in a period of expansion.

The second wave began in the late eighteenth century and consisted of traders and peaceful proselytizers for Islam, which the Manding had adopted 300 years earlier. In the beginning of the nineteenth century the westward movement—through Kédougou—into the regions of southern Sénégal Oriental and upper Casamance, took on the character of an invasion. The Diola and others were pushed west, and only the French prevented expansion farther westward and to the north. Most present-day Senegalese Manding live east of the Diola in the center of Casamance Region south of 13°30′N. latitude. Their religious, political, and commercial activities along the rivers and traditional trade routes keep them in contact with Manding in Guinea, Gabon, and Portuguese Guinea.

The Manding are cultivators, living in large, compact, and fairly autonomous settlements. They are proud of the role they played in the religious wars of the nineteenth century, and they have retained a strong sense of cultural identity.

OTHER ETHNIC GROUPS

About 10 percent of the Senegalese population is composed of relatively small segments of ethnic groups whose most important loci, except for the Lebou, are in neighboring countries. Those on the southern and eastern borders have not been deeply involved in the economic and political life of the country, either before or after independence, and they have for the most part maintained their traditional ways of life. A number of them went to Senegal because of economic opportunities.

Bambara

The homeland of the Bambara in Mali is to the northeast of the Manding, to whom they are ethnically and linguistically related. The main distinction between the two groups is that the Bambara do not trace their origin from the Manding heartland on the Niger River, although they are numerically the predominant group in the country that adopted the name of the ancient Mali Empire. Rather, they consider Ségou in Mali to be their cultural center, which from the seventeenth century was the capital of a Bambara kingdom. Another difference from the Manding is that Islam has not attracted as many converts among the Bambara, many of whom continue to adhere to traditional forms of religion. The numerical strength of the Bambara is difficult to ascertain, partly because they are spread throughout the country, partly because they have been lumped together with the Manding for statistical purposes.

The Bambara are relative newcomers to Senegal who went there in response to economic developments since about the 1920s. Some work only seasonally for others in groundnut cultivation, but others have acquired rights to work the land and have settled more or less permanently in Sine-Saloum Region. Bambara also responded to the demand for railroad labor, and a number of them settled in and near Thiès Region, site of the railroad workshops. Finally, some of the Bambara recruited into the armed forces of former French West Africa have remained in Senegal. Many who came to the country as young, unmarried men took wives from Senegalese ethnic groups. Despite their participation in Senegal's agricultural and industrial labor force, they are not yet much involved in the country's political life.

Lebou

The Lebou live along the coast of the Cap Vert peninsula from Kayar in the north to Mbour in the south. Men and women mainly fish and cultivate the land only as a subsidiary occupation. Although accounts of their history are somewhat contradictory, they seem to have gone in the sixteenth century from the Fouta Toro into the adjacent Wolof state of Djolof. Later the Lebou are said to have fled and to have settled eventually in Cap Vert. There they were for some time under the rule of Cayor, another Wolof state, until they achieved autonomy in the late eighteenth century. A kind of representative republic was established, persisting into the late nineteenth century.

During their migrations the Lebou absorbed some Wolof and Serer cultural and social elements, and they speak a Wolof dialect. But they define themselves and are defined by others as a separate group. Symbols of Lebou ethnic consciousness are the continued existence of offices that were created in the late eighteenth century. Their leaders consider themselves representatives of a distinct Lebou community.

The Lebou converted to Islam relatively recently, although their leaders were already Muslims in the late eighteenth and early nineteenth centuries. Elements of their ancestral religion survive in many aspects of their daily life. The women especially have evolved syncretic beliefs and practices, which combine Islamic and pre-Islamic features (see ch. 7).

The Lebou, like the Diola, did not develop centralized entities or social stratification. Traditional social patterns persist, although a growing number of Lebou are influenced by the nearby city of Dakar and its opportunities and pressures for rapid change. Increasingly as young men enter the labor force, there is a fairly high rate of intermarriage with Wolof and, despite Lebou conservatism and clannishness, a comparatively high rate of participation in national life.

Sarakolé

The ancestors of the Sarakolé (Soninké) formed the basic population of the Ghana Empire (see ch. 2). With the dissolution of the empire

74

and their own Islamization, many Sarakolé became itinerant traders and religious proselytizers. About 600,000 members of the group live dispersed in a number of West African countries. Their primary distribution is in Mali and Mauritania along the sixteenth parallel. The Sénégal River between Matam and Kidira marks the western end of their east-west extension. Most Senegalese Sarakolé live either in the valley between Matam and Bakel or below the confluence of the Sénégal and Falémé rivers. A few are found in upper Casamance and Sine-Saloum regions.

The Sarakolé in the valley have long been in the habit of emigrating because the locally grown crops of millet, maize (corn), and groundnuts yield barely enough for sustenance. Large numbers of Sarakolé formerly served in the French army and merchant marine. Since the early 1960s many have gone regularly to France for periods of two to three years. Together with Sarakolé from Mauritania and Mali they are said to constitute three-fourths of the African labor force in France, which in 1973 was estimated to number 70,000. When the men leave their villages the women handle all of the agricultural work, and immigrants such as Bambara from Mali come to help. These immigrants, as well as the Toucouleur who guard the cattle, are paid with the remittances sent from France by the Sarakolé emigrants.

Like many other groups in Senegal and neighboring countries, the Sarakolé have a traditionally stratified society. Specifically, they resemble some of the Manding—whose language is related to theirs—in that the upper stratum combines religious and petty commercial activity and leaves agriculture to the servile segments of the society.

Diankhanké

In Sénégal Oriental Region east of Tambacounda lives a small group called the Diankhanké. In the past they played an important role in setting up trade routes in that part of West Africa. They were the first to carry on commerce with the Arabs and the first with whom the French Compagnie du Sénégal, a French trading company, established relations in the interior at the end of the seventeenth century.

Together with the Sarakolé, to whom they are related, the Diankhanké consider themselves the earliest and most pious of Muslims. Some members of both groups are reputed to have adopted Islam in the eighth century, and many were converted in the eleventh century after the Almoravid invasion of the Ghana Empire (see ch. 2). In contemporary times at least one son in each family spends many years in Koranic studies with a noted marabout.

In the early 1970s most Diankhanké were cultivators and stockraisers who also engaged in petty trading. They lived among the Manding, whose language they had adopted and whom they provided with rudimentary Koranic teaching and Islamic amulets.

Bassari

The Bassari live west of Kédougou on both sides of the Guinean border. They are the small remnant of a population that was once much more widespread in that area but was pushed long ago into a few recesses by other ethnic groups of the region. They maintain their traditional way of life and are virtually untouched by Islam, Christianity, modern commerce, and politics. Their social and political structure is egalitarian and uncentralized.

Balanté, Mandjaque, and Mancagne

Most Balanté, Mandjaque (Mandyak), and Mancagne (Mankanya) live in Portuguese Guinea, but there are several thousand of each group south of Casamance Region in Senegal. In addition, thousands come into the country seasonally to work the groundnut crop.

The three groups are characterized by a relatively egalitarian social structure and, especially in the case of the Mandjaque, by a large proportion of Roman Catholics. Around Sédhiou a section of the Balanté lives interspersed with Muslim Manding, but there is no firm information as to how much the Balanté have been influenced by Islam. Like others in Casamance Region these ethnic groups have been affected only recently by modern political, economic, and social currents.

Maures

Maures (Moors)—the basic population of Mauritania—are an arabized Berber people, affected to varying degrees by Black African mixtures. Except for Islamic proselytizers, they are comparative latecomers to Senegal. They began to settle in isolated pockets of the north during the nineteenth century and engaged mainly in animal transport. During the early 1970s most Senegalese Maures were small shopkeepers, butchers, and jewelers in cities, especially Dakar and Saint-Louis, where they led a separate social life. They share adherence to Islam with most of the people among whom they live, but usually they belong to the Qadiriya brotherhood in contrast to other Senegalese Muslims among whom the Tidjaniya and Muridiya orders are predominant (see ch. 7).

Maure social structure has traditionally been a highly segmented one in which tribes, each of which was believed to be based on descent from a common ancestor, alternated between open hostility and more or less peaceful competition. Overt strife is no longer frequent, but Maure relationships with each other, even in the towns, are still affected by these traditional alignments.

Cape Verde Islanders

Since the end of World War II, Portuguese-African *métis* (people

76

of mixed European and African ancestry) have come in increasing numbers from the Cape Verde Islands where they constitute 85 percent of the population. They have settled in and around Dakar, the port of call for sailing vessels from the islands, working as hairdressers, shoemakers, plumbers, and house painters and in other crafts. They are Roman Catholics and are commonly called Portuguese by others.

NON-AFRICANS IN SENEGAL

Europeans

At the time of independence there were thousands of Europeans— mainly French—in the country. They included all social classes: high government officials, successful entrepreneurs, upper and middle level managerial personnel, small businessmen, and artisans. During the decade after independence most Europeans in the administration were replaced by Senegalese. Some Europeans remained in an advisory capacity, and a few continued to hold their original positions. Economic development programs brought in many foreign assistance technicians so that in the early 1970s the number of Europeans had decreased by only 26 percent. The trend, however, was definitely toward senegalization, and few Europeans expected to remain permanently.

Lebanese

For more than half a century the Lebanese in Senegal have been the small-scale commercial middlemen between the Africans and the world economy. They sell imported goods either directly to African consumers or to African retailers and buy African—chiefly agricultural— products for export, either directly or through larger European-controlled companies. Only a minority have become large-scale entrepreneurs.

Lebanese (and a few Syrians) began coming to Senegal around the 1900s. Their numbers increased in the period between World War I and World War II when Lebanon itself was under French control. They lived near or with Senegalese in the larger towns and in many of the small market centers, speaking the local language in addition to Arabic and usually maintaining cordial, if commercial and remote, relations.

An occasional Lebanese might become interested enough in Senegalese culture to write in Wolof, but most send their children to French Roman Catholic private schools or to Lebanon for their education. Most maintain their own quarters in the towns or at least have their own social life, and they have remained politically neutral. They live in the country but have not identified with it.

The distribution of religious affiliation among the Lebanese is not precisely known. Some are Roman Catholics; many are Maronite Christians, who are affiliated with Rome; and the others are Muslims, although not of the same branch of Islam as other Senegalese Muslims.

INTERETHNIC RELATIONS

Most ethnic groups are localized in specific areas, but there has been a long history of interpenetration of such territories by members of other groups. This process was intensified in the nineteenth and twentieth centuries. The activities of Al Hadj Omar, the Toucouleur leader, contributed to the dispersal of some Toucouleur elements to the south and east, and members of other groups, engaged in struggles with the French, moved into areas they had not previously occupied (see ch. 2). The gradual establishment of French control permitted and encouraged the movement of members of various ethnic groups from their traditional areas into zones occupied by others. These included marabouts and traders—often Wolof—who carried trade goods to the hinterland. Sometimes these traders settled in the areas to which they had come. Most migrants were farmers who established villages interspersed among those of the local people.

By and large, relations were neutral, and the ethnic groups involved maintained their distinctive settlements. There is no evidence that one group displaced another, probably because land was plentiful. Yet a certain amount of cultural borrowing and occasional intermarrying did occur.

The Manding thrust to the west in the Casamance area, begun in the late eighteenth century, has continued peacefully. In the course of this expansion significant segments of older Casamance peoples, particularly the Diola, have been affected by Manding ways.

The Wolof have tended for almost half a century to expand southward into Serer country and eastward where they have come into more intensive contact with the Peul. In the Sénégal River valley, ethnically dominated by the Toucouleur, there are Wolof villages in the west and Sarakolé villages in the east. Sometimes the villages of these two groups are in the same zone as those of the Toucouleur, and Wolof or Sarakolé quarters may even be found in Toucouleur settlements. Although all are Muslims the groups tend to remain separate.

The pattern of interpenetration became particularly important as the cultivation of groundnuts increased. Especially in the Terres Neuves (New Lands) where the purpose of settling was speculative cultivation, living conditions were identical for all and ethnic distinctions became less and less important (see ch. 6). Although in most traditional areas the people of a village had the same ethnic background and lived grouped around the founding family, villagers in the new areas were often of varying origin.

One peculiar institution, called "joking" relationship by outside observers (*dendirigal* in the Peul language; *masir* in Serer), facilitates social intercourse between members of specific ethnic groups. In this relationship the members of both groups owe each other services, are permitted a certain easy familiarity, and may insult each other with impunity, especially on certain ceremonial occasions.

Lebou have been paired in this way with Toucouleur. The Serer have been paired with Diola, Toucouleur, and pastoral Peul. In the latter relationship the Peul are called masters, and the Serer are called slaves, although there is no evidence that the Peul were ever really masters of Serer slaves. The Wolof are not involved in this with any other group.

Ethnic differences tend to blur in town. Senegal is among the most urbanized of African countries; 27 percent of the population lives in towns and cities (see ch. 3). In 1955 there were no less than 160 ethnic groups represented in Dakar. The three most important groups were the Wolof, who constituted 43 percent of Dakar residents, followed by the Toucouleur and Lebou. These different ethnic groups interpenetrated, adapted to each other's ways, and in some cases more or less integrated. A good example are the urban Lebou who in 1955 represented 12 percent of Dakar's population but in the 1970s had been virtually absorbed by the Wolof. Another indication is an exceptionally high incidence of interethnic marriage.

Persons whose families have lived for several generations in towns may identify themselves simply as Senegalese. A few young, educated people may even resent a query as to ethnic affiliation or suggest that it is unimportant. But on the whole, members of ethnic groups either live in specific quarters or, if they are scattered throughout the city, their social life tends to be with others of the same ethnic group.

Traditional attitudes regarding members of other ethnic groups frequently survive in the towns. According to a sociological study made in the mid-1960s at Kédougou in Sénégal Oriental Region, the Diankhanké held a special position because they were esteemed as fervent, strict, and peaceful Muslims. The socially predominant place was held by the Peul, and they had surpassed the Manding who formerly had been politically important because of their role in the Mali Empire. Both Diankhanké and Peul were reluctant to accept Western values and were rarely found in higher administrative posts. The Bassari, as non-Muslims, were looked down upon whereas the Wolof, active in commerce and administration, were held to be outside the traditional framework.

Relations between Senegalese and the French are usually amicable, buttressed by the awareness of almost two centuries of assimilation and privilege for the inhabitants of the four communes (see Glossary). At independence many Frenchmen had been concerned for their status in Senegal and expected africanization in all sectors. This has occurred to a fair degree, but the pace has been slow and cautious.

Close, informal social relationships exist between a few Frenchmen and a few Senegalese, chiefly among the highly educated members of both groups. Among the others relations are more distant, but there is no violence or fear of violence. In the days before independence the most overt competition was that between Africans and lower middle-class and working-class French, called *petits blancs*. The skilled workers, artisans, and officers feared competition from African labor, and the Africans protested what they felt to be the unnecessary immigration of French workers. Moreover, French wives often occupied jobs in sales and services that might otherwise have gone to Africans. As more Senegalese men and women acquire modern skills the number of French women in these jobs is decreasing.

The Lebanese and the Africans did not compete for the same economic opportunities until the 1960s. Most Africans who aspired beyond local petty trade tried instead to acquire the education or skills necessary for the liberal professions or for white-collar work at various levels, especially in government. Since independence some of the economic functions performed by the Lebanese have been—or are expected to be—taken over by Senegalese individuals or by cooperatives and other organizations.

The Lebanese have sought, not always successfully, to maintain good relations with Senegalese leaders and with the people, but they remain—in good part by choice—an alien people. They tend to feel superior to the Africans, and the Africans resent this and accuse the Lebanese of economic exploitation. Expressions of animosity led Lebanese active in commerce and industry to found a group in March 1970 in order to defend their economic and social interests. Members study or propose projects liable to offer them a chance for participation in national development. They also encourage economic relations between Senegal and Lebanon.

LANGUAGES

The major indigenous languages of the country are Wolof, Serer, Pulaar (the language of the Peul and Toucouleur), Diola, Manding, and Sarakolé. There are a number of others, corresponding roughly to the number of minor ethnic groups. All Senegalese languages are part of the Niger-Congo linguistic family, the majority belonging to the western branch of the West Atlantic subfamily; and Manding, Sarakolé, and Bambara, to the western branch of the Mandé subfamily. Pulaar and, particularly, Manding are widely spoken in West Africa. It has been estimated that there are about 8 million people in West Africa who speak Manding as either their first or second language. It ranks in terms of geographic spread with Hausa and Swahili.

Various efforts have been made by Africans and Europeans to transcribe some of these basically spoken languages. Pulaar is sometimes written with Arabic letters. In June 1971 the government endorsed by decree the use of a modified Latin alphabet in transcribing the country's six major languages. In June 1973 a dictionary of basic Wolof containing 6,000 words had been finished in part; a similar work on Serer was well advanced.

French, which is Senegal's official language, fills a need for administrative and technical communications inside the country and for inter-African and international relations. A small group of Senegalese—about 12 percent—are literate in French, but a far greater number speak and understand it because it continues to be the language of education (see ch. 8). A much smaller group—no more than 2 percent—has some knowledge of Arabic, including students who have studied in Arab countries and all the Maures who speak Hassania Arabic, which has an admixture of Berber words.

About 80 percent of Senegalese speak Wolof. The percentage is growing, and Wolof is well on the way to becoming a national language. The Wolof are the only Senegalese who need not learn another African language. Their language is spoken by many people who have neither a Wolof father or mother, according to a study undertaken in the late 1960s. Children of non-Wolof parents find it socially imperative to know the Wolof language as soon as they start school.

Although people continue primarily to speak Diola in Casamance Region, Serer in Thiès and Sine-Saloum regions, and Pulaar in the Sénégal River area, an increasing number of them are also speaking Wolof as a second language. It is the rare example of an African language spreading to assume national dimensions. This is partly because of the radiating influence of the cities. Wolof, mixed often with French words, is the predominant language in Dakar, and other urban centers have become relay stations for its dissemination. At Ziguinchor in Casamance Region, for example, more people know Wolof than any other language, although the population is mainly Diola, Manding, Peul, and Mandjaque.

Within the Diola cluster of languages, Fogny and Kasa (Casa) are the two most important dialects. Fogny, used by Radio Dakar and understood by almost all Diola, is spoken by about 85,000 people around Bignona. Kasa, structurally similar to Fogny, is spoken in and around the regional capital of Ziguinchor and understood throughout the area south of the Casamance River. The Diola languages are distantly related to Mandjaque and Balanté and may form together with these a special subsection of the West Atlantic subfamily of languages.

CHAPTER 5

THE SOCIAL SYSTEM

Varying combinations of traditional and modern elements characterize national and local social structures. A system of stratification that divided people at birth into different castes was typical of most Senegalese ethnic groups before French rule. Though much transformed, the caste system has survived to a large degree in contemporary society. Men of high status and some financial means who are able to attract a following and thus play an important social, economic, and political role are a modern version of the traditional nobleman with his entourage of less fortunate kinsmen, artisans, *griots* (praise singers), and slaves. In the past and in the present day such leaders and their followers were bound by mutual obligations representing vertical ties between the society's strata.

The mixture of traditional and modern social forms, however, varies. Aspects of the traditional systems are still mainly influential in ordering social relations and activities in the countryside. New status criteria, which emerged with the growth of the government apparatus, commerce, and industry and with the spread of modern education, are most effective in the urban environment. In the cities and especially in Dakar traditional elements are adapted to modern conditions or are superseded altogether, and personal qualifications increasingly modify personal status at birth. The combinations are not neatly meshed, as traditionally heavy emphasis was put on ascription to status by birth, whereas in modern society status is determined largely by achievement. Traditional criteria remain important in that they may set maximum and minimum limits to status that can be acquired by personal endeavor. The highly educated Senegalese still tend to be from high-status families, and it continues to be difficult for people of lower birth to reap all possible rewards from a modern education. In the early 1970s the upper administrative and political cadres were frequently members of prominent families, although the constitution and a fair number of the younger educated people denied the relevance of social origin.

TRADITIONAL ELEMENTS IN THE SOCIAL SYSTEM

A rigid system of stratification traditionally characterized all major ethnic groups except the Diola. People were divided into three main strata: free people, including rulers and cultivators; largely dependent artisans, including *griots*; and slaves (see table 4). Each main stratum was subdivided into substrata, or castes, that varied in number and composition from one ethnic group to another. Membership in a stratum and caste was fixed by birth. Strata and substrata were arranged in a hierarchical order of domination and subordination. The system was inflexible, with little or no mobility either upward or downward, but castes complemented each other economically. Living standards were often indistinguishable, but social differences showed in what was expected of persons in a specific status and in the manner in which they acted or were treated. In present-day society, the members of the lower castes are legally free, but the social stigma remains.

Although the major outlines of these systems resemble each other, details vary. Toucouleur society is the most complex and has the most minute distinctions. It has remained largely unchanged in the Fouta Toro (the Toucouleur home area in the middle of Sénégal River valley), partly because of geographic isolation but partly because political rule has historically been linked with religious leadership, and the religious leaders have been able to survive the upheavals of the nineteenth century.

Wolof society, originally quite similar to that of the Toucouleur, was subjected earlier and to a far greater degree to modern influences. In fact, Wolof serve as models for members of other ethnic groups not only because of their glorious past but also because of their successful adaptation to the cash economy, to pioneering agriculture, and to urbanization.

The Serer are an example of a basically egalitarian society where stratification was introduced by Manding conquerors 500 years ago. Diola society knows neither stratification nor large political structures. Sociopolitical relations are organized in terms of kinship links and residence.

Toucouleur

The traditional Toucouleur social structure consists of twelve castes, three of which belong to the upper stratum of free people (*rimBe*; sing., *dimo*); seven to the middle stratum of artisans (*nyeenyBe*; sing., *nyeenyo*); and two to the lower stratum of slaves and ex-slaves (*jyaaBe*; sing., *jyaado*). A hierarchical order prevails within the upper and lower strata but almost none within the middle stratum.

Neither Islam, nor the effects of colonization, nor the democratic goals of Senegalese leaders have been able to erase the old social divisions. The Toucouleur are still considered as belonging to the caste into which they were born regardless of their achievements, and generally they behave accordingly. Members of the upper stratum are expected to be generous and to behave with dignity, but artisans are always thought of as greedy for gain. Descendants of slaves are regarded as so

84

Table 4. *Traditional Stratification in Wolof and Toucouleur Society in Senegal*

Social category	Wolof		Toucouleur	
	Local term	Castes	Local term	Castes
Upper Stratum......	jambur......	Royal lineages (gelowar) Nobles (dom i bur) Warriors (tiedo) Cultivators (badolo)	rimɓe......	Politicoreligious rulers, religious functionaries, cultivators (tooroɓɓe) Warriors (seɓɓe) Fishermen (subalɓe)
Artisans......	ngenyo......	Metalworkers (teug) Leatherworkers (ude) Weavers (raba) Woodworkers (laobé) Praise singers, musicians, genealogists (gewel), referred to in French as griots	nyeenyɓe......	Weavers (maabuɓe) Potters (buurnaaɓe) Leatherworkers (sakkeeɓe) Metalworkers (wayilɓe) Woodworkers (lawɓe) Griots (wambaaɓe and awluɓe)
Slaves......	jam......		jyaaɓe......	Ex-slaves, freed by their masters (soottiiɓe) Slaves who remain the property of their masters (halfaaɓe)

insignificant that their advice will not be asked. This is more striking in the traditional, largely unchanged social setting of the Fouta Toro area, less pronounced in Dakar, and even less prevalent among students abroad who face a new and difficult environment and temporarily disregard traditional social divisions.

Highest among the upper stratum were the *tooroBBe* (sing., *toorodo*). They constituted by far the majority of that stratum. According to research done in the late 1950s, they accounted for 45 percent of all the Toucouleur in the Fouta Toro. They owned all the land, but there were wide variations in the size of landholdings. The *tooroBBe* included the rulers (*laamBe* or *lawakooBe*), who wielded both political and religious authority after the establishment of an Islamic federation in 1776 but lost their political power with the coming of French rule; the *seremBe*, who had purely religious functions; and the free cultivators (*demoowo*).

The work of a cultivator is considered noble everywhere in Senegal except among the nomad Peul. Despite political, social, and economic changes, the *tooroBBe* still constitute the top layer of the Toucouleur social structure.

Pride in having been the first converts to Islam and the consequent feeling of superiority unite the *tooroBBe* in spite of their mixed ancestry, which includes Peul, Sarakolé, Wolof, and Maure (see ch. 4). Yet economic circumstances have forced many of them to leave the valley and to work in Dakar as domestics, factory workers, and street-sweepers and at other jobs usually considered beneath their dignity—work they would perform neither in their homeland nor for a Toucouleur employer.

Below the *tooroBBe* socially but part of the upper stratum were the warriors (*seBBe*; sing., *ceDDo*), who had been the highest caste until the establishment of the Toucouleur theocratic federation (see ch. 2). They converted late to Islam and in 1973 were still considered rather nominal believers. They had lost their warrior function, but they often worked as guards and were still renowned for their bravery.

In contrast to the warriors the fishermen (*subalBe*; sing., *cubballo*), who represent the lowest caste within the upper stratum, have not lost their function. They remain economically independent as uncontested masters of the waters. In spite of their adherence to Islam, they retain a special set of pre-Muslim rituals associated with their occupation.

The middle stratum of Toucouleur society, which is quite small numerically, is composed of seven professional castes. Their name *nyeenyBe* means flatterers, an indication that they have an inferior position—although technically free—because they are dependent on the upper stratum for remuneration. Their skills are needed, but they inspire apprehension because of their specialized knowledge, and they usually live on the edge of villages. They are divided into two main groups: five castes of manual craftsmen and two castes of *griots*.

The weavers (*maabuBe*; sing., *maabo*) produce narrow cotton strips with precise geometric designs that are sewed together to make clothing for men as well as for women. Actually the person doing the weaving may in some cases be an apprentice of slave origin who knows his craft as well as his master, but he is always carefully distinguished as a noncaste member. On the other hand, some of the caste do not even know how to weave but are singers—specialists of genealogies who entertain at feasts organized by the weavers without being members of the *griot* castes.

Only the women of the caste of potters (*buurnaaBe;* sing., *buurnaajo*) fashion and fire items made from clay, whereas the men have no specific occupation. The wives of metalworkers and leatherworkers also make pottery without being members of the potters' caste.

Cobblers and shoemakers (*sakkesBe*; sing., *sakke*) do everything connected with leatherwork, including the tanning of hides. The metalworkers (*wayilBe*; sing., *baylo*) are divided into blacksmiths who work with iron and jewelers who fashion objects from gold and silver. In modern times it has become fairly easy to switch from one specialty to the other, but both kinds of craftsmen are still considered potentially evil and dangerous, possibly because they use fire to melt the metal. Other people will not sit on a mat on which a metalworker has sat or accept a present from him. Traditionally, he has been the circumciser.

These four artisan castes have equal social rank and can intermarry. They earn more than the cultivators because agriculture provides them with a secondary income during the rainy seasons.

The fifth artisan caste is that of the woodworkers (*lawBe*; sing., *labbo*), who are reputed to be of Peul origin and who perform services for all ethnic groups. They own large herds of donkeys, which they use for transport. The woodworkers are divided into two subcastes. One makes wooden objects for use in the house, such as spoons, mortars, and bowls. Their women are noted as makers of love potions and perfumes and as decorators of the calabashes that their husbands carve from gourds. Members of the other subcaste build dugouts for fishermen, have their own political chief, called *kalmbaan*, and feel superior to the makers of household objects. The canoe builders sometimes choose a wife from the other subcaste but do not allow their own female members to marry into it.

The *griots* are entertainers, the keepers of oral traditions, and walking archives in a society where many do not read or write. They are propagandists and specialists in public relations who help to maintain the status of lineages to which they are attached, but they also enjoy the right to mock others with impunity. They are divided into two castes. The first (*wambaaBe*; sing., *bambaalDo*) includes those who sing the praises of a family and the guitarists who know how to create musical moods on their five-string leather-covered wooden instruments in return for money, clothing, and other gifts. In former times families often had *griots* attached to them, but today few can afford such a luxury. *Griots*, therefore, travel constantly in pursuit of someone who is able to pay for their entertainment.

The second of the *griot* castes and the lowest of the professional castes (*awluBe*; sing., *gawlo*) threaten to abuse rich persons and expose them to ridicule unless they pay. They are feared, despised, and ranked almost with persons of slave origin. But they are also known for their extensive knowledge of family histories. They marry only others of the same caste.

At the bottom of the social ladder were two slave castes, one for ex-slaves (*soottiBe*) who had been liberated, and one for slaves (*halfaaBe*) who were still the property of their masters. They were of ethnically diverse and no longer known origin. In the past there were large numbers of slaves. Their forefathers who had been taken in wars and raids were integrated into the families of their masters and given the family name. They were inherited along with cattle and given as marriage payments. They cultivated the fields and worked at all kinds of other jobs. They could neither own nor inherit property. A master provided his male slaves with wives or the wherewithal for marriage. Even though a slave continued to work for his master, he gained a degree of independence as he became older.

Although slavery has been outlawed, descendants of slaves are still considered insignificant. They are usually without land, and about 80 percent of them work as tenants for their former masters. Many have become artisans—especially weavers—without, however, becoming members of the artisan castes. Through competence, some have achieved individual success.

The hierarchical ordering of Toucouleur society also becomes apparent in the rules regarding marriage. Predominantly, people marry within their social stratum and, with few exceptions, within their caste. Members of almost all the artisan castes may intermarry. Women of the slave castes occasionally marry their masters, and the children become part of their father's caste; males cannot, however, marry upward. Equally impossible is marriage between members of the upper stratum and members of the artisan castes. This prohibition has remained so strong that an artisan with a modern education and corresponding economic position tends to marry a foreigner or a non-Senegalese African. Hiding one's caste origin when marrying in order to cross social barriers is a justification for immediate divorce.

Occasionally a poor *toorodo* might seek protection and help from a rich one and thus approach servile status. Or, for lack of land, he might elect to become a fisherman, which would make it henceforth impossible for him to marry a *toorodo* woman. Religious fervor and Islamic knowledge have sometimes provided a way out of a low caste, although marabouts tend to encourage students of the upper stratum to continue their studies but send a student of artisan origin home after he has learned a few verses of the Koran.

Caste membership thus positions a Toucouleur permanently in his society. Within the caste, however, rights and duties are framed in terms of membership in a patrilineage (*leniol*; pl., *leggi*). This is a kin group that traces descent from a known common ancestor exclusively through the male line. Members of the patrilineage share the same name. Rights and duties include the permission to cultivate lineage land and an obligation to feed the aged and infirm and to give gifts at marriages, births, funerals, and other ceremonial occasions.

Generally, the members of a patrilineage are scattered among several villages, and each village tends to consist of segments of several patrilineages. Thus the most important kin-based unit for daily life—and one that has a close community of interests—is the extended family (*gallé*), of which a lineage segment is the core. The extended family consists of a husband, his wife, his unmarried children, and his married sons and their wives. The males and females in this unit are expected to cooperate in domestic tasks. The extended family is headed usually by the father or oldest brother, called *mawdo* or *dyom gallé* (master of the house).

Within the extended family the nuclear family (*pooye*; sing., *foyre*)—numbering usually four to five people and consisting of a man, his wife, and their unmarried children—is distinguished and is the seed of another extended family when the older one breaks up, often at the death of the grandfather. Frequent migrations have affected the extended family and have rendered the nuclear family more important.

Age-group associations are another division in Toucouleur society. In villages or in quarters of villages and towns, people traditionally have been grouped by age in parallel organizations for males and females, called *pelle* (sing., *fedde*). Up to the age of ten or twelve years members mostly play together but, when they become adolescents, they begin to do in common the tasks that they will perform all their lives. The age-groups thus provide means for socialization and apprenticeship. After marriage members advance to another age-grade, the function of which is, however, mostly mutual aid and participation at special events, such as a ceremony for naming a child, funerals, and they like. The bond is recognized throughout life.

Within each age-group an individual holds the social status concomitant with his particular caste. The head of an age-group is almost always a *toorodo* except occasionally in areas where the vast majority belong to lower castes. The leader presides over the meetings, directs activities, settles differences, and represents the age-group in dealing with the village chief or government administrator.

The only caste-based association in Toucouleur society is formed by persons of slave origin for the purpose of mutual aid. Living formerly with a family and now frequently on their own, they often lead miserable lives. The members of these associations help each other by contributing a small part of their millet harvest or money, which an elected chairman uses to assist those in distress.

Wolof

A strict division into castes, similar to the one existing in Toucouleur society, characterized Wolof social structure, but for a variety of reasons the Wolof have adapted more easily to modernization. The upper stratum (*jambur*) included royal lineages (*guelowar*), nobles of various ranks (*dom i bur* in Sine-Saloum), warriors (*tiedo*), and cultivators (*badolo*). The warriors were originally slaves belonging to the crown. They were commanded by a chief who was one of the most powerful persons at the king's court. Thus the warriors came to be regarded as part of the upper stratum. They were widely feared for the ransoms they exacted in return for protection.

Also belonging to the upper stratum, although outside the caste system, were the *serigne* (religious teachers and leaders). In contrast to Toucouleur society, where the marabouts became members of the ruling caste with the establishment of a theocratic regime, the *serigne* were merely counselors to the political chiefs because most Wolof did not accept Islam until the late nineteenth and early twentieth centuries. As counselors, however, they played an important role.

The middle stratum was composed of five artisan (*ngenyo*) castes: workers in gold, silver, or iron (*teug*); leatherworkers (*ude*); weavers who were also drummers (*raba*); itinerant woodworkers (*laobé*); and *griots* (*gewel*). These castes are characterized by professional specialization and inherited status. Although each caste is generally endogamous, there is some intermarriage.

The lowest stratum consisted of a vast number of slaves (*jam*) who materially were not much worse off than their masters, the free cultivators. They were never sold and were treated as part of the family.

In Wolof society before the advent of the Europeans a relatively large proportion of the people were not cultivators. Upon the establishment of French rule and the collapse of the Wolof kingdoms in the late nineteenth century, princes lost their chiefdoms; and nobles, warriors, and those specialists who had depended on the aristocracy for their living lost their function and their patrons. Added to these were landless cultivators and free slaves who wanted to get away from their masters. When the colonial regime introduced groundnut (peanut) cultivation, large numbers of people were available for pioneering agriculture. The Wolof—in contrast to the Serer and the Diola—never developed sophisticated techniques of cultivation, but the growing of groundnuts required no special qualification, only new land. The breakup of the old society facilitated mobility, and the exodus began toward the areas opened up in eastern Sine-Saloum and western Sénégal Oriental.

This was also the time for mass conversion of the Wolof to Islam. The position of religious leaders changed radically. They became the most significant figures in rural society and were able to build a new independent power structure on a modern economic base (see ch. 7). From these same strata in Wolof society came those who were willing and eager to pioneer in the Terres Neuves (New Lands) of the Sine-Saloum and Sénégal Oriental regions (see ch. 14). This was also the first generation of Wolof to settle in towns, to acquire a modern education, and to get jobs in the administration and in commercial enterprises.

Social distinctions based on caste still survived in the early 1970s, but they had weakened to a far greater degree than had those among the Toucouleur. More and more an individual's place in Wolof society was based on education and material success rather than on birth. This was particularly true in the cities. In the rural areas the values and structures of the traditional system persisted. Even in the pioneering communities of the Terres Neuves, jobs entailing leadership and responsibility—for example, in cooperatives—tended to be assigned to someone from the old ruling castes. Particularly in Muride settlements, the strong tie binding a *talibé* (follower) to his *serigne* in a reciprocal relationship of service and protection mirrored to a large degree the feudal relationship that existed in Wolof society before the introduction of Islam and the destruction of the Wolof kingdoms.

Local groups that cut across traditional status and kinship arrangements, so common in Senegal, are well developed in Wolof society. These work groups have an established esprit de corps, a local pride, and a competitive spirit that reinforce group solidarity. These groups may be adaptable to new situations but, although the work groups override the kin and caste boundaries in some contexts, they do not erase them. Moreover, the work groups have been institutionalized only for young people. Other values dominate as men grow older.

The members of each work group are of the same sex and of roughly the same age. The usual female group consists of young unmarried women and of young married women who do not yet live in their husband's compound or have not borne children. Sometimes, if the village is large enough, young married women with children form a group, as do girls who have not yet reached puberty. The men's group has a greater age range—from boys who have just passed puberty and feel capable of man's work to married men in their late twenties and thirties who have not established an independent homestead.

Traditionally, work groups have taken various forms. In the *dimboeli* several individuals jointly and spontaneously offer their help to a person in need of labor. The *nadante* is a permanent work group of several people who work successively in one another's fields. This provides a more efficient way of cultivation, especially if one member has modern equipment that all can use. The most common form is the *santaane*, a work group formed at someone's request. The head of a homestead asks his counterpart of another homestead to help form a *santaane*, whereas a simple tenant appeals to another tenant. Social pressure renders a refusal impossible. Participants expect to be amply fed, and the meal usually becomes a feast. Moreover, whoever convokes a *santaane* is under obligation to contribute his own labor for someone else. The *santaane*, organized for the cultivation of millet as well as of groundnuts, has become far more frequent since the introduction of Muridism because membership in the same religious brotherhood has provided a tie among people who in the Terres Neuves may not be related to each other. The *daara*, or Muride community, is the culmination of the long-standing Wolof tradition of forming work groups (see ch. 7).

Two kinds of lineages—patrilineal and matrilineal—and two categories of kin—traced respectively through the father and the mother—are distinguished by Wolof and have specific terms applied to them. All members of an individual's patrilineage (*genyo*—belt) are in the category of kin traced through his father (*gir*), but not all of those related through the father are in the same patrilineage. For example, a man's father's sister is of his patrilineage, but her children, although related to him, are not. Similarly, the members of one's matrilineage (*men*—breast milk) are in the category of kin linked to him through his mother (*het*—a term also used for nationality or species), but not all of those so linked are members of the same matrilineage. Thus, a man's maternal uncle is part of his matrilineage, but the uncle's children, although related to that man through his mother, are not. The adoption of Islam has given greater emphasis to the patrilineage and to kinship through the father, but the matrilineage and kin through the mother retain some importance. An individual in trouble is likely to seek help from his maternal kin, particularly from his mother's brother. Links through the mother may also be used to associate oneself with powerful persons or to acquire a following.

The patrilineage, or more usually a segment of it, holds rights in land and tends to control inheritance and succession, especially in the rural areas. Wolof prefer to establish and maintain homesteads of the same lineage in the same village, but in recent years several factors have made this difficult. The expanding population and the demand for land for cash crops may lead to the migration of some of the members of the younger adult generation from a village. In other cases some may have been permanently attracted to the towns while their kin remain in the rural areas.

This multiplicity of groups and categories, coupled with the Wolof tendency to polygyny and a high rate of divorce and remarriage, means that children of the same father may be members of different matrilineages and have different maternal kin. Children of the same mother may be members of different patrilineages and have different paternal kin.

92

The core of a Wolof domestic group is the nuclear family, which may be monogamous or polygynous. Whatever the core, however, other persons are often found living in it, sometimes permanently, sometimes temporarily. Often these are kin of some sort: the male head's unmarried or divorced sister, a sister's child, or a wife's child by a divorced spouse. Sometimes they are strangers.

In some instances a homestead of persons of slave origin may be located in a village, and the relationship between these persons and members of the free patrilineage is that of dependent and patron. A few families representing some of the artisan castes may live on the outskirts of the village.

Both parental consent and marital choice operate within a framework of Wolof social structure and values that limits the range of eligible spouses on the one hand and specifies certain people as desirable mates on the other. A major but not impassable barrier to marriage between two persons is a difference in status or caste. These traditional barriers are still effective in the rural areas and are only occasionally breached in the urban areas, even among well-educated people. A high-born male may take a woman of *griot* or slave origin as a wife or as a concubine (beyond the Islamic legal limit of four wives), and she may then be treated as a freewoman. She may not, however, be taken as a first or chief wife. Islamic law provides that the caste or slave origin of one spouse is not grounds for divorce by the other spouse if that origin was known before the marriage.

Islamic conceptions of incestuous relationships also limit the range of marital choice. In addition to the almost universal barriers to marriage between lineally related persons and between brothers and sister, uncles may not marry nieces, nor may aunts marry nephews. Islamic law permits marriage between first cousins, but Wolof custom prohibits marriage between children of two brothers or children of two sisters. Patrilineages and matrilineages are exogamous.

After these prohibitions have been taken into account, however, Wolof prefer to marry a relative. Preferred wives are either a mother's brother's daughter or a father's sister's daughter.

Serer

The traditional Serer social system has encouraged the development of a sturdy individualist peasantry in contrast to that of the Wolof, which was geared rather to political and military enterprises. Social differentiation was introduced into Serer society in the fourteenth century by Manding conquerors (see ch. 2). A thin noble upper stratum, descended from these Manding chiefs, was superimposed on an originally egalitarian society in which the cultivators (*sinig*—inhabitant of Sine) were numerically preponderant. In modern times the cultivators still constitute the vast majority of the Serer. Together with the nobles, with whom they intermarry, the cultivators form the upper stratum in

Serer society. The nobles were served in the past by warriors who in turn were served by *griots* and slaves; the free farmers also had *griots* and domestic slaves attached to their families. The number of slaves, however, was very small.

Artisans with their complementary skills—also introduced by outsiders—are less numerous and less diversified than in Toucouleur or Wolof society. The smiths, leatherworkers, and weavers are descendants either of those who came with the first Manding chiefs or, in most cases, of Wolof who settled among the Serer after the early conquest. Also in Serer country but not part of Serer society (except for a few who have settled in villages) are itinerant woodworkers, usually of Peul origin, who are held in low esteem and whose wives are soothsayers.

After the Manding conquest, nobles as well as artisans were assimilated into Serer society. They adopted the Serer language and religious beliefs. Artisans, however, kept their ancient caste status and in the early 1970s still married only members of artisan families. They practiced their crafts mainly in the dry season and cultivated during the rest of the year. They tended, for this reason, to be better off materially than full-time cultivators. In modern times descendants of slaves cannot be distinguished by their living conditions. Only the *griots* are worse off because their skills are no longer in great demand, and they have difficulty acquiring land.

For the vast majority of Serer the government and the nation-state are vague concepts. Their major concerns are for family and other near kin. Kinship solidarity is the tie that binds Serer society together and accounts for its stability. Most Serer have remained in their traditional homeland area, although during the past decade a few have begun moving toward the Terres Neuves (New Lands) in eastern Sine-Saloum Region.

All his life a Serer remains closely bound to the two families from whom he descends, even though the two ties sometimes seem contradictory. A Serer inherits his name from his father, and he is usually raised and educated within his father's homestead. He may remain there even after he is grown and have his wife come to live there.

The Serer also continues to be a member of his mother's family, which remains a close community even if dispersed. It is called the community of the breast (*den*), and the paternal line is called the community of the belt (*kourdiala*). The maternal lineage controls land tenure, and a man's right to cultivate land is given him by the head of this lineage rather than by his father. He may inherit personal effects from his father, but he inherits rights to land and cattle from his mother's brother. A son may cultivate land provided by his father as long as he lives with him and even after the father's death if there is no immediate demand for the land by a member of his father's matrilineage, but ultimately he must seek land from his own matrilineage.

The *tokor* (chief of the matrilineage) is the oldest man. He acts as the trustee of lineage property (land, cattle, cash) and uses it for the good of the group after consultation with the adult males. The *tokor* manages not only the lineage inheritance but also current earnings. A young man gives the *tokor* his earnings for safekeeping. A girl, too, entrusts her earnings to her maternal uncle or, lacking one, to her brother.

The *tokor* gives counsel in all important matters and especially plays a decisive role in marriage arrangements. He prepares for funerals and pays fines incurred by members of the matrilineage. He and the mother's brother—if they are different persons—receive marriage payments, and their consent, rather than that of a girl's father, is required for marriage. There are, however, a few Serer communities in which a father's participation in marriage arrangements is greater.

The complexities of such a system are somewhat attenuated by the widespread practice of marriage between the daughter of a *tokor* and his sister's son. Although marriages between children of two brothers or two sisters are taboo, marriages between the children of a brother and a sister reinforce family cohesion, limit strife and divorce, and keep the marriage payments in the hands of the *tokor*. Otherwise, the traditional payments of palm wine, cattle, services, and money go to another lineage.

Age-groups have been of far more importance among the Serer than among the more rigidly stratified societies. They are the means by which techniques and social values are transmitted from one generation to the next. Each individual belongs to an age-grade association (*mal*). There are parallel associations for males and females of various ages, theoretically seven in all—for small children, older children, adolescents, young adults, the married, fathers (or mothers) of families, and the very old.

Age-grades limit the activities in which each person is entitled to participate at a given age. They also provide collective apprenticeship to the young. Each grade is promoted to the next grade as the highest group is retired to inactive old age. Each Serer has a place in the age hierarchy and behaves accordingly vis-à-vis other Serer. Members of the same group regard each other as brothers and sisters throughout life. Most important is the group of young unmarried men who execute work in common for remuneration and who organize feasts under the direction of an elected responsible leader.

Diola

The Diola differ markedly from most other Senegalese in that they never have developed central political structures or social hierarchies. In some villages live so-called kings—and in one recorded case a queen—who have essentially religious roles. They have no political power, function only within a very small area, and are not distinguished by wealth.

All Diola are cultivators. There are no artisan castes and no *griots*. Anyone may learn and practice whatever skills he desires. Only the smiths (who are also cultivators) seem to inherit their specialty, but no stigma attaches to them; they freely intermarry with other Diola. There also are no slaves, although the Diola live in an area where much warfare occurred—the usual source for slaves. Prisoners taken in war or raids were either returned in exchange for cattle or assimilated into Diola society.

The Diola believe that God gave them a well-defined territory in the beginning of time and that they are all related. This is in the realm of myth and is not acted upon except perhaps in providing a feeling of solidarity among Diola when facing outsiders.

The significant social units are the patrilineage (*hukin*) and the extended family (*hak*), of which the nuclear family (*butog*), consisting of a man, his wife or wives, and their children, is a part. Two or three such nuclear families live in the same homestead, which is surrounded by a fence of palm fronds. Members do not have a common name. These various families consider themselves related through the paternal line, but no effort is made at tracing the particulars of this link, which may well be through wives or mothers. A Diola belongs to an extended family simply by living in his father's homestead. Regardless of the details of kinship, two men of the same age living there together call each other brother. Several such homesteads constitute a village quarter (*kalolak*). Named clans do exist, but their members are scattered, and they have few dealings with each other. The vital group is the local community.

In principle, the patrilineage controls the land that its members or ancestors first occupied and cleared or from which they drove earlier occupants. Effective control of landrights seems, however, to be vested in the extended family, and it is within this group that rights to land and other property are inherited.

Traditionally, land remained undivided under the control of a lineage head or the head of the extended family, and rights to its use were given to sons as needed. Only personal effects and livestock were inherited, the property of a father going to his sons, of a mother to her daughters. There appears to be a tendency to individual control over land, and sons inherit their fathers' fields.

The head of the extended family is usually the eldest man, a patriarch with religious functions who oversees the allocation of land, settles disputes, and is the intermediary between the members of the group and the spirits that preside over its fortunes. His authority is based on his long experience and his knowledge of occult forces.

A Diola's maternal kin play a lesser and different role in his life. There are special terms for the male members of one's mother's patrilineage and for the narrower group of males (mother's brothers and others) of the extended family from which she comes. One's mother's brothers are concerned, in part, with their sister's son's religious education, funeral rites, and burial.

As a rule people marry someone from outside the village or even outside the surrounding villages. Persons bearing the same name should not marry each other, but such marriages have been known to occur when relationship cannot be traced, and names have been changed to permit intermarriage. All first cousin marriages are said to be barred. The major criterion governing parental approval of a marriage is that the kin of the prospective spouses should not have been embroiled in bitter disputes and fights.

When a couple establishes its own household after marriage, the man allocates a field or fields to his wife. She must manage the ricefields and the harvest so as to contribute to the feeding of her husband and children, and she tries to grow enough extra rice to buy some things for herself. Except in areas where men have turned to groundnut cultivation and left ricegrowing almost entirely to women, the man does the heavy work in the fields, but the woman is responsible for much of the tedious labor. The role of women in rice cultivation is so important that the seasonal pattern of divorce hinges on it. A woman may not leave her husband between sowing and harvest; if she leaves before sowing, she takes nothing with her but some personal effects; if she goes after the harvest, she is entitled to half of it. A woman who fails to manage her ricefields properly is subject to scolding, beating and, ultimately, divorce.

Although the Diola are not subject to a central political power, they are governed by two forces—a firm belief in spirits that govern nature and affect agriculture, and public opinion, which exerts a strong social pressure on individuals. Each Diola tries to live in harmony with the forces of nature and with his fellowman and to fulfill the social obligations that guarantee the peace and well-being of his community.

Diola society is characterized by solidarity between men of the same family, the same age-group, and the same village. The existence of young men's and young women's groups, which are similar in form and function to the work associations of the Wolof, makes it easier to take care of big agricultural tasks, such as clearing the land for millet cultivation or the transplanting of rice shoots, or to face sickness and other disasters.

Usually such groups are organized by generation—there are parallel groups for men and for women from about the age of ten to twenty-five or thirty years and also for those who are older. In some villages unmarried persons belong to one group and married persons to another. In very large villages the associations form at the level of each quarter and, if membership is still too large for meaningful collaboration, they may be subdivided according to age. Some villages have only two associations, one grouping all the women and another grouping all the men. But they may all act together to accomplish large tasks or to organize certain big feasts. Although participation is voluntary, every Diola belongs to an association and only later in life may decide that he or she no longer wants to take part in collective tasks and feasts.

The heads of such groups are chosen by the membership on the basis of leadership qualities. They have custody of common earnings because the groups are paid for their work. Groups may also be hired by a family head who has insufficient help or more land than he can handle. The groups disband during the dry season and regroup in June, when those who have gone to work elsewhere have returned.

SOCIAL CHANGE AND MODIFICATION

Traditional societies began to change as soon as French rule in the nineteenth century brought an end to the political autonomy of the old states. As traditional rulers lost their powers and as new means for achieving wealth, power, and status were introduced, the old system of stratification—so typical for most of the groups composing the Senegalese population—was further modified.

Distinctions between substrata have begun to blur. Members of royal lineages among Wolof and Serer may still be granted some deference, but they no longer have political functions. The term *badolo*, once applied to members of the lower substratum of freemen, is now used for any poor Wolof even if he is a member of a highborn family.

Some members of artisan castes continue to be attached to specific kin groups in the upper stratum, but metalworkers (including goldsmiths and silversmiths), leatherworkers, and weavers have begun to operate more autonomously. They have gone to the towns to produce for a more general market, and the government has taken an interest in them as craftsmen without, however, wishing to perpetuate their special social status. The attachment of *griots* to upper class families is still widespread, but some perform as musicians for public audiences (see ch. 8).

The descendants of slaves have been freed of any legal disabilities, but their social status remains low, especially in the rural communities. Many Wolof of slave origin continue to help the descendants of masters and may receive gifts in return. On the other hand, a descendant of a slave may occasionally become a village headman, which was formerly impossible. Among the Toucouleur, ex-slaves have quite varied status. Some were given their freedom by their masters (in practice more effective than the formal freedom granted by decree) and have only tenuous links with them. Others have not been freed by their masters but live independently of them. Some still live as domestic help in their masters' households. Those of slave origin who migrate sometimes try to overcome their low status by refusing to acknowledge their origin.

There is little consistent evidence on the extent to which membership in a traditional stratum affects modern occupational choice. Apparently those of artisan caste or slave origin are free to engage in any occupation. A study of the railroad workshops at Thiès indicates that given the choice between working in metals and working in wood, those of the metalworking caste work exclusively in the metalworking shops. Moreover, perhaps because of their reputation as metalworkers, a fair proportion of them have become specialized workers or foremen and have no difficulty in exercising authority over their crews. On the other hand, the authority of the rare foremen of *griot* and slave origin seems to be unstable.

With the modification of the traditional system of stratification and the emergence of a money economy and new sources of wealth, a new kind of competition for status and power has developed. The competing unit is popularly called a *clan* (figuratively, clique) by the Senegalese. It consists of a man of means (a patron) and his dependents (clients) who constitute his entourage.

Although the context in which the competition takes place and some of its organizational features are twentieth-century developments, many of its elements have their roots in the traditional social structure, where artisans and slaves were dependent on a patron who dispensed food, clothing, and other gifts in return for their support, praise, and help. In the society of the 1960s and early 1970s men still clustered around a man of means whose very influence was measurable by the size of his entourage. Such a unit was likely to consist of the patron's kin, members of the artisan castes, and perhaps people of slave origin traditionally attached to his family and also included others not linked in any of these ways.

The patron provides income or opportunities for income to his followers and protects them when they are in trouble. They, in turn, provide support for him in local political and other disputes, contribute to his social standing by their numbers, and may provide other services. In this situation the patron controls the flow of a great deal of money or opportunities translatable into money, but he does not necessarily keep much of it. It is the distribution of wealth that enhances his status, although a fair amount of personal conspicuous consumption is expected and considered honorable.

In this connection a marabout with his followers may also be called a *clan*. The marabout, especially a grand marabout, is the patron; his followers, the clients. The latter provide support in political controversies and labor or money, which flows into the coffers of the order. Some of the money may also flow out in the form of alms. Much of it goes into mosques and other symbols of glory. In return the marabouts provide religious guidance and the hope of salvation. Leadership of Islamic religious brotherhoods became a new source of status in the late nineteenth and early twentieth centuries. Among the Toucouleur and some others, the role of the marabout was and, to a great extent, is a prerogative of the upper stratum. Among the Wolof, however, there is some evidence that members of lower strata who have the interest and talent can become quite influential in the religious brotherhoods and thereby enhance their status and power in Senegalese society.

Wealthy persons of low caste origin may occasionally be able to organize groups of followers. Because political power itself is a source of status in the society and because *clan* interests may be affected by government policy, *clans* and coalitions of *clans* act in a political manner as well as in ordering social and economic interaction (see ch. 7; ch. 10).

The National Elite

The new set of criteria that developed with the growth of governmental apparatus, commerce, and industry and the spread of modern education have primarily affected social relations in the towns, particularly Dakar, but they have also been influential in rural areas. They distinguish chiefly between the educated and uneducated and the occupations associated with both groups.

The status hierarchy based on occupation and education is fairly uniform in most of the country's larger communities, but only its highest category has a genuinely national scope. Virtually all of those in the higher echelons of government and private enterprise and in the liberal professions (medicine, law, higher education, the sciences, literature, and the like) know each other. Indeed, there is a good deal of overlapping among people of these categories.

Influential marabouts are not a part of this modern elite, but they interact regularly with them, at least in specifically political contexts. The elite are not homogeneous with respect to ethnic group, religion, or political ideology, but they often share memories of common experiences during their student years. Most of them live in Dakar much of the time, but their activities or assignments may require prolonged residence elsewhere, often in areas other than those of their origin. In every part of the country, therefore, there are important people who are oriented primarily to the national structure. They are few, but they have influence beyond their numbers.

Inevitably, sons are beginning to follow in their fathers' footsteps. The majority of those in the liberal professions or in administrative posts had fathers in the same occupations. The categories formed on the basis of occupational and educational criteria have not, however, hardened into neatly stratified sets of class-conscious groups. Several factors militate against the growth of a closed class system. Kinship, ethnic, and religious ties remain strong among all segments of the population. For most of those in desirable occupations the fact of their increased income and a style of life somewhat different from that of their kin and their ethnic or religious brethren does not mean that ties with them are broken. On the contrary, an entourage of these people may be essential to a quest for status of a different sort in which people of the same occupational or educational level compete with each other.

Urban Trends

Apart from the small elite that could be called members of an emerging national society, city dwellers include minor employees of government and private enterprise, independent artisans, skilled workers, and large numbers of unskilled laborers and unemployed persons. Many have come to the city to escape dependence on agricultural occupations and social pressures. Others are temporary migrants in search of work who intend to return home eventually.

Almost all city dwellers keep in contact with their home village but in varying degrees. In many cases, the children of permanently urbanized families have never gone to the traditional homeland, but they get to know the rural relatives who come to visit for one reason or another, such as to attend school. These families consider Dakar or some other city their home, and they have adopted the social values that go with urban living.

The impact of education and Western values has given rise to new strains and conflicts that affect the urban family. Traditional kinship relations consisted, in good part, of a web of reciprocal rights and obligations that in a subsistence economy led to relatively little strain; a man's obligation to his kin tended, in the long run, to be balanced by their obligations to him. In the modern situation, demands are often made in terms of traditional ties, but reciprocity may not be possible. Moreoever, the burden of such obligations may prevent a man from allocating his resources in new ways now open to him. Thus, a man who migrates to an urban center may have to support kin who follow him before he is firmly established himself. If his income is fairly high and steady, he may be unable, because of his obligations to kin, to use it for other purposes, including a higher level of living for his immediate family.

Whatever the strains imposed by what has been called family parasitism, the willingness of many Senegalese to assume old obligations in new situations provides a transitional mechanism for taking care of illiterate, unprepared rural migrants. They are supported by kin until they have found work and are given a cushioned introduction to the ways of towns. Those without relatives tend to cluster together for mutual protection and assistance in groups that are adaptations of traditional forms to a new situation. Predominantly such groups are based on ethnic affiliation or, often, on village of origin.

A basic group is formed of male newcomers to the towns who live together in one room; the Toucouleur call this arrangement *suudu*. Should someone become sick or lose his job, his part of the rent is paid by contributions from those who are employed. Members of several *suudu*, and perhaps some persons who live alone, may form an association for mutual help; all members come from the same village. They pay an admission fee and low monthly dues. Usually such groups elect a secretary who is able to read and write and who keeps the accounts. The money may be used to buy something for the home village or mosque, but it is mainly used for aiding members in need or for receiving family members or perhaps a marabout from the home village. Members meet to discuss the validity of the various demands made upon association funds. But they also meet socially, exchange news from home, or gather for special events, such as marriages or funerals. People who came originally from the same village but who have been city dwellers for a long time may entertain some tenuous ties with such an association for sentimental reasons. Women migrants do not live in *suudu*, but they form associations for social purposes and for mutual aid. Such associations comprise all the women in a town quarter, regardless of ethnic affiliation.

Among the Toucouleur, associations are often based on caste. Their purpose is also mainly mutual aid. The *tooroBBe*, however, seldom form associations; occasionally members of important families join in associations for the defense of their common interests, meeting only when a specific problem arises. Such associations are headed by well-educated influential men. On the other hand, there are associations of beggars, many of whom are former students who have lived and studied with a marabout. They often are of *toorodo* origin. They find out where naming ceremonies are to take place and go there to recite verses from the Koran. Whatever money they collect they give to their chief, who divides it among the members of the association.

Associations based on age-grades and seldom formed in the towns because most neighborhoods do not contain enough people born within the same span of years. Moreover, most of their social, educational, and economic functions have been taken over by other agencies. Children in town are educated primarily by their parents and learn their skills in school. "Brothers" of older age-groups, if they happen to live in the same town, may meet at special social occasions, such as weddings and naming ceremonies, and they continue to have feelings of solidarity.

Rural Society in Transition

Legal and political reforms, the introduction of cash crops, the building of roads and schools, and the exodus to the Terres Nueves and the cities for varying periods have brought about changes in the rural society. One major effect has been a new outlook. The traditional world of rural people is one in which constant efforts are made to accommodate the forces of nature by the proper sacrifices, by wearing the right kind of amulet, or by trying to ascertain the wishes of the spirits and acting accordingly. Although this approach is neither resigned nor pessimistic, it does not assume man's progressive mastery over his environment. In contrast, typical of a modern view is the belief that man is capable of conquering and controlling natural forces and putting them to his use. This outlook renders man primarily responsible for what happens—successes and failures alike.

Adopted principally by the younger generation, by those who have gone to school or who have spent some time away from home, such views often lead to conflict with elders and modify relations between an individual and his group. To some degree, they have brought about the fragmentation of peasant societies, which had been solidary and largely communal.

The extended family, which used to be a producing and consuming unit, loses some of its functions to the nuclear family. Although solidarity and obligations of mutual help continue to be strong among members of the larger kin groups, the group formed by a man, his wife or wives, and their children becomes the primary social cell. Local subsistence crops, such as millet, are still often stored collectively, but cash crops are increasingly cultivated and sold individually. Young Serer, for example, are reluctant to think of their incomes as contributions to the lineage patrimony and prefer to use what they earn to raise their levels of living or to buy prestige items, such as radios, bicycles, and canned foods.

Having learned to make independent decisions and to form social ties with non-kin, returning migrants find it difficult to submit fully to family heads. Moreover, if they earn the wherewithal to acquire a wife while away, they are no longer dependent on the lineage to provide the necessary payments. Frequently when young Diola marry, they build their houses outside the confines of the family homestead. Diola women, a recent study showed, adapt so thoroughly to city life that they find it even harder than men to reintegrate into rural society after their return.

Another effect of migrations has been an increased rate of divorce. Married men may go to the towns, leaving their wives and children for part of the year or longer. One source suggests that the high rate of divorce in the Sénégal River valley, particularly among the Toucouleur, may be attributed to the long periods that the men are away from home.

Nascent individualism also leads increasingly to differentiation between successful and unsuccessful farmers and to some extent between the literate and the illiterate. The more prosperous can afford the lavish feasts demanded by the work groups of young men who help with big agricultural tasks. Those who can read and write get the important positions, such as presidents and weighers in cooperatives.

CHAPTER 6

LIVING CONDITIONS

In 1973 most Senegalese were farmers, members of family groups living in villages that ranged from a few dozen to 1,000 people or more. They built huts and compounds of locally available materials, such as branches, sunbaked mud, and reeds or straw; in some areas a few of the more successful families occupied houses of cement blocks with corrugated iron roofs.

Their diet consisted primarily of cereal grains and other foods grown on their small farm plots. Many families sold a part of their crop, or one or more family members worked for large landowners during the busy season, thereby bringing the family some cash income. A minority of rural people were seminomadic herders, and a still smaller group was primarily fishermen.

Living standards were marginal among most villagers. Good or ill fortune was determined largely by the adequacy of the summer rains. In good years the farm family was able to grow and store enough food to last until the harvest of the following year; a bad year could mean a prolonged period of hunger before the next harvest, and two or more poor harvests in a row might well bring death by starvation or disease.

Some of the epidemic killer diseases, such as smallpox and yellow fever, that once ravaged Senegal and other African areas had been suppressed by immunization programs, some of which had been active since the early 1900s. In 1973 the government continued to support and expand preventive medicine programs. Treatment facilities and medical resources in general were still extremely limited, and many Senegalese had never seen a doctor. Malaria, tuberculosis, schistosomiasis (bilharziasis, or snail fever), and other diseases were widespread. Few people, particularly in rural areas, had either the facilities necessary for modern hygiene and sanitation practices or an appreciation of the need for them. Most surface water supplies were contaminated, and several serious diseases or parasitic infections were commonly spread through the use of impure water for drinking and cooking.

Migration from farms to urban areas had been an established trend for several decades and continued in 1973. Villagers who attempted to escape the rigors of farm life by joining the migrant trek were seldom able to find full-time urban jobs. Many of them joined small cooperative groups of other migrants in improvised housing in the environs of the towns. Others depended upon urban relatives to provide shelter and other aid, as required by long-standing Senegalese family customs. Despite the difficult living conditions endured by most unskilled migrants, the droughts of the 1968–73 period caused increasing numbers of villagers, especially in eastern and northern Senegal, to move to Dakar or to other towns, thereby increasing the already serious social and economic problems in the mushrooming suburbs.

Life-styles in the well-to-do sections of the largest towns, particularly Dakar, contrasted sharply with those of the villages or the unplanned new suburban settlements. In these sections a small minority of foreign and local businessmen, senior government officials, and professional men lived in European-style houses, owned automobiles, varied their diets with imported foods, and had access to modern medical care. Between the rural majority and this small minority of affluent urbanites was a middle-income group, which could not be clearly defined as a specific percentage of the total population. Most of the members of this group had only modest incomes, but they were somewhat established, if not actually secure or comfortable, in the urban milieu of Dakar or one of the other large towns. They were able to avoid some of the privations suffered by villagers and by many recent migrants to the towns. Nevertheless, many of them could not afford such amenities or services as electricity or piped water in their homes, even if such facilities were available in their neighborhood or community.

In 1973 no national unemployment insurance or compulsory government program of old-age benefits had been established, but most wage earners were covered by injury and disability benefit programs. Maternity benefits and birth allowances for the families of wage earners were also provided.

PATTERNS OF LIVING

Cultivators

For most of the rural population, living patterns and work schedules were governed by the seasons. Usually, land that had not been under cultivation during the previous year was cleared during the dry season by slash-and-burn techniques. Soil preparation and planting began as soon as the first rains of the year moved northward over Senegal in May and June. This was the beginning of a long season of hard work in the fields, lasting at least until the harvest was completed late in the year.

Every rural family accepted a fundamental reality: survival hinged upon the level of rainfall, which was by far the most important determinant of the yield from the farm plots. In good years farmers harvested and stored enough food to last until the earliest crops of the next harvest began to mature. Many farmers also sold part of their crops for cash. Some Senegalese worked on land owned by others and received a share of the value of the harvest in payment; this was a common arrangement in the groundnut (peanut) production areas in western and southwestern Senegal.

When the annual rains were light or erratic, or parasites reduced yields, or illnesses prevented the family or village from planting or caring for the crops, the food reserves for the next year could be seriously reduced. Then the *soudure*, the period of food scarcity that usually preceded the harvest, could become disastrous. Even after good harvests, food stocks were sometimes inadequate, and prolonged food scarcity weakened the people just as they were entering their busiest work season—the planting and cultivating of the new season's crops. After a bad harvest the *soudure* of the next spring and early summer might bring serious illness or death to farmpeople, many of whom might already have been weakened by a lifetime of erratic and inadequate diets, malaria, and other illnesses.

Hoping to escape the rigors and monotony of farming or forced by circumstance to look for a way to supplement their incomes, many rural dwellers left their home areas to work elsewhere. Their first work sojourns were usually temporary, possibly only for a season. Some went to other farm areas, and many migrated to distant towns. Most of the migrational patterns have been established for many decades, but the most significant movement, the trek to the towns, accelerated during the 1960–73 period (see ch. 3).

Almost always the reasons for migration were economic. Worn-out land, drought, or the difficulty of making a living even in good years in some farming areas caused many people to look for other opportunities. In the early 1970s the increasing competition for jobs in the towns and the struggle for survival in the crowded new suburban settlements had not reduced the flow of new arrivals.

For some of the migrants, their original trek to the towns initiated an extended period of seasonal movements. Many migrants returned to their families and villages each year to help with the farmwork during the planting season. Some of them left the towns to work during the growing season on commercial farms in the groundnut region (see ch. 14). Some eventually became established in the towns, possibly learned a salable skill, and settled permanently into an urban living pattern. Most of this group continued to give some help to family members in the home village and also helped new arrivals from the village to survive in the urban environment.

Other migrant workers, particularly from the Toucouleur ethnic group in northeastern Senegal, left their remote rural areas for an uninterrupted period of two or three years of work in the towns, usually in Dakar. A 1962 estimate indicated that more than one-fourth of the Toucouleur of the Sénégal River valley were working elsewhere.

Like the seasonal workers, they put up with crowded quarters and lived as simply as possible in the towns in order to save money for the family or for their own future use, possibly for bridewealth and other costs associated with marriage. After several years in the towns with few, if any, visits to the home area, many returned home permanently, but others found a more or less permanent job and settled in the towns.

Some Toucouleur and members of the Sarakolé and other groups as well made their way to Paris and other French cities for long periods of work. Whether working in Senegal or in France, they accepted low-paying jobs as laborers, busboys, or gardeners. Nevertheless, an unofficial survey in Dakar, published in 1972, showed that many of these Senegalese workers were often unemployed.

Herders

The Peul—primarily herders—constituted by far the largest group who lived by raising stock. Most of them moved about in northeastern and central Senegal. The Toucouleur near the eastern border also maintained livestock, and some members of other groups kept animals without making livestock herding their primary means of livelihood.

Most Peul have followed a seasonally nomadic life-style. They retained ties with a home village in which they spent part of the year, but they left periodically to move with their animals to fresh pastures. During this period of movement they lived in relatively lightweight huts of woven mats and skins, which could be moved with them. They were primarily cattle herders, but they also had horses, camels, sheep, or goats.

As descendants of hunters, who were celebrated in their legends, the Peul still preferred hunting. Most game had disappeared from their subdesert homelands, and the animals in most of the remaining forest areas were protected by law. As hunting had long since become inadequate as a source of food or other needs, most Peul were preoccupied with their cattle. Making a living by cattle herding, however, had also become increasingly difficult, and some of the traditional nomads had reluctantly turned to small trading or to other local commerce.

The Peul-Toucouleur area and the adjacent areas of Mauritania and Mali were a disaster area in mid-1973. The droughts of the 1968-72 period had already killed or weakened many cattle and other domestic animals. The herder families, living a marginal existence in the best of times, had also been decimated or driven from their home areas by hunger.

As the drought continued in mid-1973, many Peul in northern Senegal had moved their surviving animals southward early in the season. Many of these herders, who know no other way of life, had lost all their livestock, which was their primary and perhaps their only source of food or income. Some had come to Dakar or other towns—to them an alien environment—hoping to obtain enough food to survive and expecting to return to their parched home areas as soon as the rains arrived.

108

Urban Patterns

Living patterns in the towns included the comfort of the large homes in the well-to-do section of Dakar, the daily work routine of the typical members of the urban middle-income Senegalese wage earner, and a struggle for survival among the unemployed, unskilled migrants.

The mode of life among the small high-income group was somewhat similar to that of the well-to-do groups in France and other Western nations. General patterns of living could be deduced from the fact that this minority occupied European-style houses in neighborhoods served by sewers and other utilities (see Housing and Community Conditions, this ch.). Their work routines and leisure activities were generally similar to those of their European counterparts.

Among the middle-income groups were industrial and transportation workers, clerks, artisans, small businessmen, and civil servants. Most of them lived in crowded apartments or small houses. Typical houses were of permanent construction, but most of them had no sewer connections or other plumbing except possibly a water faucet. Some had electric lighting, but there were few other amenities or services.

Family members employed away from the home traveled to their work on foot, by bicycle, or on public buses or company trucks. Automobiles were far beyond their income, and they had few luxuries other than perhaps a radio and a few extra clothes to be worn on special occasions.

Most of their food was purchased in local markets. The typical diet was monotonous, depending heavily on rice or other cereal grains, sauces, and bread. Many urban families in the middle-income group were also feeding and providing shelter for rural relatives who were attempting to establish themselves in the urban environment.

Some rural people who migrated to the towns were not fortunate enough to have relatives in the middle-income group. Such migrants, usually young men, went to the unplanned new suburban settlements, becoming a part of the third major urban group. For these unskilled newcomers the pattern of living was primarily either a search for employment or work at an unskilled job, sometimes located miles from their quarters and without adequate public transportation. Their improvised huts and barracks were crowded and unsanitary. They survived by pooling their efforts and resources with those of other recent arrivals, perhaps with advice and guidance from a more experienced worker.

Income Levels

Average annual per capita income was equivalent to about US$250 in 1971. The data reflected sharp contrasts between the incomes of the urban population and those of the villagers. The rural majority, estimated to include approximately 70 percent of the 1973 population, received annual incomes equal to about US$130 per person, totaling altogether no more than 25 percent of the national income. Urban dwellers, constituting about 30 percent of the population, received 75 percent. Residents of Dakar had average yearly incomes equivalent to about US$580 per person. The averages for people in other towns were not available, but they were probably significantly lower than that computed for Dakar residents.

Differences in personal or family incomes within the urban population were even larger than those between average urban and rural incomes. A group that included about 1 percent of the total population, consisting of foreign-born and Senegalese business and professional men, received an estimated 13 percent of the national income during the early 1970s.

Most members of this small group had salaries ten or twenty times as high as the average incomes of farmers or unskilled wage earners. The majority of people with such incomes lived in Dakar, but much smaller numbers of people with relatively high standards of living were located in other towns.

Many of the men enjoying high incomes were senior public officials. In addition to good salaries and other benefits, they had a level of security unknown to most wage earners or farmers. Others were private businessmen or religious leaders who shared in institutionalized sources of power and could sometimes influence economic policies. Still others were professional men, such as doctors, some of whom were active and influential in business or in government as well as in their own specialties.

Many people at the high-income level had received some of their education abroad, usually in France. Others had attended the University of Dakar but had traveled, particularly to France and the rest of Europe. Whether or not they had visited or studied abroad, most of them preferred a life-style modeled after that of their French counterparts. Most of them lived in modern houses in low-density sections of Dakar. They used many imported foods and beverages, although basic day-by-day cooking might still be based on adaptations of Senegalese recipes.

At the opposite end of the urban income scale were unskilled workers, many of them recent migrants from rural areas, living in the homes of urban relatives or in crowded huts in the growing suburban settlements. Their wages were low, and during much of the year the majority of them were unemployed or underemployed.

In 1970 only about one-third of the urban work force had full-time jobs. Most of these fully employed people were paid less than the equivalent of US$100 per month, and more than one-third of all full-time wage earners received less than half that amount monthly. Even this group was better off than most, as about 70 percent of wageworkers were employed only part time, perhaps in seasonal work, and others

110

were completely unemployed. In many cases chronically unemployed or underemployed workers survived because they lived with family members who were more fully employed. In most Senegalese ethnic groups each family member was expected to share with and assist his relatives.

Single male urban workers often shared a room or shack with several other migrants from their own village. They helped each other during periods of sickness, unemployment, or other misfortune.

Between the two extremes—the wealthy and the recent rural migrant—were the majority of urban residents. Included in this middle-income group were small shopkeepers, semiskilled workers, artisans, clerks, lower echelon civil service functionaries, and others in similar occupations. On the surface they appeared to be better off than the average villager, and a minority of this middle-income urban group were able to live comfortably and to aspire to a still higher living standard. The majority of urban residents, however, could afford little more than a monotonous diet, housing that included few, if any, amenities, and a minimum of other essentials.

HOUSING AND COMMUNITY CONDITIONS

Rural Areas

Regardless of their location, the houses of rural Wolof and the arrangement of their villages generally exhibited some similarities. Family compounds were arranged along main paths through villages or were grouped around an outdoor meetingplace or a well. Structures forming village focal points often included a mosque and small shops. As a village expanded, new compounds were established along paths or streets designated in advance. Certain functions—such as grain storage—and the specialized structures associated with them, were confined to separate areas, sometimes hundreds of yards from family compounds or other functional units.

The rural Wolof family compound usually had a five-foot fence of reeds, millet stalks, or thornbush. The living area of a hut was often small and cramped. Some more elaborate structures, covering about 400 square feet, were divided into small rooms. Most houses were built of natural materials and were abandoned upon deterioration, often after a few years. Usually the floors were packed earth. Chiefs and well-to-do villagers, however, often build more permanent structures that had walls of sun-dried mud bricks, stone, or cement and roofs of corrugated iron. Such houses were not necessarily more healthful or more comfortable than a thatched-roof hut—a metal roof greatly increased the temperature inside the house—but they were more durable and were also desirable for their prestige as modern houses.

In the Cayor coastal area, many traditional-style huts were round and had walls made of rushes from local swampy areas. Other houses were built somewhat like European structures, using imported factory-made materials. The interior framework of these houses was modified to provide places to hang vegetables.

Most rural dwellers followed the traditional pattern, in which the male head of the group of families in a compound had a house or room for himself and his older sons. If his was a polygynous household, each wife had quarters for herself and her small children. Those of the group who were married, unmarried young men, old women, and servants had their own individual rooms or areas. The married sons and their wives had their own fenced-off areas within the larger compound.

Also within the compound wall there might be a roof or shelter for a horse or for sheep or goats. Harvested crops and food reserves were not usually stored within family compounds but were kept in clusters of storage huts at the edge of the village.

Except for the special importance of the living space reserved for the head of the family, the arrangement of the other living quarters and activities within the compound fences was variable. They were usually near or adjacent to the outer fence, leaving an open courtyard at the center of the compound.

Toucouleur, Diola, and other Senegalese groups built houses similar to those of the Wolof. The sites of family compounds maintained by these other groups appear to have been selected by the individual family head, showing no evidence of influence or planning by village leaders.

The Toucouleur, who lived in the central Sénégal River valley in the eastern part of Fleuve Region, built both round and square huts. Walls were usually of mud and were topped by straw roofs. Circular or oval fences of millet stalks enclosed the family homesteads of the Serer, who were located primarily in the lower river basins of the west-central area. Compounds built by families in the Serer ethnic group appeared in many instances to be somewhat isolated, separated from other compounds by some of the fields being worked by the family.

The Diola and the Manding of Casamance Region lived in compounds surrounded by fences constructed from palm fronds and other natural materials. The houses in each compound were built around a courtyard, a meeting ground and work area for the members of the several households that formed an extended family. The villages to which they belonged were relatively formless, sometimes scattered over several hills.

Some villages in this southern region were large, having as many as 3,000 people living in several clusters, each consisting of a number of family compounds. The Manding family head and his sons usually lived in the best hut, located either at the gate to the compound or near its center. These better units had several rooms and a gallery, or porch.

Urban Areas

Housing in the wealthy or well-to-do sections of the larger towns, particularly in Dakar, stood in sharp contrast to the typical rural hut with its roof of thatched straw or the barracks and improvised shelters on the fringes of most towns. Government officials, wealthy businessmen, and professionals usually lived in European-style houses or apartments in or near the town centers. Such housing was highly visible to the many visitors to Dakar, but it served only a small, elite minority of the total population. The limited areas of such housing were in most cases on planned streets and received some, although not necessarily all, of the services provided in European or other Western cities—electricity, piped water to each home, telephone service, and garbage pickup. In central Dakar and in the central core areas of a few other towns, old sewerage systems still functioned.

Beyond these special areas town growth had long since outpaced any attempts to control such growth or to provide urban services. The Médina area of Dakar is an example of an older suburb to which some of the services of the well-to-do sections—electricity, for example— had been extended. People from a variety of Senegalese and other ethnic groups were crowded into housing that was neither the best nor the worst in Senegal. A conglomeration of small houses and shops of more or less modern building materials were mixed with cruder shelters. Smaller but similar mixed areas with a limited number of services or amenities were to be found in the other major towns, especially in Saint-Louis and Kaolack.

Along with such partially planned and somewhat improved middle-income areas, every large town had a number of suburban areas of uncontrolled growth in which even the best housing was generally regarded as marginal or inadequate. Most of these unplanned settlements sprang up between 1945 and 1973, although some had appeared much earlier. They consisted of shantytowns, collections of huts and improvised shelters crowded together along narrow streets and dead-end lanes.

Water was carried by hand to these huts and improvised shelters from public fountains. Few people had electricity or other amenities in their quarters. Lighting, if any, was provided by candles or kerosine lamps.

The crowded, improvised shelters ranged from crude huts made of reeds or millet stalks to old barracks in need of various repairs. Others were made of old packing cases or gasoline tins. Some were covered with roofing paper held in place by stones.

Most residents in these areas were relatively recent migrants from rural areas. Like older brothers or others who had preceded them to the towns, they hoped to escape the difficulties and boredom of rural life and to use the urban slum as a way station, eventually moving on to better conditions in the town.

Meanwhile, because of crowded conditions, contagious diseases, and the scarcity of jobs in urban areas, the people endured living conditions that were less amenable than those of an average village, usually having all of the village's disadvantages and little of its mutual and familial support. In many cases several people shared a single hut or improvised shelter and pooled their resources in order to obtain enough food to survive.

Grand Yoff, one of the rapidly growing suburbs of Dakar, exhibited most of the problems of the uncontrolled growth of suburban settlements. A study of this suburban complex, published in 1970, showed that seven street fountains provided the only water available during the dry season for nearly 25,000 people. The runoff from a low plateau nearby sometimes flooded paths and streets during heavy rains, as there were no sewers or storm drains.

As sewage and trash were commonly dumped along streets and on vacant land, flooding compounded problems that were already serious. Although road-sweeping machines made regular trips over the main streets, other public sanitation measures were almost nonexistent. Most streets had dirt or gravel surfaces, badly damaged by flooding and heavy use. Residents placed better streets at the head of a list of desired improvements. More medical care facilities in the settlement were also listed by residents as among their greatest needs. One small dispensary in the area provided the only local medical services for 25,000 people.

Police protection and emergency services were limited and were controlled from offices outside the Grand Yoff area. A mobile post office provided mail services, but there were no public telephones. Public transportation to other parts of the Dakar urban complex was described as poor.

The lack of amenities and services, the risk of disease, and other problems of Grand Yoff were present in greater or lesser degree in most other Dakar suburbs and in the fringes of the other towns.

DIETARY PRACTICES

Average caloric intake was about 2,300 per day among most rural Senegalese. Protein content of the average diet was slightly higher than that of the typical diet in many other African countries. Millet was a primary dietary staple among most rural groups. It was being replaced in the diet of the growing nonfarm population by imported or domestic rice. Some varieties of millet had a relatively short growing season and were popular among subsistence farmers bcause the crop was among the first cereals to become available in the autumn, when food stored the previous year had been consumed. Planted in May or June after the first rains, some varieties could be harvested in November.

Corn, sorghum, beans, groundnuts, potatoes, citrons, fruits, cassava (manioc), green vegetables, and baobab leaves were also major locally produced items of diet, varying in importance according to the area and the seasons. Groundnuts are a relatively good source of protein, but they were not widely popular among the Senegalese. Most of the groundnut crop was sold for cash and eventually was shipped abroad (see ch. 14).

The most popular imported foodstuffs were wheat, rice, and sugar. Bread made from imported wheat was increasingly popular, and every important town had one or more commercial bakeries. Homegrown rice was increasingly important in Casamance Region, and imported rice—a staple of diet in the towns—was becoming more popular in other areas.

Fish was often used in sauces to go with millet, rice, or sorghum. Meat was eaten only once a week or less often, even among groups that raised livestock. The Peul cattle herders used milk, either fresh or fermented. They also traded milk or butter to members of other groups, but milk and milk products were used only in limited quantities among groups other than the Peul.

The *soudure* was often a time of serious hunger among the rural Senegalese. During this preharvest period, many families or villages had used up their food stores, put away after the previous harvests, before the current year's crops were ready to eat. During the rest of an average year, most adults were able to maintain an adequate caloric intake. Nevertheless, the diets of many people were deficient in animal protein and in several essential vitamins. Malnutrition and diet-related diseases continued, as in the past, to be prevalent.

The Diola, who live in Casamance Region, an area of relatively heavy rainfall south of The Gambia, were the people most likely to avoid serious hunger during the *soudure*. Their area produced a greater variety of grains, vegetables, and fruits than the drier regions farther north. The Diola also hunted in the local forests, gathered wild foods, and fished in the numerous swamps and rivers. Furthermore, surpluses of rice and other cereals, made available by one or more bountiful harvests, were stored away for years. Much Diola humor and gossip focused on the hidden reserves of well-to-do families—reserves that sometimes spoiled before they were used, as fresher cereals were used first if available.

Outside the Diola area, and possibly within it as well, the problems of providing adequate and balanced diets were increasing during the 1960s and early 1970s. Per person, less food was produced for local use during the 1960s than during the 1940s. Yields were declining on overworked soils in some areas; many people were leaving the farms to look for work in the towns; and droughts in the 1968–73 period were compounding existing problems. In addition to the established and growing demand for imported wheat, rice, and sugar, imports of millet and sorghum were expected to increase.

Traditional attitudes and preferences, lack of knowledge about nutritional needs, and food taboos were as important in the continuation of dietary deficiencies as the actual shortages of some kinds of food. Among some ethnic groups, customary apportionment of foods favored the men. Combined with traditional prohibitions on certain foods, these deeply entrenched customs often enforced a slow starvation upon women.

Many young children also suffered from long-established customary practices. After weaning, infants often developed kwashiorkor, a protein deficiency disease, because their parents did not provide them an adequate share of the family fare, particularly of the kinds of food that would maintain approximately the level of protein previously derived from nursing.

Poor urban families and recent migrants to the towns usually depended on the same staples, such as millet or sorghum, that were standard fare in rural areas. In Dakar those who could afford it bought rice. The trend toward rice as the preferred basic item in the diet was also well developed in other towns and, to a lesser extent, in rural areas where a market economy was strongly developed. Decorticated (white) rice, much of it imported, was preferred. The use of rice, especially white rice, by well-to-do families had given this food considerable status among people of average means. Furthermore, because rice did not require pounding, it was much easier to prepare than millet. For this reason it had an added appeal among women, who traditionally have done the work of cooking the meals and pounding the various cereals eaten in rural Senegal.

The quality of urban diets varied greatly. During the late 1960s daily average caloric intake per person was estimated to be slightly higher in Dakar than in rural areas. More than 40 percent of the urban population consumed at least 3,000 calories per person per day. Nevertheless, large numbers of urban residents, particularly recent migrants living in Dakar and other towns, ate poorly.

Most relatively recent arrivals in the mushrooming suburban shantytowns were unaccustomed to buying most of their food. They resisted the need to spend a large part of their meager incomes for subsistence. Even when they could afford a better diet, they spent their money for other things.

Rice and fish were a common combination for both midday and evening meals eaten by middle-income urban families and by others when they could afford these items. One variation from the typical rice staple was *couscous*, a processed food made from grain, accompanied by fish or meat.

Studies among established urban residents in Dakar showed that many of them had a breakfast of bread or a pancake with coffee or sweet tea or of leftovers from the previous meal. There were few variations in the use of rice or *couscous* as the basic food in the midday and evening meals. The monotony of the basic foods was relieved by different sauces based on fish, meat, groundnuts, or other foods and by a few vegetables or fruits. Wealthy people were able to buy a variety of imported foods. Those who could afford them used various European items to add variety to a basically Senegalese diet.

Diet and nutrition have been studied extensively at the University of Dakar and at other study and training centers. Research programs and nutrition courses for student nurses and auxiliary workers in health and preventive medicine programs were being guided and assisted by the World Health Organization (WHO).

Studies by independent scholars have shown that certain infections that are extremely prevalent in Senegal, such as malaria and intestinal parasites, reduce the efficiency with which the human body absorbs and utilizes food. Thus a person whose food intake appears to be adequate may continue to suffer from any of several debilitating illnesses, such as anemia, that are usually attributed to deficient diets.

CLOTHING

As in certain other aspects of Senegalese life, it was primarily the Wolof ethnic group that set the fashion in clothes. Traditional Senegalese dress for Wolof men, and to a considerable degree for men of most other groups, included wide-legged trousers and a *boubou*—a loose, lightweight, flowing robe with wide sleeves. A small cap might also be worn. At other times a man might wear a *pagne*—a length of cloth wrapped around the hips and thighs—and a short-sleeved shirt.

Officials and well-to-do businessmen usually wore European-style clothing during office hours, then reverted to the comfort of the traditional *boubou* at other times. Younger men tended to prefer European-style suits, whereas their more conservative elders remained closer to the Islamic traditions in dress, including the long robe and appropriate amulets. Some, such as the older Toucouleur men, wore simple white or dark-colored robes.

The *boubou* was also the preferred garment among Senegalese women, for whom it was usually made from bright cotton fabrics and elaborately trimmed. With it women wore brightly colored, showy hats or kerchiefs wrapped like turbans. Jeweled amulets, necklaces, golden earrings, and various other ornaments were also universally popular.

A woman's informal costume or work clothing often consisted of a blouse and *pagne*, or a rather shapeless long cotton dress, or improvised combinations of these garments. Sometimes a second length of cloth was worn around the upper body, in addition to or instead of a blouse.

The Diola in southern Senegal, an area that is more humid than the central and northern regions, preferred the wrapped *pagne* to the more elaborate trousers or *boubou*. Diola also sometimes wore a conical straw hat. A few local ethnic subgroups in remote areas in southeastern Senegal wore little or nothing other than amulets or ornamentation.

Many people throughout the country, especially the poorest rural dwellers, could afford little more than a loincloth and shirt or a simple dress or, among the herders, rough garments made of goatskins or other locally produced materials. Among them, as among most Senegalese, both men and women desired beautiful clothes and elaborate personal ornaments. Most people tried to obtain the best they could afford, spending a significant percentage of their income on clothing, and they enjoyed wearing their best outfits on any occasion that custom permitted.

HEALTH

A number of the most serious diseases that formerly were prevalent in the country have been successfully suppressed by large-scale immunization programs. Nevertheless, West Africa, which includes Senegal, continues to be troubled by a variety of communicable diseases and parasitic infections exceeding that of any other similar-sized region in the world. Knowledge gained during decades of work in Senegal by mobile health teams and other medical personnel has been incorporated into expanded programs of preventive medicine and sanitation. Planners and supervisors of these programs were advised by representatives of WHO and the United Nations Children's Fund (UNICEF).

In addition to the various diet deficiency illnesses, diseases prevalent throughout most of the country in 1973 included malaria, tuberculosis, measles, trachoma, venereal diseases, trypanosomiasis, schistosomiasis, dysentery, and several strains of influenza; various others, including leprosy, tetanus, and meningitis, were less common but still widespread. Malaria was considered to be the most prevalent infection, probably initially affecting almost everyone at a very early age. Although it was seldom fatal, malaria weakened its victims, making them vulnerable to other—possibly fatal—diseases.

Schistosomiasis was common in most of the country. Infection rates approaching 100 percent of the population were recorded in eastern Casamance Region during the early 1960s, and a high percentage of the people in the central and eastern areas were also infected. In schistosomiasis the disease-producing organisms penetrate the skin of the human foot when the victim enters a contaminated body of water. The organisms reproduce in the human liver, and some of them are returned to the soil and the water supplies through the victim's urine. One stage in the organisms' development is carried out in snails living in the swamps and rivers. Thereafter the organisms live in quiet water until they find another human host. Like malaria, schistosomiasis causes general debility and lassitude and is disabling rather than fatal. It is extremely difficult to counteract the spread of the disease.

118

Onchocerciasis, sometimes called river blindness, received increased attention during the 1960s, when mobile health teams and other medical personnel became aware of isolated pockets of the disease that had not previously been recorded. In such areas as many as 20 percent of the men have been blinded. In this illness tiny worms migrate through the body, just under the skin; in some cases the infestation drives the human into insanity. Blindness results when the tiny parasites affect the eyes. Simulium flies (blackflies), one of the main carriers of the parasite, live in river areas, especially in the Sénégal River valley. They are so painful and persistent that they cause some rural people to move their villages away from the river to other areas. Medical teams treat the local population when an outbreak is discovered and teach the villagers a few facts about the cause of the illness.

Yaws, trachoma, and endemic (nonvenereal) syphilis, which are spread by contact between human beings or by carriers such as houseflies, were most common in the central and northern areas, among nomads and other groups. In most of these areas, during at least half of each year, little water was available for bathing or for any use other than for drinking and cooking and for watering domestic animals. The prevalance of yaws and endemic syphilis could be greatly reduced by basic hygiene practices, but few rural people had the facilities for regular washing and bathing. Moreover, most adults had had little or no formal education and had not learned the importance of community sanitation and personal hygiene.

Historically, before it was nearly eliminated by vaccination programs, yellow fever crippled many West Africans, although it usually was not fatal. In 1965, after a number of years in which its prevalance had been suppressed by immunization programs, an outbreak of an unusually virulent form of the disease in the Diourbel area killed seventy-two people, mostly children under ten years of age. Health officials have speculated that other less serious cases of yellow fever still occurred but were unreported.

Cholera had not been completely suppressed, but it was suspected that the few outbreaks in Senegal since 1970 had begun when nomads brought the disease from areas outside the country. Data for 1971 indicated that 265 cases had been reported to health authorities, sixty of which were fatal. Incomplete data indicated thirty cases—six of them fatal—in Saint-Louis during August and September 1972 and a few cases in other areas. Thirty suspected cases were reported from three small adjacent communities in March and April 1973. Health teams quarantined the area and prevented a wider outbreak. The incidence of cholera had varied widely from one developing country to another during these years, and the rate of diagnosed cases in Senegal was about average.

Preventive medicine programs operating in the country during the mid-1960s were coordinated with those in neighboring African nations by personnel of the Organization and Cooperation for the Struggle Against Major Endemic Diseases (Organisation de Coordination et de Coopération pour la Lutte contre les Grandes Endémies—OCCGE). This organization, composed of seven African nations and France, was formed to coordinate the control of communicable diseases.

Both mobile teams and stationary medical services were being used in continuing programs of immunization and other procedures of preventive medicine. The concept of mobile units being followed in the early 1970s was based on mobile teams that had been quite successful in campaigns against sleeping sickness as long ago as the early 1900s. After World War II the knowledge gained from earlier programs against specific diseases was applied in simultaneous programs against several diseases, and more stationary dispensaries were set up.

OCCGE activities included studies and surveys of medical needs and nutrition as well as disease control work in the field. Aid to this organization from France was extensive during the early 1960s and probably continued to be substantial in 1973. The great majority of the doctors and other trained medical personnel in OCCGE programs were Frenchmen working under technical assistance agreements or Senegalese and other West Africans who had been trained in France. The funds committed to OCCGE by African member nations and by France had also been augmented by support from other nations, either directly or through international organizations. The United States had provided assistance through the Agency for International Development and the Public Health Service. WHO and UNICEF had also contributed, and both of these organizations had supported a wide variety of health research and educational programs in Senegal.

Four principal government-sponsored hospitals were operating in 1972: three in Dakar and one in Saint-Louis. Less well equipped hospitals were functioning in Diourbel, Kaolack, Ziguinchor, and Thiès. Three small private hospitals also were in use.

Together the principal hospitals had a total of approximately 2,590 beds. Four other less well equipped hospitals had another 610 beds; forty-six maternity centers established throughout the country added about 1,250 beds to the total; and thirty-two local treatment stations had approximately 950 beds. This made a national total of some 5,400 beds in 1970.

With three of the nation's largest and best hospitals in Dakar, the ratio of hospital beds to people in the area of the capital city— one bed to approximately 300 people—was far above the national average. Conversely, large but sparsely settled areas in the eastern half of the country had very few hospital beds. The government's goal for the decade of the 1970s was to provide at least one hospital bed for each 1,000 people in all parts of the country.

Related government policies called for continuing emphasis on prevention of disease and mass medicine in the form of enlarged programs for immunization and improved sanitation rather than expensive specialized or advanced clinics serving only limited numbers of people. Education in hygiene and other health subjects was also being stressed. The health services, which had been concentrated primarily in the towns in western areas, were to be decentralized, providing more facilities, including limited facilities for research, in local health programs.

In 1972 the country had about 170 doctors, or one doctor to each 23,000 people. Only twenty dentists and about fifty pharmacists were active. Other medical personnel included about 950 nurses, 165 trained midwives, and more than 260 medical and dental technicians and administrators.

About one-third of the doctors were French, working in Senegal under technical assistance agreements. Most of the others were Senegalese who had received most or all of their training at the University of Dakar Medical School. Other medical personnel trained at the university and at other state-supported schools, including a nursing school located in Saint-Louis.

The majority of all doctors were concentrated in Dakar and Cap Vert Region. Elsewhere an entire administrative region might have only a dozen doctors or fewer. Many communities had no contact with a fully trained physician unless he visited as a supervisor of local preventive programs.

More medical personnel were being trained, but adequate numbers of doctors and full-fledged programs of medical care for most Senegalese were far in the future. By 1972 the government had established about 260 rural dispensaries, thirty-eight small health centers, and approximately the same number of maternity centers. The dispensaries and other centers were of major importance in preventive medicine, but very few had full-time doctors. In most of these facilities treatment of disease and injury was limited to what could be done by paraprofessional medical personnel.

SOCIAL WELFARE

A voluntary program of social security, providing life insurance and retirement or disability benefits covered most industrial and commercial employees in 1973. This was a nongovernmental program, initiated in 1958 and managed by the West African Welfare and Retirement Institute. A separate system provided old-age benefits for civil service employees.

No national program of unemployment benefits was in effect in the early 1970s, but injury and temporary disability benefits were available to employed persons through government agencies. The provisions were based on laws enacted in 1932 and 1957. The employer paid the costs, which varied according to the level of risk in various industries, through a special tax levy equal to about 2.5 percent of the firm's payroll.

Disability benefits began from the day after the injury and extended until full recovery, providing 50 percent of earnings for the first twenty-eight days of disability. Other benefits were paid in accordance with complex formulas established in the social insurance laws. Permanent disability benefits were authorized, as were pensions for widows and orphans of workers whose injuries were fatal.

Data covering the 1970–71 period indicated that a lump-sum grant equivalent to about US$28 was being paid as a birth grant to wage earners for each of their first three children. This was relatively high in relation to the average wage. Limited prenatal and maternal health services were also provided for by law. Employed women who became pregnant received cash maternity benefits of 50 percent of their earnings for a maximum of fourteen weeks. Family allowances for wage earners who had one child or more had been provided for by law since 1955. Employers contributed funds equal to approximately 5 percent of their payrolls, which covered about two-thirds of the cost of such allowances. The government paid the remainder from tax funds. In 1970 and 1971 the allowance was equivalent to approximately US$2.50 per month for each child under fourteen years of age. Funds for disability, birth grants, and family allowances were maintained by the government in its Family Allowance and Employment Injuries Equalization Fund.

Formal systems of social security and welfare were well developed only among the minority of Senegalese who were on a monetary wage, working for the government or for private enterprise. Few if any people living in the rural economy could participate in these programs. Traditional and informal systems of mutual support among families provided the only welfare or social security known to most of this rural majority.

Among the various rural groups the ill, the disabled, and the elderly were cared for by the family and continued to share in whatever food or other necessities were available to the family or the village. Most rural people of any age had no other source of aid. Rural dwellers who migrated to the towns tended to retain ties to their families and villages. Earlier migrants who had become more or less established in the urban environment or who had at least learned how to cope with some of its problems offered help to new arrivals from their families or villages. Migrants in the towns, often from the same village, formed cooperative groups, pooling their resources (see ch. 5). Some sent money to help support the rural family and returned to their villages to help with the farmwork during the busy planting season.

Urban dwellers often received food from their rural relatives and brought young rural relatives into their homes to attend school or to learn urban ways. In these and other ways, people who lived primarily outside the money economy or who were only partially established in the urban or wage-earning milieu continued the mutual self-help and support programs that had been practiced for many generations.

CHAPTER 7

RELIGION

All but a few Senegalese see success and failure, misery and joy, health and sickness as consequences, at least in part, of relations between human beings and nonhuman forces. Indeed, such forces are considered so much a part of the world that Senegalese think of them as being in rather than above nature.

In 1973 it was estimated that more than 80 percent of the people were Muslims and roughly 6 percent were Christians—most of them Roman Catholics. The remainder still adhered to indigenous religious beliefs. Although some of the well educated were essentially secular in their outlook, atheism or agnosticism was quite rare.

The republic is defined as a secular state, the constitution providing freedom of religious belief and practice. Citizens are equal before the law regardless of affiliation. Religious institutions are autonomous, free of all state tutelage. The constitutional separation of religion and government notwithstanding, political leaders are well aware of the impact of religious institutions and groups, particularly the Islamic ones, on policies and programs (see ch. 2; ch. 10).

Senegalese Islam is marked by its organization. Most Senegalese Muslims—95 percent according to unofficial estimates—are members of brotherhoods that play an enormous political, social, and economic role. The scope of a Muslim leader's influence is usually purely local, but those who head the larger groups, to which local units adhere, are national and sometimes international figures.

Senegalese Islam is also marked by tolerance not only toward Christians but toward surviving elements of traditional beliefs. It has incorporated, as Islam has done elsewhere, local and Arabic pre-Islamic beliefs and rituals. Senegalese Muslims range from the few whose Islam is indistinguishable from that of a devout, learned near easterner to those whose Islam consists solely of the profession of the faith with few, if any, consequences for behavior. Between these extremes lies the average Senegalese Muslim who pays heed to many of the demands made upon him by that profession of faith. At the same time he continues to believe in and traffic with spirits who may or may not be disguised as the spirits proper to the Islamic cosmos. For the ordinary believer, this combination of Islamic and pre-Islamic belief and ritual implies no conflict. Indeed, he often does not distinguish between the two.

ISLAM

Antecedents of Senegalese Islam

In A.D. 610 Muhammad, a merchant of the Arabian town of Mecca, began to preach a series of revelations that he believed were granted him by God through the angel Gabriel. His denunciations of local religious beliefs angered his fellow Meccans, and in 622 he and his followers fled to a city later named Medina. This flight, known in the West as the Hegira, marks the beginning of the Islamic era and of the Muslim calendar. After Muhammad's death in 632 those of his words considered as coming directly from God were collected in the Koran; and the records of the prophet's teaching and doings, in the *hadith*. Together they form the Sunna (tradition), a comprehensive guide to the spiritual, ethical, and social life of Muslims.

Within a century conquering proselytizers from the Arabian peninsula spread Islam in the adjacent Near Eastern areas and North Africa. Arab traders may have carried the faith south of the Sahara as early as the beginning of the eighth century A.D. The area included in present-day Senegal was not significantly affected by Islam until the eleventh century, when the ruler of the state called Tekrur (homeland of the Toucouleur) was converted and induced his family and many of his people to do likewise. The religion spread to other ethnic groups but for centuries touched mainly the rulers who consulted the resident marabouts (religious specialists) because of their knowledge of writing and the Koran. Mass conversions occurred only in the nineteenth century during the social and political upheaval caused by colonization (see ch. 2).

Some ethnic groups, however, continued to resist Islam even then. Their memories of Islamic holy wars, which had often degenerated into slave hunts, led the Diola and Bainuk of lower Casamance to resist pressures by the Muslim Manding until the French imposed peace. Significant numbers of the Serer were not touched until the twentieth century when Wolof and others penetrated their area. Even in the early 1970s a majority of Serer remained faithful to the old beliefs, and Islamic brotherhoods had few adherents in Serer country. Many of the Peul nomads also resisted Islamization (see ch. 4).

Beliefs and Practices of Senegalese Muslims

Three elements combine in various ways to form the body of beliefs and practices characteristic of most Senegalese Muslims and Muslim communities: the prescriptions of universal Islam, the Islamic notions and customs peculiar to this part of Africa, and the conceptions and usages of particular ethnic groups that have persisted with one or another degree of modification.

Islam is a total system that embraces and governs all human activities. Islam means submission to God, and he who submits is a Muslim.

God himself is believed to have remained one and the same throughout time, but Muhammad is considered the "seal of prophets," that is, the final and truest messenger of God's will. His revelations are believed to complete the series of biblical revelations received earlier by Jews and Christians. Islam reveres as sacred only the message and rejects Christianity's deification of the messenger. It accepts the concepts of the guardian angels, of a Day of Judgment, general resurrection, heaven and hell, and an eternal life of the soul.

Generally, the emphasis is on behavior rather than on belief. One shows one's belief by the performance of appropriate rituals. All believers should practice five kinds of religious duties—the five pillars of Islam. The five duties are the recitation of the creed, daily prayers, fasting, almsgiving, and the pilgrimage. Other obligations may be imposed by virtue of membership in a brotherhood or assumed as additional signs of devotion.

The recitation of the creed *shahada* emphasizes the monotheistic character of Islam: "There is no god but God and Muhammad is his prophet." Presumably, all Senegalese Muslims have made a public profession as the first step in espousing Islam. The profession of the faith is also a routine part of prayer.

All Muslims should pray five times daily at specific times of the day: at dawn, shortly after noon, before sunset, after sunset, and at night. In Senegal few perform these prayers more than three times a day and many not that often, but there is stricter observance during the fast of Ramadan (see table 5). Prescribed genuflections and prostrations accompany the prayers, which the worshiper recites facing toward Mecca. The prayers may be said alone and in private, but public communal performances are common in Senegal. Attendance at the mosque for Friday afternoon communal prayer is often heavy. Members of brotherhoods must say specific prayers in addition to those required of all believers.

All Muslims, except the sick, the weak, pregnant women, travelers on necessary journeys, and soldiers on duty, are expected to fast from sunrise to sunset during the whole of the ninth lunar month of Ramadan and to refrain from sexual relations during those hours. The well-to-do usually do little or no work during this period, and some businesses close for all or part of the day. The fast in summertime imposes considerable hardship on those who must do physical work. Ramadan is observed rather strictly in Senegal.

The fourth obligation of a Muslim is that he give alms. The *zakat*, as this contribution is known, is no longer a state levy as it was in the old Islamic states of precolonial days. Theoretically voluntary, it is a socially unavoidable obligation in Senegal. It is collected at the beginning of the year and at the end of Ramadan. *Sadaqa*, purely voluntary almsgiving, has come to be identified with the slaughtering of a sheep at the great year-end feast and the feeding of the poor.

Table 5. Major Events in the Islamic Calendar of Senegal[1]

Month	Length of Month (in days)	Event
1. Muharram	30	10th: *ashura* (Wolof, *tamharit*); new year's celebration.
2. Safar.........	29	18th to 20th: great *magal* at Touba (Muride pilgrimage).
3. Rabia I.......	30	12th: *mouloud* (celebration of Muhammad's birthday).
4. Rabia II.......	29	11th and 12th: *gamou* at Tivaouane (Tidjani pilgrimage to Malik Sy's tomb).
5. Jumada I......	30	
6. Jumada II.....	29	
7. Rajab.........	30	
8. Shaban	29	
9. Ramadan[2].....	30	Month of fasting.
10. Shawal	29	1st: *al fitr* (Wolof, *korité*); breaking of fast—dancing, singing.
11. Zu'lkadah	30	
12. Zu'lhijjah	29[3]	10th: *al kabir* (Wolof, *tabaski*); great year-end feast; ritual sheep slaughtering.

[1]Ordinary year, 354 days; leap year, 355 days. As the months of the lunar calendar revolve through the solar year, dates occur approximately eleven days earlier from year to year in the Christian calendar; for example, 1 Muharram 1391 A.H. (after the Hegira) falls on February 27, 1971; 1 Muharram 1392 A.H. falls on February 16, 1972; 1 Muharram 1393 A.H. falls on February 4, 1973. Retrogression through all seasons occurs approximately every thirty-three years.
[2]Fasting period is set by direct observation of the new moon rather than by calculation.
[3]Thirty days in leap years.

The fifth requirement is the hajj, or pilgrimage to Mecca, if it is at all possible. One who has completed the pilgrimage may prefix his name with the title al Haj and may also wear a green turban. The pilgrimage is usually undertaken so as to reach Mecca in the twelfth lunar month of the Muslim calendar, but it may be made at any time. About 2,000 to 3,000 Senegalese make the pilgrimage annually.

The emphasis placed on the pilgrimage has led to a variety of organizational activity. Government-appointed officials arrange for transportation and other matters so as to minimize the cost of the voyage and to expedite the necessary paperwork. Some industrial enterprises hold lotteries in which one or more of their employees may win a trip to Mecca. In some towns individuals have formed associations to which they contribute in order that at least one of them may make the pilgrimage each year.

The Senegalese Islamic ritual calendar is marked by other pilgrimages. Muslims may, at any time, undertake a pilgrimage to the *zaouia* (literally, center)—which can be either the home of a leader of their brotherhood or the tomb of a founder. Of special importance is the pilgrimage known as the great *magal*, which attracts about 200,000 annually to Touba, seat of the Muridiya brotherhood and site of the great mosque and the tomb of Amadou Bamba (1850?-1927), founder of the order. The *magal* is held from the eighteenth to the twentieth of Safar and celebrates the final return from exile of Bamba and the date of his definitive prophetic vision.

The twelfth of Rabia I is the birthday of Muhammad and the occasion for general celebration. The eleventh and twelfth days have come to be the occasion for the *gamou*, a pilgrimage to the *zaouia*, or tombs, of prominent marabouts. The most important of these is the *gamou* at Tivaouane, capital of the Tidjaniya brotherhood and site of the tomb of the founder Al Haj Malik Sy (1855-1920). The numbers making the pilgrimage are fewer than those who go to Touba and may total about 100,000.

The feast of *al kabir* toward the end of the Islamic year occurs at the same time pilgrims to Mecca are engaged in ceremonies there. It is marked by the ritual slaughtering of a sheep in commemoration of Abraham's sacrifice of his son. The sheep is killed in God's name, and parts of it are distributed to the poor. Customarily the head and feet are smoked and preserved for the New Year's celebration (*ashura*) about a month later. Most Muslims prepare for that celebration by a short fast and purificatory ablutions. The day is marked by rites emphasizing prosperity in the new year. Food is shared with the poor in the belief that such sharing will help bring a good year.

Islam is a religion without clergy or ordained priests. It has teachers and leaders, usually called marabouts by French-speaking Senegalese, but other terms are also in use. The Wolof, Lebou, and Serer call them *serigne* (from an old Wolof political rank); the Toucouleur and Peul use the title *tierno*; and the Manding and Sarakolé use *karamokho* or a variation of that word.

Despite formal Islam's uncompromising monotheism, Muslims everywhere believe that God created angels and spirits. Angels are relatively unimportant in Senegalese Muslim thought. Of the spirits there are two kinds: one benevolent and believing, the other evil and unbelieving.

Believing spirits are thought to carry out God's wishes and help Him govern the world, but they have a measure of autonomy. Ordinarily spirits are considered neutral to man, but Muslims believe they may help if properly approached. Evil spirits—witches and the like—are regarded as the source of illness and other difficulties. Sometimes the spirits of the pre-Islamic religions have been assimilated to one or another of these types of spirits. They also may remain outside the Islamic categories but are, nonetheless, objects of ritual. Thus, Lebou women appeal to ancient spirits for rain, and the fishermen of the Sénégal River still perform pre-Islamic rites. Spirits are extremely important in the daily life of the ordinary rural Senegalese, for they are considered troublesome or helpful in all matters of immediate concern.

Marabouts are reputed to know how to communicate with and

appease these spirits. They make and sell amulets, which almost everyone wears around the neck in small leather bags for protection. Usually they consist of written or printed material, often from the Koran.

Islamic Brotherhoods

The rise of brotherhoods was closely connected with the development of Sufism, a mystical approach in Islam seeking a closer personal relationship to God through special spiritual disciplines. Escape from self was aided by poverty, seclusion, and other forms of self-denial; states of visionary ecstasy were brought on by group chanting of religious texts and by dances and gestures—a practice still followed. The name Sufism derives from the Arab word *suf*, meaning wool, from which the crude garment of the Muslim holy man was made. Around a mystic reputed for his piety and inspiration clustered disciples who were bound to him by personal loyalty. The size of such a *zaouia* ranged from tiny encampments with a few followers to village or town quarters with hundreds of family members, servants, teachers, and students. Some of these grew into brotherhoods organized along hierarchical lines (*tariqua* from the Arab word *tariq*, meaning way).

In principle the brotherhoods still seek, through ritual, prayer, and other techniques, to bring their members closer to God. In Senegal, however, membership is not restricted to those who have a strong tendency toward mysticism. Adherence involves little more than the repetition of a few litanies, loyalty to the leader of the brotherhood, and some obligations toward fellow members.

The brotherhood leaders play an important part in the organization and practice of Islam. Despite the theoretical absence of a priesthood, they have become not merely guides to paths to God but mediators between Him and man. They are often powers in their own right and even objects of worship. They are said to have *baraka* (a state of blessedness). As they have assumed an increasingly important role, however, the very notion of *baraka* has come to mean power rather than blessedness.

Leaders of brotherhoods became the natural heirs to the traditional rulers who lost their power to the French in the nineteenth century. The two predominant brotherhoods—the Tidjaniya and, especially, the Muridiya—eventually launched economic enterprises, mainly the cultivation of groundnuts (peanuts), as a means of acquiring power independent of the political arena. By the early 1970s they had ventured into transport, cooperatives, and other enterprises.

The majority of Senegalese Muslims belong to these two orders, possibly 57 percent to the Tidjaniya and 26 percent to the Muridiya. Of the others, perhaps 16 percent belong to the Qadiriya, and about 1 percent to various small brotherhoods. Only a few have no affiliation.

No doctrinal differences divide the various brotherhoods of Senegal.

Bamba, the founder of the Muridiya, belonged also to the Tidjaniya. Nothing prevents the *talibé* (followers) of different brotherhoods from praying together or making joint pilgrimages. The Tidjaniya is more tolerant, more flexible, and individualistic. It appeals to the free farmers, to the educated elite, and to the urban residents (see ch. 5). The Muridiya is more disciplined, more rigid, and centralized. It offers a total social system to the disinherited: the poor farmers and the ex-slaves who can only contribute the strength of their arms and the fervor of their belief. The two brotherhoods represent the two faces of Islam in Senegalese society, answering different and sometimes contradictory aspirations. Wives usually choose the affiliation of their husbands.

Qadiriya

The first brotherhood to gain a foothold in Senegal was the Qadiriya, one of the oldest and most widespread of Islamic orders. It was founded in the twelfth century in Mesopotamia by Sidi Muhammad Abd al Kader al Djilani, and its first African branch was founded by a Maure, Sidi Ahmad al Bekkaye, in the late fifteenth century. Its early influence in Senegal was limited to peoples of the Sénégal River valley—the Peul, Toucouleur, and Sarakolé. In the late nineteenth and early twentieth centuries the Qadiriya reached Casamance and the Upper Gambia, where it took root among many Manding, half of whom still belong to this brotherhood. The marabouts come from the Fouta Toro, especially from the Mauritanian side.

The Qadiriya is staid and relatively restricted in its appeal to Senegalese. It emphasizes Islamic, including legal, learning. Although chanting is permitted, the ritual tends to be quiet and nonecstatic. In 1973 the head (*cheikh*) of the Bekkaiya branch of the Qadiriya lived in Mauritania.

Branches of the Qadiriya include the Bou Kounta, named after its Maure founder. This branch established itself toward the end of the nineteenth century in the area around Tivaouane, stressing work and trade rather than learning. Another branch, the Fadeliya, which is distinguished by its relatively ecstatic ritual behavior, has some adherents among the Wolof and Manding in northwest Sénégal Oriental and Casamance regions.

Tidjaniya

In 1781, while on a pilgrimage to Mecca, Si Ahmad ben Muhammad al Tidjani, a North African, was visited by the prophet in a dream, in which the rules and the path to God of a new order—Tidjaniya—were revealed to him. Maures began to diffuse the teaching of the order to Black Africa about 1830, but the major impetus to its rapid spread in the second half of the nineteenth century came from the Toucouleur militant, Al Haj Omar (see ch. 2). His appeal was chiefly to those of his own ethnic group, but others in the valley of the Sénégal River—Sarakolé, Peul, and Wolof—were also influenced. All of these had hitherto been overwhelmingly followers of the Qadiriya. The Tidjaniya also spread to a large number of Wolof who were not yet Muslims, through the effort of Sy. Of Toucouleur origin, he had settled in the old Wolof state of Cayor at Tivao, was married to Wolof women, and had adopted the Wolof way of life.

Tidjanism guarantees more to its followers and demands less than Qadiri Islam. It does not require esoteric learning or elaborate ritual; it does, however, demand absolute loyalty. Its founder claimed that Muhammad had guaranteed positions near God's throne on Judgment Day to all faithful followers, who were assured a place in heaven despite their sins. Ideally, a novitiate is required of one who aspires to join the brotherhood, but initiation is often simplified. Prayer in groups is emphasized.

Tidjaniya is the largest brotherhood in Senegal, but it is not a solitary body. Branches of the brotherhood, organized mainly on ethnic lines and devoted to a particular leader, are the important units.

The Omariya branch of Tidjaniya is essentially Toucouleur in composition. It has several sections, headed by descendants of Omar, in different countries. Senegalese grand marabout, Al Haj Saidou Nourou Tall, grandson of Omar and a very old man in 1973, has been an important public figure for decades and, as such, spends much of his time in Dakar.

The Malikiya branch of Tidjaniya, with headquarters in Tivaouane, takes its name from Sy. It makes its primary appeal to Wolof, but members of other ethnic groups are also affiliated. The founder of the branch had a reputation for learning, and the Malikiya has emphasized the dissemination of Islamic teaching.

Despite the ethnic differences in their following, the leaders of the Omariya and the Malikiya have cooperated, and they are related by marriage. Both maintain ties with the Tidjaniya mother house in Fez, Morocco.

Muridiya

The founder of the Muridiya, Amadou Bamba, was a learned member of the Qadiriya, and the present-day leaders maintain relations with the Maure leader of that order. The reputation, organization, and functioning of the Muridiya, however, require that it be considered an autonomous brotherhood. It is essentially a Senegalese, if not Wolof, phenomenon. Only a very small minority—perhaps 10 percent—belong to other ethnic groups.

Bamba's forebears were Qadiri marabouts of Toucouleur origin, but they had thoroughly identified with the Wolof by the time he was born. Bamba taught during the last quarter of the nineteenth century, when Wolof society had become disorganized and disoriented under the impact of French penetration. His very deep mysticism, which he derived from a strict reading of the sacred texts and which made no allowance for human weakness, became a powerful magnet, drawing many Wolof

132

who had hitherto been barely or not at all affected by Islam. His thousands of early followers ranged from members of ruling lineages to slaves. Muridism became a new way of life on the one hand and a kind of passive resistance to the French on the other.

Bamba's intentions and ambitions were not altogether clear, but his reluctance to enter into direct contact with the French and the extraordinary devotion of his followers seem to have aroused suspicion. He was exiled to Gabon from 1895 to 1902 and to Mauritania from 1903 to 1907. Throughout these and later periods his kin, the M'Backé, and some devoted disciples maintained and spread his influence. Changes in colonial policy and Bamba's behavior during and after World War I led to a period of relatively good relations between him and the French and a remarkable increase in followers.

The distinctiveness of the Muridiya resides in the total dependence of the *talibé* on their *serigne*, the existence of a tight hierarchy culminating in a caliph general, and a devotion to agricultural labor as part of religious life.

Dependence on or devotion to the religious leader is characteristic of all brotherhoods, but Bamba placed heavy emphasis on it. Only through the *serigne* could access be had to the hierarchy of saints and, eventually, God. Many followers have interpreted this to mean that they could ignore all but the most important Islamic obligations and gain salvation simply by leaving the direction of their earthly life to the *serigne*. Bamba did not, in fact, absolve his followers of all their obligations, but absolute dependence and obedience seem to be consonant with the organization of the Muridiya.

The brotherhood is governed by the caliph general—first Bamba, later his successors—from the administrative center at Touba, which Murides regard as their holy city. Below him are a number of *grands serigne* (head marabouts) who are the descendants of Bamba's friends and relatives. They have their headquarters at Touba but spend most of their time within their own area of influence where they or their forefathers introduced Muridism and founded villages. The *grands serigne* are not easily accessible to the mass of the faithful.

Farther down in the hierarchy are several hundred *serigne* who constitute the basic framework of the brotherhood at the level of a village or group of villages and who are far more numerous than in other brotherhoods. They may in turn delegate some functions to others. At the bottom of the pyramid is the mass of *talibé*.

A *serigne* is consecrated by the caliph general, who chooses him for his zeal, long association, and leadership qualities. The core of Bamba's lieutenants were his kin, the M'Backé and a few close disciples. With minor exceptions, Bamba's descendants still provide the upper levels of the hierarchy. There have been some conflicts over succession, but M'Backé tend to support each other; the other *serigne* seem to follow the M'Backé lead. Moreover, Muride *serigne* are often related to each

133

other, either directly or through marriage. All of them maintain contact with the caliph general directly or indirectly through his official representatives.

Muride doctrine does not assert, as some have claimed, that work is prayer and that the former may be substituted for the latter, but Bamba did condemn idleness and stressed work as part of religion. He understood that the time of holy wars and theocratic states was past and concentrated on economic progress. The caliph general combines in his person the highest spiritual authority of a traditional chief and the economic power of a modern entrepreneur.

Confronted with followers who had little aptitude for the mystical life, Bamba and his successors sent them out to establish villages where they could work and pray at the same time in collective ecstasy. They renounce all personal initiative and give their services in return for the prayers of the *serigne*. The arrangement is voluntary and revokable and seems to be considered just by both sides, although some critics have condemned it as exploitation of religious naïveté. It places enormous power in the hands of *serigne*. The caliph general or the humblest *serigne* is first of all an agricultural enterpreneur. He can spend the profit at will, redistributing some of it among the *talibé*, investing in other economic ventures, or spending it on himself for possessions, such as cars, houses, or wives—all of which presumably redounds to the glory of the faithful. Only when *talibé* leave the religious community do they begin to work for themselves and are often set up by the brotherhood.

The *serigne* does not himself engage in manual labor, but he often deals with the commercial aspects of cultivation, either as a marketer of crops or as head of the local cooperative. Such practices are not restricted to the Murides; Tidjani marabouts have established similar communities here and there, but the Muridiya is marked by the scale and pervasiveness of these operations.

The brotherhood has played a vital role in spreading groundnut cultivation. Farming communities were established in Cayor and Baol and, after Bamba's death, in Saloum, eastern Diourbel, and elsewhere. In the late 1960s two-thirds of the great groundnut producers were Muride notables who controlled vast estates of many thousands of acres on which their followers worked for little or no immediate remuneration.

Collective work has various aspects. Muride farmers usually spend 15 percent of their working time on collective activities and also contribute every Wednesday to the cultivation of the field of their *serigne*. Moreover, a typical Muride institution is the *daara* (community of disciples), which is at once a farm and a school for Koranic education. In the *daara* the character of boys and young men (aged nine to twenty-five) is formed by hard work and austere discipline. The first *daara* was founded in 1889.

The *jawria* (representative of the *serigne*) organizes the work of the *daara.* He apportions the daily tasks, maintains discipline, and sometimes provides a little teaching by recitation of the Koran or Bamba's poems. There are no women; life is hard and isolated. Evenings are spent in religious singing and prayer. Recruitment is entirely voluntary, although the very young ones are usually enrolled by their parents. The boy learns to be a pious Muslim, to respect his elders, and to master the basic agricultural skills. His enrollment establishes a link between his family and the powerful Muride organization. Many young also come of their own volition, especially if their parents are dead or landless.

The work slackens during the dry season, that is approximately between November and May. During this time the young men perform odd jobs, such as repairing fences and huts, collecting firewood, or begging in towns and villages. They return only when the fields must be cleared for sowing. From these communities a few young people may be chosen to become *serigne.* The others may, after a time, convert the community to an ordinary Muride village.

Since the late 1950s many Murides have migrated into towns where conditions make collective work difficult. They may continue to work on Wednesday in the field of the *serigne,* often many miles distant, or they may send a fee instead. But the great majority are directly affiliated with the caliph general.

In towns Murides may form local groups called *dahira,* which resemble other voluntary urban associations with regular meetings, elected presidents, and obligation of mutual aid. Alone or with other members of this group, they may pay visits to a *serigne* or perhaps the head of their order or branch. In the city they meet members of other brotherhoods with whom relations tend to be tolerant and peaceful. The imam at the mosque where they go for Friday prayer is often a member of the Tidjaniya, which predominates in towns.

Minor Brotherhoods

The burgeoning of Islam in the late nineteenth century gave rise to a number of leaders who enjoyed a brief success but whose present-day following in Senegal is quite small. One such leader was Limahou Laye, a Lebou who, in the late nineteenth century, gained a number of followers among his own ethnic group and some others by virtue of his reputation as a holy man and healer. The Layennes have made some major modifications in doctrine and law. They consider the pilgrimage to Mecca unnecessary, and they claim that there is no limit to the number of legal wives a Muslim may take. The teaching of the founder and his son also emphasizes cleanliness of body, clothing, and dwelling as essential to purity. The Layennes constitute less than 1 percent of Senegalese Muslims.

One group, the followers of Al Haj Ibrahima Nyasse, split off from the Tidjaniya. It is important less because of its numbers in Senegal, which are few, than because of the national and international status of its leader. Unlike other important religious figures, Nyasse was born a blacksmith of low caste origin, which may account in part for the coolness between him and other Tidjani leaders (see ch. 5). He is also a learned man who has written a great deal on religious matters. He is a crusader and a Pan-Africanist, who advocates close ties with the Arab world. Nyasse is a Wolof, with headquarters in Kaolack, and manages vast fields of groundnuts that are cooperatively cultivated. He has followers in many parts of West Africa, particularly in Nigeria. His ties with Fez are less close than those of other leaders.

Cherif Hamallah, who died in 1943, founded Hamallism about the time of World War I. He preached a return to pure Tidjanism, emphasizing mystical rather than intellectual activity. He also stressed the equality of all souls, which attracted to him ex-slaves, women, and young people rebellious against the authority of the parental generation. Hamallism gave rise to several tendencies, among them a contemplative, mystical one with strong, moral emphasis and a social, revolutionary one. There are only between 7,000 and 8,000 followers of Hamallism in Senegal, many of them of non-Senegalese origin.

Trends in Senegalese Islam

Movements for reform that have affected Islam elsewhere have touched Senegal only slightly, chiefly in the form of criticism of the cult of the marabouts. Muslims are urged to abandon their reliance on them and on brotherhoods, to confront God themselves, and to acquire the learning necessary to proper Islam. In the decade preceding independence the movement assumed political overtones: chiefs of brotherhoods were accused by some reformers of cooperation with the colonial power.

Among those who have participated in the reform movement are former students at Al Azhar in Cairo, an important center of Islamic learning, where Senegalese began studying in the late 1940s. Some of the graduates stress the rational elements in Islamic doctrine and, without advocating blind acceptance of Western thought and civilization, urge adaptation to the conditions of the modern world.

The important brotherhood leaders have opposed the reformers as vehicles for Pan-arabism and spreaders of dissension among Senegalese Muslims. They have also sought to adapt themselves to their pressures, chiefly by encouraging the teaching of Arabic and by seeking to raise the level of Islamic learning. The government, as a gesture of friendship for Senegalese Islam and perhaps as a means of encouraging its modernization, has supported the teaching of Arabic in some schools and the establishment of a center of Islamic studies at the University of Dakar (see ch. 8).

CHRISTIANITY

Unlike Muslim proselytizers, Christian missionaries were not able to move freely in Senegal during the early period of French expansion and unification, which began in 1850. As whites, they were considered allies of the French. Moreover, conversion to Christianity entailed a far more profound change of the traditional social structure than did acceptance of Islam (see ch. 5).

The first mission had been installed in Dakar in 1845, and the second in Joal in 1849. During the late nineteenth century, mission stations were established among the Serer on the Petite Côte (between Dakar and Joal) and among the Diola in lower Casamance. The two ethnic groups continue to be appreciably affected by missionary efforts, although in recent years Islam has had success among both. A few Christians can also be found in almost every other ethnic group, especially among the Balanté and Mandjaque who live just south of Sédhiou in Casamance Region. Like Muslims, Christian converts often retain elements of their former beliefs.

According to papal sources, there were 249,785 Roman Catholics in 1973, distributed among five dioceses: Dakar (97,000), Kaolack (68,055), Ziguinchor (47,284), Thiès (20,491), and Saint-Louis (16,955). Senegalese clerics performed many of the parish and other duties. Of the non-African religious personnel a relatively large number minister mainly to European and Lebanese Roman Catholic populations; they operate mission schools and social centers for young people as well as libraries and various cultural activities.

The Roman Catholic Church of Senegal is affiliated with the international Episcopal Conference of French-Speaking Africa, which is the permanent organ of the plenary assembly of the bishops of West Africa. This conference was established before Senegalese independence and was retained afterward.

There were also a few thousand Protestants in the country, grouped in the Evangelical Federation. They included the Assemblies of God Mission (seat in Tambacounda), the Evangelical Mission of West Africa (seat in Ziguinchor), the Protestant Church of Dakar, and the Conservative Baptist Foreign Mission Society.

Whatever success Christian missions have had has been mainly because of the Western education they offered. Their schools, open to all, were at first largely shunned by Muslims and frequented mostly by non-Muslims and people of lower caste. Eventually they also attracted Muslims because of the opportunities they made available for modern careers. Attendance at common schools is probably one of the reasons for the tolerance and peace existing in Senegal among adherents of different religions.

Because of the mission schools, Roman Catholics play a larger role than their mere numbers would imply. They are more heavily represented among the educated elite and higher echelons of government. Quite often they have posts of responsibility in villages, where they are outnumbered thirty to one and more. In 1966 one government minister out of five, one legislative deputy out of six, and one ambassador out of three were Roman Catholics. Later figures were not available in 1973, but—significantly—the president of this predominantly Islamic country was a Roman Catholic.

INDIGENOUS RELIGIOUS SYSTEMS

Of the larger ethnic groups only the Serer and the Diola have important segments still devoted to traditional religions. Comparatively large numbers are found among members of small groups, such as the Balanté, Mandjaque, and Mancagne in Casamance Region and the Bassari in the remote southeast.

Despite differences in detail among indigenous religions, they are all this-worldly, and they assume that man must maintain good relations with those (human or otherwise) who control forces and try to influence these beings in their favor. All traditional belief systems include a creator God or Supreme Being, who is omnipotent, timeless, and remote from man. He is always associated with the sky and is rarely worshiped. He was easily adapted to Islamic and Christian beliefs by converts, who from then on gave him greater importance in prayer.

Intermediary powers—the spirits incarnate in forces of nature and thought to live in trees, rocks, water, or other natural phenomena—are considered to be either benevolent or malevolent but amenable to prayer and appeasing sacrifice. Prayers are said at tiny shrines with or without images, usually on agricultural occasions such as planting and harvest. Although spirits are not material, according to believers, they must be fed (by sacrifice of slaughtered animals), and they are annoyed if people do not pay attention to them. Attributed to them is the power to punish by illness or even madness voluntary or involuntary infringements of rules or, sometimes, failure to sacrifice. The Serer call such spirits *pango*; the Diola word is *boekin* (pl., *ukin*). In contrast to God these spirits are localized, numerous, and vary in power. Some are household spirits and are relevant only for a small group. Others are valid for a whole village or for a group of villages.

Each spirit has a priest and, sometimes, both a priest and sacrificer. In Diola society family seniors are priests for household spirits. For other spirits, Diola who have received a call by a kind of spirit-possession become priests, but these persons remain cultivators, fishermen, and so on. The only fully specialized priest is the priest-king (or occasionally a priest-queen). Not all Diola groups had such persons, and there were only two or three in the Casamance in the early 1970s. Others live in Portuguese Guinea. These priest-kings formerly had political, juridical, and religious functions, but in the early 1970s they were connected solely with traditional religion. Priest-kings are chosen from specific lineages. Often two lineages alternate in furnishing the incumbent of a priest-kingship. The power of the priest-king varies, depending on the prestige of his scepter and the loyalty of his followers.

138

In effect, he has no definite territorial jurisdiction.

Diola do not stand in awe of their spirits. They are there to be dealt with: one makes the appropriate sacrifices, says the appropriate words (words are powerful), and expects results. A Diola is quite capable of telling a spirit who has failed him that he will ignore it.

Below the spirits and capable of communicating with them are the souls of dead ancestors. They may be asked to intercede with spirits. Ancestors are the makers and guardians of tradition and thus, essentially, the arbiters of morality. They are intimately involved with everyday happenings. Death is not an absolute end to life, and the family name and power are maintained through successive generations. There is also widespread belief in the existence of ghosts as souls of people who have not been given proper burial and therefore are restless.

For the Diola the universe consists of a coherent hierarchical system in which man occupies a privileged position in the middle. Below man in the hierarchy are animals and inanimate objects, which are alive in some respects but without consciousness. The most important of these animals are symbols of clans, and members may not kill or eat them.

President Léopold-Sédar Senghor, a Serer, has described the religious beliefs of his people as a coherent system that provides man with a total vision of the universe in which he is in permanent contact with all life forces—visible as well as invisible ones. There is no dividing line between the mundane and the sacred. The underlying reason for rites and sacrifices is to reconcile those life forces that bring fertility to fields and to women.

Belief in various forms of magic is widespread, and witchcraft and sorcery are used to explain misfortune in personal terms as the consequence of acts of witches and sorcerers. Malevolent men suspected of witchcraft are often more deeply feared than evil spirits. Details of belief and practice vary, but the Wolof pattern indicates their general tenor.

A Wolof witch (*doma*) is believed to attack and eat others. His behavior is often involuntary, but he is compelled to act by a supernatural power inherited from his mother. Extraordinary precautions are taken against witches at crucial events in the life cycle, and much money is spent on amulets to ward them off. Witches are believed to hunger for blood and for the heart, liver, and fat of the young. Childbirth is therefore dangerous for the mother and child, circumsion for the initiate, marriage for the young bride, and nightlife for the young man. Witches also are believed to seize and eat souls that wander about during a person's sleep.

It is thought that witches turn into animals or other beings, and their appearance can paralyze most people. They then enter the victim's body to consume the organ they want. Many Wolof assert that God gives witches the power to penetrate the body without a mark.

Witches may cause illness, but they also enter a body when it is weakened by illness. A sick Wolof is therefore reluctant to be visited at night, nor does he care to acknowledge a weakened condition for fear that a witch, overhearing him, will attack.

A victim can identify the witch responsible for his illness. Formerly, a witch was beaten, killed, sold into slavery, or forcibly exiled; he may still be ostracized. Ordinarily, however, a medicine man, often a marabout, gives the victim a magical powder to enable the victim to speak if he is paralyzed. If the victim refuses the powder it is assumed that he has been "eaten" and must die. If the witch is identified, the medicine man usually places his name in the center of a magical drawing of Arabic origin. The witch should then withdraw and return the organ, but some are able to resist any magic used against them.

Accusations are most often leveled against outsiders of low status groups, but anyone, including close kin or friends, may be a witch. This possibility is anxiety provoking, but Wolof feel that they have some control through protective magic, and they do not live in constant fear.

Possession cults appear in some societies. The Lebou, for example, consider *ndop* (possession) to have therapeutic qualities. Their traditional religion centers on women and the notion of fertility, which guarantee the continued existence and well-being of the group. It is the women who experience *ndop* during which supernatural forces take possession of them, directing their speech and actions. This is believed to reconcile the spirits and dead ancestors who were responsible for an unsuccessful fishing expedition, a bad harvest, lack of pregnancy, or other misfortune.

Just as Muslims and many Christians are still affected by elements of traditional religions, so those adhering to such religions are affected by elements or ideas derived from their Muslim or Christian neighbors. Thus, Serer may wear amulets containing bits of the Koran and prepared by local marabouts, or Diola may sometimes appeal directly and without sacrifice to their high god, having been influenced by the Christians among them.

Sometimes certain aspects of traditional religions that were closely linked to specific social arrangements have changed. For example, the funerals of Serer chiefs cease to be central elements in Serer society, and a whole class of Diola spirits has been forgotten except by the very old because the way of life of the Diola has changed. Moreover, because indigenous religious beliefs are usually localized within the traditional order, they often lose their validity for individuals who migrate to the cities and find a place in modern society.

CHAPTER 8

CULTURAL EXPRESSION AND EDUCATION

As Senegal entered its second decade of independence, the dominant theme expressed by the country's intellectuals and government leaders was the search for national identity. Senegalese intellectuals had been among the first Africans to reject the French concept of assimilation and had led the move to reassess the value of African traditions (see ch. 2). President Léopold-Sédar Senghor was generally credited with having made one of the most significant contributions of all African intellectuals to the development of the concept of *négritude*—a term used loosely to denote a reassessment of African culture—and was leading the move to transform it into an ideology for national development (see Intellectual Activity, this ch.).

The reassessment of African traditions implied by the concept of *négritude* was an essential step in the synthesis of indigenous traditions and the heritage of the colonial experience into a national culture. It was assumed that this synthesis would better serve the needs and realities of a twentieth-century African state than would its component traditions. That the nature and direction of the synthesis were still open to debate in 1973 reflected definitional disagreement by the factions advocating *négritude* as well as the basic flexibility of the concept. It also reflected the vitality of intellectual movements in Senegal.

The country possesses a rich tradition of cultural expression. For the majority of the population the most significant areas of traditional art forms are music and oral literature, and artistic expression is closely linked to particular social functions. As early as the nineteenth century, however, a small urban elite evolved from the formal educational system established by the French. Its members not only enjoyed, but came to participate in, forms of Western cultural expression. During the twentieth century this elite gained an international reputation first for literary works and later for scholarship in the social sciences and for contributions to the visual and motion picture arts. Participation in Western forms of cultural expression remained largely an urban experience.

Since independence in 1960 the government's role in national development has included the support of cultural expression—ranging from direct financial aid to the sponsorship of exhibitions—and the direction of educational development. Educational policy has stressed the importance of improving the quality of educational facilities already available in the country over simple increases in enrollment and, during the first half of the 1960s, priority was given to improvements in elementary education. About 40 percent of the population of elementary school age attended school. During the last half of the decade the government initiated various studies of the educational system inherited from the French. Of particular concern was the nature of post-elementary education and the relevance of secondary and higher education to the social and economic needs and resources of the country. Government modifications of the educational system included the elimination of certain specializations. Student reaction to the government's educational reforms in the early 1970s led to violent demonstrations and to the destruction of public property, providing a major source of political disruption and threats to public order (see ch. 10; ch. 16).

ARTISTIC EXPRESSION AND SOCIETY

Artistic expression has been judged traditionally by the Senegalese in terms of the fulfillment of tasks regarded as essential to the survival of particular social groups rather than on the basis of each form's aesthetic merits. Under such a perspective, objects and acts are designed to fulfill a specific social, religious, or technical function, the significance of which is greater than—but does not exclude—the ability of the object or the act to please the ear or eye. So defined, artistic expression in traditional Senegalese society attempts to control the social and natural environment. Thus, although the recitation of oral literature provides a measure of entertainment, the more fundamental purpose is to strengthen group cohesion and to establish guidelines for social action, including the socialization of children to facilitate the transmission of myths, sacred beliefs, and traditional histories.

The concept of beauty in Senegalese art differs from the standard Western conception. The Wolof word for beauty, for example, translates best as "that which is suitable." It is assumed that music, ceremonial masks, and poetry will affect the audience; their beauty derives not from the fact that they affect the beholder but from their ability to produce the specific effect considered suitable to the occasion. The Bambara have a more versatile set of words for beauty, one of which corresponds to "beauty of and for itself." In general, however, this concept is not applied to artistic expression.

The functional emphasis of traditional Senegalese art places greater attention even in the visual arts on the process through which an object is created or with which the object is associated than on the object itself. Objects obtain their meaning not from their own form but from the essence with which they are invested and which can be reassigned to another object. Thus the object itself is not valued, and no great concern is shown for its preservation. The use of durable materials for art objects is of minor importance, and decayed objects are replaced by new ones.

Although certain requirements define the form of ritual objects, the need for representational art is not stressed in art. Meaning is sometimes accorded to an object by geometric markings, the meaning of which may be understood by only a small group or may be interpreted differently by members of various groups. Abstract forms suggestive of the essence or spirit that resides in the ritual object is more important than the creation of an exact physical resemblance. To a degree, realism has been restricted by the Islamic prohibition against the representation of living forms. Islam did not become a dominant cultural force, however, until the nineteenth century, and this restriction tended to serve as an additional reinforcement for tendencies already inherent in Senegalese visual art forms rather than as a limitation on previously evolved forms.

In the performing arts the competence of individual performers is assumed and, although individual excellence is often rewarded, there is greater stress on the communal function of the activity than on individual performance. Music and dance tend to be group activities, sometimes led by an individual or a small group. Extemporaneous performance by certain individuals—because of their status in the community or their function in a task at hand—is common, but even spontaneous expression tends to be limited by convention.

With the exception of songs and chants related to work and the celebration of certain holidays, group gatherings for singing and dancing occur mainly in the evening after the completion of daily tasks. Songs and dances are frequently related to religious occasions or to seasonal events, such as crop planting and harvesting. Some are associated with occurrences in the life cycle of group members, such as birth, puberty, marriage, and death. Similar celebrations are sometimes used to repay social debts or to demonstrate social position or wealth.

Small sums of money or token gifts may be given even to non-professional performers. Aristocratic Wolof women, who do not dance in public—at regular intervals and frequently in a formal manner—present coins to the drummers accompanying the dancers. Sometimes the women serve as intermediaries for men who wish to reward the musicians. Young women are often given the head scarves of older women or are given groundnuts (peanuts) by men in the audience. When a dancer receives a gift it is usually assumed that she will share a portion of it with the drummers.

Specialization is common in both the performing and the visual arts. Moreover, the social status of those engaged in the arts varies. Religious specialists in oral recitation—especially among Islamic groups—and those who are literate are usually highly regarded. Among the educated, modernizing segment of the population, the composition of literary works is a symbol of prestige. Lower status is accorded to craftsmen. Although the popularity of entertainers in urban areas has modified the traditionally lower status of performers, professional musicians still have low social positions.

A special caste known as *griots* perform multiple functions, serving often as musicians. They attend ceremonies or travel about the countryside singing the praises of a family, group, or individual by whom they are temporarily employed or to whom they are permanently attached. They serve as historians and genealogists and spread news and satirical forms of social criticism. Respected only for the role they perform, they possess low social status and are subjected to socioreligious restrictions, including matters of dress, housing, and burial rites. They are, however, granted considerable divergence from group standards in both their social criticism and general behavior (see ch. 5).

HANDICRAFTS

The tradition of handicrafts is an old one among Senegalese. Most ethnic groups have artisan castes, including smiths, weavers, dyers, leatherworkers, woodworkers, basket weavers, and potters (see ch. 5). Sometimes both the husband and wife are artisans in traditionally coupled fields; for example, the wives of smiths are potters, and wives of leatherworkers are dyers. The excellence of the work of one group is sometimes highly regarded by other ethnic groups and obtained either through trade or from itinerant artisans. Thus Wolof jewelry is valued over a wide area, and the *laobé* (itinerant woodworkers) do decorative carving for all ethnic groups.

Handcrafted utilitarian objects are common among groups throughout the country. Pottery is made either by shaping a mass of clay with a tool or by turning it to the desired shape on a potter's wheel. Baskets serve various purposes, and in some areas houses and granaries are made of thatch. Among the Bambara extremely fine mats with woven geometric, varicolored patterns are used for sitting and sleeping. The Bambara also dye fabrics with a background color obtained from a tree sap and then bleach out intricate patterns with lye taken from corrosive soap.

The pastoral Peul are especially noted for their leatherwork, including a variety of utilitarian and ornamental articles. The leather is often dyed bright colors, punched, carved, or embroidered with narrow leather strips. Most of the designs are geometric, in keeping with the Muslim prohibitions on producing likenesses of living things. Leatherwork is also produced by the Manding and other groups.

The highest artistry has been achieved by jewelers who work in gold and silver, producing elaborate bracelets, necklaces, earrings, and pendants in delicate filigree work. Examples of such jewelry made several hundred years ago—especially by Serer and Manding craftsmen—can be seen in museums in Senegal and France; that present-day art is practically unchanged. Demand for the jewelers' work is as high among European as among Wolof women, who were the original customers. Placing great value on personal adornment, Wolof women have long demanded high standards of design and workmanship from local craftsmen.

The changes in traditional values under way in the early 1970s had led to a reduction in the importance of certain rituals, and the quality of workmanship evident in masks and other ritual objects had declined. Some craftsmen had turned to producing inexpensive art for the tourist trade, and some coastal carvers were attempting to duplicate the plaster of paris saints found in Roman Catholic churches in the country. Competition from industrial goods—particularly items of plastic—had displaced a number of traditional handicrafts. Rather than modify and improve their methods to meet the demands of modern life, many artisans were abandoning their crafts for other occupations.

Efforts to preserve the quality of handicraft production in the country were first initiated by the French and have been continued by the national government. Training programs for craftsmen were initiated; information campaigns stressing the importance of traditional crafts were launched; and a small artisans' village was constructed on the outskirts of Dakar. Experimentation with new techniques as well as traditional methods was encouraged, and special exhibits featuring traditional crafts have been sponsored locally and abroad. The revitalization of traditional crafts remained an uncertainty in the early 1970s.

THE VISUAL ARTS

Although early stone sculpture and small objects of clay and metal have been excavated, Senegalese development of the visual arts has been rather limited. Those objects on which carving is found are usually designed for ritual performances, utilitarian purposes, or personal adornment, but small fertility statuettes are found sometimes among the Bambara. Most objects are made of wood and are usually the work of *laobé* or their wives. The most common utilitarian items on which carving appears include wooden mortars and pestles used for crushing grain and beating sticks used in the preparation of linen cloth.

The Bambara and Manding both make, for ritual use, elaborate wood and fiber masks and headpieces, which are completely or partly carved. The masks and their manufacture are controlled by initiation societies. The masks are used for rituals in which the participants gain worldly and spiritual knowledge in their passage to adulthood. Most masks combine human and animal features. Similar helmetlike masks are made by the Diola but are usually of woven matting. They present a comic appearance with their tubular eyes and are often topped by antelope horns. The reduced importance of initiation societies made it increasingly difficult by the early 1970s to find authentic examples of these masks, and many inferior ones were being made for the tourist trade. A modern version of a particular style of headpiece with a young antelope riding on the back of an adult antelope were being imported in large numbers from neighboring Mali by Bambara traders as well as being locally produced for marketplace sales.

After the introduction of formal education by the French in the mid-nineteenth century, a limited number of Senegalese artists began to express themselves in formerly unknown mediums, such as painting and lithography, and approached sculpture from a more universal perspective than that found in traditional carving. At first these artists sought to duplicate the styles and themes current in France. Some were highly competent, but the appeal of their work was rather restricted. Experimentation and deviation from previous standards typified their work in the 1950s. By the 1960s two different schools began to emerge. The first sought to express universal concepts in abstract styles of international appeal; the other was more representational and used natural motifs such as flowers and animals to reinterpret traditional themes.

As in the case of traditional crafts, the government was attempting to encourage and support the development of visual arts. Most training efforts were centered in the National School of the Arts in Dakar. Special exhibits were sponsored featuring both traditional and contemporary art objects. Some artists had been offered positions designing sets and costumes for the national theater, and 1 percent of the construction budget for new public buildings was required by law to be devoted to the inclusion of artistic decoration. By the early 1970s the government had sponsored special exhibits of contemporary art in various foreign countries, including Brazil, Sweden, Morocco, Cameroon, and Nigeria. Individual Senegalese artists had participated in various international art festivals, and the government had also helped arrange for one-man shows of Senegalese artists abroad. The work of these artists was well received and had in several instances been purchased by museums such as the Museum of Modern Art in Paris.

THE PERFORMING ARTS

Music

Music plays a significant social and religious role in Senegalese society. Specific songs, melodies, and kinds of music have special purposes, and there are often strict rules governing when and by whom they may be performed. Much of the daily work in the villages and rural areas is accompanied by music and singing. Work songs set a pace that helps to ward off fatigue and to create a communal spirit that motivates the worker and makes his task seem easier. In other situations instrumental and vocal music are frequently associated with dancing rather than independent performances. Regional variations occur not only in the style of music but also in the kind of instruments used.

Traditional instrumental music is produced chiefly by percussion instruments, particularly drums. The art of drumming is highly regarded and is extremely popular. It is taught to boys at an early age. In addition to rhythmic effects, drum music achieves tonal contrasts by the use of different drumming techniques and by the use of various kinds of drums at the same time.

Drums vary in size, shape, bracing, and the kind of drum head used. Some are beaten by hand and others with strikers. The *tamal*, a drum shaped like an hourglass and played under the arm of the player, provides different tones according to the pressure with which it is held. Other percussion instruments include wooden xylophones and a variety of rattles, gongs, and bells.

Although not as common as percussion models, various stringed instruments are found. The most common form is the *khalom*, a type of lute, of which there are three varieties that differ in size and musical range. All have resonators, usually made of gourds, over which tanned cowhide has been stretched; all but one have five strings. The exception is the one-string lute or *molo*, which is found in the north. A more complicated harplike instrument with twenty-one strings called a *cora* is used in the southern Casamance area. Highly specialized musicians use this instrument to create polyphonic music. Less common wind instruments include whistles, horns, and simple flutes.

Through schools and Christian missions the people have long been exposed to European music and influenced by it. Formerly unknown rhythms and harmonies found their way into local music, and in some areas where European influence was particularly strong a new style evolved. Similar to South American and Caribbean rhythms, variations of this form of new music are found in many coastal, urban areas of West Africa. Most variations resemble popular dance music. During the 1960s jazz music became highly popular in Dakar and other urban centers. Local concerts were well attended, and clubs that held weekly jazz sessions were formed. Local critics generally welcomed the efforts of young musicians to develop an African style of jazz, especially because of African influence on the early development of jazz in North America. Reaction to rock music introduced in the 1970s was not as enthusiastic.

Some educated Senegalese who had been steeped in the French culture prefer classical European music to local musical forms. Many children in larger cities take piano lessons or study other Western instruments. Small concerts featuring Western classical music are held frequently in Dakar; they are usually well attended. Performances are provided by a variety of local choirs, cantata groups, small orchestral ensembles, and military bands as well as by visiting groups from abroad. Concerts by the company of the national theater, however, continue to feature traditional musical forms.

Dance

Dancing is the principal means of self-expression and the focus of

147

much artistic activity. It permeates all aspects of life; men and women, young and old, dance at the slightest provocation—at religious ceremonies, at social or political gatherings, or simply from sheer joy of living. In the past, elaborate ritual dances evolved for recurrent formal occasions marking points in the life cycle, seasonal change—such as the coming of yearly rains and the beginning of harvest—or the setting out on a hunting or raiding expedition. On such occasions the ritual dancing was part of a religious ceremony and often called for elaborate symbolic costuming.

Although the style of Senegalese dancing is more expressive than formal, deriving its effect from the interpretation, through body movement, of a character or mood rather than from precise, disciplined footwork or gestures, tradition prescribes certain forms for specific occasions. Improvisation takes place only within the limits of this prescribed form. Emphasis is on collective performance, with group dancers moving in lines to simple rhythms often accompanied by instrumental music and chanting. Short solos may be offered by one or each member of the group.

Dance forms that initially evolved to serve traditional ritualistic expression were adapted to serve Islam and were modified during the colonial experience. Multiple variations of these dances continued to be an integral aspect of village life and to be regarded by educated urbanites as an important aspect of traditional heritage. Various local dance troupes toured the country, as did the national dance company affiliated with the national theater in Dakar. In 1971 this company was selected as one of four groups to tour the United States in a privately sponsored Afro-Asian Dance Festival, and the company was scheduled to tour Europe in the fall of 1973.

Drama

Drama had its origin in traditional religious and social celebrations, notably in the ritual dances that had all the elements of a dramatic presentation. In some cases these constituted a rudimentary play with characters and a simple plot, which was transmitted through costumes, mimicry, and song. The traditional love for theatrical spectacles was utilized by missionaries and French administrators as an educational medium. Sketches and tableaux on religious and educational themes were presented by amateur groups in all parts of the country to impress specific points on the local population.

Professional drama had its start in the 1930s when a group of students at the William Ponty Normal School formed a theatrical troupe. Staging plays both of their own creation and of standard European repertory, their presentations were aimed entirely toward the French-speaking urban elite. Their plays often satirized African traditions.

In the two decades after World War II professional Senegalese drama stagnated. The only semiprofessional dramatic company was that of the Alliance Française, the French cultural organization in Dakar, and it was composed almost entirely of French actors. Although some of the old plays were occasionally produced by amateur groups, they were considered outmoded and did not attract large audiences. Senegalese writers showed only a marginal interest in the theater during that period, and theatrical presentations offered little of interest to a people preparing for independence. Most Senegalese actors went to France in order to find more profitable and rewarding career opportunities.

During the early 1960s the government expressed concern over the state of the theater in Senegal and established a special committee to advise the secretary for cultural affairs in the Ministry of National Education and Culture on problems faced by the theater and to assist in the creation of a national theatrical company. Plans were drawn for the construction of modern theater facilities in Dakar. Senegalese actors were urged to return from abroad to staff the company, and a program was established under the drama section of the National School of the Arts to train additional actors and technicians.

The new Daniel Sorano Theater in Dakar—named after a Senegalese actor who earned considerable fame in France—was completed in the early 1970s. The theatrical company housed in the theater was composed of three troupes: a dance company, a company of singers and musicians, and an acting company. The troupes toured separately but also presented cooperative performances. Actors' salaries and production costs were supported by the state, allowing tickets to be sold at low cost.

To celebrate the tricentennial of the death of Molière, the national theater company presented an adaptation of the playwright's *Imaginary Invalid* in 1973. Although the production closely followed the original French script, the seventeenth-century play was flavored with Senegalese music and dance. A more liberal interpretation of Shakespeare's *Macbeth* had been presented, setting the play in the context of an African kingdom and providing the characters with modified African names.

Major developments in the film industry as a dramatic medium occurred during the 1960s. The artistic accomplishment of Senegalese producers was impressive from the start, and by the early 1970s filmmaking was clearly becoming an important form of cultural expression in the country (see ch. 12). Both short-subject and feature-length films were being produced, and several had received international awards. The first Senegalese films were largely French productions. In 1973 film production still depended on French processing facilities, but the actors and technicians were mainly Senegalese. The country clearly was a leader of filmmaking in Black Africa and was the headquarters of the African Filmmakers Association (Fédération Panafricaine des Cinéastes—FEPACI). Film viewing had assumed social importance, and special clubs existed for the viewing and discussion of films.

The first films produced by Senegalese concerned the problems faced by African students abroad, village life, and the issue of independence and related problems. Increasingly, films shifted to problems related to alienation from traditional society and the anomie in urban society. Various perspectives of *négritude* also began to be reflected in films. Of the more than ten major producers Ousmane Sembène, who received a prize for his Wolof-language film *Le Mandat* at the Venice Film Festival in 1968, had the greatest international reputation. Sembène's films followed the form and aesthetic treatment of neorealistic Italian films to show both the universal and particular problems that faced the Senegalese.

LITERATURE

Traditional Literature

The people have a rich tradition of oral literature—legends, myths, fables, and proverbs—transmitted from generation to generation by storytellers and *griots*. There are numerous legends and epics about tribal ancestors and great warriors, myths of the supposed origins of families and tribes, and legends explaining social customs or natural phenomena, such as fire, thunder and lightning, the sun, the moon, and the stars. Moral and cautionary tales point out the virtues of good behavior. In many of these, animals and insects are the main characters. Proverbs, problems, riddles, and puzzles also form part of the folklore.

Storytelling is an art that was developed to its highest level by *griots*. Part narrative, part song, and often accompanied by music, it involved all the teller's dramatic abilities. Good storytellers may have a wide reputation, and in the past they often became the subjects of legends composed by others. This folk literature is the medium to record events and to educate the young in the history and traditions of their society. It mirrors the values of the people and is a commentary on human relations. Some of it has been translated or transposed into French by missionaries, colonial administrators, or ethnographers.

After the introduction of Islam in the eleventh century, written literature was introduced to the portion of West Africa occupied by present-day Senegal. The ability to read and write Arabic was restricted to higher clerics and court scribes (see ch. 5). Even in the nineteenth century when Islam gained popular acceptance, the number of written texts in Arabic was limited.

Adaptations of Arabic script were used to transcribe Pulaar—spoken by the Peul and the Toucouleur—and Wolof. These adaptations were first used to record some of the old oral literature. Later on they were used to write original works based on Arab models. Many of these poems are epics of a religious or historical character, but there are also poems that reflect on aspects of everyday life. It is generally recognized that the utilization of scripts adapted from Arabic resulted not only in Arabic influences on the structure of the indigenous languages but also in Islamic influences on the thoughts of the indigenous writers. The extent of this influence, however, remained an open question.

Modern Literature

Although the growth of modern Senegalese literature can be traced back to the last half of the nineteenth century, the quality and quantity of literary works during that period were limited. During the 1930s, however, Senegalese writers began to produce what has subsequently become a substantial body of literature in French. Much of it is poetry—the usual form of traditional oral literature—but other forms, including novels, short stories, and essays, have been popular. Although written in refined French and initially for an audience of Europeans and assimilated Africans, this literature had dealt almost exclusively with African themes and situations. Much of the early work represented attempts by educated and assimilated Senegalese— many of whom had spent or were spending extended periods of time in Paris—to assert themselves against cultural and political domination by the French. Increasingly, the writing came to reflect the social and cultural problems of the Senegalese environment.

One of the principal themes of these writers has been the idealization and glorification of Africa and things African. This is especially evident in the early poetry of writers such as Senghor and David Diop, which is both passionate and romantic. Two other common themes found mainly in the novels of the late 1930s and the 1950s are the difficult adjustment between traditional African and modern European cultures and the social and economic problems resulting from rapid urbanization. Ousmane Socé's *Mirages de Paris* (Paris Mirages) and Cheikh Amidou Kâne's *Aventure Ambiguë* (Mixed Adventure) are both concerned with the confusion and loneliness faced by the African who has become estranged from the traditional values and way of life through exposure and adaptation to modern European culture. Abdoulaye Dadji's two novels, *Maimouana* and *Nini*, treat the same theme in connection with the social and economic problems of urbanization.

Several authors have drawn heavily on the customs and traditions of their people as subjects of their writing. Socé's *Karim*, the story of a boy growing up in the Senegal of the early twentieth century, is one of the most widely read pieces of modern African writing, and it has gone through more than five printings. It is extremely popular in Senegal, as are the short stories of Birago Diop, which are based on Senegalese traditions and follow the style of folktales and fables. Diop is often considered the modern *griot* of Senegal. Many of his stories have been published in newspapers and periodicals, but the best known are those contained in *Les Contes d'Amadou Koumba* (The Stories of Amadou Koumba) and *Les Nouveaux Contes d'Amadou Koumba* (The New

Stories of Amadou Koumba), collections of the stories that he remembers having heard as a child from his family *griot*, Amadou Koumba.

The growing interest in Africa throughout the world since the 1950s has been accompanied by an increasing interest in African literature. This has resulted in a great deal of analysis and criticism of African writing in magazines and periodicals, at conferences concerned with Africa, and in prefaces and introductions to works by African writers. Many of the critics, both European and African, see in the writing specifically African characteristics that distinguish it as a body from other literature. Others see it as part of a world literature that is African only inasmuch as it was written by Africans. All agree, however, that it has become an important part of the cultural heritage of the Senegalese people. Thus, although readers in Senegal still indicated a strong interest in French authors—especially classical masters such ae Victor Hugo, Molière, and Jean La Fontaine—they were especially interested in the early 1970s in works by Senegalese and other Africans. Their favorite authors were Senghor, Aimé Césaire, Diop, Socé, and Abdoulaye Sadji.

International respect for Senegalese literary efforts was widely expressed. Particular regard was held for the past work of President Senghor, who had published five major collections of poetry. During the 1960s the president received seven international literary awards, including one for his most recent collection of poetry, entitled *Nocturnes* (Night Pieces). The contribution of younger writers, many of whom had turned to writing motion picture scripts, to this literary heritage during the 1970s remained to be seen.

INTELLECTUAL ACTIVITY

No consideration of cultural expression in contemporary Africa is complete without a discussion of the concept of *négritude*; no single discussion, however, provides a complete explanation of what is meant by the concept and how it is relevant to a particular society. In simplest terms, *négritude* calls for a reassessment of the origins, evolution, and uniqueness of African culture and the rebirth of African dignity after colonial subjugation. Further definition is complicated by the fact that, although certain core concepts and values of the original leaders of the *négritude* movement have remained fairly constant over time, changes in emphasis and accommodation to the political, social, and economic realities of individual societies have occurred. Moreover, successive generations of political and intellectual elites, who did not share in the initial formation of the concept, have sometimes distorted the basic tenets of *négritude* in order to fit it to such personal interest as criticism of imperialism, support for revolutionary tactics, or justification of domination by a particular elite group. The relevance of *négritude* to cultural expression in Senegal stems from the predominant role played by President Senghor in the evolution of the concept and Senegalese attempts to apply it to the needs of national development.

The conceptual evolution of *négritude* is divided by Irving Markovitz, one of the most respected authorities on the concept, into three periods: the 1930s, the period after World War II, and the period after independence in 1960. These periods can be differentiated not only on the basis of the definitional focus of African intellectuals during these years— especially in the writings of Senghor—but also, and perhaps more importantly, in terms of changes in the motivation leading these writers to discuss the concept and their perspective of its relevance to the needs of their respective societies.

The *négritude* of African intellectuals during the 1930s was an extension of their individual search for personal identity. Exposed to the nationalist writings of men such as Maurice Barré, André Gide, and the French socialists as well as writers such as William Dubois, the young Africans began to doubt the necessity of cultural assimilation by the French and the exclusion of their own heritage. The advocates of *négritude* during this period sometimes overcompensated in their writing; some advanced the idea of African superiority or of revolutionary rejection of European values. Both aspects were rejected by the end of the decade, opening the way for support by French existentialists such as Jean-Paul Sartre. The main issue became the cultural rebirth of the African.

After World War II *négritude* became motivated by a search for national identity. It became less concerned with the philosophical and psychological issues of racial origins, and African leaders began to look at the problems they shared in common rather than in terms of their differences. The interest in a redefinition of African-European ties was not seen as a rejection of association with France but rather as an attempt to obtain a level of association offering the theoretically promised equality on which cooperation had been based (see ch. 2).

Senghor's presentation of the African case in terms evolved by the French culture as a demonstration of African cultural evolution through legitimate channels was to come under attack by more radical opponents as being overly cooperative. Differences also began to develop over Senghor's concept of African socialism as an alternative to capitalistic economic development (see ch. 10). Senghor continued to advocate cooperation as evidence of preparedness for independence rather than alienation leading to violent dissociation. By the mid-1950s, however, general dissatisfaction with attempts to forge a mutually satisfactory political union between France and its colonies led to support for separate independent status (see ch. 2).

In postindependent Senegal the concept of *négritude* developed in two somewhat divergent directions. On the one hand, under the influence of Teilhard de Chardin, Senghor sought to compare *négritude* and French culture in universal terms. On the other hand, he sought to

153

develop out of *négritude* an ideology for national development. In this approach science and technology were to replace philosophy in the solution of the more pressing problems of development. The concern shifted to production, motivation, and the mobilization of human and natural resources. A synthesis of African and European traditions was an ideal only when it was relevant to the realities of African development.

The acceptance of Senghor's concept of *négritude* as a national ideology for the masses has necessitated modification and dissemination of what was originally designed for elite consumption. Senghor's position as president and the assumption of political roles by other intellectuals, who played lesser but important roles in the conceptual evolution of *négritude,* have facilitated this transfer. As a national ideology *négritude* has become a catchall concept used to rally support for government development efforts as well as to evaluate national planning.

National attention was first attracted to the concept with the government's sponsorship in 1966 of the first Festival of Negro Art in conjunction with the United Nations Educational, Scientific and Cultural Organization (UNESCO). This was followed by a new interest in African languages in the schools and the establishment by the Senegalese Progressive Union (Union Progressiste Sénégalaise—UPS) of a touring program of lectures and debates on various aspects of *négritude.*

In 1971 the special Colloquium on Négritude, which included representatives from various states in Africa, Europe, and the Americas, was held in Dakar. The various papers presented reflected continued debate over what constituted *négritude.* The argument raised by some young intellectuals that the concept was no longer relevant to their problems, was too generalized, or was not radical enough for their needs was also recognized by the colloquium. Clearly, however, in the early 1970s the concept remained a useful meeting ground for intellectual and pragmatic dialogue.

SCIENTIFIC RESEARCH

A portion of the intellectual community that evolved after the establishment of the French educational system showed an interest in scholarly activity in the natural and social sciences. As in the early literary movement scholars initially tended to center in Paris, where there were greater facilities and opportunities. Their number remained small. A major stimulus to scholarly research in the country occurred in 1938 with the establishment in Dakar of the French Institute of Black Africa (Institut Français d'Afrique Noire). Although preceded by the establishment of several other institutions, this center was created specifically to encourage original West African research in the physical sciences, ethnology, and economics and to preserve African culture and crafts. Branches were established in the capitals of other

African territories, and the institute became the nucleus of Black African scholarly activity. At the same time the French administration began to encourage local intellectual activity by sponsoring award competitions for original scientific and literary works and by providing grants for research and for lecture tours.

Research facilities and programs expanded rapidly after World War II, especially during the 1950s. In 1973 there were about fifteen different research organizations in the country; almost all were located in Dakar. In addition to these institutes, there were close to twenty research centers and institutes associated with the University of Dakar that were engaged in research as well as in instruction. Several of these published occasional papers as well as quarterly or annual periodicals and reports (see ch. 12).

Among the oldest research facilities were the Pasteur Institute (Institut Pasteur), which was founded in 1906 to sponsor medical research, and the National Center of Agronomic Research of Bambary (Centre National de Recherches Agronomiques de Bambary), which was founded in 1921. The latter was specifically interested in fundamental and applied agricultural research and was under the direction of the Institute of Agronomic and Tropical Research (Institut de Recherches Agronomiques et Tropicales—IRAT). The various facilities of the Overseas Bureau of Scientific and Technical Research (Office de la Recherche Scientifique et Technique d'Outre-Mer—ORSTOM) engaged in highly specialized research in soil biology, botany, ecology, entomology, hydrology, ornithology, zoology, and other fields.

The French Institute of Black Africa was reconstituted in 1959 as the Basic Institute of Black Africa (Institut Fondamental d'Afrique Noire—IFAN). In 1963 the institute became associated with the University of Dakar and continued its various research activities under the sponsorship of the national government. Throughout the 1960s the number of Africans staffing the institute increased, and in the early 1970s a Senegalese was named director of the organization. The facilities available at the institute were drawing scholars from throughout the world to conduct research there. Institute bulletins were divided into a series on the natural sciences (with emphasis on geology, entomology, zoology, and botany) and a series on the social sciences (including anthropology, history, and sociology) in which the writings of Senegalese scholars and other experts on Africa were published. The theories of Cheikh Anta Diop, linking Black Africa to ancient Egypt, the geographic research of Assane Seck, and the historical work of Abdoulaye Ly represented some of the more noted contributions associated with the institute.

LIBRARIES AND MUSEUMS

Although the country possessed an established tradition of scholarly research, most library facilities that existed in 1973 came into being after World War II. In 1973 there were four major libraries in the country, all of which were located in Dakar. The oldest of these was the collection of the Archives of Senegal founded in 1913. It contained a collection of about 14,000 volumes and 850 periodicals. The library of IFAN had about three times as many volumes as well as collections of microfilm, maps, photographs, and slides and an extensive document file. The library of the Alliance Française dated back to 1948 and contained 10,000 volumes, most of which pertained to the arts and letters.

The largest facility was the Central Library of the University of Dakar. This library was established in 1952 to serve the newly founded university from a core of about 4,000 volumes and forty-five periodicals formerly in the collection of the African School of Medicine. Acquisitions for the departments of law, letters, and sciences were joined to the main collection, but they were separately housed. In 1965 the collection was consolidated in a new facility constructed on the campus of the University of Dakar. This modern air-conditioned building with a mosaic facade was designed to house 450,000 volumes as well as to provide reading and lecture facilities. By 1972 the library collection had reached about 185,000 volumes, 11,700 pamphlets, and 4,800 periodicals.

In addition to these major facilities, small specialized collections were held by the various independent research institutes in the country and the various centers and institutes attached to the university. The American Cultural Center in Dakar had a library of about 5,000 volumes. There were ten public libraries having a total of about 52,000 volumes, and reading materials were available at local information and cultural centers. The latter collections were limited, however, and were used mainly for entertainment. Information on holdings in school libraries was incomplete. Teachers were able to obtain materials on loan from various research and library facilities, but information detailing the operation and the effectiveness of this program was not readily available.

In 1973 all museum facilities in the country were operated by IFAN. The Museum of African Art of Dakar (Musée d'Art Africain de Dakar) was established in 1936 and housed a general ethnographic collection of Senegalese and African artifacts. The History Museum (Musée Historique) and the Museum of the Sea (Musée de la Mer) had displays on fishing and oceanography. Both were located on the island of Gorée.

EDUCATION

Development of Westernized Education

Although Western education was introduced during the first half of the nineteenth century, it was not until the last half of the century that an organized education system was established. The first school was opened in 1816 by a Roman Catholic priest in Saint-Louis. Various

Roman Catholic orders operated elementary schools to teach French and manual skills, and by the 1840s the four major elementary schools in the territory had a combined enrollment of just under 600 students. The first secondary school was opened in Saint-Louis, but it was forced to close in 1849 because of financial and administrative problems.

The real basis for Western education was laid by Governor Louis Faidherbe. In 1857 he asked the Frères de Ploermel to open several secondary courses for children of Europeans and of *métis* (people of mixed European and African ancestry) in the colony, and he established a school known as the School for the Sons of Chiefs and Interpreters in Saint-Louis to train children of African chiefs and notables as colonial administrators. Then he organized all the existing schools into a state school system but left it under the administration of religious orders. In 1901 the school system was secularized, and in 1903 it was integrated into the expanded system of the French West African federation.

The educational system of French West Africa was designed to serve two often contradictory purposes—to train the farmers, artisans, clerks, interpreters, and teachers who were needed to assist the French in operating the colony and, at the same time, to inculcate the African people with French culture. The second purpose tended to dominate educational policy throughout the colonial period, and the structures and content of education in Senegal increasingly came to follow the system of metropolitan France.

Initially, elementary schools (*écoles primaries élémentaires*) were divided into village schools, offering a three-year course of reading and writing—both in French—and arithmetic, and regional schools where the best students from the village schools could complete their studies for the French certificate of elementary education (*certificat d'études primaires élémentaires*). After 1927 they were combined into a single kind of primary school in an effort to make the school system more closely correspond to that of France. Curricula in rural schools were modified to include agricultural training, but urban schools came to follow the standard French curriculum.

Secondary education following the French model became available in 1911 with the founding of the William Ponty Normal School, which offered a three-year course and had separate programs for training teachers and junior administrators for government and business positions. Although it was not the only secondary school in French West Africa, it was the only all-African secondary school that consistently maintained high standards. It was attended by students from all the French territories and played a major role in the development of Africa's educated elite. In 1918 the African School of Medicine was attached to the William Ponty institution, and limited higher education preparing Africans for a local degree in medicine, pharmacy, or veterinary science was made available.

In 1927 the School for the Sons of Chiefs and Interpreters was transformed into the Blanchot Advanced Primary School offering a three-year course following the certificate of elementary education, which trained students for junior clerical positions in government and commerce. At the same time the Pinet-Laprade Professional School in Dakar offered a three-year course that trained craftsmen. A number of other institutions in Dakar and Saint-Louis were established, and they followed programs sanctioned by French certificates and degrees. The most important were the Lycée Faidherbe, founded in Saint-Louis in 1919, and the Lycée Van Vollenhoven, established in Dakar in 1936.

Changes in colonial policy and political reforms immediately after World War II led to the establishment of a new twenty-year plan. The mission of the plan was to give the population at large the basic education necessary for responsible citizenship in a westernized society and to prepare the more gifted students to assume leadership in their communities. During the 1950s educational facilities were expanded, enrollment increased sharply, an extensive scholarship program for advanced study abroad was instituted, and an institute of higher education was established (later it was incorporated as the University of Dakar). The educational system continued to reflect the French colonial policy of assimilation and followed the structure and curriculum of the metropolitan system.

The School System

At independence the Senegalese inherited a fully developed educational system whose curriculum and standards were modeled on those found in France. The system tended to produce a small number of highly qualified specialists and large numbers of students whose elementary school certificates prepared them to read but not to find employment. The system was in need of major modification; but the overall scarcity of human and social resources, the disruptive effect of introducing major modifications of the education system too rapidly, and the problem of establishing and coordinating commonly agreed-upon guidelines for long-term development complicated both the conception and implementation of reforms. With the exception of certain reforms, the country continued to rely on this basic system in 1973.

Public facilities under the system were free and provided for elementary, secondary, and higher levels of education (see fig. 6). Each of these three educational levels was divided into alternate short and long cycles, the completion of which usually entitled the student to hold specific certificates. Students were required to pass qualifying examinations in order to advance to the next higher level; they could not do so simply on the basis of holding a certificate that indicated completion of the preceding level.

Preschool education was provided by private nursery schools, most

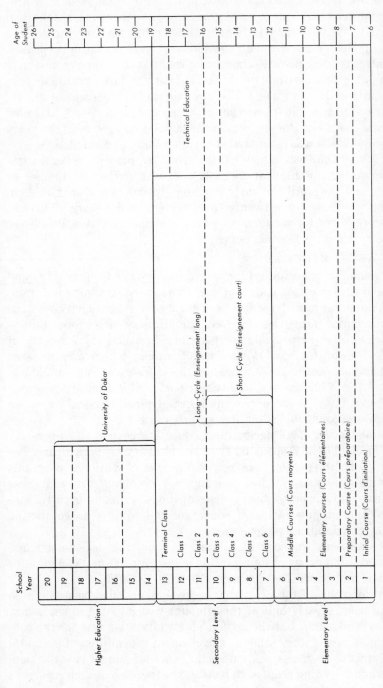

Source: Adapted from Martena Sasnett and Inez Sepmeyer, *Educational System of Africa: Interpretations for Use in the Evaluation of Academic Credentials*, Berkeley, 1966; and Jerry B. Bolibaugh, *Educational Development in Guinea, Mali, Senegal, and Ivory Coast*, Washington, 1972.

Figure 6. Educational System of Senegal, 1970

159

of which used the Montessori method. Private elementary and secondary schools were allowed to operate, provided they followed a government-approved curriculum, used government-approved textbooks, and employed licensed teachers. Under these conditions private schools were eligible for government subsidies to meet operating expenses. Students attending private schools who wished to continue their education in public schools could do so after taking standard state qualifying examinations. In the early 1970s approximately 25 percent of all elementary students and 13 percent of all secondary students attended private schools. For the segment of the population aged fourteen years and over, literacy was estimated at between 5 and 10 percent.

The school year was scheduled for about ten months, several vacations breaking up the year. Schools opened in either September or October and ran until the early summer. Instruction was in French. Grading was based on a twenty-point system, and a score of at least ten was required for passing. Six years of elementary education were compulsory, but the law was not enforced.

Administration and Financing

The major responsibility for the administration, financing, and control of the educational system in 1973 was divided among four ministries, but other ministries also were engaged in educational activities. The four major ministries included: the Ministry of National Education, which was responsible for general education; the Ministry of Technical Education and Vocational Training, which administered technical and vocational training; and the Ministry of Popular Education and the Ministry of Youth and Sports, which jointly operated youth programs in civic service and sports, trained physical education teachers, and conducted adult literacy programs.

Administration of all agricultural education beyond the secondary school level was the responsibility of the Ministry of Agriculture. The Ministry of Information was responsible for educational programs employing the mass media. Coordination problems between these ministries and various other agencies of the government greatly complicated the administration of education and resulted in conflicting planning and duplicate programming.

Education was financed by allocations from the national budget, local funds, and external sources. Under the Third Four-Year Plan for Economic and Social Development (1969/70–1972/73), almost CFAF8 million (for value of the CFA franc—see Glossary) had been allocated for education. Nearly half of this amount was invested in secondary education programs, but the largest single allocation was for the construction of elementary schools. Government expenditures for capital improvements in the education sector, such as school construction, were gradually being reduced to balance the increase in such recurrent expenditures as salaries for teachers in the new facilities.

Local funds were used largely to finance the construction or improvement of schools. During the first half of the 1960s this method of financing helped to increase the number of elementary schools offering a complete six-year program. In some cases, however, expenditures did not match those projected in national plans, and there were no funds for staffing the locally improved facilities.

Within the Ministry of National Education was the Office of Planning and Control. Although seeming to be a center from which educational planning should be coordinated, it lacked the staff and budget to do so. The publication of educational statistics was one of its major functions. Various sections within the ministry were responsible for prescribing curricula, textbooks, teaching methods, qualifying examinations, and teacher certification.

An office of health inspection and school sanitation in the ministry is responsible for maintaining health standards in the schools and for administering periodic medical examinations and smallpox vaccinations. Each child must have been vaccinated against smallpox before he can be admitted to school, and the vaccination must be repeated at fixed intervals. Inspectors, usually experienced teachers who have had additional special training for their position, have the duty of visiting each school at least once a year to pass on its compliance with government regulations, to evaluate the performance of teachers, and to recommend promotion or demotion.

External sources of revenue were especially important to educational development and provided over 40 percent of education expenditures during the late 1960s. France provided the majority of external aid, but contributions also came from Canada, the Federal Republic of Germany (West Germany), Israel, Switzerland, and the United States. The major multilateral souce of aid was the European Development Fund of the European Economic Community (EEC, known as the Common Market), but important contributions were also made by the United Nations Special Fund and UNESCO.

Elementary Level

Elementary education was composed of six years of schooling that included a one-year initial course, a one-year preparatory course, a two-year elementary course, and a two-year middle course. Students were awarded the certificate of elementary education (*certificate d'études primaires élémentaires*) at the completion of the program. This certificate increasingly was becoming a prerequisite for salaried employment. Students were allowed to repeat a maximum of two years and still remain in the program.

The goal of elementary education—apart from its function as a base for further study—was to develop basic language and mathematical skills suitable to lower level employment and to teach skills essential to participation in the emerging social and political system of the country. The program consisted of about thirty hours of instruction weekly.

During the first two years emphasis was on learning the French language. Mathematics was also important, and history, geography, and the arts were included in the curriculum.

In the 1969/70 school year there were about 258,000 students in public and private elementary schools. Although this constituted an increase of about 100,000 students over enrollment figures in the early 1960s, as a result of population increase the percentage of the school-age population attending elementary schools had remained constant at slightly over 40 percent. Not quite 40 percent of all elementary school students were girls, and about 20 percent of all students were repeating a year. In all there were 1,312 schools and 5,722 teachers for elementary instruction.

Secondary Level

Students interested in attending secondary schools were required to pass an entrance examination. They could then enter general academic, technical, or teacher training programs. General secondary education was divided into long and short cycles. Students following the four-year short cycle (*enseignement court*) received a first-cycle study certificate (*brevet d'études du premier cycle*). Those following the seven-year long course (*enseignement long*) received a secondary school certificate (*baccalauréat*), which entitled them automatically to enter the university if they so chose.

The purpose of general short-cycle education was to supplement elementary education so that the graduate could either pursue further academic or technical studies or enter the labor market. Most holders of the first-cycle study certificate did continue with some form of additional secondary education. The study of a modern foreign language was required of all secondary level students. Initially English was the required language, but Arabic was later made an alternate choice. Literature, mathematics, history, geography, and basic science were standard in both long and short cycles. Students studying for the *baccalauréat*, however, also studied chemistry, physics, classical languages, philosophy, and mathematics.

In the 1969/70 school year there were 48,905 students enrolled in general secondary school programs. This was an increase of over five times the enrollment figures for the early 1960s. About 25 percent of these students were girls, and slightly over 10 percent of the total students were repeating a year for a second time. There were more than 152 schools and 1,709 teachers for general secondary school instruction.

Higher Education

Higher education was first introduced to the country in 1918 with the establishment of a medical program designed to train Africans to serve as physicians, although initially it did not provide the complete training available to medical students in France. In 1950, under the auspices of French universities, the Institute of Higher Education was established in Dakar. In 1957 the medical program and the institute were incorporated as the University of Dakar and attracted students throughout French-speaking Africa. Jurisdiction was transferred to the national government at independence in 1960, but cooperation with French institutions continued. The university gained an excellent reputation, and its degrees—including those granted to medical doctors—were recognized internationally as comparable to those granted in France.

The university originally had four faculties: law and economics; medicine and pharmacy; sciences; and arts and social sciences. In 1973 the number had been increased to six through the addition of the Faculty of Veterinary Sciences and the division of the Faculty of Law and Economics into two separate faculties. The programs and requirements of each faculty varied widely. With the exception of medicine and pharmacy, university education was divided into three stages. Two-year programs led to the receipt of a general license (*licence libre*) or a teaching license (*licence d'enseignement*), the most commonly acquired university degrees. A four-year program provided a certificate of higher study (*certificat d'étude supérieur*). A doctorate (*diplôme d'étude supérieur*) was obtained from varying combinations of additional study, presentation of a thesis, or both.

In addition to the seven faculties, there were about twenty different institutes and centers attached to the university offering specialized programs that led to the award of terminal certificates and diplomas. Among these were the University Institute of Technology (Institut Universitaire de Technologie), the Center for the Study of Information Sciences and Techniques (Centre d'Études des Sciences et Techniques de l'Information), and the School for Librarians, Archivists, and Documentationists (Ecole de Bibliothécaires, Archivistes, et Documentalistes). In 1970 more than 140 students were also studying abroad in programs of higher education.

Admission to the university was open to anyone with a *baccalauréat* or a recognized equivalent and to persons over twenty-one years of age who did not have a degree but could pass a special entrance examination. Annual fees for registration, library, laboratory, examinations, and medical service were modest. Housing for both single and married students was available, but most students preferred off-campus facilities to those provided by the institution.

Since its inception Senegalese higher education has been devoted to specialization. Having reached this level the student was supposed to be thoroughly grounded in general culture and able to decide on a field of particular interest. To matriculate he enrolled in a specific program in one of the faculties or institutes and followed the year-by-year curriculum prescribed for the program. Program changes were possible but, as the curricula were highly specialized, few credits could be transferred. Modifications of the rigidity inherent in this system were under way in the early 1970s. These efforts also reflected modification of the elementary and secondary programs, which sought greater relevance to the needs and resources of Senegalese society.

Enrollment in the various faculties and institutes providing higher education for the 1969/70 school year totaled about 3,000 students. This compared with 2,000 in the 1962/63 school year. The total number of Senegalese students had increased during this period from 36 to 52 percent of the total student body. The number of female Senegalese students increased during this period from about 3 to 16 percent. Statistics also indicated that, of the foreign students in attendance at the university, 60 percent came from other African countries and about 32 percent, from France.

Almost 40 percent of all Senegalese students were enrolled in studies of the humanities, letters, and French language and civilization. The next largest enrollment was in law and economics. Foreign students, however, were interested primarily in medical study. There were about 650 professors in the higher educational system, about 10 percent of whom were women. Although about 40 percent of all professors were foreigners, over half of them were from African countries.

Technical Education

The Ministry of Technical Education and Vocational Training operated most of the various schools that provided vocational training in technical and agricultural fields. It supervised forestry and fishery training programs and cooperated with the Ministry of Agriculture in the direction of postsecondary level agricultural training. In addition to providing training for students before they entered employment, programs were also operated for improving the skills of rural and urban workers.

There were two types of specialized secondary technical schools. Training centers (centres de formation) offered a three-year program leading to a professional skill certificate (certificat d'aptitude professionelle). Technical agents schools (écoles d'agents techniques) provided a four-year program leading to diplomas attesting to specialized qualifications, such as the agricultural technical agent diploma (diplôme d'agent technique de l'agriculture). Most of those following these programs were being trained as foremen and technicians. Some continued their education with postsecondary level technical study, but modifications under the third four-year development plan were redirecting those who desired such advanced technical training to general secondary schools.

Current enrollment figures were not available in mid-1973, but during the late 1960s about 9,000 students had been enrolled in the twenty-five schools administered by the Ministry of Technical Education and Vocational Training. There were about 1,400 students enrolled in short training programs offered by the National Center of Professional Courses (Centre National des Cours Professionnels), and some students were following short courses in private schools. The University Polytechnic Institute (Institut Universitaire de Technologie), which was

164

established in 1964, had an enrollment of more than sixty students and was expected to grow in importance during the 1970s.

Although some agricultural training facilities offered short courses for farmers, few of the students attending secondary level agricultural training programs were interested in farming as an occupation but sought positions in government agricultural programs, municipal projects, and the park services. The total number of students attending various secondary level agricultural courses was about 500 in the late 1960s.

Teacher Training

Students interested in becoming elementary-school teachers entered an upper level secondary program at one of the normal schools after the completion of the first cycle of general secondary education. Assistant elementary-school teachers went directly into one-year training programs offered at regional teacher training centers after having received the first-cycle study certificate.

Students training as first-cycle secondary teachers entered a two-year program at the Higher Teacher Training School (Ecole Normale Superieur). Those interested in teaching at the second-cycle level took a four-year program offered jointly by the University of Dakar and the Higher Teacher Training School. The number of students qualified to enroll in these programs and low teachers' salaries limited the number of students who entered and completed teacher training programs. The training of teachers for technical or other vocational teaching was especially low. Most continued to be trained abroad, and local programs continued to be heavily staffed by expatriate Frenchmen.

Adult Education and Literacy

The government—mainly through the Ministry of Popular Education—operated various adult education programs both independently and in conjunction with regional information and cultural centers. The most dynamic and extensive of all these programs began in 1964 as a pilot project conducted in cooperation with UNESCO. The purpose of the program was to test the effectiveness of audiovisual media in adult education. Experimental television programs presented a series on health and nutrition to women in Dakar, who gathered at special viewing centers. A more extensive educational and cultural program entitled "Rencontres" (Encounters) was added in 1966. During the late 1960s project expansion included literacy programs for factory workers, radio broadcasts to villages and rural areas, and a series of films for both urban and rural viewing.

The Dakar program had three primary goals. It was designed to demonstrate the feasibility and effectiveness of audiovisual media on adult education in an African setting. It was also seen as a means of helping to discover the most effective strategy to be followed by governments in use of the media and to provide a training program for

African personnel. The program has been judged highly successful in the achievement of these goals as well as in the effect it had on the establishment of television broadcasting in Senegal (see ch. 12).

In addition to the achievement of the primary goals of the program, observation of changes in the attitudes and behavior of project participants reflected the multiple dimension of adult education. The groups of women in the initial project became involved in organized community action groups and social clubs. Discussion following the telecasts, moreover, allowed the women to discuss issues more openly. The extensive adoption of Western foods, for example, as an index of social status, was replaced by a comparison of the relative values of traditional and processed foods and personal taste preferences.

Educational Reform

Provision for educational reform has been tied to the formulation of national development plans. The preparation of these plans has been an involved process, the responsibility having been shared by a higher council and a multiplicity of subordinate planning committees. The process has been further complicated by the division of administrative responsibility for national education among four ministries rather than by confinement to a central agency.

During the first half of the 1960s major emphasis was on expanding elementary school facilities and on increasing primary school enrollment. As a result, no major modification of the educational system was undertaken. During the last half of the 1960s the relevance of higher education to national needs was examined. The decision was made during the 1968/69 school year to close certain departments in the university that did not closely fit the aims of the development plan. In the Faculty of Arts the departments of philosophy, sociology, psychology, and the classics were to be closed. Implementation of this policy was delayed by a student protest that followed because of this and other issues related to the university.

Various innovations were instituted to modify school curricula and teaching methods. Curricula changes were designed to make instruction more relevant to the African environment. Consequently, greater emphasis has been given to African geography and history, both of which were only marginally treated under the French. Concentration on flora and fauna native to the region had been introduced in biology and zoology classes.

Modification in policies regarding textbooks used for instruction has also occurred. Until 1965 textbooks were selected for each area by its elementary school inspector. After 1965 selection was made on a national basis. Most books were published in France but were adapted for use in Senegal or Africa in general. Frequently, however, adaptations were superficial revisions, and the Ministry of National Education had obtained aid from UNESCO to prepare a limited number of texts for school use.

Experimentation with courses introducing new methods of mathematical instruction were under way in the early 1970s, but extensive use of audiovisual materials remained limited as a result of financial considerations. The Applied Linguistics Center of Dakar (Centre de Linguistiques Appliqués de Dakar—CLAD) had successfully introduced a program called "Pour Parler Français" (In Order to Speak French) using the direct method of language instruction for teaching French in the first three years of elementary school. As of 1970 all student teachers were required to be trained in the new method. Revision of methods used to teach Arabic had also been implemented.

Provisions for modifying elementary and secondary level education were included in the third four-year development plan. Transition to the new system was to be on a phased basis and would be completed by the mid-1970s. The time devoted to elementary education would be reduced by one year. Elementary school graduates would enter first-cycle secondary schools or postelementary practical training schools offering an agriculturally oriented program. The first-cycle technical schools would be eliminated, and those students wishing an advanced technical education would first complete the four-year short cycle at a secondary school and then transfer to a two-year, second-cycle vocational program. A transitional year would be provided so that the top 5 percent of the students in practical training schools could be transferred into the second year of first-cycle secondary school programs. Initiation of the phasing was delayed by at least one year, and further information on the status of modifications was not readily available in mid-1973.

Education and Society

Traditional Education

Traditional society placed emphasis on the continuity of the family and community, and from an early age children were instilled with the traditions and mores of their society by various means, including recitations and the singing of songs relating sacred myths. Most of their games were imitations of adult roles the children would later assume, and from an early age children were given simple tasks such as gathering wood or herding animals. At the age of about eight, children began to receive training in the occupation they were to follow as adults. Most ethnic groups had occupational castes that limited the choice of occupations.

Formal education of boys was restricted to Koranic schools associated with local mosques or the households of more affluent families. Girls did not usually attend these schools, but some girls of wealthier families were educated at home. Students were taught to recite portions of the major prayers and verses of the Koran in Arabic as well as to know the practices of Islam. Sometimes they were taught to read and write Arabic as well. The possession of literacy skills was highly valued and provided a means of status and social mobility. The social system tended to perpetuate itself, however, and generally only children of upper class families received more than superficial Koranic educations.

During the nineteenth century, Koranic school education began to displace the importance of initiation rites among those groups gradually accepting Islam. The introduction of Western education by the French did not, however, displace Koranic schools and, even in the 1970s, Muslim boys received Koranic educations. Sometimes they attended the religious schools before or after going to public school, and their absence from the latter was sometimes excused so that they might participate in some form of traditional education. The values and orientations of the two systems were not similar, and confusion sometimes arose in the minds of children as a result.

Education as a Social Force

In 1973 it was difficult to fully appraise the all-embracing role education had played in the evolution of the Senegalese social and political system since independence. Education has not been the panacea that some educators initially had presented it to be. In some cases, it had helped to generate social and political conflict (see ch. 5; ch. 10). Adjustment of the educational system to the needs and realities of the people and the exploitation of those aspects of the system that would promote political and social stability were of particular interest to national planners in the early 1970s.

Studies of urban and rural attitudes indicated a high value accorded to education both as an end in itself and as a means of gaining better employment; prestige was accorded to occupations considered to be intellectual. Civil service positions were highly preferred for the security they offered and the prestige they held. As a result, students tended to favor academic education over technical training, and the labor force had suffered. This set of priorities was manifest throughout the entire system of education, including the university.

The situation was complicated by the number of students who terminated their education at the elementary level, having received an education structured along academic lines, or who dropped out of school before completing a particular educational cycle. Dropout rates for various levels were often as high as 45 percent, and in one sector the rate was 65 percent during the mid-1960s. The reliance on French as the language of instruction contributed to the failure of some students who had not been exposed to the language before entering elementary school. Experimentation was under way to determine the effect of nursery schools and preelementary language instruction on the dropout rate.

The effect of school failure or the inability to find employment of the kind valued by school-leavers holding certificates was differently interpreted. That these people would experience frustration as a result of their failure to succeed or profit as a result of their encounter with the educational system would be natural. Similarly their education had contributed to their alienation from traditional society and to their insecurity in the transitional or modernizing society. Although the degree of frustration could not be readily determined, it did represent a social cost.

The educational system was supposed to function as a means of social mobility for persons attempting to enter the modernizing society or to advance through its ranks. The Islamic prohibition on the integration of the sexes placed a restriction on the education of women, especially in elementary and secondary schools, and retarded their rise in the social system. The proportion of female students had increased significantly during the 1960s, however, and women were taking increasingly important roles in national development as a result of the skills provided by the public educational system.

Access to education was not balanced geographically, and the distribution of secondary schools favored those living in Dakar and in the vicinity of Saint-Louis. The effects of class values and urban upbringing on educational success were also projected as sources of imbalance. Some programs sought to deal with these problems, but the overall dimension of the problem and the effects of the programs designed to compensate for them were differently interpreted.

Dissent by students enrolled in higher educational facilities represented an increasingly disruptive factor in the quest for national development and stability. University students had become a subgroup evolving within the social system and had developed social institutions such as university student organizations and cultural associations. Students associated their personal future, as well as that of the nation, with the educational system. They watched modifications of the system with great care and diligently guarded their social prestige as university students.

Agitation developed in 1968 over government plans to eliminate certain university departments and later over additional changes, such as restrictions announced in 1971 limiting the students' free choice of specialization. Student dissatisfaction with the government's efforts at conciliation led to violent demonstrations, to the boycott of classes, and to the destruction of public property (see ch. 10; ch. 16). Students had come to assume a political role. In mid-1973 the government and the students had not resolved their differences.

169

SECTION II. POLITICAL

CHAPTER 9

THE GOVERNMENTAL SYSTEM

In 1973 the country was governed in accordance with a highly centralized constitutional structure that placed nearly all power in the hands of the national administration. From 1963 until 1970 President Léopold-Sédar Senghor had performed the functions of both head-of-state and head-of-government. The appointment of a prime minister in 1970 still left most powers in the president's hands.

President Senghor's position was further strengthened by his leadership of the ruling party, the Senegalese Progressive Union (Union Progressiste Sénégalaise—UPS), which he had founded. The UPS had held all seats in the National Assembly for almost ten years. The executive committee of the party reviewed and approved government policy weekly, thus forming in effect a fourth branch of government. The UPS is not named in the constitution, but Senegal is a one-party state, and any significant power struggles go on within the higher echelons of the party rather than between the UPS and other parties.

Despite the existence of a dominant figure in the government and the party and the centralized form of control, an independent judiciary and the ingrained customs of the people left individual liberties substantially intact. President Senghor and his party maintained their rule by striving for consensus not by intimidation (see ch. 10).

CONSTITUTIONAL DEVELOPMENT

The country's experience with the European kind of political institutions has been both long and rich. The coastal cities had first known municipal self-government over 200 years ago. For over fifty years Senegal was the capital of the federation of French West Africa (Afrique Occidentale Française—AOF), from which the other territories were governed (see ch. 2). Thus a small but influential group of citizens had a background of generations of experience with government as the French practiced it. These men had the opportunity to attend school, vote in elections, run for office, and participate in a civil service that administered not only their own territory but also a major European country.

From 1914 until independence, the country sent Africans as elected representatives to the French National Assembly, where they

171

participated in the complicated and instructive French legislative process. As early as 1919 a Senegalese, Blaise Diagne, held a subcabinet position in the French government. Shortly after World War II Senegalese began to be given posts at the executive level of government as senior civil servants, involved in the actual day-to-day administration of the country.

As independence approached, the country adopted a constitution and government institutions that were closely patterned on the French models. They were not so much in imitation of the French as they were an indication of the political and administrative experience of their leaders. One of the features acquired in part from this French administrative experience was a strict pyramidal structure that emphasized strong authority on the part of the central state apparatus.

The Senegalese were in the forefront of early endeavors to form independent regional federations. Between 1956 and independence they sought to keep the former AOF states together but, when self-government was granted in 1958, only the former French Sudan (now Mali) joined with Senegal in what was intended as a federation of French-speaking West Africa. The federation achieved its independence from France on April 4, 1960. The union fell apart four months later, less than two years after its founding, as its politicians split over the question of who would serve as its leader.

The first constitution of independent Senegal, written after the break with Mali, came into operation on August 26, 1960. The constitution provided for a careful balance between the halves of a dual executive consisting of a president, elected indirectly, and a premier. The unicameral assembly was elected by direct universal suffrage. Personal freedoms were elaborately protected. The system was parliamentary, like its French model; the prime minister (president of the Council of Ministers) was approved by the National Assembly but selected his ministers after his investiture. The judicial branch was declared independent.

The prime minister could request a vote of confidence, and the National Assembly could initiate a motion of censure. Either a vote of no-confidence or one of censure spelled the demise of the government. A censure motion voted in December 1962 was the climax of a political crisis within the ruling party and finally led to the drafting of the 1963 Constitution (see ch. 2). The new constitution, accepted by popular referendum and signed into law in March 1963, abolished the office of prime minister and gave broader powers to the president, who was to be elected by direct suffrage rather than indirectly. The president and members of the National Assembly now had simultaneous terms of four years.

The National Assembly had no power to censure the president. Although he could no longer dissolve the legislature, the net result of the changes was to strengthen the power of the president. This brought the governmental system of the country more into conformity with those of other African states, many of which had already established the strong executive as the outstanding mark of their governmental structure. In telling the people about the constitution, the president and his ministers stressed the innovation of the separation of powers, by which the ministers could no longer be members of the National Assembly, emphasizing the new distinction between the legislative and executive branches. Although the office of prime minister was restored in 1970, real power over all important decisions remained under the control of the president.

BASIC CONSTITUTIONAL PRINCIPLES

The basic principles on which the 1963 Constitution rests are set forth in a preamble and in the first few articles in which the people proclaim their independence and attachment to the fundamental rights as defined in the French Declaration of the Rights of Man of 1789 and in the Universal Declaration of Human Rights of 1948. The preamble also states that "the Republic of Senegal will spare no effort for the realization of the unity of Africa," citing an awareness of the "historic, moral, and material imperatives" uniting West African countries and of the necessity "for a political, cultural, economic and social unity, indispensable for the affirmation of the African personality."

The 1963 Constitution, like its predecessors, is unusually explicit about human freedoms and civil liberties. Such guarantees are especially pertinent in a country where 75 percent of the population comes from ethnic groups with slave and caste traditions (see ch. 5). Security of person is inviolable, the state having the obligation to respect and protect it. All individuals are equal before the law, regardless of sex, status, or family or ethnic origin.

Freedom of expression and propagation of ideas are guaranteed, as is the right to form associations. The constitution also guarantees secrecy of correspondence and telecommunication. All citizens have the right to settle anywhere in Senegal—a right that cannot be limited by law. The right of property is guaranteed, although the power of eminent domain with just compensation is provided in the constitution. The home is inviolable, and a search requires a warrant, which may be obtained only under conditions specified by law.

Dealing with individual liberties in the realm of marriage, the family, and education, the constitution declares that "marriage and the family constitute the natural and moral base of the human community" and are under the protection of the state. The state, charged with assistance on the physical and moral plane, is to aid parents in their "natural right and duty" to bring up their children and to see to it that children are neither exploited nor morally neglected. The state is to create public insititutions that guarantee the education of children, although private schools may be authorized under control of the state.

Religious institutions and communities are to remain free from state control, are recognized as means of education, and are guaranteed philosophic and religious freedom.

Everyone is accorded both the duty and the right to work. The right to strike is explicitly recognized but may be controlled by law and may not in any way interfere with the rights of others to work.

Nearly all of these civil guarantees are cushioned by clauses stating that the right granted may be limited by law or regulation to ensure the welfare of other individuals or society as a whole. The record of the first twelve years of independence, however, in the main shows a real effort on the part of the government to respect these rights and liberties.

Initiative for constitutional amendment rests concurrently with the president and the deputies. To be enacted, an amendment must be voted by a three-fifths majority of the National Assembly or by an absolute majority followed by approval in a national referendum. The republican form of government may not be the subject of an amendment.

ORGANIZATION OF GOVERNMENT

The President

From 1963 to 1970 executive power was concentrated solely in the hands of the president. He was elected by direct universal suffrage for four years. In 1970 the constitution was altered so that any future president could be reelected only once. He must be a Senegalese citizen and at least thirty-five years old. Election arrangements were spelled out in considerable detail in the constitution.

The president was the guardian of the constitution and repository of the executive power. He determined and directed the policies of the country; assured the execution of the laws; had the power of decree; was responsible for civil administration and national defense; was chief of the armed services; presided over the Supreme Defense Council; appointed judicial, diplomatic, military, and administrative officers; negotiated and ratified treaties; and exercised the right to pardon.

The president was aided by ministers and state secretaries, who were appointed and assigned their duties by him and required no confirmation by the National Assembly (see fig. 7). They could not simultaneously be deputies in the legislature or engage in other public or private professional activity. The president could address the nation and deliver messages to the National Assembly, in person if he so chose. The messages were not, however, subject to debate.

The president may be held personally responsible for his action in the exercise of his official functions only in the case of high treason. The National Assembly is the impeaching body. Impeachment requires a three-fifths vote of the full membership by secret ballot, and the

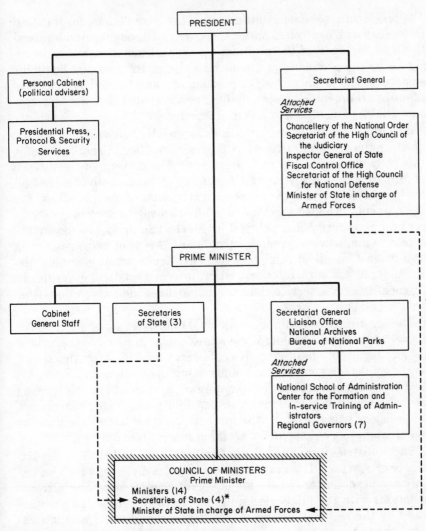

PRESIDENT

Personal Cabinet
(political advisers)

Presidential Press,
Protocol & Security
Services

Secretariat General

*Attached
Services*

Chancellery of the National Order
Secretariat of the High Council of
the Judiciary
Inspector General of State
Fiscal Control Office
Secretariat of the High Council
for National Defense
Minister of State in charge of
Armed Forces

PRIME MINISTER

Cabinet
General Staff

Secretaries
of State (3)

Secretariat General
Liaison Office
National Archives
Bureau of National Parks

*Attached
Services*

National School of Administration
Center for the Formation and
In-service Training of Admin-
istrators
Regional Governors (7)

COUNCIL OF MINISTERS
Prime Minister
Ministers (14)
Secretaries of State (4)*
Minister of State in charge of Armed Forces

*Three in office of Prime Minister; one in Ministry of Foreign Affairs.

Figure 7. Senegal, Organization of the Executive Branch, 1973

impeachment is tried by the High Court of Justice. Ministers and state secretaries are also subject to impeachment procedures in the case of a plot against the security of the state. As with the president, the National Assembly brings the impeachment, and the High Court of Justice tries it.

The changes that reestablished the post of prime minister in 1970 also assigned a considerable number of duties to his office and made the rest of the cabinet responsible to him. It was the president, however, who continued to determine the policies of the government. He retained the power to appoint and dismiss the prime minister at will.

The president also remained the head of the High Council for National Defense, which controlled national security. Although general legislation was the work of the prime minister, all legislation had to be cosigned by the president, and some sensitive matters required only his signature. The prime minister's position was also limited by a restoration of parliamentary responsibility, which made the prime minister again liable to dismissal by a vote of censure.

The ministers and state secretaries formed the Council of Ministers, of which the prime minister was the presiding officer. Constitutionally, this body was defined as the government. The makeup of the Council of Ministers changed with some frequency, in terms both of men holding the portfolio and of the names and attributes of the ministries. The departments grouped together in ministries varied according to current administrative and political exigencies. Subjects covered by the departments, however, remained standard. Areas of responsibility in any given Council of Ministers included development planning, defense, foreign affairs, interior, justice, information, local government, finance, the civil service, labor, agriculture, industry, education, health, and public works.

The organization within the individual ministries generally followed a similar pattern. At the top, the minister was assisted by a personal cabinet invariably limited to five civil servants. This body functioned as the minister's general staff, supervising the implementation of his decisions and overseeing the operational echelons of the ministry on his behalf. Within the ministry, responsibility was highly centralized, all decisions being taken by the minister or in his name. The director of his cabinet served as chief of staff but not as his deputy.

The ministries were divided into first level units called either departments or services. The next level was called a division, which served only as a headquarters for the major operating elements—the bureaus. Relations with the ministries' units in the field were actually supervised by the regional governors (see Regional and Local Administration, this ch.).

A second organ of the executive branch, in addition to the Council of Ministers, was the office of the president, or the presidency. This was divided into the president's personal cabinet and the Secretariat General. The cabinet included only his personal political advisers and his press, protocol, and security staffs. The Secretariat General, on the other hand, became a major organ of government. During the years of presidential rule, the man in charge of directing the administrative affairs of the government, the secretary general, was given ministerial rank.

This situation ended with the appointment of a prime minister, but a number of important services remained within the Secretariat General. In 1973 these included the High Council of the Judiciary, the High Council for National Defense, the Inspectorate General, and the Fiscal

Control Office. One very important cabinet member, the minister of state in charge of the armed forces, was also associated directly with the presidency.

Most of the other responsibilities of the Secretariat General were transferred to a new and similar secretariat within the office of the prime minister. Three junior cabinet members—the secretaries of state in charge of youth and sports, environmental matters, and special projects to improve living conditions—were assigned to the prime minister's office. In addition, the seven regional governors were attached through this office directly to the executive, although regional government in general was under the minister of interior.

Both secretariats served as places where interministerial conflicts were resolved and as the final filters through which affairs had to pass to be given consideration by the president or the prime minister. As a result of this and of the general habit of passing questions to the top for decision, many matters that might have been expected to be dealt with elsewhere were actually resolved within the secretariats.

The National Assembly

Under the constitution sovereignty rests with the people and is exercised through their representatives, gathered in a unicameral legislature called the National Assembly. Members of the body, called deputies, are elected every four years, at the same time as the president, by direct universal suffrage. Until 1973 there were eighty deputies and twenty substitutes elected on a single national list, so that the party winning the election gained all eighty seats. Deputies have parliamentary immunity, which may be—and has been—lifted under certain circumstances. No deputy may be simultaneously a minister or a state secretary. The number of deputies was increased to 100 in 1973. The additional twenty members were chosen to represent social and economic interest groups.

The assembly holds two regular sessions a year. The budget must be debated in the first session. No ordinary session may last longer than two months. A special session may be called either on the petition of a majority of the deputies or at the request of the executive. Such a session may not last more than two weeks except in the case of a special session on the budget, which may last until the budget is approved. Sittings of the assembly are usually open to the public, and debates are generally published verbatim in a special *Journal Officiel.*

The organization of the legislative body includes an executive committee known as the bureau and headed by the president of the assembly, who is the second most influential figure in the government. The members divide themselves into standing committees for the review of draft legislation before it is put to a vote. The rules provide for the establishment of special committees as needed. In addition, some of the deputies are assigned to several public and semipublic agencies on which the assembly has regular representation. These agencies include such institutions as the national press agency and the National Office of Veterans.

For a measure to have the status of law it must be passed by the National Assembly, with two important exceptions. The constitution provides for the delegation of legislative power to the president under specified circumstances and provides a mechanism for referring bills to the people. The president negotiates and ratifies treaties, but peace treaties, commercial treaties, and agreements relative to international organizations or changes in the territorial extent of the state must be approved by the assembly.

Special conditions are laid down for fiscal legislation. In the usual legislative process a bill may be introduced either by the government (in which case it is called a *projet de loi*) or by deputies (*proposition de loi*). Once introduced, the bill is referred to committee, where amendments are often made and where members of the government may be heard and questioned. The bill is then debated on the floor, usually in open session. After a bill has been passed—and in most cases passage requires a simple majority—the president of the assembly signs it and sends it to the chief executive.

In practice, most bills are introduced by the government. It is rare for such measures to be defeated, but alterations to bills or to their applications are made by the government to satisfy criticism voiced on the floor. In most cabinets a minister has been placed in charge of relations with the assembly and has had to keep the executive informed of the mood of the members on all issues. When discontent or opposition is expected, the concerned members may be invited to discuss the matter with a cabinet member or the president. Most politically sensitive measures have been reviewed by the party leaders before presentation so that they already represent an acceptable compromise (see ch. 10).

In the late 1960s there were nine standing committees with defined areas of competence; for example, foreign affairs, defense, and public works. Bills and other matters for discussion by the legislature are referred automatically to the concerned committee. Because the committees are permanent, the government apparently takes seriously its duty to provide them with information. Most members of the assembly apparently belong to no more than two committees; therefore, the members develop a degree of competence in their areas of responsibility. Most of the committees do, however, cover several broad areas, overseeing the operation of two or three ministries.

Within two weeks after receiving newly passed legislation, the president of the republic must sign it into law or return it for a second consideration. In the latter case the National Assembly is obliged to reopen debate on the bill, and a three-fifths majority of the full membership is required for passage the second time. The president must then sign the bill into law. When all the proper signatures are affixed, the law is printed in the *Journal Officiel* and enters into force.

Following the French model, the constitution is complemented by organic laws specifically called for in that document. An organic law requires the vote of an absolute majority for passage and can only be promulgated when the Supreme Court, at the request of the president, has declared it to be in conformity with the constitution. Organic laws are called for to regulate such matters as the eligibility and election of deputies, the special conditions for financial laws, and the organization and functions of the Supreme Court and the High Council of the Judiciary.

Relations between the executive and the legislative authorities are carefully delineated. Those matters that are restricted to law (that is, legislative acts of the assembly) are in two categories. The first is the establishment of rules concerning such basic matters as electoral systems; civil rights; nationality; personal law, law codes, organization of the courts, and the status of the judiciary; the issuance of currency; the basis, rate, and methods of collection of all taxes; the nationalization of any private enterprise; and the creation of new public agencies.

The second category concerns the determination of "fundamental principles" in several areas of legislation, leaving the details to be worked out by regulations issued by the government. The subjects in this category are limited to educational matters; property rights and civil and commercial obligations; all legislation pertaining to employment, unions, and social security; the general organization of the armed forces, the police, and local government; and the pay schedules of state employees.

All other matters are of a regulatory character, implying that residual powers rest with the executive. The president's authority to submit to the assembly bills of social, economic, or financial import not within the realm of stated legislation does not change the principle that what is not assigned to the assembly is within the realm of presidential action.

In addition, the assembly may delegate its powers over specific matters to the president, allowing him to take action generally within the realm of law. The procedure for this is carefully spelled out. Such powers may not concern organic laws or amendments to the constitution.

A declaration of war also must be authorized by the National Assembly. A state of seige (*état de siège*) or a state of emergency (*état d'urgence*) is decreed by the president.

When institutions of the republic, the independence of the nation, its territorial integrity, or the fulfillment of its international commitments are seriously threatened, the president may take such immediate measures, including notifying the nation, as are required to ensure the regular functioning of the public authorities. (This arrangement is distinct from a state of siege or a state of emergency.) He may not, however, amend the constitution under these circumstances. In any of these cases the assembly meets by right and remains in session for the duration of the crisis. During that time the president acts as his own legislature, but at the end of the period his decrees must be approved by the assembly in order to continue to have the force of law.

The Supreme Court is the final arbiter in case of disagreement between the executive and the legislative branches. Before asking the Supreme Court for an opinion, however, the assembly has other approaches to control the executive. Ministers and state secretaries may be questioned in writing or orally, with or without debate. A committee of inquiry may be constituted under serious circumstances. After 1970 the assembly could force the fall of the Council of Ministers.

The Economic and Social Council

The Economic and Social Council is an advisory body created to provide a formal voice for organized interest groups within the modern sector. The council must be consulted by the government on all major economic and social activities and on planning projects. With the exception of the national budget, all such matters submitted to the National Assembly are first given to the council for study. Although its opinions are purely advisory, the government makes every appearance of giving considerable weight to its advice and to the detailed studies that it produces. As an additional duty it is charged with encouraging the involvement of businessmen and professional people in national development efforts.

The council is composed of forty-five members sitting for six-year terms. One-third of the posts are vacated every two years. Its chairman holds the post for his full six-year term. Of the forty-five members, nine are nominated by the labor unions to represent employees in government and private enterprise; eighteen, by professional bodies representing commerce, industry, and the professions; and nine, by rural economic interests. Finally, nine are chosen by the president because of their competence in social, scientific, cultural, or economic matters. The council's membership at times has included a number of Frenchmen. The council, which holds two sessions each year, has a permanent bureau functioning under the chairman.

The Judicial System

The legal system was derived from that of the French colonial period. The source of all law is codified legislation rather than common law or judicial precedent.

Until the end of World War II, two broad judicial jurisdictions had been recognized. Europeans, and Africans who had gained French citizenship, were subject to the general body of French law, administered by French courts sitting in the colony. Other Africans were bound in general by the customary law of their particular community, administered by customary courts and by the system of colonial disciplinary law known as the *indigénat* (civil status of subject people). In 1945 the *indigénat* was abolished and, as a result of subsequent reforms, all inhabitants, regardless of race or affiliation, were brought under the exclusive criminal jurisdiction of the courts that administered the French penal code. The duality of the civil law, however, persisted.

The body of law in force at the time of independence was retained by a constitutional proviso, but since that time it has been progressively adapted to the needs of the new nation. Among the more important innovations were the ending of adherence to the French principle of separation of ordinary and administrative law tribunals and the establishment of a new, unified court system to administer both the general body of French law and customary law.

Under the constitution the judicial authority of the state is independent of both the executive and the legislature. In addition to the High Court of Justice, the constitution specifically provides for the High Council of the Judiciary and the Supreme Court. Other organs are established by enactments of the National Assembly. The High Council of the Judiciary assists the president in nominating judges, in exercising powers of clemency, and in guaranteeing the independence of the judiciary. The president presides over the council; the minister of justice is its vice chairman; and other members are appointed from the ranks of the judiciary.

Below the Supreme Court the court structure has three levels. At the bottom, the law provides for a petty court at the capital of each department. Eventually, one will sit in each district. Each case is heard by a single justice of the peace (*juge de la paix*) who has original jurisdiction in cases involving petty offenses and certain specified misdemeanors, in minor civil suits, and in certain actions under customary law. The cases last named are tried with the aid of assessors or, in certain cases involving Muslim law, by a *cadi* appointed to sit as a justice of the peace.

The colonial regime had permitted African and Muslim customary law to retain considerable legal authority, particularly in civil and personal matters. Muslim and customary courts continued to exist in 1973, but all were scheduled to be abolished. Their duties were to be completely taken over by the petty courts.

Tribunals of first instance, located in each of the regional capitals, form the intermediate level of courts. Each has a presiding judge, a public prosecutor, and a varying number of associate judges; but all cases are heard by a single judge. The courts have original jurisdiction in civil actions and in criminal cases that exceed the competence of petty courts, as well as appellate jurisdiction over most judgments of such courts. In action involving customary law the bench is assisted by assessors.

Matters classified as *criminelles* (major criminal offenses for which the punishment can exceed five years in prison) are all tried before the courts of assize. Four of these are located in Dakar, Saint-Louis, Ziguinchor, and Kaolack. These are the only courts utilizing a jury system.

The Court of Appeal, sitting in Dakar, serves the entire country. The bench is usually composed of three judges and, under some circumstances, of five. The court hears appeals from judgments of the lower courts. Further appeal lies to the Supreme Court.

The full bench of the Supreme Court consists of the chief justice (*premier président*), three presiding justices for sections of the court (*présidents de section*), and six associate justices (*conseillers*). A prosecution department is headed by an attorney general (*procureur général*) assisted by two solicitors. Ten civil servants known as *auditeurs* are assigned to assist in preparing and hearing cases. Members of the court have the same immunity as deputies in the National Assembly.

In full court the Supreme Court rules on the constitutionality of laws and international agreements and approves organic laws before promulgation. These constitutional sessions are not open to the public. The full court also sits as the general consultative assembly to give advice on draft legislation, regulatory decrees, and administrative problems at the request of the government or of the president of the National Assembly.

For most of its work, however, the full court is divided into three sections, each consisting of a presiding justice and two associate justices. The *auditeurs* are divided among the sections as necessary. One section serves as the court of final appeal in civil and criminal matters. A second section handles final appeals involving jurisdictional decisions. The third section is responsible for overseeing and annually auditing government accounts and the financial transactions of state enterprises of an industrial or commercial character.

Judges are appointed by the president on the nomination of the minister of justice and may not be removed. Usually, no judge may be transferred, even for a promotion, without his express prior consent. Although independent of the government, the judges are under the authority of the minister of justice for administrative purposes. While serving as judges they may not engage in any other public or private enterprise or hold elective office, although this provision may be waived under certain circumstances. The major source of judicial personnel, prosecutors, and lawyers is the Faculty of Law of the University of Dakar, although many older members have been educated in France.

Lawyers are divided into three categories: advocates, notaries, and legal counselors (*conseillers juridiques*). Only advocates may plead cases before a court. In addition to having a law degree, an advocate must have spent from three to five years as an intern in a law office or court. Notaries are not allowed to plead cases and are not law school graduates, but they are entitled to prepare and record legal documents. Most have completed an extensive apprenticeship and have passed competitive examinations.

Any person may serve as a legal counselor, but such a counselor may not appear before the courts or prepare legal documents. All advocates must belong to the bar association, which has the power to discipline its members.

In addition to the courts of the regular legal system, there are several types of specialized courts. The most important but least used of these is the High Court of Justice, created by the constitution for the sole purpose of trying high government officials for treason or malfeasance in office. The fourteen members of this body are chosen by the National Assembly—two from the ranks of the judiciary and twelve from among the legislature's own members.

A second body, also distinct from the regular judiciary, was created by law in September 1961. The Security Court, consisting of a single judge and two assessors, was created to try political cases and to provide for preventive detention in cases involving a threat to national security. Any case involving crimes committed with a political motive could be referred to it at the decision of the government. There was no appeal from its decisions. It was not clear if it was still in existence in 1973.

Under a 1963 revision of the Code of Military Justice, the Court of Appeal and the tribunals of first instance and courts of assize at Dakar, augmented by military members, have jurisdiction over offenses committed by members of the armed forces in time of peace (see ch. 16).

Labor courts are established by a decree that fixes the location, territorial jurisdiction, and administrative organization of each court. The courts are agents of the minister of justice. Composed of a judge and two expert advisers each for labor and management, labor courts adjudicate disputes between workers (individually or collectively) and their employers concerning contracts, working conditions, health, safety, and social security. Decisions may be appealed through the regional court system.

The Public Service

Civil servants are appointed by the president. The Supreme Council of the Public Service advises on matters concerning the public service, but it has only consultative powers. Civil servants have the right to organize and strike within the limits of public security and may hold no other posts simultaneously without special permission. They may, however, hold elective office. While campaigning, they must take leave without pay but, once elected, they receive leave with pay during the meetings of the elective body on which they serve.

All civil servants are required to be Senegalese citizens, and to rise in rank they must be graduates of the National School of Administration (see ch. 8). The French employees of the Senegalese government, who had numbered over 1,300 civil servants and specialists in 1963, had been greatly reduced in number by 1973. Most were paid by the French government through foreign assistance programs (see ch. 11).

In the early 1970s, because of the place it plays in the country's economy and the demand for jobs that exists among graduating students, government employment seemed to be a major factor in the country's stability. The civil service, however, had actually grown at a fairly moderate rate, increasing from 30,000 at independence in 1960 to 38,000 a decade later. Although these figures included all government civil employees, except for municipal employees and teachers, it did not include the sizable number of employees of commercial and transportation organizations owned by the government (see ch. 13).

The civil service was divided into two major groups: functionaries and agents, the first group having permanent tenure. Of the functionaries some 1,500 were in general administration posts, and about 16,000 were in technical and specialized posts. Of some 18,000 agents roughly 13,000 were contractual or temporary employees.

There was a large concentration of civil servants in Dakar because of the desire for the comforts and prestige of the posts in the country's largest city and also because of the concentration of powers in the national capital. Very few civil servants willingly served in the remote parts of the country. Although the populations of the capital area and Casamance Region were almost identical, the capital contained 42 percent of the government's employees; Casamance Region had only 0.5 percent of the total.

REGIONAL AND LOCAL ADMINISTRATION

For purposes of administration the country is divided into regions, departments, *arrondissements* (districts), villages, and—parallel to this structure—municipalities, or urban communes. Cap Vert Region, surrounding the capital of Dakar, has a special structure. The regions and communes are the only two units with any semblance of self-government.

The seven regions of the country are drawn, according to the government, to correspond roughly to the natural economic regions, modified to some extent by ethnic and communications considerations. At the head of each region is an inspector of administration known as the governor, who is directly responsible to the president. The governor functions as the delegate of the president and the Council of Ministers, representing each of the ministers. His duty is essentially that of coordinator rather than administrator. He receives instruction on general policy from the president and on specific policies of each ministry from the appropriate minister; in turn, he reports back to the central government on the administration of the departments in his region.

Two deputy governors, one for administration and one for coordinating economic development, assist each governor. Because the development plan is so encompassing and important in Senegal, the role of the deputy governor for economic development is a key one (see ch. 13). In their economic capacity the governor and his deputy are assisted by the Regional Development Center (Centre Régional d'Assistance pour le Développement—CRAD). The governor, his deputy for economic development, and the CRAD director all have responsibility for seeing that the development plan is carried out in their region. They are assisted by a regional development committee, which includes the chiefs of the technical service units and local political leaders. Their work involves rural construction programs, rural cooperatives, and liaison with the central agricultural marketing agencies and the National Development Bank (Banque Nationale de Développement du Sénégal— BNDS).

Regional assemblies were established in 1960, when members were elected for five-year terms by universal suffrage (exclusive of residents of municipalities, which did not participate in the regional government). These assemblies, whose size varied from twenty to sixty members, approved the budget, financed by taxes imposed in and for that region, within the limits set by the National Assembly.

The seven regions appear to exist primarily to provide a workable link between the central government and the twenty-seven departments. Almost all local administrative activities take place at the department level or lower. The head of the department, the prefect, is appointed by the president. He is the depositary in his area of the powers of the national government and again represents each of the ministers. He reports to both the unit of the Ministry of Interior responsible for regional and local government and directly to the president through the governor. Until after 1963 the departments had been called circles (*cercles*) and their heads, commandants.

The prefect is the figure to whom local leaders look as the voice of the government. His is therefore the key post in the government's link with the people—the one upon whose success or failure any effort to introduce new ideas and progressive changes most heavily depends. One of his principal duties is to inform the central government of the attitudes of local people.

With the assistance of his deputy, who handles administrative matters, the prefect is responsible for maintaining order and has full police powers. He also controls the public servants employed in his department. All their correspondence with their ministries has to pass through his hands. The prefect himself is usually a civil servant, although along the troubled border with Portuguese Guinea the post invariably is assigned to a military officer instead. The majority of the prefects were graduates of the National School of Administration (see ch. 8).

A prefect has under his authority the heads of the *arrondissements* into which each department is divided. In 1970 there were eighty-five *arrondissements*, with a rural population in almost all cases of between 10,000 and 35,000. The *arrondissements* are essentially amalgamations of the old colonial cantons, which had been headed by a local chief. In 1973 the *arrondissement* chief was a civil servant named by decree. Under the prefect, he was responsible for public order and safety and could utilize the small detachment of the Republican Guard at his disposal. He was responsible for arrests and for full investigation of offenses against the law, as well as the registration of births and deaths and control of elections. He supervised the collection of taxes by village chiefs and served as the prefect's representative in the local rural development center. In many areas the *arrondissement* chief was regarded in the same way that the traditional tribal leader or the colonial official would have been.

Each *arrondissement* is made up of from 100 to 600 villages. Arrangements are made to consider nomadic and seminomadic groups of families as villages. The minister responsible for local government confirms local notables as village chiefs (*chefs du village*) on the advice of the prefect. Village heads collect taxes for the higher authorities, but aside from that their powers are limited, and they have little initiative. Because they are in closest contact with the people, however, they are in a position to foster or obstruct the effective implementation of decisions made at higher levels. The chief is assisted by a council; formerly this was a council of notables, but where the change has actually been effected, it has become an elected council.

The Communes

Municipalities are labeled urban communes. In the early 1970s there were thirty-four of these purportedly self-governing towns. Although many of them served as capitals of a region or department, they had a separate administrative structure from the region in which they were located. Theoretically, to qualify as a commune, a town must be able to balance its budget. A municipal council is elected by universal suffrage for a six-year term, and a mayor is elected by the council from among its members. The mayor receives no salary but is granted expenses and a small annual allowance. He is a voting member of the municipal council, over which he presides. He supervises such matters as traffic, sanitation, and licensing. Security functions of the commune are handled by the regional governor or by the local prefect. The mayor implements laws and regulations on behalf of the central government and often serves as unofficial arbiter of differences arising between citizens of his commune.

The municipal councillors number between thirteen and thirty-seven, depending on the population represented. The members are unpaid and meet in only four regular sessions a year. The council has certain functions laid down by law, such as recordkeeping, maintenance of cemeteries and streets, provision of public lighting and water, and supervision of markets. In theory, it has financial autonomy and votes its own budget annually. In fact, the government, by setting the number and wages of communal employees, giving or withholding approval of proposed taxes, and itself supplying most of the money spent by the communes, firmly controls all but about one-fifth of the average communal budget and exercises negative control over that fifth.

Even in matters other than finance, the central government exercises considerable control over the communes, despite their purported self-governing status. The cities are supervised by the Ministry of Interior through the regional governors and prefects. Any municipal council that acts in conflict with the laws or in a way that the ministry determines is not in the population's best interests can be suspended by decree. This has been a very common occurrence. Until the government permits elections to be held, the communes thus affected are governed by appointed officials.

All regional and department capitals are located in towns with the status of urban communes. Although the communes' administration and their lack of representation in the regional assemblies put them in a separate administrative status from the departments, the prefects exercise considerable control over municipal government. Officially, the prefect serves as the counselor of the municipality in its relations with the central government. He participates in municipal council meetings, and all the commune's correspondence with the central government is transmitted through him. Despite the objections of some urban leaders in the early 1970s, the central government planned to continue its close controls over the municipalities and to postpone decentralization efforts until the 1980s.

Dakar has a special status within both the regional and municipal framework. In January 1961 Cap Vert Region and the commune of Dakar were divided into six *arrondissements*, each of which had a council, a mayor, and an assistant mayor. Over these officials was imposed the municipal council of greater Dakar, a body that included all eighty *arrondissement* council members. The greater Dakar council elected its own mayor and assistant mayor. Beginning in 1972 an additional twenty members were nominated by local social and economic organizations.

The mayor of Dakar has almost no powers, his large budget being used mostly by the governor of Cap Vert Region, who is the only governor to have direct administrative powers. The governor has police powers for Dakar and is responsible for such services as health, roads, water supply, public lighting, and fire protection. He is accountable to the mayor of Dakar for the funds spent. Beginning in 1972 officials with the rank of prefect were assigned to handle the administrative affairs of the *arrondissements*.

Mayors, and to a lesser extent municipal councillors, are important in Senegalese political life. Over half of the deputies in the National Assembly at times have served simultaneously as municipal councillors or mayors. A number of former mayors have served as ambassadors or have held other important posts. The mayor, in short, spends less than full time administering his commune.

Changes Under Way in 1973

Extensive changes in the regional administration and local government were envisioned by legislation passed in early 1972. By mid-1973, however, many of these changes had been carried out in parts of only one region, which was to serve as a test area for the new reforms before they were applied throughout the country.

Under the reforms the regional assemblies, which had never actually played the role they were designed for, were to be replaced by the regional councils. The new councils were to be purely advisory bodies. They also differed from the assemblies in that they were to include representatives of the urban communes and members nominated by local social and economic interest groups. Similar councils were to be created at the department and *arrondissement* levels. The *arrondissements* were to be renamed subprefectures, headed by a civil servant of increased rank.

Finally, a new level of administration was to be created in the form of rural communes headed by rural councils. The communes, approximately one-fourth the size of the *arrondissements*, are intended eventually to give the rural people management over their own affairs. Their formation was expected to follow only after local agricultural cooperatives had been successful in linking several villages in cooperative enterprises.

Two-thirds of the rural council members are to be chosen by popular election, and one-third are to be nominated by the members of the communities' cooperative organizations. Changes in the administration of those urban communes that are also regional capitals are also called for. An appointed official will take over the administrative duties of the mayor, leaving him solely with duties as the chairman of the municipal council.

These and many of the other planned changes were decided upon as part of a policy labeled deconcentration, that is, the placing of more responsibility on the shoulders of civil servants rather than concentrating power in ministerial hands. The policy was adopted primarily to solve what President Senghor had often termed the country's major governmental problem, a very widespread and ingrained practice among civil servants and politicians of avoiding responsibility by passing all matters for decision to the top. This practice, depicted by the president as "Pontius Pilate-ism" left so many petty decisions in the hands of officials at the top levels of management that it interfered with their primary duties.

CHAPTER 10

POLITICAL DYNAMICS AND VALUES

Political power in Senegal is based on the personal popularity of a leader and on his ability to handle the coalition nature of Senegalese politics. President Léopold-Sédar Senghor has continually demonstrated his political strength on both counts. He had first won the support of the rural majority in the late 1940s by being the only politician to seek to represent their interests. In late 1973 he retained his rural popularity, in part through his adroit political contacts with the Islamic brotherhoods. The leaders of these brotherhoods exercise considerable influence over the majority of the country's population. President Senghor's appeal did not fully extend to the older sophisticates in the cities nor to the young intellectuals at the university, but the great mass of the population, mobilized through its traditional local leaders, kept him firmly in office.

The ruling party, the Senegalese Progressive Union (Union Progressiste Sénégalaise—UPS), is a mass-based party that operates down to the village level throughout the country. Despite the absence of legal barriers to the formation of opposition parties, the UPS had complete control over the government and in 1973 had been virtually unopposed for five years. It had come to power through the abilities of its leaders—particularly the skills of President Senghor—to mobilize and retain the support of the vast majority of the people in open competition with other parties and their leaders in the late 1940s and 1950s. The opposition parties had continued to contest elections until 1966, although they were unable to make more than small dents in the appeal of the UPS. Their disappearance six years after independence resulted from the realization by their leaders that they would have a better chance of obtaining their objectives by working within the dominant party. After their absorption in the UPS the former opposition leaders were granted voices in decisionmaking out of proportion to their political strength but in line with their personal skills.

The only vocal challenges to the UPS came from the remnants of a small communist group, the African Party of Independence (Parti Africain d'Indépendance—PAI) and from certain radical elements among Dakar's secondary and university students. Neither had any significant following.

All meaningful political activity took place within the UPS, where factions advocating modern objectives sought the support of

189

traditional groups that still formed primarily along religious or ethnic lines, although such traditional divisions were not particularly hostile. Basic policy differences among the political factions were limited to disagreements over the speed with which major changes were to be accomplished. Most significant political maneuvering was actually the result of clashes between competing personalities. The political skills and popular preeminence of President Senghor allowed him to reconcile and control such clashes.

MAJOR POSTINDEPENDENCE POLITICAL EVENTS

Political Opposition and Change

President Senghor weathered his most serious political crisis in December 1962 with the attempted coup and later arrest of Prime Minister Mamadou Dia (see ch. 2). This was followed in early 1963 by a national plebiscite, which approved a new constitution placing the great bulk of authority in presidential hands and abolishing the post of prime minister (see ch. 9).

A political opposition continued to exist in the form of two or three small opposition parties, the most important of which was the African Realignment Party of Senegal (Parti du Regroupement Africain-Sénégal—PRA-Sénégal). Legislative and presidential elections in December 1963 were marred by violent riots in Dakar by PRA-Sénégal supporters and others who had formed a united front to oppose the UPS candidates. The riots were suppressed by the police and military forces. In the next two years the UPS won over many of the PRA-Sénégal supporters, and PRA-Sénégal leaders decided to dissolve their party and join the UPS in June 1966. Three of these leaders were immediately named to ministerial posts in the national government.

Of the thirty-odd parties that had contested elections in the 1950s, only two very small communist parties—both illegal—remained in existence. Other forces, however, still disturbed the political tranquillity.

The government's major problems came from the students of Dakar, primarily those in the university. Following the examples of rioting led by left-wing radical elements at European universities in May 1968, the students of the University of Dakar went on strike, demanding major educational reforms at first but later issuing demands for major changes in Senegalese society. Their first demands were for a reduction in the French government's influence in the university and changes in the curriculum at all educational levels that would make courses more relevant to the African society. They were joined in their protest—first by secondary students and later by the workers of Dakar in a general strike, without the sanction of their unions. Violent rioting broke out; in the rioting and the subsequent suppression by military forces a number of Senegalese were killed.

In 1969 the government was again compelled to control student protests, this time accomplished without a significant degree of violence. In addition to suppressing the rioting, the government also undertook a number of reforms to lessen the grounds for complaint. These changes were still being announced and implemented in 1973. They included an end to the supervision that the French Ministry of Education had exercised over the university and the adoption of curriculum reforms. The salaries and working conditions of the lowest paid urban workers had been improved, and in mid-1973 the government announced legislation to force the pace of africanization in private industry. In order to lessen the resentment of the younger generation, younger men were brought into important posts in the party and the government.

The most important of these men was Abdou Diouf, who at the age of thirty-five in early 1970 was appointed to fill the newly re-created post of prime minister. The new post was left clearly subordinate to the president in matters of major political importance, but Diouf exercised control over all the day-to-day operations of the government. Observers considered Diouf President Senghor's handpicked successor, a point made more important by a 1970 constitutional change that barred the president from seeking reelection in 1978 (see ch. 9).

Elections of 1973

In the January 1973 national elections President Senghor received the support of 97.1 percent of the registered voters in his quest for a third full five-year term. At the same time, 96.9 percent of the registered voters cast ballots in support of the UPS list of 100 candidates for the National Assembly. There were no opposition candidates. Even if there had been, the president's popularity and ability to mobilize his supporters was such that outside observers felt there would have been little difference in the percentage of votes he received.

Although the 100 candidates on the party's electoral ticket for the assembly could not lay claim to similar support, their selection by the party was not arbitrary. Almost all of the eighty candidates drawn from regional constituencies and most of the twenty representing social, labor, youth, and other interest groups had gained the nomination by a competitive selection process conducted within the party (see ch. 9). They were the choice of the strongest voices in the local party unit, and in the traditionally organized communal society they were thus the persons best able to attract votes in their own districts.

A small number of candidates were selected by a decision of the party's national leadership in order to ensure a voice for ethnic or social minorities or to reward a particularly helpful leader for his assistance. In an open, single-member constituency election, there was little doubt that few of these candidates would have received anything like 96 percent of the votes, and some undoubtedly would have been defeated. Senegalese elections, however, are conducted by the single national list system. This system provides that all voters cast a single vote for an entire list of candidates compiled by party leaders to fill all 100 seats. Even if the electors had had a choice between two or more complete lists, there is little doubt that the vast majority would have given its support to the UPS ticket as a whole regardless of their attitude toward some of the individual candidates.

DEVELOPMENT OF PARTY POLITICS

Since the nineteenth century, citizens of the communes (see Glossary) have organized to elect representatives, although not in the form of modern political parties. For the first few decades of the twentieth century, the political organizations served primarily as a means of distributing patronage—an element of political activity that was still of importance in 1973. The other heritage of early electoral political activity was its elite nature. The early political groupings were of and for citizens of the communes and virtually ignored the subjects who made up the rest of the population. It was not until the beginning of a progressive extension of the franchise in 1946 and 1947 that politicians, following the example of Senghor, began to court the nonurban majority of the population (see ch. 2).

With the new political climate after World War II and the beginning of the ground swell that was to result in statehood and independence, political parties proliferated. The educated, relatively wealthy, assimilated city people who formed the core of an established socialist party associated with the French Socialist Party were unable to ride the new crest. Senghor, one of their most promising politicians, broke away in 1948 and, taking advantage of the popular reaction to the older party, founded his own. His qualifications were his having been a subject and not a citizen, his willingness to campaign for days on end in the villages and smaller towns of the back country, and his operation of the party on a relatively decentralized basis. He quickly won the support of the growing electorate outside the communes. His victory—that of the "new citizens," both rural and urban, against the "old citizens" of the communes—came in 1951, and in the 1957 election he easily carried all parts of the country except the urban strongholds of Dakar and Saint-Louis. Although after 1960 he had support from most townspeople as well as from those in the country, the political cleavage between town and country still persisted. For example, the anti-Senghor vote during the March 1963 constitutional referendum was twice as large in Dakar as it was anywhere else, although even there it was small in absolute terms.

Senghor left the established Socialists not over an ideological argument but because he felt that the party could not survive the way it was run. He resigned over what he called the dictatorship of its leader, Lamine Guèye, and over Guèye's persistence in ignoring large segments of the population and catering almost exclusively to the urban dwellers. (Guèye later came over to Senghor's side to join the UPS and was president of the National Assembly during the 1960s.) Senghor did not renounce socialism; in fact, there has never been a party in Senegal that did not profess some form of socialism. Senghor, in setting up his own party, put the emphasis on a smoothly running machine designed to win elections rather than on a community of ideas; and this approach was successful from the first.

Senghor built up his party after 1948 as a series of coalitions, and the coalition continues to be one of the outstanding features of Senegalese parties. Not only did Senghor successfully manage to keep afloat a series of intraparty coalitions but, by devising interparty coalitions and making them palatable, his own organization merged periodically with others to form new coalitions.

Out of this welter of factions and followings four parties had emerged by the time independence was obtained in 1960. Senghor's UPS was in control and was trying to form a coalition with the two legal opposition parties. One of these, the PRA-Sénégal, had a considerable following but almost no real strength and no representative in the National Assembly. The other, the Bloc of Senegalese Masses (Bloc des Masses Sénégalaises—BMS), had one deputy in the assembly and a small and ill-defined following of old-line socialists. The outlawed PAI, which was very close to the French Communist Party, had a small, dedicated following but no strength or geographical base.

Senegalese Progressive Union

According to the constitution of the Senegalese Progressive Union (Union Progressiste Sénégalaise—UPS), membership is a formal act involving the purchase of a party card. In 1967, at the end of the annual drive, 540,000 cards had been distributed. The party's total strength was more accurately indicated by the results of the 1968 elections, when over 93 percent of the electorate voted as Senghor, his lieutenants, the Islamic brotherhoods, and most clan (see Glossary) leaders had suggested.

The core of Senghor's strength has always rested in the area around Thiès, Diourbel, and Kaolack—the area dominated by groundnut (peanut) cultivation—and in the Muridiya, the strongest of the Islamic brotherhoods (see Political Interest Groups, this ch.). The small farmers all over the country, except in Casamance Region, can be counted loyal UPS supporters.

The base units of the party are the 2,500 village or neighborhood committees, which were established in occupational as well as geographic groups. These local committees elect their many officers, who generally reflect the various factions, clans, ethnic groups, and occupational groups in the area involved. The village committees are brought together into some 400 subsections, which in turn form sections at the department level; in Dakar, neighborhoods are grouped into sectors and divided into subsections.

Above these party units are seven regional unions, and at the top of the party structure is the national council (formerly the executive committee), comprising UPS ministers and deputies; members of the Youth Movement of the Senegalese Progressive Union (Mouvement de la Jeunesse de l'Union Progressiste Sénégalaise—MJUPS); and the delegates from the departments on the basis of overall and party population. These delegates must outnumber the ministers and deputies, and total attendance of the national council is about 300 at its quarterly meetings. The national council elects the executive bureau, the top administrative body of the party, and committees to deal with finances and internal conflicts. The executive bureau has thirty-eight members, of whom four are delegates from the MJUPS. The president of the republic and the president of the National Assembly are members by right. This body is the real policymaking organ in the country.

The party constitution calls for a national congress to be held every two years, at which time the executive bureau reports on party policy in various fields. Representation, proportional to the membership in each section, is fixed by the bureau before each congress.

The higher in the pyramid the party unit is, the more control or attempted control is exercised from Dakar. The national party officials decide not only who will be elected to party posts at higher levels but also whom the party members on municipal councils will choose as their mayors.

After national council meetings the delegates are expected to return home and hold meetings at which they pass on to the local population decisions made at the national level. The role of the party, according to Senghor, is to elaborate the governmental program and doctrine at the party congress and to "orient and control" the assembly and the government through national council and executive bureau meetings. Once the administrators have been oriented, they are to be left alone by the party in carrying out their administrative tasks.

The MJUPS is in theory a parallel structure to the party for all people between eighteen and twenty-five years of age (and up to thirty if desired by the individual). No one may belong to both the UPS and the MJUPS at the same time. The MJUPS considers its role to be that of the avant-garde within the party. Members are often recruited from the younger youth group, Pioneers of Senegal (Pionniers du Sénégal). The other organization aimed at young people within the party is its student organization. In 1973 there was no indication that this group had either influence or a significant number of members. It claimed to be related to but not a part of the MJUPS; students in both Dakar and Paris were members of its bureau. All youth groups were affiliated in an overall federation, the National Union of Young People of Senegal (Union Nationale de la Jeunesse du Sénégal—UNJS). To assure the political course of the federation, its president was the secretary general of the MJUPS. The women's organization that was supposed to exist within the party actually functioned only in the form of a few local women's groups in the cities.

The party publishes a daily newspaper, *Le Soleil du Sénégal*, and subsidizes the weekly party newspaper, *L'Unité Africaine*, to which all members are expected to subscribe if possible (see ch. 12). The executive bureau exercises editorial supervision over the newspapers.

The party's formal arrangements for finance, structure, and membership are based on foreign models, especially on the constitutions of French parties of which Africans had been members. These models do not reflect the local political realities and therefore cannot provide for the actual operation of the party. Consequently, it is difficult for the nonparty member to determine how the UPS really works.

African Realignment Party of Senegal

The African Realignment Party of Senegal (Parti du Regroupement Africain-Sénégal—PRA-Sénégal) had counted most of its support in the early 1960s as being in Casamance Region, where it had some 300,000 followers (over half the population). In addition, there were estimated to be another 3,000 to 4,000 supporters, mostly among recent university graduates in Dakar and in Saint-Louis. These latter tended to support PRA-Sénégal rather than the UPS because they looked down on what they considered to be the "party of the hacks" and the mass-party appeal of the UPS. After 1962 many urban PRA-Sénégal adherents were technicians of the development plan who had supported Mamadou Dia when he was prime minister. The party had no basic ideological disagreement with the stated aims of the government or with the development plan, although some members felt that Senghor was not moving fast enough. PRA-Sénégal was continually split by serious internal dissensions. Its leaders, like those of the other parties, were UPS dissidents. The formal structure of the party was similar to that of the UPS. Communication between the political bureau and its village committees was difficult after the party newspaper, *Indépendance Africaine*, was banned in September 1960.

In 1963 the PRA-Sénégal became the major member of a front that included the PAI, members of the then-dissolved BMS, and the supporters of the jailed Dia. Its turn to violence in the 1963 elections was apparently planned and was a reaction to the futility of its efforts to gain electoral support. By 1966 the party was eager to accept President Senghor's offer of unity.

Bloc of Senegalese Masses

The Bloc of Senegalese Masses (Bloc des Masses Sénégalaises— BMS), a breakaway from the UPS, represented some of the more conservative commercial and dissatisfied religious elements who were formerly associated with the various socialist parties and Lamine Guèye. Although Lamine Guèye did not join the BMS, his nephew and law partner, Boubacar Guèye, was one of the national leaders and the only deputy in the National Assembly not a member of the UPS. Many of these national leaders had broken with the UPS over the dissolution of the Mali Federation (see ch. 2).

The party was abolished by a government decree in October 1963, but shortly after it was re-formed as the Senegalese National Front. Because the front attracted the support of the former supporters of Dia, the government again brought pressure to bear against it. It finally dissolved in late 1964.

African Party of Independence and Other Marxist Groups

The African Party of Independence (Parti Africain d'Indépendance— PAI), outlawed since 1960, was still able to maintain a covert existence in 1973. It has remained closely associated with the Soviet and French communist parties. Its small size had never allowed it to be an electoral or an effective conspiratorial organization, but it managed to retain a following of about 2,000 to 3,000 members. Despite the party's espousal of communism, its members are drawn from among the middle-class recent university graduates. Their courtship of the Senegalese proletariat remains largely unrequited. They have no real geographic base but have been active in Saint-Louis and at the University of Dakar. Their organization is the most rigid of all the parties because of their communist connections. The basic unit is the cell (noyau), which has very few members, who may be chosen by geography or occupation. In theory, above the cell are sectors, regional groupings, and the national bureau. In actual fact, there appears to be no organizational apparatus between the cell and the national level. A very small pro-Chinese communist splinter faction, the Senegalese Communist Party (Parti Communiste Sénégalaise—PCS) split from the PAI and was promptly declared illegal by the government in 1965.

A large number of PAI and PCS members (reportedly 170) had been convicted of subversion and imprisoned in 1965 and 1969. A number of the other members were in exile, mostly among the sizable Senegalese community in France. Nevertheless, the PAI claimed that its Central Committee was able to hold its annual meeting in Dakar, at least in 1971.

During the 1950s and 1960s the PAI actively sought to form a united front with other groups opposing the UPS but had little success in such efforts (except for a brief period at the time of the troubled 1963 elections), largely because it was widely recognized as a part of the international communist movement. This failure, and its stated policy of opposition to the power of the Muslim religious brotherhoods, prevented the PAI from gaining any support among the rural majority.

The University of Dakar has also been the center of other radical

Marxist-oriented groups. The combined efforts of these groups in the late 1960s and early 1970s had been limited to disrupting the academic community, notably during student riots in the 1968/69 school year. The primary objective of the rioters at the University of Dakar was the reduction of French domination of the educational facilities and curriculum.

The other center of radical left-wing activity among the students had been the Democratic Union of Senegalese Students (Union Démocratique des Etudiants Sénégalais) and the Union of Dakar Students (Union des Etudiants de Dakar), both of which were declared illegal organizations in February 1971. Other radicals could be found among the members of the Teachers Union of Senegal (Syndicat des Enseignants du Sénégal—SES), which was banned in early 1973, and the General Union of Senegalese Workers in France (Union Générale des Travailleurs Sénégalais en France). In 1973 these were the only labor unions that could be considered in any way opposed to the government. The influence of these groups spread as the new graduates left the university to join the teaching profession, but their numbers and influence were still very small in 1973.

POLITICAL INTEREST GROUPS

Successful party building in Senegal consists of making a grand coalition out of several interests. Ethnic groups, generation, caste, Muslim brotherhood, labor union, or veterans association may be far more important to an individual than membership in a political party.

The UPS leadership is also the government leadership, and there is a strong tendency to conceive of the government and party as interchangeable. In principle, the party is paramount and gives instructions to the government but, since the party can and does change its makeup, there is a nameless amalgamation of party and government that is the source of power and patronage—the way to get things done for one's country, one's friends, and oneself.

Senghor's party coalition has always reflected the basic social structure of the country. Groups that the Senegalese call *clans*, consisting of a leader and his followers (who are generally from a single ethnic, religious, or kinship group) along with the brotherhoods, are the significant units in the political system (see ch. 5). The men commanding these groups are those to whom Senghor turns. The *clans* are in many ways more important to politics than are issues, although *clans* themselves are an issue. Everyone professes to be against *clan* politics, but it is widely practiced and is in effect almost the only way to conduct politics in the country.

Members of a *clan* fully support their leader, and he looks after their interests on a patron-client basis. A *clan* leader does not seek formal political power so much as he seeks influence and status as a means of assuring the group's welfare. As an institutionalization of personal

197

relationships, the *clan* provides an obvious vehicle for political influence. Members give their leader their votes, among other things, in return for whatever he can obtain by delivering their votes.

The Islamic Brotherhoods

The Islamic brotherhoods and their leaders, the marabouts, are the major controllers of public opinion and organs for mobilization of political support in the country. The marabouts also dominate much of their followers' economic life as well, as they control large portions of land, particularly in the groundnut production areas. The brotherhoods, to which as much as 75 percent of the population belong, dominate the lives of the small farmers throughout the country, except in Casamance Region. The marabouts provide the earthly as well as the spiritual leadership for their followers. Their domination varies from group to group but is sufficiently strong in almost all cases so that the government feels its necessary to deal with the people through the marabouts in all efforts to mobilize support for its policies. In order to seek or retain the support of a major element of the population, political leaders regularly take sides in conflicts within and between the brotherhoods, such as which order should control an important mosque or which claimant should be recognized as a great marabout's legitimate successor.

The portions of the Islamic community that belong to the brotherhoods are divided into three major orders (see ch. 7). Two of these, the Tidjaniya and the Qadiriya, are further split into several different branches, giving the country six major and several minor divisions. Each separate branch or united brotherhood is headed by a chief marabout, generally called a great marabout or caliph. All other religious leaders are called marabouts, without distinction as to whether they lead 100 or 10,000 men. They are, however, in a hierarchy, and the great marabout is their leader. Each man owes obedience to his own marabout, to the marabouts heading the larger units above him, and ultimately to the great marabout of his branch or brotherhood.

This obedience extends to civil and political matters as well as to religious questions. Thus the six major divisions (the united Muridiya brotherhood and the five important branches of the two other large brotherhoods) form the major political divisions among the country's rural population.

The control that a marabout actually exercises varies from group to group as well as with the personal capabilities of the individual leader. Moreover, many of the marabouts who possess considerable authority over their followers have not developed any strong interest in most political questions. The Muridiya, however, forms a tightly disciplined force and follows leaders who have generally demonstrated considerable political interest, at least in matters that they see as affecting them. Because of this, President Senghor has usually supported the

Muride leaders when they have come into confrontation with other groups and has generally made major efforts to appease the Muride caliph. The government automatically seeks the support of the Muride leaders on all issues.

The branches of the other orders have at least the latent political ability to interfere with governmental plans on a national scale and do severely affect or control government activity at the regional level and below. The national government is therefore careful to placate the leaders of the other orders, although assigning a lower priority to this effort than to maintaining the support of the Muride leaders.

Despite its outward unity and discipline, even the Muridiya is a loosely structured body. The great marabout must be obeyed, but the lower ranking marabouts are free to feud with each other. They seek to influence the great marabout or to boost the men they are associated with into positions of influence and power, both within their brotherhood and in governmental posts.

Marabout influence is strong in the groundnut areas of Thiès, Diourbel, and Sine-Saloum and strongest of all in those sections within the groundnut area that are dominated by the Muridiya brotherhood. The marabouts have less control over their Toucouleur adherents in Fleuve Region; however, during much of the 1950s and the postindependence period, Saidou Nourou Tall, the leading marabout in Fleuve was perhaps the most politically minded of all the religious leaders. The brotherhoods have little influence in Casamance Region, where the population largely adheres to traditional religions, or in Sénégal Oriental Region, where population density is very low (see ch. 3). In highly urban Cap Vert Region surrounding Dakar, the brotherhoods retain their religious leadership over the many people who have migrated from the interior, but the government has other channels to influence the people on political matters.

At least in some of the branches and brotherhoods, the great marabout is assisted by a council of marabouts, comprising the principal figures in the brotherhood. The marabout may consult the council before making important decisions and generally announces such decisions in its presence. His personal retainers, however, ordinarily advise him on political matters. They also serve as his ambassadors to the other orders and to the national government. The great marabout of the Murides, for example, considered himself officially represented in Dakar during the 1960s by a relative, Bamba Guèye, who was named to cabinet minister rank, and by his own general secretary, who regularly called upon President Senghor as the marabout's personal representative.

At the local level, at least in the heartlands of the brotherhoods, most people turn to the powerful marabouts whenever they need assistance. They are fully aware of the influential voice the marabouts have in government circles. In their efforts to obtain support from the national government for projects within their region or district, it is not even uncommon for regional government officials to seek the assistance of the leading marabouts.

The government officials regularly use the marabouts at all levels as their channels of information to the rural people. The degree of marabout involvement in local administration varies with the degree of power of the branch or brotherhood.

A man seeking a government position, an ambitious official wishing promotion, or a person seeking party nomination for an elected post will also cultivate the support of a powerful marabout. Those who are most successful at obtaining the marabout's backing become known as his protégés. They often function as his representatives in a particular government agency to the detriment of efforts to reduce nepotism and to increase efficiency. Those who turn to the marabouts for support include younger men who have European educations and ministers of the national government as well as traditionalist members of the National Assembly.

The government also found it necessary to continue the colonial practice of giving gifts of cash to the politically important marabouts. Throughout the colonial period the French sought to bind the brotherhoods to them by giving gifts to the leading marabouts, particularly the heads of the orders. They in turn used such gifts either to reward their own closest disciples or to provide feasts and other celebrations for their followers. As a result, the marabouts came to expect to receive money from the French in return for supporting their policies. In return, on all public occasions, the French expected and received speeches from important Islamic leaders, praising their policies. Fortunately for the government's treasury, only a few hundred of the more than 5,000 marabouts were influential outside their own villages in 1973, and not more than a handful of these exercised any power at the national level.

In each major political crisis President Senghor and the UPS have expected and received the major bulk of their political support from the Islamic brotherhoods. For this reason the UPS has, at least at times, limited its efforts to adopt social reforms favored by its leaders in order to be sure of retaining the support of the conservative marabouts. This has affected the party's chances to adopt measures that might attract left-wing elements into the party.

In addition, the government has had difficulty dealing with marabouts who oppose its policies, not only because of the support they can expect from their followers but also because, as religious figures, they cannot be threatened as can opposition political leaders. On two occasions when the government did arrest and briefly detain an important marabout, it took great care to publicly justify and explain its actions. There are no practical means for the government to deal with a marabout who withholds the support of his followers other than buying his support.

Because of this, many Senegalese among the modernist elite, including the factions of the UPS leadership that favor rapid or radical changes, regard the power of the marabouts as the largest single block to national development. They look upon the marabouts as feudal lords who prevent the liberation and improvement of the country's peasantry. They feel that the marabouts act as a privileged class whose members can disobey the government almost at will, setting precedents that others attempt to follow.

On the other hand, President Senghor and other moderate leaders recognize that the marabouts, although major forces obstructing change in some cases, are in other instances the channels through which government efforts to bring about change can succeed. Identical problems—or worse ones—block government efforts to introduce change among that portion of the population (about 15 to 20 percent, mostly in Sénégal Oriental and Casamance regions) that is not associated with the brotherhoods but maintains strong ties to a traditional society. Desirable changes in the social and economic order are blocked more by the lack of funds and resources necessary to carry them out than by any resistance from the traditional elements of society.

Despite the importance that the UPS leadership places on good relations with the marabouts, the latter do not in any way dominate the party. They represent the major portion of traditional rural interests and thus the majority of the population, but the party is actually led by modernists dedicated to bringing about social and economic change. The major division among the modernists concerns the rate at which these changes should be made. Those favoring gradual transformation as well as those favoring relatively rapid change, however, have objectives that will result in the liberation of the peasants from the near-feudal system imposed by the brotherhoods' present-day structure. The government's policies must, therefore, ultimately come into conflict with the interests of the marabouts, or at least with their worldly interests.

Labor Unions and Other Groups

Labor unions, as organizations, are not a potent political force. Whatever political role they have is played not by the rank and file but by their *clan* leaders. The National Confederation of Senegalese Workers (Confédération Nationale des Travailleurs Sénégalais—CNTS) was affiliated with the UPS. Most of the leaders were in the government, and some were in the higher echelons of the UPS. The executive bureau of the party tries to ensure coordination of policy betwen itself and the union leadership. Only when the party is so divided that the split has become public knowledge does the coordination of party and labor break down. Then the difficulties of both the party and labor are manifestations of the same "deterioration of the social climate," to use Senghor's phrase. The union's leaders were split badly at the time of each political crisis from 1962 to 1973. After upheavals in the union governing body, the party has often stepped in and forced a change.

The CNTS supports national construction, unity, and education and has been charged by the government with seeing to the interests of the agricultural population, which far outnumbers the salaried workers on whom the unions are based. Labor union influence is exercised rarely in public but rather in the privacy of party councils where the real decisions are made. The unions, like the Muslim brotherhoods, exercised a negative power instead of presenting a cohesive opposition to the government or being an active political force for a given program.

Politically important in the sense of being a potential pressure group are the Senegalese veterans of the French army, reported to number more than 15,000 in 1959. The veterans in Senegal are well organized and close to the government. Veterans early received the franchise from the French, and many of them have pensions, permitting such amenities as radios, which give them added status in their village or neighborhood (see ch. 2). There is a national Senegalese veterans organization built on regional ones. The local president appears on the platform at almost any political event, such as a campaign rally, and representatives of the organization are put on a variety of national committees. Their interests are looked after by an office of veterans affairs attached to a ministry and advised by a committee of deputies.

The Dakar communities of Frenchmen, Lebanese, and people from neighboring Portuguese colonies have little impact on party policies. Individual Frenchmen and Portuguese Guineans, however, are personally involved in the UPS.

Casamance Region receives special political attention from Senghor to counteract a sectionalism that stems in part from geographical isolation. That people in Casamance still describe a trip to Dakar or Thiès as "going to Senegal" symbolizes the government's problem.

A somewhat different version of sectionalism pertains in the valley of the Sénégal River among the Toucouleur. To a depressed economic situation and more than the usual land tenure problems are added an ethnic pride and cohesion that sometimes take the form of resentment of the preponderant Wolof. It is the Toucouleur, for instance, who most resent the frequent use of the French and Wolof languages on the radio. Once away from the river valley itself, they tend, perhaps more than other peoples, to form ethnically based special-interest groups, such as the Toucouleur students of the University of Dakar, the UPS Toucouleur workers of Dakar, and the UPS committee of the Toucouleur of Thiès.

POLITICAL PHILOSOPHY AND ISSUES

Over the years Senghor, steeped in Roman Catholic and socialist thought, a theorist at heart and a poet by profession, has thoroughly articulated his intellectual approach to the problems and policies of Senegal. The president, and to a lesser extent several other Senegalese political figures (including Mamadou Dia), has been instrumental in formulating two philosophical concepts that have had a major political impact, not only in Senegal but also throughout the African continent. These two interrelated primary concepts are *négritude* and African socialism. *Négritude*, according to President Senghor, is the total of the values—cultural, social, and political—that are characteristic of all people of Black African ancestry (see ch. 8).

African socialism, like *négritude*, is neither a precisely defined philosophy nor a political action program. Rather it is the name for a related group of concepts that are intended to serve as the theoretical basis for such practical political programs. President Senghor's African socialism is derived from his reaction to the study of European political and social traditions and their adaptation to what he regards as the underlying values and realities of African society.

His African socialism rejects the capitalist economic mode, largely because African countries have neither the accumulated capital nor the traditions of commerce that would be required to establish a base for a capitalist economy. Although African socialism's originators have been thoroughly familiar with Marxist and later communist thought, African socialism completely rejects their major conclusions. In general the philosophy appears more akin to the British Fabian or Swedish Socialists. Its primary association, however, is with twentieth-century Roman Catholic social thinkers, most notably the Jesuit Pierre Teilhard de Chardin. In line, however, with President Senghor's desire to assimilate foreign ideas without adopting them wholesale, the major portions of the philosophy differ considerably from all other doctrines labeled socialism, drawing on the experiences of the Europeans without trying to copy from any of them. President Senghor feels that this will allow the Africans to select the best elements of the other systems and permit them to retain their unaligned posture in foreign affairs (see ch. 11).

Although the Marxist idea of the dialectic (that change is brought about by synthesis resulting from the clash of two opposing ideas or forces) is accepted, virtually all other major Marxist concepts are rejected. Marxist materialism is regarded as the absolute opposite of the most important African values, those that emphasize and give primacy to the spiritual and the sensate. Determinism, the Marxist concept of the inevitability of history, is in complete conflict with the African's view that man can elect to change his own environment and does not have to await the historical process.

As of mid-1973 the inevitability of a class struggle was rejected as requiring the encouragement of divisions and conflict in a society whose primary need is for unity. In addition, although classes exist in

Senegalese and certain other African societies, they do not control the state and are weakening under the impact of modernism and government-forced reform rather than growing more rigid as Marx's ideas would require.

President Senghor's espousal of socialism had not caused him to create plans to have the state take control of foreign-owned industrial and commercial interests. A major portion of local commerce was replaced in the early 1960s by the creation of state agencies for the purchase and marketing of agricultural produce and the supplying of farmers with agricultural needs (see ch. 14). In mid-1973 the government had newly announced plans to force foreign companies to hire Senegalese and train them to replace European employees, but this did not include any announced threats to have the state take over their businesses (see ch. 13). Rather, Senegalese businessmen were to be encouraged to supplant the Europeans wherever possible. A share of wholesale trade in certain commodities was also to be reserved for Senegalese traders (see ch. 15).

The dominance of humanistic themes in President Senghor's political philosophy would seem to support personal freedoms and, indeed, civil rights are given considerable protection in practice as well as in theory. Nevertheless, the primacy of the role of a single dominant party in governing the state is an important part of the African socialist philosophy. The emphasis of party over the individual is a direct result of the great stress put on rapid national economic and social development. According to the Senghor philosophy, such rapid development requires centralized leadership with continuity of control, and both of these objectives can best be obtained with a single, unchangeable party in charge. Further, control over the party itself should be centralized, and the members of the party should participate in the decisionmaking process but should give complete obedience to the party's leadership once the decision has been made.

Subordination of the individual to the party is justified on two grounds. First, the general good of the people is deemed more important than that of any individual, and the work required to obtain results that serve the public's welfare can only be mobilized through forceful leadership. Second, the support that the party receives at the polls, even if its candidates are uncontested, demonstrates that the party must be accomplishing the tasks that the people desire.

President Senghor has also insisted that the party leadership must exercise a strong guiding role in decisionmaking because of the limited educational level of the people and the dominance over their lives of traditional structures (see ch. 5; ch. 8). For this reason, the educated elite alone is regarded as having the knowledge and experience required to make the right decisions. In the president's opinion, supremacy of the party included absolute control over the machinery of government at all levels, both to ensure continuity and direction and to prevent the civil service from actually controlling the country. Control by the civil service constituted a real danger in a society in which the concentration of the modern educated minority in government posts tends to cause the civil service to form a class by itself, distinct from the rest of society.

An immediate objective of the president's philosophy has been the creation of a communal society in the countryside. A major step in this direction was the creation of rural cooperatives, which were intended philosophically as vehicles for uplifting the lives of the peasants. On a practical scale, the cooperatives, which were formed throughout most of the country in the early 1960s, were intended to provide the means for the small farmers to improve returns from their groundnut and other crop production. Attempting to make a success of such rural structures occupied a major part of the efforts of the regional governments and economic ministries. Their efforts, however, did not block the *clans* and brotherhoods from controlling these rural units, thus distorting their intended purposes (see ch. 9; ch. 14).

Political Role of Theoretic Concepts

African socialism and *négritude* are important intellectual points. But important as they may be to the elite and despite constant reference to them by the president, it is doubtful that either term, as a philosophical concept, means much to the mass of the people. Never having been alienated from their original culture and traditions, they feel under no compulsion to reassert their Africanness, to define the essential difference between themselves and the Europeans. Theories of *négritude* and African socialism, like other political issues, are important for what they have come to mean to the people as political slogans.

Négritude has been brought into play for political purposes to a much lesser extent than has African socialism. The tradition of sharing in village life and labor is upheld by President Senghor as among the essential virtues of *négritude* as applied to the cooperative movement. African socialism in government documents is also primarily used in reference to the national development plan. It has come, however, to mean all things good to all Senegalese, a political word for the traditional life of the compound and village as joint and successful centers for a just and useful economic life. Leaders and politicans at the local level are apt to define African socialism or tout it variously as "the rational organization of human society," "the merciless struggle against injustice and dishonesty," or simply as "abundance for everyone."

As an agreed ideal, socialism becomes a slogan for a system to increase production. On the one hand African socialism is humanism and human society; on the other it is groundnuts and millet. Socialism thus becomes the optimum development of wealth and its fair distribution. Socialism, the development of production by the most modern technical means, is the way to overcome sickness, misery and ignorance, thus to bringing about the well-being of each citizen.

When asked to define his domestic policy, President Senghor has replied, "The policy of Senegal is based on development, development, and always development." This policy has been given concrete form in a series of four-year development plans (see ch. 13).

Despite the official urgency of national development, Senghor keeps reassuring the people that his government does not propose to exploit one generation for the benefit of the next. Austerity programs to reduce nonproductive expenditure did not seriously encroach on the level of living of the more affluent minority.

Other Permanent Issues

Some influential issues other than African socialism, development, and *négritude* are important in terms of the time spent discussing them but have little relevance to the life of the people. One such issue is democracy. During the referendum for the 1963 Constitution, the opposition maintained that both the new constitution and the president himself were undemocratic. The lines were clearly drawn, and the issue had symbolic value. But what the terms *democratic* and *undemocratic* meant to the speakers or the voters is not only unknown but irrelevant. One of President Senghor's arguments for a single party is, that democracy is practiced within the single party. Again, democracy is not defined.

The campaign against corruption is another such issue. Everyone is against corruption, and the issue is used by everyone. Other issues are anticolonialism and neocolonialism.

In contrast to these contrived issues are some that are seldom mentioned but really matter to the people. One is the proper interaction of the state and religious bodies. The formal situation is set forth clearly in the constitution (see ch. 9). But problems of land tenure, public begging, and education, to mention only a few, all involve the relationship of the state to the Muslim brotherhoods, and all are involved in national development. The issue is active but almost unmentioned, and the president—an accomplished compromiser who is not of the majority religion—juggles and balances the various religious and governmental forces.

Another such issue stems from the position of the entrenched elite of Dakar and Saint-Louis, who cling to city comforts and a much higher level of living than can be found in the countryside. Most young people who aspire to advancement seek the same urban status; opportunities, however, are limited, and the main need is for skills and leadership to spur development in the rural regions. The resulting pressures for urban opportunities, questions concerning undue privileges, and differences about the reasons for lagging economic development form a complex political undercurrent.

VALUES AND ATTITUDES

The drive to forge a nation and develop a viable economy implies a set of broad standards and values, a view of the world held by the elite but not necessarily by the majority of the Senegalese population (see ch. 5). The governing elite is faced with the task of creating a modern, unified nation from the communes and hinterland of the colonial past. In the eyes of the government this task involves bringing the whole population into participation. The distance between the few and the many (literate and illiterate, urban and rural, modern and traditional) must be narrowed if the country is to become truly a nation.

All public speeches—whether by national political leaders, important religious figures, or local notables—urge or at least acknowledge that the nation and its strength and welfare be the primary focus of loyalty. It is doubtful, however, that any but a few persons regularly and naturally think in national terms rather than local ones. On the other hand, there is no strenuous antinational or transnational loyalty. It is simply that other interests tend to be paramount. These interests are not necessarily fixed or rigid. In some contexts it is the kin group; in others it is the village or ethnic group, a religious organization, or— rarely—a region.

Attitudes Toward the Nation

A number of factors, both traditional and modern, have tended for several years to facilitate the identification of the people with their country as a political entity. These are not unifying factors in themselves but can often be used by government and party leaders in their efforts to implant the ideas of citizen and nation.

Islam, with its pilgrimages, fast periods, and perspectives, reaches into almost every corner of the country and often is a stronger identification than ethnic group or region. Eating habits and dress do not vary greatly, and one language, Wolof, is understood by the great majority of the population. These elements facilitate adjustment for those moving about the country and make intermarriage between people of different ethnic groups or areas a not uncommon occurrence.

Thus, there is a kind of homogeneity on which, although it is weaker in the rural areas than in the towns, the government is trying to build. In the urban situation unifying factors tend to mitigate factors making for division. Education, for those who have received it, has provided a common experience and, to a varying extent, a common set of standards and ideals. Labor unions (in the towns) have afforded their members an allegiance that cuts across ethnic and regional lines and can be carried over to the state with some ease. In a country where one-fourth of the population lives in larger towns and cities, urbanization is to some extent itself a unifying, equalizing force. For many decades town dwellers coming into contact with the French found themselves considered not as Wolof, Lebou, or Serer but as *Senegalese*, a term applied to the inhabitants of the four communes and to the indigenous units of the entire French West African army. There is, however, evidence of regional feeling among the Toucouleur in the north and, more especially, among the geographically isolated people of Casamance Region in the south.

The very fact that education and urbanization have led some people to begin to think of themselves as Senegalese, however, paradoxically widens the gap between the elite and the mass of the population. One of the major problems the government sees is the need to narrow this gap and to mold the population into a cohesive whole.

Several factors are involved in slowly bringing the people in rural areas to a nascent sense of nation. The UPS is one of these factors. The UPS and its 2,500 base units are trying to bring the general population into contact with national political life, using both programs and activities such as elections and committee work. Such participation is often new to the people involved. During the colonial period the major part of the population was on the receiving end of government administration rather than participating in it.

The UPS has been trying to act as a bridge between the government and the people. It is the job of the party rank and file to understand the needs and aspirations of the people—specific people in specific villages—and then to communicate these desires to the higher echelons of the party. They must also make the people see how the party's aims are relevant to themselves and help them understand what is being done in their name and why. To the extent that this system functions in the 2,500 villages and neighborhoods, it is bound to have some effect.

When talking to the people, President Senghor and other leaders try constantly to relate national life to the known quantity of village life and to help the peasant see his nation as a larger village—that is, to have a higher community allegiance. The development plan, the principal political program, is designed to help all the people and is to take place in all the villages; the plan can only be successful if all the people contribute under such banners as "organization, discipline, work, and union."

The problem as the leaders see it is to build the kind of socialism they envisage on the foundation of native communalism, where the traditional unit (and then later the modern unit of the nation) is that for which the citizen works and to which, in many respects, he subjects himself. Thus the establishment of schools, community radio listening posts, and the construction of roads (linking the parts of the country and one community with the next) help to expand the sense of identification with the village into a feeling for the larger unit of state and nation.

The rural development programs not only provide, at their best, a sense of participation in national development but also bring together the elite (sent out from the city to administer the program) and the rural population. These people might otherwise have little or no first-hand knowledge of each other.

Elections, although uncontested since 1963, are regarded as serious political events, as they provide the opportunity to express national solidarity and loyalty to the party and the government. The constitution states that sovereignty rests with the people. The act of going to the polls and casting a ballot, even on a single list, is considered the periodic expression of this sovereignty, an act of consent registering participation in the new state (see ch. 9).

Educated urban Africans, who have been in close contact with the French, tend to measure themselves by French standards. These men and, in fewer numbers, women are the elite, those setting forth the government program or even articulating it. It is the urban dwellers who are involved in the national life and, in an economic sense, the marabouts of the groundnut region as well. These are the people with money to spend and ideas about how to spend it, who have radios and who therefore can hear the government broadcasts. In addition, the elite tend to want to work for the government. Jobs in the administration are highly favored over jobs in commercial or industrial establishments. For this reason it is very difficult for the government to hasten the process of africanization of commerce and industry, but the tendency to work for the government increases the sense of personal identification with the new state.

In the present day, although the majority of Senegalese probably lack the desire for, and the habit of active participation in, national government and although their political life is dominated by a few national leaders and their traditional local leaders (that is, by the force of personality and custom), they are politically aware. Those who have access to a community listening post eagerly await the news broadcasts in their own language (see ch. 12). They enjoy most the programs in a language they can understand depicting Senegalese heroes in a historical context. The government feels that this preference indicates a groping search for the dignity of an African past. Some have been caught up in the excitement of local rural community development projects; many have participated in the rollicking good fun of pre-election and postelection rallies.

Government and party leaders have consciously developed and disseminated a well-defined image of the ideal citizen. He knows that Senegal is his country and that the government is his government. To act against the government or the laws is to act against his country, against his fellow Senegalese and, hence, against himself. He does not evade taxes or default on seed payments and loans because that would be robbing Senegal and betraying his fellow citizens. If he does not fulfill his duty as a citizen—to work conscientiously and to be honest—he is being a bad Senegalese. Senegal is the mother country, and he treats it as he would treat his mother. To criticize or speak ill of the laws and institutions of his country—no matter when, where, or to whom—is to injure his leaders who were democratically elected by the whole population, and to work against the country. He defends his country at every opportunity, and his patriotic duty is to make it better, stronger, richer, and more united. The term *Senegalese* is constantly reiterated in public speeches.

The citizen himself is largely unaware of either the legal or the official ideal definition. He has heard the exhortations to do this and not to do that, but when they conflict with his own way of life they mean little to him. He works hard when and where he considers it important, but hard work for the sake of capital accumulation means little to him. The city holds the lure of money to be earned, however, and migrants to Dakar may well return home with new ideas, broadened horizons, and a smattering of French.

Many young people think of the new nation and national tasks as an escape from traditional restraints and as an opportunity for individual self-expression and material advancement. Questioning the older values, they grasp at ideas and ideals presented to them by teachers and other representatives of the new ruling class.

Appointment to a government post is generally based on brotherhood, family, or *clan* alliance. Civil servants as well as politicians retain their primary allegiances. They are expected to and do regularly obtain whatever favors they can for their group. No tradition of service to the state exists to conflict with this loyalty to their group. Those in public office use their authority and even the public money that they may control to increase the power and prestige of their family or brotherhood. Despite President Senghor's efforts to require officials to accept a modern moral code, the majority of the people consider this a perfectly natural political practice as long as it is aimed at benefiting the group.

Along with such nepotism, President Senghor regards indecisiveness as the major problem inhibiting the growth of an effective civil service. The political culture that stems from the tradition of the marabouts has left little if any room for public servants or lower ranking leaders to accept responsibility and even less for challenges to the leadership by the rank and file. Policy in the traditional order and in the modern government, despite the president's efforts, is expected to result only from the decisions of the leader at the top. No one below the level of the leader has ever expected to do anything more than make personal recommendations to him. For any subordinate to make a decision himself would be a potential affront to the leader's supremacy.

Attitudes Toward the Government

It is doubtful that the large majority of the population can make any meaningful distinction between the ruling party and the government. This simplifies life, however, for most citizens and perhaps speeds the process of their recognition of themselves as Senegalese. In addition, as the leading symbol of nation, government, and party, President Senghor is generally held in high esteem throughout the country. The average citizen and his marabout seem satisfied with the president and have been willing to vote overwhelmingly for him. This of course does not exclude dissatisfaction among elements of the elite, both within and outside the party. The elite corps of the government seems to have a feeling of cohesiveness, even to the extent of feeling itself separate from the rest of the population. This has been true for some years, and Senghor in fact got his political start by capitalizing on the rural resentment of this kind of administrative clique.

For some years after independence, the attractiveness of government employment tended to mute would-be critics of the government, such as some of the university students. President Senghor's often-stated precept that the proper and most effective avenue for criticism is inside the dominant or single party may make party membership more attractive to some of the elite.

But there are areas of potential dissatisfaction outside the group on which the civil service can call. The government itself has been working hard to raise expectations. Heightened expectations mean the desire to spend rather than to save money (capital accumulation), the desire to have a desk job rather than to do manual labor, and sundry other problems with which the government is beset. The government is trying to teach its people that their world is improvable and then to teach them how to help to improve that world without indulging in what the government considers unnecessary private aggrandizement.

The programs propounded by the leaders make little difference to the peasant and voter. A new well, school, or road for his town makes a comprehensible issue, but larger policies are too remote for him, unless his marabout, for instance, alerts him to them. Likewise, foreign policy issues are all but meaningless. Ethnic friendships and rivalries exist in border areas; Islam is international in character (although the brotherhoods may not be), and France, when considered, is on the whole looked upon as a friend. But beyond that, even such "African" issues as Pan-Africanism are beyond the interest of most people, although there must be very few who actively object to the Pan-African ideal.

CHAPTER 11

FOREIGN RELATIONS

President Léopold-Sédar Senghor has been the country's only important foreign policy decisionmaker since independence. Few others expressed any interest in challenging his leadership in this area. As a result, Senegalese foreign policy in most details reflected his personal philosophy and ideas of national needs. Basic to his concepts was the desire to retain a special relationship with France while participating actively in the development of stronger African unity.

Underlying forces included the need for external aid to accomplish the projects the country required to enhance its own development and the assurance of markets in the developed countries for the agricultural products that dominated its economy (see ch. 15). Growth would be stimulated by the opening up of a market in neighboring states for the goods produced by Senegalese factories. This market was generally sought in an area that before independence served as Dakar's economic hinterland, French West Africa.

Senegal also sought to strengthen the special relationships that existed for natural or historic reasons with The Gambia, Mauritania, and Mali. Its most difficult relations, on the other hand, were with its other two neighbors, Guinea and Portuguese Guinea (referred to as Guinea-Bissau by the Senegalese). Although the problems with Guinea were of a peaceful nature, resulting primarily from the different ideologies of the two governments, those with the Portuguese were much more fundamental and on a number of occasions have led to armed, if brief, conflicts. Their basis was Senegalese opposition to the continuation of white minority rule anywhere in Africa and its resulting support of the liberation movement that was attempting to oust the Portuguese from the only remaining colony in West Africa.

In this as in all other international differences, however, Senegalese government policies showed a preference for a peaceful solution. President Senghor made major efforts to encourage a dialogue between the hostile parties. Major emphasis also was placed on cooperation through international organizations, both at the level of the United Nations and, more important, through continental and West African regional bodies.

PRINCIPLES AND OBJECTIVES OF FOREIGN POLICY

The country's foreign policy has been based on three principles. The first principle is nonalignment. This is not a policy of neutrality but one

213

of freedom to choose between alternatives without following the lead of any other country or power bloc. The foreign minister has defined nonalignment in practice as being the right to consider the solution to international problems independent of the East and West.

The second principle is a belief that peaceful solutions should be sought to international problems through dialogue—open, face-to-face discussions—between the opposing parties. In part this principle is based on the country's own practices: modern political conflicts have generally been resolved by talks and compromise in the traditional format of a palaver; for example, supporters of all points of view talking until a consensus is finally reached. It also strongly reflects President Senghor's belief in peaceful solutions.

The third principle is expressed as a belief in cooperation, which for the Senegalese means cooperation between nations as equal, sovereign states meeting together in international organizations. This cooperation must be with countries of all political persuasions.

Cultural relations play an important part in the Senegalese concept of foreign relations, again reflecting President Senghor's influence. The president sees Senegal as the crossroads of two cultures, French and African. Special links are viewed as existing with other states on the basis of the ties of a common association with French language and culture. The country was in the forefront of efforts in the late 1960s to form a semipolitical worldwide association of all French-speaking states.

The major cultural connection, however, is with the rest of Africa in particular and all the black-skinned peoples of the world in general. The president's philosophy of *négritude* sees everyone of Black African ancestry as holding a common cultural tradition that can provide an important addition to a broader world culture (see ch. 8).

The government's degrees of interest in foreign areas may be described as extending in concentric circles. First priority is given to forming firm associations on the basis of common economic interests with Senegal's closest neighbors: The Gambia, Mauritania, and Mali. Portuguese Guinea is physically within this first circle but, because of its threat to Senegalese peace and security, it is placed in a different category. At times Guinea is also included in this first priority grouping, but political differences between the two states have tended to push it into the second circle.

The second circle includes the other French-speaking states of West Africa as well as those English-speaking states of the area that express any interest in joining cooperatively in regional ventures. The first two circles are also of importance as the primary areas of potential markets for the products of Senegal's nascent industrial development.

A third circle included all of western and central Africa, down through the Congo River basin. President Senghor conceived of this as a natural area of cooperation because it included all of those African states facing the Atlantic and their inland neighbors. At successive levels there is a united Africa; there is also an Africa associated with its natural markets and historic colonizers in Europe. The rest of the world is of interest only as it interrelates with Africa, particularly through assistance to African development.

Three major exceptions may be made to this simplified description, however. First is the special place filled by France and the French culture; to most Senegalese France hardly fits into the category of a foreign country at all. Second, as fellow recipients of French culture, a special place is reserved for other French-speaking countries, particularly in Africa. Third, given its self-recognized needs for foreign financial assistance, relations with states outside Africa fluctuate according to their prospects as donor states.

THE GOVERNMENT'S ROLE IN FOREIGN RELATIONS

After 1963 constitutional authority and political practice left foreign affairs primarily in the hands of the president. The constitutional changes that created the post of prime minister in 1970 did nothing to change this situation (see ch. 9). The president still set national policy in all matters. Moreover, foreign affairs and national defense were constitutionally his specific prerogatives.

The executive apparently kept the Foreign Relations Committee of the National Assembly informed on all policy issues, but the legislature took little interest in foreign affairs. The foreign ministry was headed throughout the 1960s by a close confidant of the president. He was regarded as the senior member of the Council of Ministers, but this did not reflect any importance of the ministry itself, which had little influence on decisionmaking. Not only was policy left in presidential hands, but many of the technical ministers continued to conduct their relations with foreign governments and international organizations with a considerable degree of freedom from the foreign ministry.

At the head of the ministerial staff were the director of the minister's cabinet and the secretary general of the ministry (see ch. 9). The director served as the minister's chief personal adviser, with responsibility for handling policy definitions and diplomatic and political matters. The secretary general directed the administrative affairs of the ministry. Somewhat detached from the rest of the ministry was the protocol service headed by the ranking diplomat.

The ministry proper is divided into three offices. The first of these, the Office of Administrative Affairs, has divisions for administrative and financial matters, for consular matters, and for courier and communication services. The second is the office of International Economic and Technical Cooperation. It is a major portion of the ministry and is concerned exclusively with foreign aid and other economic matters. In actual practice much of the administration of foreign technical

215

assistance programs is carried out within the secretariat general of the office of the president. The third major element of the ministry is the Office of Political, Cultural, and Social Affairs. It has divisions for international organization affairs, cultural relations, and geographic sectors. The last division is further subdivided into four regional bureaus, dealing respectively with Africa, Europe, the Americas and the Near East, and the Far East.

The foreign service in 1973 was divided into three categories of officers. Graduates of the diplomatic program of the National School of Administration were admitted directly to the senior category. Competition for admission to the services was not keen, as men with similar educations could obtain much more desirable posts in other government agencies. The entire foreign ministry has only about 300 men, and promotion of younger men—regardless of their educational qualifications—is slow.

In 1973 the country had twenty-three resident ambassadors and four other resident missions at stations around the world. These ambassadors were accredited to about thirty other countries, the busiest in this regard being the ambassador to Great Britain, who also covered Austria, Switzerland, and the Scandinavian countries. There was a total of seven permanent posts in Western Europe, including separate representatives to the United Nations Educational, Scientific and Cultural Organization (UNESCO) and to the Vatican.

Eleven posts were active in Africa, including three in North Africa. Because Senegalese relations with The Gambia were carried out directly by the chief executives of the two states, the Gambian post was a consulate general. There were three Senegalese embassies in the Middle East. The country's only embassy in Asia was in the People's Republic of China (PRC). Two other posts were in communist countries: the Soviet Union and Yugoslavia. Finally, there were three posts in the Americas: the United Nations in New York, the United States, and Brazil.

During 1973 plans to appoint ambassadors to Albania, the United Arab emirates, and Qatar were announced, but the ambassadors were apparently to be based elsewhere. There were diplomatic representatives from at least forty-four states stationed in Dakar.

Senegal is a member of the United Nations and of the following United Nations related agencies: the Food and Agriculture Organization, the General Agreement on Tariffs and Trade, the International Atomic Energy Agency, the World Bank Group (see Glossary), the International Civil Aviation Organization, the International Labor Organization, the Intergovernmental Maritime Consultative Organization, the International Monetary Fund, the International Telecommunications Union, UNESCO, the Universal Postal Union, the World Health Organization, the World Meteorological Organization, and the United Nations Economic Commission for Africa.

RELATIONS WITH OTHER STATES
France

Senegal's special relationship with France has probably been closer than that between any other metropolitan authority and its former colonial state in Africa. During the long colonial history there had been few actual conflicts between France and Senegal. French civilization had been adopted by the Senegalese in the coastal enclaves nearly two centuries before independence in 1960. Schools had begun to produce an elite educated in the French tradition as early as 1817 (see ch. 2). Senegalese had long participated in the French government, rising to the highest levels in the era after World War II.

President Senghor has described the Senegalese elite as at one and the same time fervent francophiles and militants of African culture. Ties of language, education, economy, administrative practice, legal form, and personal association bind the two countries more closely than could any links of diplomatic or political origin. This was almost as true for the younger generation and the small radical opposition as it was for the older ruling elite.

In the early 1970s the long-standing relationship with France was still clearly visible. Some 30,000 Frenchmen still resided in the country. These included one cabinet minister (who, however, had Senegalese citizenship); more than 300 technical assistance personnel who filled key advisory posts at many levels in every ministry; and nearly every teacher in the technical schools, secondary schools, and higher education posts.

Until 1964 Frenchmen had remained in positions of leadership, including the posts of regional governor and director of ministerial cabinets. By 1965, a desire to diminish the image of the French presence had led to their withdrawal from regional government and from all command positions. Their actual loss of influence was slight, however, as they continued to work as advisers to the same Senegalese personnel who had previously been their assistants.

This continuity of preindependence and postindependence administrations resulted from a policy of President Senghor, who preferred to ensure governmental efficiency, which the continued presence of impersonal French administrators would provide. As generally disinterested foreigners, they could be expected to make decisions on technical bases, whereas Senegalese, if left to make such decisions themselves, would be influenced by political, ethnic, and personal considerations.

The French were particularly numerous in all of the technical ministries, but it was their presence in large numbers in the ministries of finance and education that was most politically sensitive. In 1969 the finance contingent still included six members of the ministerial cabinet. In education, Frenchmen filled many policymaking positions as well as dominating the teaching posts. In addition, the University of Dakar drew its primary financial support directly from the French Ministry of Education.

The technical assistants form a network throughout the administration and a group separate from the Senegalese civil servants within each ministry. Often ingrained habits and the lack of experience of their Senegalese employees lead cabinet ministers and other executives to turn first to their Frenchmen for advice and even to allow decisions to be implemented along the interministerial network these men form. The French, in turn, accidentally perpetuate this system by ignoring to a considerable degree their major assigned responsibility, which is to provide practical training to the Senegalese civil servants assigned to work with them.

The Gambia

The country's closest natural ties are with The Gambia, a narrow enclave that juts for some 200 miles into lower Senegal. The tiny country straddles the navigable Gambie (the Gambia River), extending outward from each bank about ten miles (see fig. 1). Senegal and The Gambia are bound together by ethnic factors as well as by geography. The 300,000 Gambians are largely Muslim Wolof groundnut (peanut) farmers. Most of the differences between the two countries grew out of varied colonial traditions—The Gambia having been a British colony almost as long as Senegal was a French possession. Gambian opposition to joining what otherwise appears to be a natural union has as its basic cause the fears of its educated elite that they would be swallowed up by the French culture of the larger state surrounding them.

Both President Senghor and the Gambian leaders expressed a favorable attitude toward ultimate unification, but they were only able to agree on a very limited number of steps in that direction. Before obtaining complete independence from Great Britain in 1965, the Gambian prime minister, Sir Kairaba Dawda Jawara, proposed the creation of a federation that would leave complete control over internal affairs in Gambian hands. Senegal rejected this offer, motivated largely by apprehensions that such a federal form in its midst might encourage the Casamance regional separatist movement that was then active. Instead, the two countries settled for a treaty of cooperation that came to cover many subjects the two states had in common. A permanent interministerial committee to discuss problems that might arise was created, but it met only eight times in nine years.

The major problems caused by the lack of unity resulted from smuggling and interruptions to transportation. Differing currency and customs rates and the undefinable border encouraged smuggling on a major scale. The very existence of the strip of land splits the majority of Senegal from easy contact with the potential granary of Casamance Region.

The lack of a greater degree of cooperation has impeded the planned construction of a bridge across the middle portion of the Gambie that would generally facilitate transport between the two halves of Senegal. Preliminary studies were also under way to consider the river's use to Senegal as a transportation route, although it parallels the existing rail line and might take trade away from Senegal's own ports (see ch. 15).

The Rest of West Africa

The government's attachment to the idea of a regional federation springs from several sources. Dakar had profited greatly from its position as the capital of French West Africa during the colonial era, predisposing its politicians to wish for their country again to serve as the capital of an independent federation. President Senghor continued to view the French-inspired creation of eight separate states as part of an effort to balkanize and thus to weaken Africa. He regarded the individual countries, each with few resources and a limited population, as lacking the strength that a federation, with a large combined population and a broader economic base, would be able to produce in the worldwide competition for development assistance. It would also make possible a more efficient search for solutions to the many problems these countries had in common.

The Sénégal River Basin States

President Senghor's primary desire for the creation of a regional federation took the form of continuing support for a grouping of the Sénégal River basin states: Mauritania, Mali, and Guinea. The long river and its major tributaries rise in northern Guinea, flow through Mali, and form the boundary between Senegal and Mauritania. The river is an actual or potential transportation route and source of electric power, irrigation, and groundwater for a large arid and poor region (see ch. 14). A unified approach by the states involved is required by the international nature of the waterway and the scale of foreign aid needed to complete the desirable projects.

As of mid-1973 President Senghor's line of reasoning about the river had met no opposition from the other three governments involved, but for a long time he was the only active proponent of such a regional body. Until the mid-1960s the animosity created by the breakup of the Mali Federation blocked almost all friendly contacts with that country (see ch. 2). The Mauritanian government, while maintaining particularly close relations with Senegal (including an agreement after independence to divide customs revenues), remained preoccupied with other major development projects and with its relations with North Africa.

Finally, Guinea, which had the least involvement with the river, was divided from Senegal by major ideological differences and was troubled by internal difficulties. The two states were at opposite ends of the spectrum in terms of economic policies and relations with France. The

Guinean government claimed that Senegal, along with France and Ivory Coast, was supporting opposition efforts to overthrow the Guinean government. Many thousands of Guineans had left their country because of economic and political problems, and the majority of these had settled in Senegal. During many periods the Guinean government radio broadcasts were designed to be as hostile to the Senegalese leaders as possible.

The temperamental relations with Guinea led each to close its embassy in the other country. President Senghor made major efforts to reconcile the differences between the two and generally ignored the hostile statements coming from Guinea.

The four states had formed the joint Sénégal River Basin Development Commission in 1964, but this agency had never had a chance to function. In March 1968, after a summit meeting between the four heads of state, a new body, the Organization of Sénégal River States (Organisation des Etats Riverains du Sénégal—OERS), was formed with an elaborate administrative structure and with considerable hopes. The government of Mali, however, was overthrown by a military coup later that year. Although the new Malian government was not opposed to the OERS and was on friendly terms with Senegal, Guinea refused to recognize the new government and for this reason withdrew from the joint body.

A restoration of friendly relations in 1970 brought a brief resurgence of OERS negotiations, but renewed disagreements with Guinea led once again to a decline. By 1972 President Senghor was ready to go ahead without the participation of Guinea. The three more compatible states formed the Organization for Development of the Sénégal River (Organisation pour la Mise en Valeur du Fleuve Sénégal—OMVS) in March 1972 (see ch. 15).

West African Economic Community

President Senghor was willing to go ahead without Guinea in the OMVS because he hoped the Guineans could be brought into a new and much larger grouping then being formed: the West African Economic Community (Communauté Economique de l'Afrique de l'Ouest—CEAO). Throughout the 1960s President Senghor had led successive stages in the creation of such an economic federation, which was to include all the states of West Africa. The CEAO came into being in June 1972.

The new organization included six full members—Senegal, Mauritania, Mali, Upper Volta, Niger, and Ivory Coast—and two associate members, Togo and Dahomey. This included all of the former French territories of West Africa except Guinea. It did not include any of the region's English-speaking states, as President Senghor had hoped it would. The opportunity was left for them to join it in the future. It did, however, represent the first stage in linking together an area with a population of over 28 million people.

The CEAO was to constitute a customs union, to encourage economic cooperation, to create common investment conditions, and to allow for the free movement of money and people (see ch. 15). The new treaty was not to come into force, however, until January 1974. A general secretariat was to be created to act as the body's administration, carrying out directives of a council composed of two ministers from each member state. Its supreme body was to be a conference of the heads of state. The Senegalese viewed the CEAO as an imperfect instrument having many problems to be faced but also saw it as a fresh starting point for the development of more meaningful unity in the future.

Ivory Coast

After the 1950s Senegal's rival for leadership of French-speaking West Africa was Ivory Coast and its leader, President Félix Houphouët-Boigny. The two countries' internal policies were very similar. Their rivalry had originated in differing policies toward regional federation, which Senegal—then the capital area of French West Africa—had regarded as being to its advantage. Ivory Coast, the wealthiest of the French West African states, supported complete separation, which Senegal condemned as a balkanization of Africa. The Senegalese believed that Ivory Coast opposed a federation at that time primarily because it did not want to share its revenues with the other, poorer states. Ivory Coast objected to what it felt was Senegal's inequitable control over the combined territories' revenues.

This rivalry and Ivory Coast's opposition to Senegal's plans for regional federations continued throughout the 1960s. Ivory Coast, through its economic strength in the loose customs union it had formed with three of the other French colonies, was able to block Senegal's initiatives within the regional and francophone bodies on many occasions. By the early 1970s, however, the difference had largely come to an end. Solidarity was confirmed in a joint treaty of cooperation signed by the two governments in December 1971. The potential for further rivalry in West African leadership remained, however, and both leaders took special precautions in dealing with matters that might again stimulate conflicts.

Inter-African Organizations

The country is a member of the African, Malagasy, and Mauritius Common Organization (Organisation Commune Africaine, Malgache, et Mauricienne—OCAM). OCAM is composed of French-speaking states, including several former Belgian and British—rather than just French—colonies. The Senegalese government has expressed strong attachment to the Organization of African Unity (OAU)—a body that includes all the independent African countries. President Senghor has long been active in the leadership of OCAM and in the OAU's major efforts at peacekeeping throughout Africa and the Middle East.

221

Membership in both bodies is in harmony with the Senegalese foreign policy principles of cooperation and dialogue.

Attitudes Toward Portuguese Guinea and Southern Africa

Since independence Senegal has continually voiced its strongest opposition toward the white minority regimes in Portuguese Africa, Rhodesia, and South Africa. In contrast to its belief in bringing all questions before international bodies, Senegal has continued to demand the expulsion of these countries from the United Nations and has urged all other states to break off both diplomatic and economic relations with them. Nevertheless, the government did, as part of its general philosophy, support the opening of a dialogue between South Africa and the OAU.

Personal sentiments, derived from their own history, of anticolonialism and opposition to racial discrimination were the motivating forces in the adoption of this policy by the Senegalese. Attitudes toward Portuguese Guinea—the only one of these territories outside southern Africa—were influenced by the fact that it was on Senegal's border.

Senegal has been a member of the OAU's African Liberation Committee since it was founded. The committee assesses and controls the contributions of African states through the OAU to liberation movements that seek to oust the white minority regimes by force. Senegal is one of the few member countries that has constantly met its financial obligation to the committee and, in fact, urged that assessments be doubled to speed the success of the insurgent efforts.

Portuguese Guinea was the only one of the six white-ruled territories in which the rebels were able to present a real threat to continued colonial rule in the 1960s and early 1970s. The key to their success was the support they were able to receive from the two adjacent independent countries, primarily from Guinea but to a lesser extent from Senegal.

As a result, after 1961 Senegal suffered numerous brief incursions by Portuguese security forces. In most cases these attacks, which included bombings, shellings, and ground assaults on Senegalese villages, appeared to be aimed at fleeing insurgent forces or refugees. The frequency of the attacks increased after 1967. In that year the Senegalese government had switched its support from a moderate, militarily ineffective group based in Senegal, known as the Liberation Front for the National Independence of Guinea (Front de Libération pour l'Indépendance Nationale de la Guinée—FLING), to the African Party for the Independence of Guinea and the Cape Verde Islands (Parti Africain pour l'Indépendance de la Guinée et des Iles du Cap-Vert—PAIGC). PAIGC was based in Guinea and was under strong Marxist influence from its leader, Amilcar Cabral, who was assassinated in 1973. Despite their political and ideological differences with both PAIGC and its host government, the Senegalese decided to support PAIGC because it had proved itself to be an effective force. The Senegalese did not allow PAIGC to operate from bases in Senegal or to receive arms shipments there, but the country clearly served as a place of refuge for noncombatants. PAIGC maintained a medical center in the Casamance regional capital, and more than 80,000 Portuguese Guineans—roughly one-seventh of the colony's population—were receiving assistance in Senegal. Many of these people were members of ethnic groups that straddle both sides of the border, which in some cases actually splits villages in two or splits villagers from their farms. As a result control over cross-border movement is extremely difficult.

In addition to supporting the nationalists and condemning the Portuguese before world bodies, President Senghor had sought a constructive role by making a major effort to bring the Portuguese government and PAIGC to the conference table. Between 1969 and 1973 he attempted to interest the Portuguese in negotiating a gradual granting of independence to the colony within a Portuguese-speaking commonwealth. The assistance of the Brazilian government was sought, and the agreement of PAIGC was obtained. The Senegalese foreign minister presented an appeal directly to the Portuguese government. The Portuguese, however, never reacted publicly to the offer. Thus sporadic hostilities along the border continued in 1973 (see ch. 16).

The United States

Relations with the United States have been friendly. Although much smaller than that of France and the European Economic Community (EEC, known as the Common Market), aid from the United States has been considerable, totaling the equivalent of US$43 million by 1972. Most of this assistance was in the form of food staples. Other significant elements included a small Peace Corps contingent and a military aid mission, which limited its duties to providing the army's engineer battalion with equipment, materials, and training for both military and civic development projects. United States influence has remained very limited, however, because of the dominant position of France and because of differences in policies on several major international questions. These included the Chinese representation in the United Nations and United States involvement in Southeast Asia. The major difference concerned the United States position toward the Portuguese African territories, particularly its failure to support the Senegalese position in several votes at the United Nations on Portuguese military incursions into the Casamance border region.

Asian Communist States

In accordance with the principles of its foreign policy, in 1961 Senegal became one of the few states in the world to extend diplomatic recognition to both the Republic of China (Nationalist China) and the PRC. By 1962 Nationalist China was represented in Dakar by an embassy, although this was reduced to a foreign assistance office from 1963 until 1969. The PRC opened an office of its New China News Agency in Dakar in early 1964. The Senegalese expelled the agency the next year because of PRC support for efforts to overthrow legitimate governments elsewhere in Africa. The office was allowed to reopen about 1967, but two of its staff were expelled on the eve of the 1968 student riots.

After 1961 Senegal actively supported efforts to admit the PRC to the United Nations. Until after its admission actually took place in 1972, however, the Senegalese government favored seating PRC representatives without expelling those from Nationalist China.

The improved world attitude toward the PRC led Senegal to establish formal diplomatic relations with the PRC, which opened an embassy in Dakar in May 1972. At the same time a Nationalist Chinese presence continued, as its embassy was again transformed into a foreign assistance office to administer the agricultural training programs, which had been in operation in Senegal for a decade.

In April 1973 President Senghor finally announced the gradual ending of his two-Chinas policy. Informing the public of plans for a state visit to Peking scheduled for May 1974, the president explained that the Communists would gradually replace the Nationalists in the existing aid programs. By the end of that month more than fifty Communist Chinese agricultural advisers had arrived in the country for this purpose.

In mid-1973 the Senegalese embassy in Peking was the country's only diplomatic post in the Far East, but several other Asian countries had embassies in Dakar. These again reflected Senegal's nonalignment and dialogue policies, as diplomatic ties were maintained with both the Democratic People's Republic of Korea (North Korea) and the Republic of Korea (South Korea) and with both the Democratic Republic of Vietnam (North Vietnam) and the Republic of Vietnam (South Vietnam). Recognition had also been extended to the procommunist government-in-exile of Cambodian Prince Norodom Sihanouk. In July 1973 the country carried this policy one step further by extending recognition to the Provisional Revolutionary Government of South Vietnam (Viet Cong) while continuing relations with South Vietnam. In explaining this step, government spokesmen said that it was a measure designed to aid in the dialogue between the two claimants to legitimacy and in line with the Paris accords bringing a halt to war in that country.

The Middle East

President Senghor served as one of four African heads-of-state who sought to ease the Middle East crisis in 1971. The group was sent out by the OAU to support the efforts of the United Nations mediator. At that time President Senghor stated that his people could well understand the feelings of persecution of both the Arabs and the threatened Israelis. Diplomatic relations were maintained with Israel and the

224

Arab Republic of Egypt as well as with a number of Arab states in North Africa and the Middle East.

Religious ties linked most of Senegal's people to the Arab world, particularly to Saudi Arabia and Morocco. The former is looked upon as the birthplace of their religion. The majority of the Senegalese Muslims are members of the Tidjaniya brotherhood, which has maintained its historic ties to its place of origin in Morocco (see ch. 7).

Motivated in part by these historic ties, Senegal drew closer to the Arab states in the early 1970s. After a state visit by the king of Saudi Arabia in 1972 and the signing of economic assistance and cultural cooperation agreements, Senegal associated itself with the twenty-eight-member Islamic Foreign Ministers' Conference, serving on a peace mission on its behalf to the Philippines. The Senegalese embassy in Saudia Arabia had been opened to serve the several thousand Senegalese pilgrims who made their way to Mecca each year. By 1973, however, its chief duty was maintaining contacts with the Arabian peninsula governments that represented new potential sources of foreign aid, as their increased oil revenues made them interested in loans to developing countries.

CHAPTER 12

MASS COMMUNICATIONS

In 1973, despite the circulation of printed media and the existence of radio and television broadcasting facilities, news reached the majority of the Senegalese peoples by the traditional channel of word of mouth. A variety of interpersonal situations arising from the living habits of a rural population offered ample opportunity for face-to-face dialogue (see ch. 5). As a source of information for topics extending beyond local affairs, however, traditional channels were often unreliable mixtures of facts and rumor.

Although the number of persons reached by the modern media represented a small portion of the total population, those who relied on its elements for information tended to be the most politically active. The impact of information disseminated through modern media channels was strongest among those living in urban areas.

From their inception radio and television broadcasting have been owned and operated by the government. The role of the press as a forum for the expression of opposition opinion was reduced as a result of the creation of a unitary party political system in the mid-1960s and indirect government control of the one daily newspaper as well as direction of the national radio broadcasting system (see ch. 12). The use of the mass media for political purposes by the government had not, however, eliminated the open discussion of current issues.

The interest of the government in the qualitative improvement and quantitative expression of the mass media was seen as a means not only to reinforce the mass support upon which the ruling political party, the Senegalese Progressive Union (Union Progressiste Sénégalaise—UPS) had structured its ascent to power but also as an integral part of development planning. Government use of the media had as goals both the creation of national identity and the mobilization of natural and social resources. Adult education programs emphasized civic education as well as literacy. Printed materials written in indigenous languages or for beginning readers in French were in short supply.

Efforts by the government to improve the media involved a considerable amount of aid from France. Mutual agreements included both short- and long-term arrangements and ranged from the provision of broadcasting equipment to the supply of taped programs for radio and television transmission. The extent of literacy in the French language in urban areas, moreover, provided the information service of the

French government greater access to the Senegalese people. Such efforts generally were not seen as neocolonialist by the Senegalese and were accorded a somewhat higher degree of validity than that granted to the information services of other foreign countries.

TRADITIONAL CHANNELS OF COMMUNICATION

News and other information have been communicated traditionally by word of mouth within small groups meeting for social purposes or to perform work. The most common examples were gatherings of families and larger kinship groups, people engaged in cultivation or herding, religious bodies, and the numerous traditional and voluntary associations to which the people belonged (see ch. 5; ch. 6). Although Senegalese did not regard participation in these groups primarily as a means of gathering information, such encounters nonetheless provided a primary channel for exchanges regarding local affairs.

The number of such associations in which an individual participated varied depending on the ethnic group to which he belonged and his individual interests. Such assemblages were supplemented as media of communication by less formally structured gatherings where exchanges occurred at marketplaces, cultural clubs, and wells and other sources of water.

Traditionally, information received from a source outside the group was often treated with suspicion, but information attributed to a prestigious source, such as a regional religious leader, was more often believed. The continued relevance of this attitude was reflected in 1973 by the reluctance of northern groups seriously affected by the drought to move to southern water holes, which they were told existed but none of the leaders had seen (see ch. 3). Customary style continued to be an important factor in communication among traditional groups, and the exchange of traditional and introductory pleasantries was often an essential step that had to precede the discussion of any substantive issue or problem.

Most groups had individual leaders or formal decisionmaking bodies that not only served to settle issues in dispute but also acted as evaluators of information coming from sources external to the group. Although the exclusiveness of this function had been eroded by the growth of the mass media, it remained a feature of traditional groups— especially among the Islamic brotherhoods—and was present to various degrees in many more recently organized groups, such as agricultural cooperatives and community groups (see ch. 7; ch. 14).

The exchange of information between groups was sometimes the assigned task of specific individuals, such as runners who would take news from one group to another. Among most ethnic groups the *griot* caste fulfilled a variety of functions that ranged from serving as the official spokesmen of the chief to composing songs detailing the most recent achievements of the family to which they were attached (see ch. 5). Sometimes traveling from group to group to spread official news—often combined with public entertainment—the *griots* provided information not only in the performance of their official task but also in their informal conversations along the way.

More typically, however, information spread between groups as the result of interaction not specifically intended to serve the flow of information. Migratory herders and semisedentary peoples in the north, for example, often picked up news from conversations with the village residents with whom they traded or from village radio receivers. These reports, as well as the listeners' interpretations of them, were later passed on in the course of agricultural activities, during religious or social occasions, and sometimes during contacts with other villages. The structure and regularity of group contact varied widely. Some groups used the same source of water without variance and traveled only short distances. The patterns of movement of almost all groups, however, had been severely disrupted as a result of the drought the country was experiencing in 1973.

Some castes or ethnic groups traditionally have been assigned certain tasks that required moving from one group to another or that were performed for other ethnic groups in which the social structure did not include artisan castes. Both the Wolof and Diankhanké have served as traders. At one time their trade networks had been extensive, and in modern times the two groups continued to serve as petty traders. The *laobé* caste—originally of Peul ancestry—moved in gypsylike fashion as woodworkers for all ethnic groups.

Seasonal and short-term migrations of laborers also served to spread information. Some groups such as the Bambara seasonally moved to the lands of other groups to cultivate groundnuts (peanuts), and the Diola moved to urban centers for short-term labor. For some groups such as the Toucouleur poor economic conditions at home required longer periods of employment away from home. They continued to be identified with the place of their origin and would often return with their savings for extended periods of residence and then again seek work away from home.

Although modern technology had eroded the traditional importance of communication by word of mouth, it also offered alternate occasions for face-to-face communication. An example is provided by the introduction of motor transport in Senegal. The use of trucks to haul passengers as well as freight increased the ease with which individuals could move through the country. The truckdrivers themselves, moreover, had come to be prestigious figures from whom information was sought at each stop.

MODERN MASS MEDIA

The Role of the Government

Government emphasis on development and support of the modern mass media was in part reflected by the allocation of CFAF618 million (for value of the CFA franc—see Glossary) for the Ministry of Information in Charge of Relations with the National Assembly—subsequently referred to as the Ministry of Information—in the projected national budget for fiscal year 1973/74. This represented about 1 percent of the total budget, which was more than was allocated to industrial development. Additional programs financed by the Ministry of National Education and the Ministry of Culture were administered in close cooperation with the Ministry of Information.

Constitutional provisions assigned responsibility for control of information within the country to the Ministry of Information. A variety of legal restrictions existed, based largely on patterns of French metropolitan press laws. Although the media were not directly subjected to censorship, the formation of a one-party political system in 1966, the government operation of all domestic broadcasting facilities, and the party's control of the editorial policy of the country's single daily newspaper reduced the likelihood of even mildly antigovernment expressions by the national media.

The Ministry of Information was responsible for the accreditation of all journalists in the country, and both foreign correspondents and reporters working for the local press were required to apply to the minister for a press card in order to work. Laws regulated the local dissemination of information by foreign embassies and information services. The government's attitude, which welcomed cultural and information programs of a nonpolitical nature, was not generally regarded by most foreign government information services as excessively restrictive.

The Ministry of Information had undergone varying degrees of reorganization at several points since Senegalese independence in 1960, but its overall structure and functions remained unchanged. There were both functional divisions and regional offices. One of the major functions of the ministry was the direction of Radio Senegal (Radiodiffusion-Sénégal), the only broadcasting service in the country. This section was scheduled to be reorganized in mid-1973 in order to accommodate the administration of the newly established television service.

The Senegalese Press Agency (Agence de Presse Sénégalaise—APS) was under the Ministry of Information and produced a daily bulletin, *Info Sénégal*. The information service of the ministry, in conjunction with APS, used these daily bulletins as the basis for articles written for publication by the ministry in a series of reviews. Other sections directed by the ministry included a film service, a photography service, and a documentation center.

The Ministry of Information, in coordination with other government ministries, was responsible for the direction of the Research and Production Center for the Information and Education of the Masses (Centre de Recherches et de Production pour l'Information et l'Education des Masses—CIEM). Research and program planning by CIEM included the provision of reading materials for children, educational radio and television programming, efforts to increase adult literacy, and poster campaigns. It was a major government attempt at program coordination and maximization of scarce resources in development planning.

In each of the administrative regions, the ministry also maintained a Regional Information Center (Centre Régional d'Information—CRI). In 1971 there were twenty-eight centers distributed among the seven administrative regions of the country (see ch. 9). The programs offered by each of the centers differed widely in type and quality. All of the centers had originally been given small libraries and reading rooms, but the book and periodical sections of some of the centers no longer existed. Others possessed modern audiovisual equipment as well as library holdings of several hundred volumes. The centers sponsored various activities such as photography expositions, and the upgrading of center facilities was envisioned by the ministry in the early 1970s.

Although control of the film industry was a joint responsibility of the Ministry of Information and the Ministry of Culture, the censorship commission that judged the individual merits of films was composed of representatives of several other ministries as well. Films were evaluated on the basis of political, social, educational, and moral criteria. Any film lacking approval by the commission could not be shown within the country.

Government efforts to improve the modern media included the utilization of regional and international organizations. Cooperation had been particularly close with the United Nations Educational, Scientific and Cultural Organization (UNESCO). A recent example of a UNESCO-sponsored project was a seminar in 1970 that sought to stimulate the training of journalists as well as the development of rural newsletters, utilizing existing duplication facilities.

Senegal was an active member of the African National Radio-Television Union (Union des Radio-Télévision Nationales Africaines—URTNA). This organization was composed of nearly twenty African states as well as representatives of the French Radio-Television Broadcasting Service (Office de Radiodiffusion-Télévision Française—ORTF). In addition to providing a forum for the discussion of media promotion, the organization also annually awarded a prize to the best radio or television program of the year. The 1971 annual meeting of URTNA took place in Senegal.

Attitudes Toward the Media

In mid-1970 a survey of Senegalese use of and reliance on the modern media as sources of information revealed a significant, if incomplete, attitudinal pattern. Included in the survey were about 500 politicians, government officials, community leaders, agricultural leaders, students, and members of the academic community. Those interviewed indicated that they relied on radio and newspapers as their major source of domestic and foreign news. Word-of-mouth channels, however, remained an important source of news for half of the group, and nearly all admitted having regular discussions of news events and their interpretations with friends and professional associates. Only a few respondents included members of their families as sources of news. Civil servants tended to regard their colleagues—followed by radio and the press—as sources of news, and journalists tended to rely heavily on the wire services.

Radio was a major source of information for participants of the survey group. Most members listened to Radio Senegal, but some dissatisfaction with the quality and objectivity of the station's approach to news handling was indicated. Although many expressed reservations about the credibility of foreign radio news programs, most listed foreign broadcasts as a major source of news. Radio Guinea was the only foreign broadcasting station that appeared to have a Senegalese audience for music. The Voice of America (VOA) was the most popular of all the non-African broadcasts. Although its credibility was not as high as French broadcasts, which were not regarded by the survey group as "foreign," VOA musical features were popular among some students. The most popular times for listening to radio broadcasts were in the morning, early afternoon, and midevening.

Most respondents relied to some degree on the local press as a source of information. They followed articles on sports, Pan-African affairs, Senegalese development, and—to a lesser degree—international events. Most of the group read foreign newspapers and periodicals and gave French publications the highest rating as valid information sources. The news bulletins of foreign embassies were read by only a few of the respondents.

Although 75 percent of the survey group attended a film once a month, most regarded the viewing of the film as entertainment rather than as a source of information. They showed little interest in newsreels or documentaries. The respondents usually saw them only when attending the presentation of a feature-length film and generally felt that short subject films were intended primarily for the masses.

French sources of information served almost as an integral part of the Senegalese modern media. Some respondents felt that French sources were superior to those of domestic origin, and few indicated that they regarded French sources as foreign. The reliance on the French media, however, had not broadened Senegalese readers' interests; most of the replies showed little concern with international events that were not related to the African continent. United States Information Service (USIS) programs were second only to those of the French, but their indicated influence was considerably less.

Student attitudes varied from the general group pattern. These representatives of the survey group obtained most of their news from radio broadcasts, followed by the local press. Students were generally more suspicious of foreign publications, but they accorded greater credibility to foreign radio broadcasts than did people thirty years of age or older. Students generally attended motion picture theaters more frequently. They did not indicate a reliance on conversations with their professors as a major source of news.

Radio and Television Broadcasting

In 1973 radio was the most effective element of the mass media, especially in the rural areas where a low rate of literacy and a distribution problem limited the effectiveness of the printed word. The value of radio was reinforced by the use of Wolof—which was rapidly becoming a national language—as well as French and other languages in broadcasting (see ch. 4). Broadcasts in French were aimed at the more educated segments of the population, but a series of programs providing French-language instruction was also offered as a part of the government's education efforts.

The early development of radio broadcasting in Senegal was the result of the selection of Dakar by the French in the early 1900s as the capital of French West Africa. Radio French West Africa in Dakar later became one of the most important broadcasting stations on the African continent. In the 1950s expansion of broadcasting facilities was placed under the direction of the French Overseas Radio Broadcasting Company (Société de Radiodiffusion de la France d'Outre-Mer—SORAFOM), the central offices of which were in Paris.

When Senegal became independent it inherited the most powerful broadcasting installations in French-speaking West Africa. Responsibility for their operation was transferred to the Ministry of Information, and by the early 1960s the vast majority of the service's personnel were African. Technical cooperation with France, including equipment needs and programming, was continued under SORAFOM, which was reconstituted in 1963 as the Radio Broadcasting Cooperation Service (Office de la Coopération Radiophonique—OCORA). In 1969 the activities of OCORA were transferred directly to ORTF.

In 1973 the system was known as the Radio Broadcasting Service of Senegal (Radiodiffusion du Sénégal). The International Network (Chaîne Inter) broadcast programs in French, Arabic, English, and Portuguese. The daily schedule offered one hour of morning programs, two hours in the afternoon, and six hours in the evening. Total broadcast time on the weekends was longer. Transmissions were sent over three different shortwave frequencies, the power and broadcasting hours of which varied.

The National Network (Chaîne Nationale) broadcast in French but also offered newscasts in Wolof, Serer, Sarakolé, Manding, Diola, and Pulaar (see ch. 4). The daily schedule provided twenty hours of programs beginning at 6:00 A.M. The programs transmitted on one mediumwave frequency and two shortwave frequencies. Transmitters were located at Dakar, Saint-Louis, Ziguinchor, Kaolack, and Tambacounda.

Programming was planned in Dakar by the broadcasting service— sometimes in conjunction with other government services—and also by the regional stations, which possessed a certain degree of autonomy. The service relied heavily on programs prepared in Paris by ORTF. The service was also supplied taped programs by the VOA, and the USIS produced a program locally for domestic broadcasts. The service placed heavy emphasis on cultural and educational programming. Regularly programmed features included series on such topics as the school, the family, health advice, and literature.

Various experimental programs initiated in conjunction with the Ministry of National Education have led to the establishment of regularly broadcast educational programs designed to coordinate with the country's educational system. The development of School Radio (Radio Scolaire) was the responsibility of CIEM and included several programs designed for hearing during the schoolday. These programs were of particular help for those learning basic skills and for new teachers (see ch. 8). Printed materials for use by listeners during the broadcasts were available.

Innovative programming also focused on the problems of economic development and the creation of national identity. A special program was developed as part of a UNESCO pilot project, which began in the mid 1960s for the use of audiovisual media in adult education. This program featured rural and cooperative leaders, who discussed in local language the most pressing problems their people faced. Listeners from other communities were encouraged to follow the broadcasts with discussions and to correspond with the local station. Listeners were not only able to share solutions to common problems but were helped to see their common development problems in terms of overall national development planning. Perhaps one of the most popular programs of this kind in 1973 was a Monday evening feature called "Speaking Directly with...," during which journalists questioned members of the government, members of the bureaucracy, and administrative directors, as well as religious and community leaders on various issues of national interest.

In the early 1960s there were an estimated 150,000 radio receivers in the country, and transistor radios were popular in Dakar. In the early 1970s the number of receivers was estimated at 212,000, and transistor radios were found in even the more remote villages. Radio sets were not taxed, and a special program existed whereby the government provided free batteries for transistor radios, which it also recharged at low cost. Local and regional administrative centers provided facilities for group radio listening, and a project in the Ziguinchor area provided radio services to over 600 homes by means of individual loudspeakers connected in a network that resembled a telephone system. It was estimated that these government programs made radio broadcasts available to at least 630,000 people, or about 15 percent of the population.

In addition to Radio Senegal, various foreign broadcasts could be heard. ORTF broadcast for the greatest number of hours each week, most of which was relayed from Congo (formerly, Congo Brazzaville). The VOA and Radio Guinea, however, had the largest regular audience. Other broadcasts were received from Great Britain and the Soviet Union. The government welcomed such broadcasts as long as they were of an apolitical nature and required all governments with which it maintained diplomatic relations to agree to restrict their transmissions to French-language broadcasts. The government sought to maintain the Radio Senegal monopoly over broadcasting advertising and in 1971 had passed a law providing fines of up to CFAF2 million and bans on Senegal-based firms that advertised in foreign broadcasts beamed to Senegal.

Television broadcasting began in 1964 under a five-year experimental pilot project sponsored by UNESCO. The carefully controlled project was one of several investigating audiovisual media and adult education. Programs in Wolof were broadcast over a fifty-watt transmitter two days a week to groups of up to seventy persons gathered in community-viewing facilities at various locations in Dakar. Each program lasted from fifteen to forty-five minutes and was followed by an evaluation session in which the participants were asked questions about the broadcast they had just seen. The results of this experiment not only enabled Senegal to judge how television could be best developed to fit national needs but also provided useful guides to other African countries as well.

At the conclusion of the pilot project, the government began planning its own service, which was put into operation on a limited scale in September 1972. Broadcasts provided 3½ hours of programming daily, but the implementation of an expanded schedule was expected in June 1973. Estimates of the number of television receivers in the country were as high as 1,500. The National Assembly had adopted a resolution in January 1973 to reduce the 100 percent tariff on television sets imported into the country. Receivers from the European Economic Community (EEC, known as the Common Market) were to be subject to a 35 percent duty; those from the United States were to carry a tariff of about 44 percent; and those from countries with which Senegal had but general tariff arrangements were to carry a charge of 67 percent.

Press

The first locally published newspapers appeared during the last two decades of the nineteenth century. The three most important were Le Réveil du Sénégalais founded in 1885, Le Petit Sénégalais founded in 1886, and L'Union Africaine founded in 1896. Their development represented a response to the demands of the increasing numbers of French and *métis* (people of mixed European and African ancestry) and, as such, they were produced for and by the French community. The focus of these newspapers was on French metropolitan politics and issues of economic interest to local commerce. Until the mid-1930s only French citizens were allowed to publish newspapers. In accordance with the French policy of assimilation there was a tax on the import of newsprint and printing machinery, which was designed to encourage the importation of French publications (see ch. 2). Even mission groups were slow to establish publications.

One of the first politically oriented newspapers, *L'Afrique Occidentale Française*, appeared in 1907. It was an organ of a local section of the French Socialist Party and was published on a somewhat irregular weekly basis. During the 1930s restrictions on the citizenship of publishers and increased African participation in the decisionmaking process led to the appearance of several irregular daily newsletters supporting various African candidates running for local offices. Typical of these were *La Bastille, Le Periscope Africain*, and *L'Echo de Rufisque*. Most of these were short lived, but *Le Periscope Africain* had a correspondent in Paris and for some time was a major source of news.

The most significant development, however, was the founding of the weekly *Paris-Dakar* in 1933. Established as part of what was to become the Breteuil chain, the newspaper became a daily in 1935. Initially intended for European readers, the publication—which later changed its name to *Dakar-Matin*—began to play an increasing role in the local information system.

Although political awareness increased in the years immediately after World War II, it focused mainly on metropolitan politics. Numerous newspapers appeared as organs of the various short-lived political parties that evolved during this period only to follow the fate of the parties for which they spoke. An information weekly, *Afrique Nouvelle*, however, was established in 1947 by the Roman Catholic White Fathers. It aimed at interterritorial distribution, offered international news coverage, and became a first-class publication. Its editorial independence from the administration gave it a steadily increasing circulation.

Although an independent, private press failed to evolve in the 1950s, several small party newspapers were established. Two of the more notable were *Afrique Noire* and *La Condition Humaine*; the latter was published by Léopold-Sédar Senghor. These newspapers, however, never reached the circulation or the level of professionalism of *Afrique Nouvelle* and *Dakar-Matin*.

During the 1960s *Afrique Nouvelle* became the most professionally respected newspaper in French-speaking Africa. Editions were published twice weekly and were flown all over Africa. It sought a moderate political position and the advancement of African unity and development. Increasingly, it became a publication produced by Africans—only some of whom were Senegalese—but remained under the control of the Roman Catholic Church. At its zenith, circulation reached over 20,000. By the early 1970s, however, circulation began to drop. Increasing postal costs and currency devaluations were among the reasons cited for the indefinite suspension of publication in June 1972. Attempts had been made to renew publication, but the final outcome of deliberations within the church was not clear in mid-1973.

During the 1950s the editorial policy of *Dakar-Matin* supported French government policy and was slow to encourage the African independence movement. After independence it shifted its support to the government of President Senghor, who was a personal friend of the editor. When the newspaper disapproved of a government position, it usually avoided comments on the issue. Once in 1962 the newspaper even ceased publication until the official government position was clarified.

The newspaper continued to be basically French in both the emphasis of its content and its form. It did provide an important source of local news, however, and many readers regarded its system of correspondents in cities throughout the country as being more effective than the government news agency, the APS. Its conservative editorial policy may have been one reason for a decline in circulation after the mid-1960s. In 1970 the newspaper ceased publication and was replaced by a new daily, *Le Soleil du Sénégal*, produced basically by the same personnel in the same facilities but in closer cooperation with the UPS. The newspaper contained twelve pages printed in full-size format. The firts page was usually devoted to international news, followed by about two pages of national events. Other full pages were devoted to sports, films, and regional news. Advertisements, especially for air transport and automobiles, were included. Regular features also included a crossword puzzle, legal announcements, articles on cultural events, a daily television schedule, and horoscopes.

In 1973 *Le Soleil du Sénégal* was the only daily newspaper in the country (see table 6). It reported an increased circulation during the three years since its incorporation. The only other locally issued daily was *Info Sénégal*, a mimeographed news bulletin published by the APS. There were three major weeklies. The largest circulation was held by *Le Moniteur Africain du Commerce et de l'Industrie*, which focused on commerce and economics and was circulated to other African countries. *L'Unité Africaïne* was a UPS newspaper, and the third, *La Semaine à Dakar*, was a theater magazine.

There were more than twenty other major periodicials published in the country. *Bingo*, a popular picture monthly founded in 1952, was slanted toward urban African youth and was circulated throughout French-speaking Africa. *Afrique Médicale* was also circulated regionally, as was *Médecine d'Afrique Noire*. Two monthly publications,

Table 6. *Principal Newspapers and Periodicals of Senegal, 1973*[1]

Name of Publication	Circulation	Remarks
DAILY:		
Le Soleil du Sénégal	20,000	Published by Senegalese Progressive Union.
Info Sénégal[2]	n.a.	Published by Senegalese Press Agency.
WEEKLY:		
La Semaine à Dakar	n.a.	Theater magazine.
Le Moniteur Africain du Commerce et de l'Industrie	10,000	Commerce and economics subjects.
L'Unité Africaine	5,000	Senegalese Progressive Union.
PERIODICALS:		
Africa	n.a.	Economics subjects.
Afrique Médicale	n.a.	Medical review.
Afrique, Mon Pays	n.a.	n.a.
Amina[3]	10,000	Women's magazine.
Awa[3]	n.a.	Do.
Bafilia	n.a.	n.a.
Bingo[3]	100,000	Popular sports and news.
Bulletin de l'Institut Fondamental d'Afrique Noire	n.a.	Historical and sociological journal; originally under French direction.
Bulletin Statistique et Mensuel[3]	n.a.	Published by government statistical service.

Publication	Circulation	Notes
Etudes et Documents[3]	n.a.	Ministry of Information publication.
Journal Officiel de La République du Sénégal	n.a.	Government publication.
Médecine d'Afrique Noire[3]	10,000	Medical review.
La Nation Sénégalaise	n.a.	Bilingual French and Arabic; Ministry of Information publication.
Notes Africaines[3]	n.a.	Private, academic journal.
L'Observateur Africain	n.a.	n.a.
Sénégal-Actualitiés[3]	n.a.	Ministry of Information publication.
Sénégal d'Aujourd'hui[3]	5,000	Do
Sénégal-Carrefour[4]	n.a.	Do
Sénégal-Documents[5]	n.a.	Do
Terre Sénégalaise[3]	n.a.	Farm magazine.
La Voix des Combattants	n.a.	Ecole al Hadj-Malick Sy publication.
Yaya[6]	10,000	Children's magazine; published by Research and Production Center for the Information and Education of the Masses.

n.a.—not available.
[1] All published in Dakar and all in French, unless otherwise noted.
[2] A mimeographed bulletin published daily.
[3] Monthly.
[4] Every other month.
[5] Quarterly.
[6] Monthly except during school vacations.

Amina and *Awa*, were women's magazines. The *Bulletin de l'Institut Fondamental d'Afrique Noire* was originally a French research publication covering all of French-speaking West Africa, but by the early 1970s its focus was on Senegal, and it was largely a Senegalese operation. Other major periodicals included six publications of the Ministry of Information. Less important government reports and irregular serials also appeared.

The APS, founded in 1959, provided a limited news service. It had but a small staff in Dakar and no regional reporters. Although it did receive information from the regional information centers, local coverage was not adequate for events outside Dakar. Until 1972, when foreign offices were opened in Paris, Addis Ababa, and Washington, the APS was totally dependent on other foreign news services for foreign news. About 80 percent of its foreign coverage came from the French Press Agency (Agence France Presse—AFP). Other foreign news services in the country included those of the Soviet Union (Novosti and TASS) and Great Britain (Reuters), and Deutsche Presse Agentur, the news service of the Federal Republic of Germany (West Germany). The information services of several embassies in Dakar also provided news bulletins.

In addition to newspapers and periodicals produced within the country, various foreign publications were available. Most of these were in French. *Le Monde, France-Soir,* and *Le Figaro* were the most popular newspapers; the most popular foreign magazines included *Jeune Afrique, l'Express,* and *Paris Match.*

Publishing and Book Distribution

In addition to government printing facilities, there were six major publishing houses in 1973; all were located in Dakar. The Grand African Printing House (Grande Imprimerie Africaine) was founded in 1917 and specialized in law and administration. Clairafrique published works dealing with politics, law, and sociology. The House of Books (Maison du Livre) featured fiction and classical literature. The press of the Basic Institute of Black Africa (Institut Fondamental d'Afrique Noire—IFAN) produced a variety of scientific and humanistic studies. The two remaining publishing houses were the African Publishing Company (Société Africaine d'Editions et de Publication) and the Publishing and African Press Company (Société d'Edition et de Press Africaine). Information was unavailable concerning the number and kinds of publications produced by these companies.

Adult Senegalese readers indicated a strong preference for owning books rather than borrowing them from libraries. With the exception of a few shops in Médina, Thiès, and Kaolack, almost all bookstores were in Dakar. Limited numbers of selected books were sold in rural areas by some religious groups and commodity cooperatives, and some bazaar shopkeepers offered books in villages at prices higher than those asked in Dakar. The seven bookstores and two art stores that sold books in Dakar in the early 1970s offered a variety of locally published and imported texts. All of these outlets were operated by Europeans. Some customers reported difficulties in getting the shops to order books that were not on the shelves.

Films

Although films were produced by an industry still in an embryonic stage in 1973, the country was the fourth major producer of full-length films in Africa and possessed the most dynamic motion picture producers in Black Africa. The first film directed by a Senegalese was produced in 1955, but it was not until the early 1960s that films began to be produced in their entirety in Senegal with any regularity. By the early 1970s over thirty films had been made. About one-third of these were full-length features, and the remainder included documentaries and other subjects (see ch. 8).

Local processing facilities were generally able to handle only black and white films; most color and feature-length films were processed in France. Although various local directors had established their own production firms, financial limitations usually required cooperation with foreign film companies. Major financial support was arranged through an international audiovisual film consortium sponsored by the French government.

The popularity of films continued to increase, but the opportunity to view them regularly was limited largely to those people living in the larger urban centers. Estimates of the number of permanent theaters in the country ranged from seventy to 120. All theaters were owned by French companies. Estimates of the total seating capacity ranged from about 35,000 to about 50,000. Most films were shown with French sound tracks or subtitles.

The importation and distribution of most films were handled by two private French film companies operating in Senegal. Most full-length features were imported from the United States and France, but films from India and Egypt were also highly popular. Official film exchanges had been instituted with the Soviet Union, several East European countries, and various other states, including Spain and Argentina. Local distribution of films produced in other African countries was on the increase.

In early 1973 the government announced the establishment of a state-owned film company with capital assets of CFAF48 million. Designed to control the production of cultural and educational films, the company was also to oversee the importation of films and aid government programs for increasing the country's literacy rate.

The government information service itself produced a variety of films for local viewing and for distribution abroad. In addition to educational films, a weekly filmed news series was distributed to local theaters and various European television networks. The service also operated mobile film vans, which took educational and technical films to groups living in remote regions of the country.

In addition to commercially imported films and those produced locally by the various government services or private individuals, the information services of several foreign embassies in Dakar had film loan programs. Most showings were for special groups, such as schools, labor unions, and cultural organizations (see ch. 8). The Senegalese government required that such films be of an apolitical nature, and foreign information service films were also subject to the approval of the censorship commission. The USIS was a major distributor of such materials; in 1972 about 60,000 Senegalese saw films produced and lent by USIS.

SECTION III. ECONOMIC

CHAPTER 13

CHARACTER AND STRUCTURE OF THE ECONOMY

Even before it was hit by the disastrous drought of 1972, the country was facing difficult economic problems of retarded growth, localized rural overpopulation, high urban unemployment and underemployment, and diminished foreign exchange reserves. In contrast to some of the other West African countries affected by the drought, however, Senegal was in a relatively sound position. Despite its poor climate and soils and its apparent lack of readily exploitable mineral resources, the country at independence had been among the more advanced economically in former French Africa. Because of its excellent natural port at Dakar, it had been the commercial and administrative center of former French West Africa. A relatively effective transport network had been established, and access to the West African market had led to the development of manufacturing capacity around the port at Dakar.

By promoting peasant groundnut (peanut) production for export, the colonial authorities had also developed a product in some demand on world markets that could provide the basis for a domestic processing industry. Groundnuts were relatively resistant to the recurrent droughts that ravaged the country, and they were the only commercial crop that could be grown in the poor soils over much of the land area (see ch. 14). Cash crop cultivation had facilitated widespread use of farming methods that in the early 1960s were among the most advanced in Africa, but it had also led to rural overpopulation and soil depletion in parts of the western plains that intensified the effects of the drought. Heavy dependence on a single export crop had also contributed to the radical fluctuations in yearly earnings that retarded the country's economic growth during the 1960s.

In 1972 the country's per capita gross domestic product (GDP—see Glossary) was estimated at around the equivalent of US$250, a relatively high level by African standards; but this included exceptionally high incomes accruing to foreign residents (see ch. 6). Moreover, the rate of growth in per capita income had been minimal during much of the 1960s. Particularly in the rural areas, there were pockets of poverty, and in much of the western plains peasant cash earnings had been stagnating even before the drought of 1972. The result was growing peasant social malaise and political disaffection toward the end of the 1960s, which in turn inspired a central government effort in 1971 and 1972 to introduce reforms in farm price policy and the central marketing administration and to reduce corruption or indifference in the local farm marketing cooperatives and political party organizations (see ch. 14).

There was a dramatic revival in agricultural production in 1972, accompanied by an acceleration of the already favorable rate of growth in fishing and manufacturing. Just as the success of the government's policy seemed assured, however, the consequences of the scantiest rainy season in sixty years hit the economy, devastated large areas of the north and west, and decimated the livestock population. With fiscal and foreign exchange resources at a low ebb, the government was obliged to look to foreign loan financing for much of its planned recovery effort and was seeking to implement sound domestic policies that would ensure a stable and favorable economic climate to attract and effectively utilize the required foreign aid and investment.

PATTERNS OF GROWTH AND
RESOURCE ALLOCATION

By the end of 1972 it was evident that in the twelve years since independence growth had been slow in the economy as a whole. According to one estimate, real domestic product per capita, in constant prices, had not increased at all in the ten years since 1962. Over the same period GDP at current prices had increased by an average rate of about 4.9 percent a year, but it was thought that most of this growth had been absorbed by increases in prices and in population. Urban unemployment had been swelled by the exodus from the countryside and by 1970 was estimated at about 7 percent of the labor force.

By the mid-1960s the country's industrial sector had largely recovered from the loss of its West African markets at independence and was once more operating at full capacity or going on to expand capacity and output in several lines. Other sectors of above-average growth were tourism and fishing. The nonproductive tertiary sector of activity, comprising transport, commerce, and services, accounted for a disproportionately high share of total value added (GDP) in the form of profit margins, wages, and salaries. In 1967, for example, wages paid by the government amounted to CFAF45.5 billion (for value of the CFA franc—see Glossary), or 12 percent of GDP. A sizable but unquantified share of commercial profits was thought to be remitted abroad by French-owned wholesale or retail firms (see ch. 15). Salaries and profits accruing to foreigners were also relatively high in manufacturing, where costs had been reduced since independence but continued to be burdened by high incentive pay for skilled European personnel.

The main factor retarding the rate of growth during the period had

244

been agricultural production. In most of the country the main crops were millet and sorghum for subsistence consumption and groundnuts for oil exports. The strongest single determinant of export earnings and the overall rate of growth was the value of the year's groundnut harvest (see fig. 8).

A year-to-year zigzag pattern in exports and GDP had typified the entire period from 1960 to 1973. The even-numbered years had been years of favorable harvests and crop marketing (December to May) following adequate rains during the preceding May to September growing season. The poor harvests of odd-numbered years had an impact on earnings not only in farming but in industry, where oil-pressing mills generated a substantial portion of value added (see ch. 14). The level and distribution of rainfall were the chief but not the sole causes of poor crop earnings. The world market price of edible oils was a modifying factor that may not have had its full impact during the period under review. Preferential price support for Senegal's groundnut oil on the French market had been gradually reduced after 1962 and finally abolished in 1967. This was a factor in reducing the share of agriculture in GDP in the mid-1960s, but by 1971 the world market price had risen above the previous protected French price. In 1973 price competition among edible oils on the world market thus constituted a potential danger rather than an immediate threat to the country's economic growth and foreign exchange position.

Forecasts concerning the future world market for oilseeds, edible oils, and byproducts were thrown into some disarray by the world grain and feed shortage of 1973. Studies published in 1971 by both the United States Department of Agriculture and the United Nations Food and Agriculture Organization had concluded that annual increases in world production of oilseeds, fats, and oils would outpace the growth of demand during the 1970s and 1980s, resulting in a decline in free market prices. Demand for oil cake and meal for animal feed was on the increase in Western Europe, however, and there was thought to be a reserve of untapped demand in Eastern Europe and in the People's Republic of China (PRC). Soybeans accounted for more than half of total world oilseed production and 70 percent of world trade in oilseed meal. The United States was regarded as a prime source of potential competition. The leading seeds for edible oil production also had a high feed meal content so that, if a feed shortage continued, it might have some influence on world prices for edible oils, which were trending strongly upward in mid-1973.

Nevertheless, the International Oilseed Crushers Congress at Killarney in mid-1973 warned that developing countries dependent on exports of vegetable oilseeds and oils were confronting three serious problems. The first was short-term price fluctuations; the second was the probable long-term downward trend in prices because of narrowing markets; and the third was that of trade barriers in major import

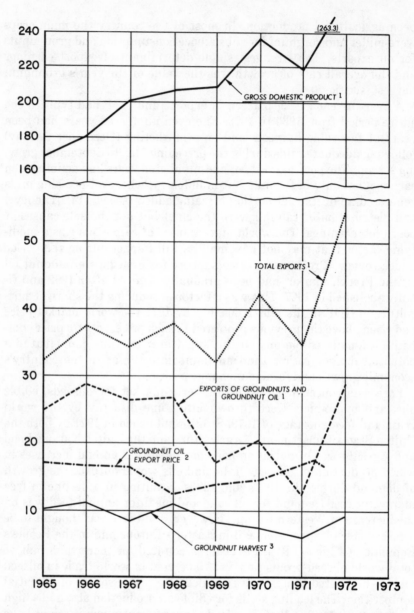

[1] In billions of CFAF. For value of CFA franc, see Glossary. Devalued August 1969. Revalued upward December 1971.
[2] In dollars per hundred pounds.
[3] For crop year beginning in December of previous calendar year. Quantity in million quintals (100,000 metric tons). Harvest estimates are approximate because of subsistence consumption and smuggling.

Source: Adapted from International Monetary Fund, *International Financial Statistics*, Washington, June 1973; and *Marchés Tropicaux et Méditerranéens*, Paris, February 23, 1973.

Figure 8. Groundnut Oil Price and Selected Economic Indicators, Senegal, 1965-72

markets. Through the United Nations Conference on Trade and Development (UNCTAD) and through negotiations with the expanded European Economic Community (EEC, known as the Common Market) Senegal and other oil-exporting countries were seeking reduction of tariff barriers, elimination of tariff differences between crude, refined, and processed products, and price stabilization or compensatory payments arrangements to counteract the effect of volatile price fluctuations (see ch. 15).

On the domestic front the government was pursuing its efforts to diversify the economic base to reduce dependence on groundnut earnings as a source of GDP. The primary effort would be a long-range program to reduce dependence on rainfall, and its effects would not be felt in the short term. Besides a program of well drilling and construction of dams and irrigation channels, a time-consuming program of peasant extension training would be required to improve cultivation methods. At the agricultural experimental station at Bambey, demonstrations carried out during a season of scanty and erratic rainfall in 1972 had proved that methodic cultivation and use of green manure and mineral fertilizer could triple the amount of moisture retained by the soil a month after the rains and double the groundnut yield per acre. Such methods, within the reach of the average smallholder, could modify, if not eliminate, the extreme fluctuations in crop output in response to climatic factors.

Somewhat more effective in the short term were the efforts to diversify production by promoting a variety of cash crops and by reducing reliance on agriculture as a source of GDP. By 1970 only about 5 percent of the country's farmers were thought to have been reached by programs to diversify crop production, but there had been marked progress in output of rice, cotton, and vegetables. Exports of phosphates and of manufactures had increased, so that by 1970 groundnut products had a less dominant role in determining the level of export earnings. The fishing fleet had been largely modernized, and the commercial catch was increasing rapidly. In the late 1960s the output of manufacturing had been growing by about 14 percent a year in current prices.

The proportionate share of each sector of economic activity in GDP had fluctuated from year to year in response to crop variations (see table 7). The share of agriculture had declined from around 30 percent in the years 1966 through 1968 to only 25 percent in 1972, which was a good crop marketing year. The estimate of value added in agriculture may also have reflected the artificially low level of producer prices for groundnuts (see ch. 14). It was not readily apparent whether the profits realized by the government's Groundnut Stabilization Fund on groundnut sales accrued to GDP in the commercial sector. The peasants' loss of interest in groundnut production, culminating in the 1970/71 growing season, is thought to have increased the share of agricultural GDP

Table 7. *Origin and Use of Gross Domestic Product
and Other Resources, Senegal, 1967–72*
(in billions of CFA francs)[1]

	1967	1968	1969	1970	1971	1972
Origin:						
Agriculture, fishing, forestry ..	58.8	66.3	56.3	63.4	47.9	66.4
Subsistence production	(28.1)	(32.9)	(28.2)	(31.3)	n.a.	n.a.
Industry[2]...................	31.9	35.1	37.2	41.6	41.7	48.1
Transport..................	10.0	10.2	} 71.0	76.1	73.2	89.9
Commerce...................	54.2	57.8				
Government[3]	29.1	29.7	} 52.9	55.5	57.1	58.9
Households[4].................	8.4	8.6				
Other tertiary service activities	8.4	8.8				
Gross domestic product (GDP)	200.8	216.5	217.4	236.6	219.9	263.3
Resource gap (+) filled by net imports of goods and nonfactor services[5]	+5.0	+7.3	+19.4	+11.4	+25.8	+15.9
AGGREGATE RESOURCES.	205.8	223.8	236.8	248.0	245.7	279.2
Utilization of Resources:						
Private consumption	162.6	186.1	192.8	206.7	n.a.	n.a.
Public consumption	10.7	11.2	13.8	14.6	n.a.	n.a.
Gross private investment (capital formation)	18.3	12.5	16.7	17.3	n.a.	n.a.
Gross public investment	14.2	14.0	12.0	7.2	n.a.	n.a.
Change in inventories.........	n.s.s.	n.s.s.	1.5	2.2	n.a.	n.a.
Annual percentage change in GDP at current market prices	−2.8	+7.8	+0.4	+8.8	−7.1	+19.7
Annual average rise in consumer prices (percent)	n.a.	+0.4	+3.3	+3.8	+5.0	+5.8
Gross fixed investment as percent of GDP	n.a.	12.2	13.2	10.3	n.a.	n.a.
Gross domestic savings as percent of GDP	n.a.	8.8	5.0	6.5	n.a.	n.a.

n.a.—not available.
n.s.s.—not separately specified in source (probably included in private and public investment).
[1]At current market prices; for value of the CFA franc—see Glossary.
[2]Including mining, manufacturing, electric power, construction, and public works.
[3]Wages and other value added by government.
[4]Wages of domestic servants and other value added by households as such.
[5]Equivalent to current balance of payments. Because data are in current prices, this does not provide a measure of the real resource gap, which may be partly filled by a rise in prices.

derived from subsistence food grain production, which had averaged an estimated 47 percent in the years 1966 through 1968. No detailed breakdown of the value added in rural activities was available for 1972. In 1970 fishing had accounted for CFAF8.9 billion, or about 3.8 percent of total GDP, and forestry for CFAF5.4 billion, or 2 percent.

Over the years the share of industry in total GDP had increased from around 13 percent in 1962 to 18 percent in 1972. Although the industry sector included mining, electric power, construction, and public works, most of its share consisted of value added in manufacturing and was evidence of the country's relatively well-developed processing capacity. In 1970 CFAF4 billion of the value added in manufacturing had accrued to the oil-pressing industry, CFAF4.3 billion to the textile and leather branch, CFAF4 billion to the mechanical and electrical branch, CFAF3.3 billion to the chemical and related industries, and CFAF2.3 billion to the French-owned flour-milling industry, which was subsidized by the French government.

The relatively high proportion of available resources devoted to consumption was among the factors that retarded growth during the 1960s. Over the period as a whole the aggregate of private and government consumption expenditure averaged about 92 percent of GDP. Total investment had increased rapidly from an annual average of CFAF15 billion in the years 1960 through 1962 to CFAF23 billion in 1963 through 1965 and CFAF29 billion in 1966 through 1968. Even in the last period, however, it was equivalent to only about 13 percent of GDP. The excess of consumption and investment expenditure combined over GDP was derived from net imports. The share of aggregate gross domestic expenditure covered by resources from abroad had been increasing since the early 1960s. More than 40 percent of gross fixed capital formation was supplied by foreign financing, principally official loans, along with some grants and private foreign direct investment (see ch. 15). During the 1960s private investment, which was mainly in industry, accounted for more than half of total investment. Public investment had increased from about CFAF5 billion in 1960 to about CFAF14 billion in 1968. A large share of it was spent under the four-year economic development plans.

Between 14 and 18 percent of private consumption was met by subsistence production. Private cash consumption expenditure and private investment were the chief sources of fluctuation in gross domestic expenditure. Government consumption (operating) expenditure showed an upward trend toward the end of the period despite an official policy of restraint. Public investment expenditure had declined at the end of the 1960s but was increased marginally in the early 1970s in an effort to stimulate expansion (see Public Finance, this ch.). The outlook was that a growing share of development financing would be sought from abroad.

The high level of consumption expenditure during the period generated some pressure on the external balance of payments, symbolized by the growing resource gap. The pressure on domestic prices, however, had been restrained during most of the period, and the upward trend of prices in the early 1970s was judged by the authorities to be the result of shortages of certain foodstuffs and of higher import prices rather than of mounting demand pressure.

FOREIGN PARTICIPATION IN THE ECONOMY

In 1973 the private enterprise sector of the modern economy was still strongly dominated by foreign ownership and management. The foreign element extended from giant French firms that did business on a worldwide basis to small family-operated and -staffed stores owned by Lebanese or French families. Many of these smaller scale operators had left the country at independence, but a number survived. A census of industry (manufacturing and artisan enterprise) indicated that as many as half of the small enterprises employing from ten to twenty workers and 90 percent of businesses employing more than twenty workers were foreign owned. Little was known about enterprises employing fewer than ten workers.

In the late 1960s nearly all the leading positions in industry, commerce, services, and in chambers of commerce and employers' organizations were filled by Frenchmen. One-third of the doctors were Frenchmen or other non-Africans, and large numbers of Frenchmen were also found in the middle levels of the public administration and the educational system (see ch. 8; ch. 9).

LABOR

In 1973 there had been no comprehensive census of the economically active population, and data concerning the labor force were largely based on speculation. The level of unemployment in the towns had been alarmingly high even before the 1972 drought further accelerated the exodus from the rural areas. Statistics were kept on applications for employment, but it was thought that only a minority of the unemployed registered at unemployment offices. One source estimated that only about 30 percent of the workers in Dakar had full-time jobs.

The active population, consisting of people aged fifteen to fifty-nine inclusive, was estimated in 1973 at 2,167,871. The percentage engaged in rural activities—cultivation, herding, fishing, or forestry—was commonly placed at around 75 percent but sometimes estimated as high as 87 percent. An official source published in 1965 had divided the estimated active population by sector of economic activity as follows: cultivation, 66 percent; mixed cultivation and stockraising, 8 percent; stockraising alone, 2 percent; fishing, 1 percent; industry, 5 percent; artisan activity, 6 percent; transport, commerce, and services, 12 percent.

Most of the active population consisted of unpaid family workers employed either on family farms or in small family commercial or artisanal enterprise in the towns. This labor force engaged in the traditional economy escaped enumeration but was thought to constitute about 90 percent of the active population. In the modern economy in 1973 there were 65,000 wage and salary earners in government employment and 71,447 in private employment. Of those employed in the private sector, 88.8 percent were Senegalese and other Africans; only 1.4 percent were women. Africans predominated heavily in middle-level and upper middle-level positions; but in jobs requiring high technical qualifications employment of non-Africans was still high.

As the number of new jobs opening up in government slowed during the late 1960s, there was increasing concern over employment opportunities in the private modern sector, which was largely foreign owned. Senegal was one of the leading countries in Africa in the rate of replacement of non-African employees, having a proportion of less than 7 percent foreign employees in industry and less than 10 percent in commerce. More than three-fourths of technical and managerial positions were occupied by Europeans, however. Only about 27 percent of employers and upper management and 18 percent of technicians and cadres were Senegalese or other Africans. This contributed to the generally high cost level of Senegalese industry: to attract foreigners with the necessary technical or managerial qualifications, employers had to offer salaries almost twice as high as the applicants would earn in Europe. Non-Africans made up only 4 percent of the country's employment but accounted for 31 percent of the wage and salary bill.

Because the cost of capital was low relative to the wage and salary bill, the new industries established by foreign investors tended to be relatively capital-intensive rather than labor-intensive. The loss of Dakar's economic hinterland in former French West Africa also contributed to the stagnation of employment (see ch. 14). Employment in the modern sector of the economy accordingly declined from 135,000 in 1960 to 125,000 in 1968. By 1973 it had again surpassed 135,000, but the number of those seeking employment in the towns was growing rapidly. In mid-1973 a cabinet minister noted that during the preceding ten years overall economic activity had progressed at an average annual rate of between 5 and 6 percent at current prices and that profits had grown at the same rate, but there had been no real progress in employment.

By May 1973 popular dissatisfaction was mounting, and the National Confederation of Labor demanded that government policy give priority to full employment and to greater pressure on private employers to hire and promote Africans. The government authorities, in response, publicly accused the private firms of dragging their feet on compliance with government directives. In a speech entitled "The New Slave Trade, or the Second War of Independence," President Léopold-Sédar Senghor asserted that "European neocolonialism" was "attempting a veritable reconquest of Africa." He referred not only to the continued employment of Europeans in African subsidiary firms but also to employment of low-wage African labor in France and other European countries, a practice in which scandalous abuses had been revealed by several press exposés during the preceding year.

In March and July 1973 the government launched an accelerated policy of *sénégalisation*, as the replacement of foreign employees is called. A predominant share of domestic trade in major consumer goods was to be expressly reserved for Senegalese wholesale and retail

251

traders (see ch. 15). All private firms already established in the country would be obliged to submit a written plan for *sénégalisation* of their personnel by the end of the year or face prosecution. Potential new foreign investors must make written commitments of the same kind as a part of their application for admission. Private firms were to begin at once to hire African counterparts for all their European employees, to be trained on the job. The official target was to double the number of employees in the private sector, not only by eliminating residual employment of foreigners but by expanding foreign investment and government participation in the creation of new industrial capacity.

Many foreign firms operating in the country pursued common employment policies that are familiar to job applicants in developed countries but that in the local context could easily give rise to accusations of deliberate discrimination against nationals. One such practice frequently denounced was the requirement that new employees should possess previous job experience in addition to appropriate education. Since few new graduates had any means of acquiring the necessary experience unless they were hired by the firms concerned, this practice had the practical effect of excluding them from employment, and new employees with job experience were then allegedly imported from abroad. At a public meeting on June 29, 1973, that included a number of cabinet ministers and scholars, this practice was unanimously denounced as evidence of bad faith on the part of foreign-owned enterprises.

Although an increased commitment by foreign-owned firms to provision of on-the-job training might interfere with the maximization of profit in the short term, it was thought that it could pay dividends in goodwill and inhibit the growth of popular dissatisfaction with the government's encouragement of foreign investment. The government was seeking to reduce the high price level vis-à-vis foreign competition, but high domestic prices resulted in part from the employment of foreign nationals at relatively high salaries. The short-term effect of employing untrained personnel might thus be offset in the longer term by the replacement of the higher salaried foreigners.

Labor unions were based on the French model and grouped in the National Confederation of Senegalese Workers (Confédération Nationale des Travailleurs Sénégalais—CNTS). Labor unions in Cap Vert Region, where most modern sector employment was located, were grouped in the Senegalese Progressive Union (Union Progressiste Sénégalaise—UPS). Despite the government's efforts to maintain a wage freeze, Senegal in 1972 had the highest wages of any French-speaking African nation. Between 1960 and 1970 the average annual pay of a wage earner in the private sector had increased from around CFAF180,000 to CFAF300,000, and the average annual income of a government employee had increased from CFAF360,000 to CFAF500,000.

By contrast, the average annual income of a peasant was thought to have fluctuated over the same period between CFAF10,000 and CFAF50,000. Many peasants came to the towns to live at the expense of a wage-earning relative, perhaps with the hope of finding an urban job.

The traditional family system was a disincentive to effort by wage earners, as increased earnings might not mean increased welfare for the nuclear family but only a larger number of kin to support (see ch. 6). Some urban wage earners were reportedly responsible for the livelihood of as many as twenty-five relatives. Moreover, wage levels in the 1960s were generally unrelated to productivity. Many African workers showed a preference for wage employment in less productive activities, such as government, commerce, or services. A study of Senegal's industrial labor published by a visiting American scholar in 1968 concluded that the operation of the labor market was completely distorted by social and political factors. He placed much of the blame on the persistence of colonial attitudes and of inappropriate French models and pointed out that government wage policy might contribute to retarding the replacement of foreign by Senegalese employees. He recommended that wage policy should discriminate in favor of more productive employment sectors and that more effective training should be provided for prospective wage earners.

The educational system was based upon the French model and catered to an elite that would go on to acquire a university education (see ch. 8). Of those completing college preparatory education, only about one-third had majored in science or technical subjects. A 1970 planning commission report had recognized the need to make the educational system more relevant to the country's practical needs.

Accordingly, the government in 1972 as part of its effort to improve employment possibilities for Senegalese nationals introduced certain reforms in the educational system designed to orient more students toward vocational training and toward studies in the scientific and mathematical fields. In May 1973 the prime minister approved the new Department of Human Resources and the establishment of a detailed human resources plan to be periodically revised. Follow-up programs for former elementary and secondary school and university students were to be expanded, and coordination between employment and technical training services improved.

DEVELOPMENT PLANNING

In the French overseas territories there had been some form of centralized investment planning for more than forty years, in the early years often involving the conscription of indigenous labor for public works. After World War II formal development plans were introduced but were confined to public investment. The plans were drawn up in France and treated all of French West Africa as an integrated whole, inextricably linked with the French economy. Emphasis was upon facilitating the export of raw materials to France and exports of manufactures from France or from French-owned African enterprises to the West African market. In the 1947–59 period, CFAF 25.8 billion was invested by the French economic development agency in Senegal, representing one-third of the total development spending for all seven French West African countries. Of Senegal's share, CFAF12 billion, or 47 percent, was investment in infrastructure; most of the remainder was for social or administrative projects. There were two postwar development plans before independence, the first a six-year plan for 1947 to 1953 and the second a five-year plan for 1954 to 1959.

After independence the new government initiated a series of four-year development plans. The first four have been defined by the authorities as essentially indicative programs of action, setting desirable targets of achievement to be fulfilled by private as well as public investment and designed to stimulate overall growth in per capita income. Their expectations of domestic investment have not as a rule been fulfilled, but they have also left numerous projects to be financed by foreign investment, which has not always proved forthcoming.

The First Four-Year Plan for Economic and Social Development (1961–64) emphasized investment in transport and social infrastructure, including administrative buildings, housing, and urban water supply. Only 20 percent of its investment target was earmarked for the rural sector. Planning was poorly coordinated and almost totally lacking in follow-up provisions. The cumbersome administrative machinery was slow to take action and lacked flexibility of response. Despite the plan objectives, therefore, the economy was stagnant in the early 1960s, with an average rate of growth estimated at about 1 percent a year in real terms (constant prices).

The level of public investment was subsequently increased under the Second Four-Year Plan for Economic and Social Development (1965/66–1968/69) and the Third Four-Year Plan for Economic and Social Development (1969/70–1972/73). The share of total financing devoted to the productive sectors increased from 24 to 45 percent, and rural investments tripled in quantity and improved in effectiveness. The shift in policy was too late, however, to have much impact on growth until after 1968. There was some progress in rural diversification and in industrial capacity, particularly in import substitution; but recurrent drought and the government's producer price and marketing policy interfered with the achievement of overall production targets in agriculture (see ch. 14).

The country had not inherited any planning structure at independence, because plans had previously been formulated in France. During the 1960s administrative problems had often led to delay in the utilization of foreign aid once it had been obtained. Moreover, desirable projects were not always prepared and justified in adequate detail to attract foreign aid within the proposed time period. By the introduction of the fourth four-year plan in 1973, however, the government's capacity to prepare and implement development projects had reportedly been improved.

The Fourth Four-Year Plan for Economic and Social Development (1973-77) was adopted by the National Assembly in July 1973. It projected an overall investment target of CFAF181 billion for the entire plan period, against CFAF116 billion actually invested under the preceding third plan. The official objective of the fourth plan was to attain an annual rate of growth of 5.7 percent overall, 4.6 percent in agriculture, 6.5 percent in industry, and 6 percent in the tertiary sector (commerce and services).

Financing of the fourth plan presented numerous difficulties. It was proposed that three-fourths should be obtained from foreign sources. The declining trend in public savings had coincided with trends militating against increased taxes. There was also limited scope for increased deficit financing, which would place undue strain on the foreign exchange balance and inhibit credit to the private sector. Loans obtained from abroad would have to be found on relatively easy terms to avoid an unmanageable increase in the debt service burden as a result of the decline in the proportion of grant aid. Grant aid had constituted as much as 85 percent of total foreign aid in the years 1964 through 1966 but had declined to 55 percent in 1969 through 1971 and was expected to drop still further.

Of the total investment proposed under the fourth plan, 26.2 percent was earmarked for the rural sector. Groundnut production was to be increased to 1.2 million tons by the end of the period, compared with a previous high of 1,005,100 in 1968 and a low of around 500,000 in 1973. Food grain production targets were 750,000 tons for millet and sorghum, compared to a previous high estimated at 86,000 tons. Cotton output was to be increased to around 60,000 tons, from 23,000 tons in 1973. There would also be increased emphasis on diversification of crop production, including irrigated production of rice, sugarcane, and vegetables. A dam-building program was to be initiated, and CFAF11 billion was to be allocated to a program of drilling wells and boreholes. This program would improve the water supply of remote villages and facilitate livestock development, which had lagged under previous plans and was seriously set back by the 1972 drought.

Industry would receive CFAF26 billion, or 16.9 percent of investment, under the plan. This would include CFAF12 billion for the establishment of new enterprises. Priority would be given to enterprises oriented toward export or those favoring industrial decentralization or having a relatively high labor requirement. The target was a growth of 11 percent in industrial output by the end of the plan period. Investment projected under the plan did not include proposed financing of several large-scale projects, such as a new petroleum refinery and a dry dock for supertankers, for which approval had been obtained in August 1973 from the International Bank for Reconstruction and Development (IBRD—also known as the World Bank).

About 23.8 percent of total investment would go for commerce, tourism, and other services. Tourism would have high priority with a scheduled CFAF20.8 billion in investment. Education would get CFAF10.3 billion, and health facilities CFAF3.6 billion.

PUBLIC FINANCE

Like many developing countries, Senegal has rather meager tax resources. Because the current operating costs of government are relatively high and have a tendency to grow, there is little flexibility for the use of public finance as an instrument of economic or social policy, to influence the business cycle, restrain prices, or redistribute wealth among social groups. During the 1960s the government had followed a generally conservative fiscal policy designed to maintain price stability. The overall tax burden, as measured in percent of GDP, had increased only moderately, to around 21 percent in 1969 and 1970; but its incidence on consumers and wage earners was high. Because economic growth was limited, yields from the tax base at existing rates had not greatly expanded, and the economic and social climate did not encourage further rate increases. Low per capita income limited the direct tax base, and the government must rely heavily on indirect taxes on consumption, imports, and exports.

A feature common to the public finance systems of many developing nations has been the use of the official marketing system to skim off a share of earnings from peasant export production for the national treasury. The Groundnut Stabilization Fund was intended in principle to support the groundnut price to the peasant producer in years when the world market price had slumped; but in practice, throughout the 1960s, the government consistently maintained the producer price at a level well below the export price, and the profits were used to cover a portion of the deficit resulting from central government operating and development expenditure. This practice resulted in widespread peasant discontent, and the low producer price inspired the groundnut crisis of the mid-1960s (see ch. 14). Consequently, the government in 1971 undertook to use the stabilization fund in the future to support the producer price at a level somewhat higher than in the past.

Another reform introduced in 1972 was designed to give the local governments greater independence in determining the use of revenues collected at the local level (see ch. 9). The reform was initiated on an experimental basis in Thiès Region and by mid-1973 appeared to be so successful that it was to be introduced in other regions.

Since independence Senegal had pursued a policy of relative stability in its public finances, holding the current operating expenditures of government below the level of current revenues and using the resulting public saving to finance a portion of development expenditure. The annual rate of increase in the price level had accordingly been kept within manageable proportions, but there had been little stimulus to expansion in the economy. During the early 1960s the government had placed primary spending emphasis on administration rather than development, but in the second half of the decade a more energetic investment spending policy was pursued. The expansionary effects were not felt, however, until after 1968.

Through fiscal 1969 there had been a decline in public saving. On the one hand, both ordinary and investment expenditures were growing; on the other, tax receipts remained largely stagnant, owing to increased tax exemptions on the country's imports.

After fiscal 1969 there was a recovery in public saving and in extra-budgetary treasury receipts (see table 8). Rising international groundnut oil prices produced some sizable stabilization fund surpluses in good crop years. After fiscal 1969 tax yields rose, as rates had been increased and collection improved; but there was no further improvement through mid-1973.

In 1973 the government appeared to be committed to a more energetic policy of development expenditure. In principle, it sought to contain the growth of government operating expenditure, notably expenditure on personnel. In practice, however, it was anticipated that current as well as investment expenditure would grow more rapidly than tax revenue during the 1970s. The authorities did not have concrete plans for new taxes or for higher tax rates. The tax burden was already relatively high; and the social climate was regarded as unpropitious for further increases because of widespread unemployment, peasant discontent, and the hardships attendant on the drought. Although it was hoped to avoid a current budget deficit, there was a possibility that after 1973 a deficit on the current operating budget might have to be financed by domestic borrowing and by credit from the central bank and that development expenditure would be increasingly financed by foreign borrowing.

Revenue

In 1970 the share of direct taxes in total tax revenue had reached CFAF17.2 billion, or 40 percent of the total of CFAF43.5 billion (see table 9). It had been on the rise throughout the second half of the 1960s as a result of higher tax rates and better methods of collection but on average in fiscal 1967 through fiscal 1971 had nonetheless provided only about one-fourth of budgetary revenues. In this period between 15 and 20 percent had come from taxes on personal or business incomes and 3 or 4 percent from the rural head tax and livestock tax. Tax rates on personal income were progressive and varied according to the source of income. Because of low average personal income levels, only about 100,000 individuals paid income tax. As is characteristic of developing

Table 8. Treasury Operations and Financing of the Deficit, Senegal, 1968-73
(in billions of CFA francs)[1]

	1968	1969	1970	Year[2] 1971	1972	1973 (forecast)
Current budgetary revenue.............	35.4	36.5	41.0	40.7	45.8	45.5
Current budgetary expenditure........	-34.5	-36.5	-36.6	-39.8	-41.1	-44.4
Current surplus (public saving).....	0.9	0.0[3]	4.4	0.9	4.7	1.1
Development budget expenditure[4].......	-4.0	-5.0	-2.9	-3.3	-4.2	-4.0
Pension funds and other operations (net)	0.4	...[5]	-0.5	-0.4	-0.7	-0.8
Overall treasury surplus or deficit (-)	-2.7	-5.0	1.0	-2.8	-0.2	-3.7
Financing:						
Commodity stabilization fund surpluses......................	1.0	1.0	0.4	2.8	1.5	...[6]
Operations of public enterprises.....	n.a.	n.a.	-1.4	-1.3	-0.3	-1.0
Foreign borrowing.................	0.5	1.6	0.1	...[5]	2.9	1.2
Deposits with central bank (increase -).....................	1.4	2.0	0.6	1.0	-0.6	1.5
Nonbank domestic borrowing, transactions with French treasury and other entities................	-0.9	0.4	-0.5	-0.6	-2.5	...[6]
Change in treasury cash balances (increase -).....................	0.7	...[5]	-0.2	0.9	-0.8	0.8
Current budget revenue as percent of GDP[7].............................	n.a.	n.a.	17.3	18.5	17.4	18.9
Current budget expenditure as percent of GDP[7].............................	n.a.	n.a.	16.8	18.1	15.6	18.5
Expenditure on personnel as percent of GDP[7].............................	n.a.	n.a.	8.2	9.5	8.2	9.4

n.a.—not available.
[1]For value of the CFA franc—see Glossary.
[2]Fiscal year ending June 31.
[3]0 means none.
[4]Excludes development projects directly financed by foreign aid.
[5]Less than half the unit.
[6]Because data for 1973 are only forecast, estimates on financing of the deficit are incomplete and add to less than anticipated deficit.
[7]Gross domestic product.

countries, the relatively small number of wage and salary earners, particularly government employees, were a prime source of personal income tax because their incomes could be more readily identified. The major source of income tax revenues was industrial and commercial profits. Business also paid a payroll tax, and in 1973 a special tax on firms employing foreigners was augmented to discourage the hiring of non-African personnel. Under the investment incentive code, enterprises engaged in priority activities might enjoy an initial tax holiday of five to eight years, as well as other tax advantages.

Under the reforms introduced after 1972, the rural head and livestock taxes were gradually to be taken over by the rural councils to be used for local development expenditure. In 1973 these taxes were forgiven in many areas because of the drought.

Table 9. Structure of Taxation, Senegal, 1969-70
(in billions of CFA francs)[1]

	1969[2]	1970[2]
Taxation of imports	14.8	15.1
Taxation of exports.............................	2.8	1.8
Other indirect taxation...........................	8.2	9.4
Direct taxes paid by enterprises......................	4.0	4.5
Direct taxes paid by households.....................	9.8	12.7
TOTAL	39.3	43.5

[1]For value of CFA franc—see Glossary.
[2]Calendar years.

Source: Adapted from "Les Comptes Economiques du Sénégal, 1969-1970," *Marchés Tropicaux et Méditerranéens* [Paris], XXVIII, No. 1424, February 23, 1973, pp. 605-606.

Indirect taxation provided between 65 and 70 percent of government revenues in fiscal year 1967 through 1971, the residue being supplied by nontax sources, such as licensing fees, income from government property, and the national lottery. The largest single source of revenue was taxes or customs tariffs on imports, which accounted for more than 40 percent of the total. Import tax yields had dropped by about 10 percent in fiscal 1966, when goods from Common Market countries were granted full exemption from duty (see ch. 15). Withdrawal of French military personnel in the mid-1960s had also brought a decline in imports of the kind of luxury goods subject to the highest duties and excise taxes, and a steadily growing share of total import value consisted of essential products that were duty free or subject to minimum import tax, such as raw materials and capital equipment. There were six categories of import taxes: customs duties, fiscal duties, a statistical tax, a standard tax on transactions, an import turnover tax, and a refinery tax on petroleum products.

Despite exemptions provided for essential goods, the burden of import taxes was high relative to that in other countries. In fiscal 1967, for example, the customs service reported that taxes and tariff duties constituted 38 percent of total import value in Senegal, compared with 19 percent in Ivory Coast and 10 percent in Mauritania. There were special protective tariffs for some goods produced domestically, and on some items not produced domestically but taxed as luxuries the rate was also well above average. On automobiles, for example, the tax burden exceeded 100 percent.

The yield of export taxes fluctuates sharply from year to year, depending primarily on the level and price of groundnut oil exports. The rate of the tax on groundnut exports was lowered in 1965 and 1967 after the loss of price support on the French market, and receipts have since declined. Export taxes provided about 8 percent of total revenues in fiscal 1967 and 4 percent in fiscal 1971.

Receipts from excise duties and other consumption taxes provide 12 to 14 percent of total revenues, and the domestic turnover tax provides about 7 percent. Excise duties were levied on alcoholic beverages, cigars and cigarettes, soft drinks, kola nuts, green tea, and certain petroleum products. In 1969 a new excise tax on coffee was introduced, and the taxes on kola nuts and petroleum products were increased. A tax on edible oil was extended to include all fats and oils.

Expenditure

At independence the country had inherited a costly and top-heavy administrative structure based upon its former position as the capital of French West Africa. Its educated elite looked to the government as the natural source of employment. After independence the nationalization of existing agencies and creation of new government enterprises and other public entities accelerated the proliferation of jobs on the public payroll. Overstaffing and inefficiency were rife. Indignation over the incidence of corruption and diversion of public funds reached from the peasants of remote villages to President Senghor himself.

In fiscal 1973 salaries had continued to make up more than 50 percent of current operating expenditure. The government had undertaken to contain the size of the administration as far as possible through attrition, insisting on the mandatory retirement age and failing to replace retiring personnel. The economic climate was not considered propitious, however, for outright reductions in staffing, and some increase in salary levels was expected.

There is no breakdown of final expenditure by function performed. The budget allocation of resources to individual ministries is not always an accurate indication of function because administrative allocations include many catchall categories. In fiscal 1971 the allocation included the following categories: education and sports, 21.0 percent; defense, 12.6 percent; general administration, 10.0 percent; justice and police, 9.7 percent; health, 9.4 percent; transport, urbanism, and public works, 7.1 percent; agriculture, 6.0 percent; and service of the public debt, 4.5 percent. In fiscal 1973 there was an increase in public debt servicing and in transfer payments from central to local government.

MONETARY AND BANKING SYSTEM

There are four commercial banks, as well as the National Development Bank (Banque Nationale de Développement du Sénégal—BNDS), the National Savings Bank (Caisse Nationale d'Epargne du Sénégal), and other financial intermediaries, such as the postal checking system, the treasury, and various insurance and pension funds. Senegal is a member of the French franc area and of the West African Monetary Union (Union Monétaire Ouest-Africaine—UMOA). With the other members of the union it shares a common central bank, the Central Bank of the West African States (Banque Centrale des Etats de l'Afrique de l'Ouest—BCEAO), which functions as the bank of issue for their common currency. Until 1973 the union had seven members: Senegal, Ivory Coast, Niger, Upper Volta, Togo, Dahomey, and Mauritania. Mauritania left the union on June 31, 1973, when it withdrew from the French franc area and established its own currency independent of the CFA franc. Togo and Dahomey were reported to be considering following suit.

The CFA franc is the common currency unit of the African Financial Community (Communauté Financière Africaine—CFA), which consists of African members of the French franc area. It is tied to the French franc at a fixed parity of CFAF50 equal 1 French franc. The CFA franc has followed the successive devaluations of the French franc, changing its par value in relation to the United States dollar each time. The rates of exchange per United States dollar were: from 1958 through 1968, CFAF246.8; from August 10, 1969, through November 1971, CFAF277.8. From December 1971, when the United States dollar was first devalued, through January 1973, the rate was CFAF255.79 per United States dollar; after the second dollar devaluation in February 1973 it was CFAF230.2. Coins and banknotes issued by the BCEAO are legal tender in all member countries of the union, but CFA francs from other African countries are not usually accepted.

The BCEAO was the lineal descendant of the old common bank of issue of the French West African countries in colonial times. This had originally been a commercial bank, but its title was changed to the BCEAO in April 1959. It was then dissolved in 1962 and replaced by a new central bank with the same name but with a board of directors consisting of representatives of the member governments of the UMOA and of France. The operations of the BCEAO are governed by the UMOA treaty of May 1962 and by the cooperation agreement with France of October 1962.

The member countries hold their foreign currency reserves in an operations account with the French treasury. Transfers between member countries and France are unrestricted, but transfers of foreign exchange reserves to other countries require French approval. The French treasury, however, guarantees the convertibility of all holdings in the operations account into any foreign currency needed. It thus stands behind the parity of the CFA franc and guarantees its stability. In return, France exercises a measure of control over the monetary and fiscal policies of UMOA governments through its representation on the board of directors of the BCEAO.

The management of the union's monetary policy is entrusted to a board of directors and five monetary committees, one for each member country. The monetary committees have general competence over the operations of the central bank in their respective countries and specific powers over credit distribution in the country. The chief implements available for credit control are rediscount rates and credit ceilings.

Ever since the monetary union was established in 1962, however, the basic discount rate has been maintained unchanged at a low 3.5 percent. The credit ceilings are determined semiannually by the union's board of directors on the recommendation of the monetary committee for the country concerned. The national monetary committee then decides upon the allocation of the ceiling among the banks and the treasury. The ceilings are enforced by moral suasion.

The generally cautious monetary policy followed by the BCEAO and by other African franc area institutions had brought franc area arrangements under attack in the early 1970s. The Malagasy Republic and Mauritania withdrew from membership, and other countries were calling for revision of their basic economic cooperation agreements with France. In December 1972 President Senghor asserted that Senegal had benefited from the relative stability of the CFA franc. He also emphasized that no country could hope to achieve true monetary autonomy, because all were under the domination of North America, Europe, and Japan in monetary matters. At the same time, however, he concurred with the demand for franc area reforms presented to the French government by the president of Niger in January 1972 and particularly with the complaint that BCEAO policy had emphasized stability at the expense of economic development.

President Senghor proposed that the BCEAO be replaced by a West African bank for development, retaining the same functions but providing in addition more flexible means for financing member government treasuries. He also suggested that its statutes be modified to permit decisions by a two-thirds vote instead of the existing requirement for unanimity. This would give the non-French members a greater voice. He also proposed that the monetary committees for the individual member countries be given an expanded competence. The BCEAO already had stronger African representation on the board of directors and monetary committees than did the corresponding central bank for central African countries, but President Senghor recommended that it should have a higher proportion of Africans on its administrative staff and provide the requisite training.

During the 1960s and the early 1970s the BCEAO kept the general level of interest rates low in order to encourage the expansion of investment and production. Because interest rates were so much lower than those prevailing in France, however, many businesses transferred their profits to French banks and then borrowed from banks in Senegal to finance their expansion. In general, it was thought that the low level of domestic interest rates was not conducive to the needed mobilization of domestic saving for development. The outflow of savings to abroad was particularly marked after 1966.

Uniform banking legislation for the members of the UMOA was provided for in its 1962 treaty and was introduced in Senegal by a law of July 10, 1964, and a decree of 1965. These banking regulations established minimum capitalization and reserve requirements for all the country's banking institutions. Total bank credit is regulated by the BCEAO and its monetary committees, but supervision of banking safety requirements, admission of new banks, and determination of other banking terms and conditions is the province of the National Credit Council. A commission for banks and financial institutions supervises the application of both credit policy and banking regulations.

The country has four commercial banks, three of which are owned by foreign interests, predominantly French. One of the commercial banks, the Senegalese Bank Union for Commerce and Industry (Union Sénégalaise de Banque pour le Commerce et l'Industrie—USB), is jointly owned by the Senegal government, the BNDS, and foreign interests. The other three are the General Banking Company of Senegal (Société Générale de Banque au Sénégal—SGBS), the International Bank for Commerce and Industry of Senegal (Banque Internationale pour le Commerce et l'Industrie au Sénégal—BICIS), and the International West African Bank (Banque Internationale pour l'Afrique Occidentale—BIAO).

In Senegal the national treasury also performs certain banking operations: it may receive deposits from public or semipublic institutions and accepts customs duty bills in payment of certain import taxes. The post office operates a postal checking system for the public on the European model. Other financial institutions include the General Company for Automobile Credit (Société Générale de Crédit Automobile—SOGECA) and the National Savings Bank. A French government agency with headquarters in Paris, the Central Fund for Economic Cooperation (Caisse Centrale de Coopération Economique—CCCE), operates in Senegal as it does in other French-speaking African countries, extending medium-term or long-term loans to public entities or for projects undertaken by private companies.

In the early 1970s two special credit guarantee funds were created to facilitate the granting of bank credits to small or medium-sized enterprises owned by Senegalese nationals, as part of the program to promote Senegalese participation in the private business sector. The first of these guarantee funds was established at the end of 1970 as part of the Industrial Promotion Fund (Société Nationale d'Etudes et de Promotion Industrielle—SONEPI). Another was created in August 1971 as an autonomous semipublic entity, the Guarantee and Assistance Fund for Commerce (Société Nationale de Garantie et d'Assistance au Commerce—SONAGA).

The main source of medium- and long-term credit in the country is the BNDS, which was created in 1964 by the merger of two previous banks. Its purpose is to provide financing and technical assistance for projects conducive to economic and social development. Through 1970 it extended credit to industry as well as for agriculture and housing construction. After October 1970, however, the USB commercial bank took over much of the financing for projects in industry and commercial construction, and BNDS credits have gone largely for agriculture and housing. The BNDS also provides short-term crop financing, and after mid-1970 its share of groundnut crop financing increased to 80 percent. The bank's medium- and long-term lending bogged down after 1968, when a high proportion of its loans outstanding consisted of bad debts. In 1969 the government began a reorganization of the bank's affairs which was still under way in 1973.

CHAPTER 14

AGRICULTURE, FISHING, AND INDUSTRY

In 1970 the rural sector of the economy, including crop production, stockraising, fishing, and forestry, was thought to provide the livelihood for about 77 percent of the population. Roughly 66 percent were dependent upon cultivation alone, and another 8 percent upon the combination of cultivation and stockraising. Only about 2 percent were wholly dependent upon herding for their livelihood, and about 1 percent upon full-time fishing. Some 170,000 farm families were engaged in the production of groundnuts (peanuts) for export, usually in combination with subsistence production of drought-resistant sorghum and millet.

Cultivating methods were among the most advanced in West Africa but, because of poor soils and low and erratic rainfall through most of the northern and central portions of the country, average yields were low. Population pressure in the longest settled rural areas in the west meant that many cultivating families did not have enough land to ensure subsistence. Earnings from rural sector activities furnished only 33 percent of gross domestic product (GDP) in the crop year 1970. Another 21.6 percent derived from industry, of which the groundnut-crushing edible oil mills accounted for an important share. In 1972, for the first time, gross turnover from the traditional and industrial fishing fleets exceeded gross turnover in agriculture.

The industrial sector, heavily dependent upon processing of agricultural crops, suffered from the recurrent full or partial crop failures of the late 1960s, just as it was surmounting the difficult process of readjustment after loss at independence of its markets in the former federation of French West Africa (see ch. 2). The crucial groundnut export sector was hard hit in this period by the increasingly severe droughts that came every other year, by loss of its price protection on the French market, and by government policy on cooperatives, marketing, and producer prices—which contributed to the mounting peasant malaise and groundnut production crisis of the late 1960s.

In 1970 and 1971 the government accordingly undertook an energetic program to restore peasant confidence by reforming its crop price and marketing structure, and in the 1971/72 season there was a strong revival of groundnut production. Concurrently, the authorities were drawing up their Fourth Four-Year Plan for Economic and Social Development (1973-77), which was to coordinate heavy new investments and foreign aid projects designed to increase productivity in

265

existing crops; relieve population pressure by organized settlement of new lands; and diversify crop production to improve food supply, to reduce heavy food imports, and to alleviate the disadvantages of heavy dependence on groundnut oil exports. By mid-1973, however, a new and serious crisis for agriculture had come with the disastrous consequences of the 1972 drought.

MAJOR PROBLEMS OF THE 1960s AND EARLY 1970s

Regional Population Pressure and Land Use Patterns

In the late 1960s less than 15 percent of the country's total land area was thought to be under cultivation. The area cultivated had been extended by about 40 percent between 1960 and 1967. Assessment of the amount of potentially arable land was uncertain, but in the early 1960s one source placed it at nearly 30 percent of total land area. Most of the cultivated land was in the overpopulated Groundnut Basin of the west where, on only one-seventh of the country's surface, 60 percent of the population lived and farmed (see fig. 9). Growing population pressure on the land in large portions of this region had resulted in badly depleted soils and in declining yields.

The Groundnut Basin (or Groundnut Triangle) extends from between Saint-Louis and Louga in the north to Kaolack in the south, including the regions of Thiès, Diourbel, and most of Sine-Saloum. The northern half, often known as the Old Groundnut Basin, is densely populated and relatively arid. In an average year it receives less than twenty-six inches of rainfall; and in the drought years 1966, 1968, 1970, and 1972 it suffered badly (see ch. 3). The southern half, and particularly its southeastern portion, is less densely settled, has better soils, and averages between thirty-six and sixty inches of rainfall a year. Plans for resettlement of excess population from the west and for the expansion and diversification of agricultural production are therefore focused on the use of less densely settled portions of southeastern Sine-Saloum, western Sénégal Oriental, and the river basins in Casamance and along the Sénégal River in the north.

Population density in the Groundnut Basin is about 230 inhabitants per cultivated square mile, compared to an average of forty-nine per cultivated square mile for the country as a whole. Given the poor condition of the soils and the methods of cultivation in use in most of the basin, 2½ acres must be cultivated to provide enough food for one person during an average year. With the techniques in use in 1973, one active adult had the capacity to cultivate three acres. Because of growing population pressure, however, the average active adult in the basin had access to only about one acre for cultivation. The result was endemic malnutrition and a death rate among children that reached nearly 20 percent in some parts of the basin.

The progressive reduction of fallow periods and exhaustion of soils

266

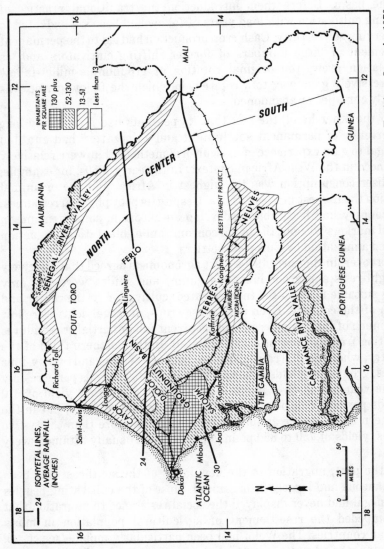

Source: Adapted from André Vanhaeverbeke, *Rémunération du Travail et Commerce Extérieur*, Louvain, 1970.

Figure 9. Senegal, Density of Settlement in Agricultural Regions, 1960s

in the older parts of the Groundnut Basin were sometimes attributed not only to population pressure but to excessive concentration on production of groundnuts for export. Groundnuts were first introduced as a cash crop by the French around 1840, so that by 1970 they had been under cultivation for more than 100 years in the northwestern portion of the basin. Before their introduction the traditional practice of shifting cultivation with long years of fallow had been well adapted to conserving soil fertility. Cash crop production had led to the permanent settlement of large numbers of former shifting cultivators and, as population grew, the original rotation of groundnuts-millet-fallow progressively gave way to a rotation in which the fallow period was greatly curtailed or abandoned.

On the other hand, the fact that its peasants had a relatively long experience of permanent settlement and cultivation had enabled Senegal to gain experience of agricultural methods that were relatively advanced in the West African context. In the early 1960s, for example, fertilizer consumption was the highest in Africa, and use of animal traction the highest in West Africa. Despite its poor physical resources, the country had been able to develop an export in some demand on world markets without the usual concomitant of plantation production or land annexation by European settlers.

Moreover, in the early 1970s most agronomists agreed that relatively drought-resistant groundnuts, sorghum, and millet were the only crops suitable for rain-fed (nonirrigated) cultivation in the center and north of the country. Even with these crops, average yields were low over much of the basin because of recurrent full or partial crop failures resulting from too low or erratic rainfall. In the northern third of the country, where annual rainfall ranges between sixteen and twenty-four inches, groundnut yields attain an average of 450 pounds per acre only in one year out of two. In the central third an average yield of 670 pounds per acre can be attained in two years out of three; but in the southern third, where annual rainfall averages more than thirty-two inches, yields of 750 to 850 pounds per acre are usually attained every year.

In the past, migration to the new lands of the southeast had been spontaneous and largely disorganized. Most of the cultivating peoples of Senegal had never displayed the social resistance to migration that has impeded the resettlement of agricultural population in many African countries. The Wolof had been particularly mobile (see ch. 4). Ever since the advent of commercial groundnut production in 1840, the farm population and land under cultivation has been expanding gradually eastward and southward. From 1840 to 1885 groundnut production and farm population had been concentrated largely in the regions surrounding the ports of Saint-Louis and Mbour. After construction of the rail line from Dakar to Saint-Louis in 1885, the entire "rail region," extending from Joal in the south to Saint-Louis in the north and considerably to the east of the railroad, became a center of rural population and groundnut production. Between 1909 and 1912 groundnut production and population followed the eastward extension of the railroad, and after 1912 Wolof members of the Muslim Muridiya brotherhood began to migrate eastward from the Groundnut Basin to settle part of the Terres Neuves (New Lands), in the eastern half of Sine-Saloum. After 1960 migration of Muridiya pioneers reached a rate of about 5,000 a year. In consequence the districts around Kaffrine and Kongheul had been almost fully settled by 1970, and soil exhaustion had become a problem. Thereafter new land was available for settlement only in the more easterly part of the Terres Neuves area and farther east.

The chief obstacle to resettlement in the early 1970s was the lack of rural feeder roads and other economic and social infrastructure in the southeast. Moreover, although social resistance to migration was much less entrenched than in most African countries, many young men were reluctant to break off family ties in the old village and to learn the new techniques and cropping practices required by the different soils and climate of the southeast. Most of the impoverished inhabitants of the northwestern Groundnut Basin lacked the food or cash resources needed to maintain them for a year until the first harvest on the new land.

For the government to provide the required roads, schools, health facilities, and farm inputs in the Terres Neuves and to assume the cost of moving families and maintaining them until the first harvest would be a very costly operation. Moreover, if the mistakes of previous spontaneous and planned resettlement were to be avoided, it was apparent that supervision and extension services would be required for a time to prevent rapid depletion of the soils. A ten-year pilot project for resettlement of 300 families in the eastern Terres Neuves region was therefore initiated in 1972 to test costs and methods for larger scale resettlement efforts in the future (see Agricultural Improvement Programs, this ch.).

Similarly, agricultural diversification programs for the river valleys and other irrigated areas were being initiated on a limited scale with a view to future extension. In areas of eastern Sine-Saloum, Casamance, and Sénégal Oriental regions, considerable progress had already been made with cotton, rice, tobacco, and maize (corn); and there were plans for increasing production of sugar, fruits, and vegetables.

Drought and Water Supply

Low and erratic rainfall has been a consistent problem over large areas of the country (see ch. 3). Beginning in the mid-1960s, however, the customary cycle of one drought year in four gave way to droughts of increasing severity every other year. Droughts in 1966 and 1968 were followed by a more severe drought in 1970, and the drought of 1972 was the worst since 1913. The effect on the water table and vegetation cover was cumulative, and it was feared that in some areas of the country it might prove permanent.

The usual rainy season extends from May through October in the south, from mid-June to mid-October in most of the central portion of the country, and from July to September in the north. This is the growing season for groundnuts and food crops. In 1972 the rains came early in June and July and, after a long period without any rain, precipitation was scant in August and September and too late in October. The effect on the 1972 harvest and on 1973 food supply was catastrophic.

The entire country suffered from the 1972 drought, even as far south as Casamance, where the rice harvest was about half that of the previous year. The 1972 growing season was particularly disastrous in the most populated two-thirds of the northern portion of the country. By May 1973 between 80 and 95 percent of the rural population of the northern and north-central areas had been hard hit by the consequences of the drought, and the exodus to the towns was alarming the authorities. Certain areas had been designated for priority relief on the basis of the percentage of crop loss. Group three, with losses between 76 and 100 percent, had highest priority. Thiès Region, with 227,225 disaster victims, and Diourbel Region, with 493,630, were in this category. The *arrondissements* (districts) listed for priority assistance were mostly located in a triangle lying between Thiès, Saint-Louis, and Linguère. Farther east, the Ferlo had become an unrecognizable desert. To the south, around Kaolack in Sine-Saloum Region, losses were estimated at between 50 and 75 percent. In Fleuve Region the Sénégal River in the north had reached a high-water mark of only sixteen feet compared to its customary thirty feet in flood season, which is the cultivating season. On the modern development projects irrigation could not be assured, and traditional cultivators of the river valley were able to plant only about 10 percent of the area usually cultivated.

The cumulative effect of six years of drought on the water table had dried up wells and streams and devastated the natural vegetation cover in the traditional grazing areas, and the herders had been forced farther and farther south or had sought refuge in the towns. The distance between watering points should not be greater than ten or twelve miles, but some livestock owners had to drive their herds hundreds of miles in search of water and grazing. Livestock losses from thirst and starvation could not yet be estimated in mid-1973, but in the department of Louga southeast of Saint-Louis, where much of the cattle herd had sought refuge, about 65 percent had already died, and considerable further losses were expected as disease spread among the starved and weakened animals.

Because only about 2 percent of its total population is thought to be wholly dependent on livestock for survival, Senegal was somewhat less hard hit in this respect than some of the other five Sahelian countries that suffered from the drought: Mauritania, Mali, Chad, Niger, and Upper Volta. Quite apart from the short-term suffering involved, however, long-term plans to reduce the need for imports of meat and dairy products and to improve the productivity of the livestock herd would obviously be set back by many years. The program for drilling new wells and establishing watering points along the traditional grazing itineraries had also received a grave setback, and massive new investment in the program would be required.

By mid-1973 short-term famine relief supplies mobilized by bilateral and international aid agencies had reached the ports of West Africa, but the onset of the rainy season in June threatened to inundate roads to the interior. Press reports were full of accusations that not enough had been done to ensure the smooth operation of the distribution program. The main lesson of the disaster, however, was said to be that it could have been avoided if cooperation between the Sahelian countries of West Africa could have been achieved ten years earlier on the vital problem of water control in the river basins.

The drainage pattern of the river basins, which determines the water table of the entire Sahelian region, cannot be effectively controlled without an active degree of cooperation among the states involved. Regulation of the flow of the Sénégal River, for example, will require, at the very least, agreement between Senegal, Mali, and Mauritania, the remaining members of the Organization for Development of the Sénégal River (Organisation pour la Mise en Valeur du Fleuve Sénégal—OMVS), which was founded in 1972 after the old Organization of Sénégal River States (Organisation des Etats Riverains du Sénégal—OERS) foundered upon Guinea's withdrawal (see ch. 15). Discussion had been under way for decades on the most suitable location for a main regulating dam and subsidiary dams and, if action had been taken in time, some commentators believe that the impact of the 1966–72 drought cycle might have been greatly reduced if not averted altogether. Among possible locations discussed for the main dam, Manantali in Mali was favored. Other possible damsites included one on the Falémé River along the eastern border between Senegal and Mali.

Even if the coming rains were abundant, it was predicted that restoration of the water table in the area might take five to eight years and that an effective program to regulate river flow and drainage in the area by means of dams might take thirty years to carry out. The short- and long-term aid efforts were being coordinated by the United Nations Food and Agriculture Organization (FAO), which had created the special Fund for Aid to the Sahelian Zone. A suitable pattern for a successful long-term water-control program was cited in the project carried out by the FAO in cooperation with the Moroccan government in the Rharb River Plain of Morocco. Initiated in 1967, the program was expected to take twenty-five or thirty years to complete, but it had already resulted in some improvement.

Senegal was mobilizing foreign aid commitments for an accelerated program of well drilling in the areas most affected by the drought and for construction of a dam on the Sénégal River Delta. By May 1973 six stationary well-drilling brigades and one mobile well-drilling brigade had been equipped. United States aid technicians were already engaged in a well-drilling program in Thiès Region. New watering points were to be connected up to the channel from Lac de Guiers Reservoir, which furnished Dakar's dwindling water supply.

An interministerial council meeting in late March 1973 announced that more than CFAF8 billion (for value of the CFA franc—see Glossary) would be required for a ten-year action program in the center and north to restore vegetation and agriculture in Diourbel Region and in the areas of Cayor and Ndiambour, all in the center and north, which had become virtually a semidesert.

For the cultivating population of the north and center, there would be no 1973/74 harvest unless the seed were put into the ground at the onset of the rainy season in June 1973. Most cultivators had been forced to consume all their seed from the previous year's harvest, and the distribution of new seed supplies to the interior was therefore one of the most urgent tasks confronting the authorities. Short-term efforts to relieve the immediate suffering of the population also included the distribution of fish to inland villages and the cancellation of debts incurred to the cooperatives for supplies during the 1972 growing season.

Government Policy and the Peasant Malaise

Producer Price Policy

Since the country's groundnut exports lost their protection on the French market in the 1960s, agricultural price support has become an exclusively domestic responsibility. It was carried out by the commodity stabilization funds, of which the most important was the Groundnut Stabilization Fund, established in 1958. Payments to the fund were intended to provide support for producer prices in years when the international price has slumped; but in practice, throughout the 1960s, the government consistently maintained the producer price well below the export price and used the resulting surpluses paid into the stabilization fund as a source of general revenue for government.

Preferential high prices on the French market were gradually reduced after 1962 and finally abolished in 1967. Thereafter, Senegal's groundnut oil had to compete on the world market against a wide range of other edible oils. The impact of declining export prices on the peasant producer was heightened when the authorities, fearing loss of government revenue, made a sharp reduction in the producer price. The low price did not offer sufficient incentive to production, and many peasants forsook groundnuts for millet and sorghum. The result was to accelerate the decline in groundnut production caused by the droughts of 1966, 1968, and 1970.

Moreover the authorities, dissatisfied with groundnut quality and

272

with the financial management of the marketing cooperatives, decided to withhold about 4 percent of the producer price in the 1967/68 and 1968/69 seasons pending investigation and reform. To make matters worse, the system paid the producers at harvesttime in promissory notes, making the cash payment only several months later, after the crop had been exported and the accounts of the marketing cooperatives verified. Most farmers were in severe need of cash by harvesttime and could not afford to wait for payment. Speculation in the promissory notes by usurers developed, and the farmers incurred burdensome debt in return for immediate cash. Substantial quantities of groundnuts, estimated at about 10 percent of the crop, were smuggled into The Gambia, to be sold for cash at the higher prices prevailing there.

The increasingly severe droughts of 1966, 1968, and 1970 also made it difficult for the peasants to repay the charges incurred for the use of farm supplies and equipment pressed upon them by the cooperatives. Because of the droughts the use of improved seed, fertilizers, and implements did not result in the improved harvest promised but only in an onerous burden of debt, contributing to peasant impoverishment and resentment against the authorities. The 1970/71 groundnut season was the worst in twenty years, and by March 1971 only about 30 percent of the peasants' debt for farm supplies had been recovered by the marketing cooperatives. Faced by a crisis of production and a crisis of confidence, the government decided in mid-1971 to forgive the remainder of the debt.

Already, in mid-1970, the government and ruling political party, faced with mounting peasant unrest, had undertaken to hear the grievances of the peasants and had come up with certain interim price reforms. Cash payment had been reintroduced in the 1969/70 season, and for the 1970/71 season the producer price was increased for the first time in several years. Special premiums were added to the basic producer price. In the subsequent 1971/72 season, prices were raised by 16 to 27 percent, and with more favorable weather there was a dramatic recovery in groundnut production. Thereafter the government undertook a commitment to support the producer price at a level that would pay the farmer to maintain a reasonable proportion of his land under groundnuts. The concurrent reorganization and reform of the cooperative system and of the government marketing agencies were designed to restore peasant confidence as well as to reduce administrative costs and improve financial efficiency.

An illustration of the cost composition of the groundnut price in a good market year under the new policy projected the 1973 price at the equivalent of CFAF50,000 per ton in the shell, at European port of entry. Of this, an estimated 24 percent would represent a surplus to go into the Groundnut Stabilization Fund. Eight percent would go for transportation to the port, 13 percent for cost of insurance and freight, 5 percent for the export tax, and 5 percent for miscellaneous expenses, including the commission of the marketing cooperative. The farmer would be left with the official gross producer price of CFAF23,000 per ton, or about 45 percent of the export price of the raw product in the shell. Actually, by 1973 the country was crushing all of its own ground-nut production (except for eating peanuts, which are only shelled). The output was then exported in processed form as oil or feed cake. A sizable share of the final export earnings thus consisted of processing earnings accruing to industry.

The official farm gate price to the producer is gross, not net, of the farmer's production costs. Thus the price of CFAF23,000 per ton in 1973 does not represent what a peasant actually receives. The cooperative first deducts from this price the cost of supplies and equipment provided to the farmer: seed, fungicide, fertilizer, implements, and services. The cost of these supplies includes a profit margin for the government. An official report published in 1970 estimated that the peasants may effectively have received a net return equivalent to only 55 to 60 percent of the official farm gate producer price.

Marketing Policy

Until independence, crops had been purchased from the farmers and marketed by private traders, although producer prices were fixed by the government. Private traders also dealt in fertilizer, seed, and farm implements. In 1960 a government decree provided for association of farmers in reorganized local marketing cooperatives and established government agencies to control the marketing of crops and farm supplies. For a few years private traders continued to operate in competition with the official cooperative-marketing agency system, but the cooperatives took over an increasingly important role, collecting 22 percent of the recorded groundnut crop in the 1960/61 season and 63 percent by the 1966/67 season. After the licenses of most of the private traders had expired and an official collection and marketing monopoly had been decreed, the cooperatives collected 98 percent of the recorded crop in the 1967/68 season. That portion of the crop that was consumed for subsistence, smuggled into The Gambia, sold surreptitiously to itinerant traditional African traders, or exchanged with nomadic herders probably did not enter into recorded crop statistics at all.

During most of the 1960s two or more government agencies participated in the marketing operation, which involved considerable over-staffing, inefficiency, and financial loss. Even before the crisis in peasant confidence of the late 1960s, economic advisers had been urging the authorities to streamline the marketing bureaucracy and procedures. In 1968 a three-year program for this purpose was launched with funds from the International Development Association and advice from an Italian consultant group. In November 1971 the former Agricultural Marketing Board was abolished and its staff and functions merged with those of the government's National Cooperation and

Development Assistance Office (Office Nationale de Coopération et d'Assistance pour le Développement—ONCAD). ONCAD thus assumed sole responsibility for collection and marketing of certain crops, including groundnuts, millet, and sorghum. The agency's personnel had been reduced and the effectiveness of its operations improved, although there remained room for further improvement. In 1969 it began to register a small surplus. Collection of crops from the farmers and distribution of farm inputs remained the function of the local cooperative. ONCAD's responsibility was collection from the cooperative and sale as exports or to the oil mills.

Its intermediate role in the collection of crops was only one of the functions of ONCAD. It was responsible for the functioning of the system of cooperatives. Along with the Agricultural Development Agency and the National Development Bank, it also had responsibility for carrying out the government's major rural development program in the Groundnut Basin. In this connection it managed the stock of improved seed and distributed seed through the cooperatives in May, to be paid for in kind out of the harvest in December. It ordered, imported, and distributed other farm supplies required by the cooperatives and their members, including farm equipment. It sustained the credit burden entailed by the delay between cash payment for the crop at farm gate and eventual reimbursement by oil mills or exports. For this purpose it received credits from the National Development Bank and from private commercial banks.

Cooperatives

The postindependence cooperatives had been preceded by the providence societies (later, mutual societies) established at the village level by the French authorities after 1910. These societies were viewed by the French as cooperatives in the village interest, and they did perform certain traditional functions of a European cooperative, such as the provision of credit for seed, fertilizer, and implements. They also protected their members from the worst excesses of village usury, although their own rates of interest were very high. They did not attempt to eliminate the foreign private middleman in crop collection and export. Moreover, they tended to be dominated by local French administrators, and their peasant members usually viewed them as simply another manifestation of colonial authority. Because this authority was often exercised through the local notables, this already privileged group was favored in the operation of the cooperatives. They also tended to perpetuate or increase social inequalities by providing credit and means of production by preference to those in the best position to achieve rapid increases in productivity.

The period 1947 through 1953 also saw the spontaneous growth of a number of purported cooperatives formed by local notables to exploit the government, on the one hand, and the peasant, on the other, for their own private gain. They often used the local political

275

party organization to obtain loans—ostensibly for productive purposes but actually primarily to "line the pockets" of the notables.

After 1960 the new government took the initiative in establishing new marketing cooperatives at the village level, which were to be restricted to three basic functions: collection of the crop, extension of credit, and distribution of farm supplies. Geared to the nationalized marketing agencies, the new system was intended to eliminate the French and Lebanese businessmen who had previously dominated the groundnut trade from the interior. The official line was that the new system would end the evils of colonial exploitation, under which the traders had kept the peasants in a perpetual condition of indebtedness.

As licenses for private traders were progressively withdrawn, membership by farmers in the local cooperative lost its theoretically voluntary character, until by 1968 they had virtually no other legitimate outlet for their production. As in most tropical African countries, the official ideology placed great stress on the precolonial village tradition of mutual aid as the democratic root of the new cooperative system, which in contrast to the cooperatives imposed by the Europeans was supposed to have a grass-roots, national character. In practice, however, it was acknowledged that the cooperative form of organization must be imposed from above by the government, and it was sometimes viewed as a means of mobilizing political support and financial revenue at the rural level.

The ideological zeal invested in the local cooperatives waned after the fall of socialist prime minister Mamadou Dia in 1962 (see ch. 2). The cooperatives began to revert to the pattern familiar in preindependence days. Toward the mid-1960s they were criticized as the vehicle of political and economic control and exploitation by the central government and party bureaucracy and the local notables. The use of the official monopoly and marketing system to skim off a sizable share of earnings from peasant production for the national treasury has been common practice in emerging nations, which have had few other sources of revenue, and is defended on ideological and development grounds. In the mid-1960s, however, critics contended that these revenues were not being used for productive purposes. Moreover, the level of bureaucratic corruption and misappropriation of funds had been denounced by the president as alarming. There were growing accusations of corruption and mismanagement within the local cooperatives and the marketing system. Even in their legitimate operation, the cooperatives, like those of the colonial period, had tended to augment social inequality by favoring the larger producers and by increasing the wealth and power of the local notables.

The crisis of the cooperative system contributed to the peasant malaise of the late 1960s (see ch. 13). Village resentment was reportedly directed primarily against the central elite rather than against the local notables, whose traditional patronage system was sometimes accepted as a form of partial return for the benefits they exacted from the peasants and from the system. Peasant disaffection resulted in an aversion to the groundnut, regarded as the vehicle of exploitation, and there was a widespread return to the cultivation of subsistence crops instead.

Reform of the cooperative system has been part of an energetic effort launched by the central government in early 1971 to eliminate the major causes of peasant unrest. Measures were introduced to give the members greater control over operations of the cooperative. An effort was initiated to teach members to read and write and to read scales so that they could not be easily victimized by the local elite acting as weighers, presidents, or other officials of the local cooperative. Fixed payments for weighers and other officials were established. In combination with the three-year program for reorganization and reform of ONCAD begun in 1968, these measures somewhat improved the effectiveness of the marketing system. Supplemented by higher producer prices and premiums and by the good crop weather of the 1971/72 season, they helped to produce the revival of groundnut production after the 1970/71 slump. By 1973 it was not yet apparent, however, whether there had been any permanent restoration of peasant confidence in the system.

CROP PRODUCTION

Food Supply

In the 1960s all the principal staple food crops were being produced almost entirely for subsistence consumption, so that the growing urban population was dependent upon imports of rice. In an average year more than 30 percent of the nation's imports consisted of foodstuffs. The price ratio between exported groundnuts and imported rice had worsened considerably after both crops lost the special protection they had enjoyed under the French colonial system in Africa and Indochina. In the 1960s it was necessary to produce 220 pounds of groundnuts to pay for eighty pounds of rice.

The chief staple food crops are millet and sorghum, followed at some distance by cassava, rice, and maize. These field crops are supplemented by kitchen garden crops of niebe beans, yams, sweet potatoes, and assorted vegetables and condiments. Truck gardening of vegetables has developed around the main towns, and sugar cultivation is being actively promoted by the government.

Drought-resistant sorghum and millet are the only rain-fed staple food crops that can be grown satisfactorily with the low and erratic rainfall and poor soil conditions over most of the country. Both have a short growing period, permitting them to mature during the short rainy season that in a good year lasts from mid-June to mid-October in the central plains and from July to September in the north. They stop growing during a dry spell and start up again after a rain. In the arid conditions that characterize most of the country, the average yield of sorghum is twice as high as that of millet. In published writings and statistics, sorghum is often considered as a variety of millet, so that it is usually impossible to differentiate between the two. Wherever sorghum and millet are reported, therefore, either or both may be meant.

The government's target for production of millet and sorghum had been 700,000 to 750,000 tons for 1973; presumably it would be deferred as a result of the 1972 drought. From 1966 to 1971 estimated annual production had fluctuated between 400,000 and 650,000 tons (see table 10). In poor crop years the government was obliged to import quantities of sorghum. Although much of it was imported under the United States Food for Peace program of emergency assistance, the rural population found it costly, providing a powerful incentive to increase subsistence production.

Millet and sorghum are grown chiefly in association or in competition with groundnuts, all three crops requiring similar soils and climate. More than 90 percent of all the land under cultivation in 1970 was thought to be devoted to these three crops. The official estimate was approximately 2.5 million acres under groundnuts and 2.5 million acres under sorghum and millet.

The two food grains are commonly said to be grown in rotation with groundnuts, although all three crops must be sown at the first rains and matured during the short rainy season. In the older and more over-crowded portion of the Groundnut Basin, the traditional rotation sequence was groundnuts followed by millet or sorghum, followed by another crop of groundnuts, followed by a long period of fallow. Pressure on available village land frequently led to elimination of the fallow period and progressive soil deterioration. Sometimes millet is intercropped in rows between the groundnuts. Where adequate land is available, as in the newer portions of the Groundnut Basin in eastern Saloum, separate fields of food grains and groundnuts are maintained.

The groundnut crisis of the late 1960s, when the peasants lost confidence in commercial production and turned increasingly to subsistence production of food grains, indicated that millet is to some extent an alternative to groundnut production, rather than a constant by-product as might be expected from a fixed pattern of rotation. Despite the evident disadvantages of excessive reliance on groundnut production and the need to increase the domestic food supply, the authorities were alarmed at the shift to subsistence production, which resulted in loss of export earnings and government revenue and an overall economic slump. After taking measures in 1970 and 1971 to revive confidence in groundnut production, they sought for the future to maintain a balanced increase in the associated production of groundnuts and food grains.

A study of settlements of Muridiya pioneers in eastern Sine-Saloum

Table 10. Senegal, Estimated Area and Output of Principal Crops, Crop Years 1966–71*

	1966/67	1967/68	1968/69	1969/70	1970/71	1971/72	1972/73 (forecast)
Food crops:							
Millet and sorghum:							
Production	423.0	654.9	450.3	634.8	411.0	601.0	322.0
Area	2,389.5	2,854.8	2,603.7	2,563.2	2,410.2	n.a.	n.a.
Cassava:							
Production	141.0	239.5	232.3	176.7	133.0	n.a.	n.a.
Area	158.1	156.2	154.4	99.3	96.6	n.a.	n.a.
Rice (paddy):							
Production	125.0	137.5	58.3	155.9	90.5	102.0	52.0
Area	217.5	250.1	159.6	253.5	217.5	n.a.	n.a.
Maize (corn):							
Production	42.0	86.5	25.3	48.8	38.7	n.a.	n.a.
Area	133.4	177.1	89.7	136.9	125.0	n.a.	n.a.
Vegetables:							
Production	35.0	41.0	41.0	40.0	40.0	n.a.	n.a.
Area	6.4	7.9	7.7	7.7	7.9	n.a.	n.a.
Cash Crops:							
Groundnuts (peanuts—unshelled):							
Production	923.0	1,005.1	830.4	789.0	583.0	920.0	489.0
Area	2,753.0	2,875.8	2,943.0	2,355.1	2,592.1	2,594.6	n.a.
Cotton (unginned):							
Production	1.2	4.1	9.8	12.0	11.6	21.2	23.3
Area	2.5	7.7	16.1	24.2	33.6	45.2	n.a.

n.a.—not available
* Area in thousands of acres; production in thousand metric tons. Crop year December through May.

Region during the 1966/67 season indicated that, in deciding on the relative effort to be devoted to cultivation of food grains and of groundnuts, the farmers were influenced partly by relative prices and partly by more traditional factors. The ratio was influenced by weather conditions as the season progressed and by the size of the family to be provided for. In both the old and new portions of the Groundnut Basin, the Wolof devoted approximately twice as much time to groundnuts as to food grains. As the input of laborsaving equipment and the amount of land under cultivation increased, the acreage devoted to millet increased more rapidly than that under groundnuts. On holdings under 3.5 acres groundnuts tended to be favored; above 3.5 acres the amount of land devoted to millet and sorghum began to exceed that for groundnuts.

In its campaign to improve domestic food supply, the government has emphasized the need to increase production of rice, the customary diet of the urban population. In 1964, however, it also launched a combined groundnut and millet productivity program, providing improved seed, fertilizer, and animal-drawn farm implements to increase yields of both food grains and groundnuts. Although it was demonstrated that yields under the program were higher than they would have been without these inputs, the increasingly severe droughts of the period tended to cancel out any improvement in the overall level of production.

During the 1966–71 period annual domestic production of rice, most of which went into susbistence consumption, averaged about 110,000 tons of paddy a year. This was equivalent to only about 30 percent of estimated national consumption requirements of 250,000 tons of white rice a year. Rice imports cost the equivalent of about US$25 million a year in foreign exchange. The target of government production programs was self-sufficiency in rice by 1977. Both swamp rice and upland rice were traditionally grown. Most swamp rice came from Casamance Region, which provided about 80 percent of national production. Casamance alone, however, did not have the potential to fill domestic consumption requirements, so that the development planners were also concerned to open up new areas of production.

Several rice productivity projects were launched during the 1960s, but results were generally disappointing. Because of low productivity, the domestic rice was considerably more costly than that imported from the Far East. An official agency, the Cereal Equalization Fund, had a monopoly of rice sales and used the profits realized from imported rice to make up the losses on sales of domestic rice.

Truck farming of vegetables for export and for the urban markets of Dakar and Thiès expanded in the 1960s. In February 1972 the minister of rural development announced that about 9,890 acres were devoted to truck farming, about 80 percent of it around Dakar in Cap Vert Region. Some 40,000 people were employed in the activity, which was thought to provide a livelihood for more than 200,000. About two crops a year were produced on the average, or a total of more than 100,000 tons of vegetables a year. This included tomatoes, onions, cabbage, lettuce, potatoes, turnips, carrots, and french beans. The industry was subject to a number of problems, of which lack of water for irrigation and encroachment of desert were perhaps the worst.

Average annual per capita consumption of vegetables was thought to be around sixty-five pounds, compared to an average of between 150 and 220 pounds in European countries. High market prices discouraged consumption by the lower income population of the towns (see ch. 6). To increase consumption, the government sought to lower urban vegetable prices by increasing productivity; improving transport; regulating prices; staggering production by mastering new techniques; and establishing permanent, more efficient sales circuits. It also aimed at reducing imports of vegetables and increasing exports of Senegalese vegetables and flowers, for both of which there was some foreign demand. In late 1971 a private firm with Dutch and American ownership had obtained financing from the Senegalese government and from the International Finance Corporation to establish a subsidiary in Senegal. The new firm was to undertake large-scale industrial development of truck farming for export in the area around Lake Takhmat in Cap Vert Region and the area around Thiès. It hoped eventually to have more than 7,000 acres under production.

Sugarcane production was to be initiated in 1975 on the Richard-Toll government agricultural estate on the Sénégal River in the north, where a rice production project had proved unsuccessful. The goal was eventually to meet the entire domestic requirement for sugar, estimated at about 60,000 tons in 1971, which was being filled by imports. The project was to be carried out by a private, foreign-owned firm on about 18,000 irrigated acres at Richard-Toll. It would also involve construction of a sugar mill, a refinery, and an alcohol distillery.

Groundnuts

In the mid-1960s Senegal ranked fifth among world producers of groundnuts for edible oil, after India, the People's Republic of China (PRC), the United States, and Nigeria. It was first among world exporters of groundnut oil. Before Senegal began crushing its entire production of the oilseed in 1973, it ranked second to Nigeria in exports of shelled groundnuts. Despite the termination of protection on the French market, most of the groundnut exports continued to go to France.

In these years groundnuts were generating about 25 percent of GDP and furnishing 70 or 80 percent of exports. In 1968 the groundnut oil mills accounted for 30 percent of the total turnover of industry. Groundnut production provided about two-thirds of the money income of the rural population. Each additional ton produced was estimated to generate an increase in GDP three times the increment in income to the producer and an increase in government revenue equivalent to 60 percent of the increment in income to the producer.

In 1970 groundnuts provided more than 40 percent of total exports and an estimated 14 percent of GDP. Despite the groundnut crisis of the late 1960s and the disastrously poor rains of 1972, the crop retained its crucial importance to the economy. Efforts at crop diversification had as yet involved only about 5 percent of the country's farmers and were confined chiefly to river valleys or the environs of the towns.

In the late 1960s some 170,000 farm families were thought to be engaged in production of groundnuts, usually in combination with subsistence food crops. Most of the farms were quite small, although the number of large-scale producers was increasing. Official statistics on acreage under cultivation represented mainly an informed guess, but about 40 percent of the total was thought to be devoted to groundnuts. An estimated 85 percent of the crop still came from the Groundnut Basin. In the 1967/68 crop year—the last so-called normal season before 1971/72—there were an estimated 1,312,000 acres under groundnuts in Sine-Saloum Region, 743,700 acres in Diourbel Region, and 389,000 in Thiès Region. The areas of most rapid expansion were the Terres Neuves of eastern Sine-Saloum and western Sénégal Oriental regions.

Cotton

By 1972 the country was filling most of the needs of its own cotton spinning mills and was able to export a share of its cotton production. There were plans to triple production in order to promote export and to meet growing domestic requirements. The country's cotton cultivation was entirely rain fed, attempts at irrigated production on the Richard-Toll estate on the Sénégal River having been abandoned as unsuccessful. Because the rainfall requirement for cotton growing (thirty-four to forty-four inches a year) was too high for most of the center and north, production in 1972 was concentrated in three departments in the south of Sine-Saloum Region near the border with The Gambia, in one department in western Sénégal Oriental Region, and in one department of Casamance Region. In the 1969/70 crop year about 10,000 acres were thought to be under cultivation. The goal was 25,000 acres by 1972/73 and extension of production into certain adjoining departments.

As in most other former French African countries, cotton production was under the guidance of the French Company for the Development of Textile Fibers (Compagnie Française pour le Développement des Fibres Textiles—CFDT), a company of mixed government and private ownership that had had notable success in promoting advanced cultivation methods to increase production. The cotton program was largely financed by official French foreign aid funds. The price to the producer was fixed by the government, and CFDT received around 2 percent of sales plus a portion of the surplus to be reinvested in production. Cultivation methods were generally less advanced in Sine-Saloum Region, where the program had been under way only a short time, than in Casamance and Sénégal Oriental regions, where almost all the farms were cultivated with animal traction, mineral fertilizer, and repeated use of insecticides.

LAND TENURE

Because of the country's ethnic diversity, the mosaic of differing traditional land tenure systems has remained quite complex. The confusion has been increased by the superposition of an Islamic hierarchy on traditional hierarchies in some areas and by the changes resulting from large-scale migrations to new areas, from the spread of permanent cash crop production during more than a century, and from various attempts to modify land use made during or since the colonial period. Consequently, the application of existing general descriptions of land tenure to any particular locality may be subject to challenge.

In general, the traditional structure of landrights was quite egalitarian among the Diola of Casamance but more hierarchical among most of the cultivating peoples living north of The Gambia, in accordance with the rigidly stratified nature of their traditional societies (see ch. 5). In the longest settled portions of the Groundnut Basin, the tenure systems of the Wolof and Serer have retained certain feudal characteristics resembling those of Europe in the Middle Ages. In principle, royal lineages, chiefs, and nobles have eminent domain; but the real function of chiefs is to redistribute the land by giving cultivation rights to families who do not have land. In practice, those who exercise landrights may do so more by virtue of long family occupation of the land than by the will of the ruler. In the same village some families may have the "right of the axe" or "right of the fire," deriving from the fact that they originally cleared the land; whereas others may derive their rights simply from a grant by the chief or ruler.

In principle, every freeman not belonging to one of the artisan castes or descended from a former slave family has a right to some land to cultivate, although not to sell or dispose of as he wishes. In some areas, however, the local notables appropriate all the best land surrounding the village, leaving to the ordinary peasant the more distant or inferior fields. Moreover, the status of the freeman varies from one group to another. In the traditional hierarchy of some peoples, such as the Wolof, many cultivators must pay annual tribute to a local notable for the right to cultivate. In some communities such tribute may be owed to the Islamic leader. Former slave families owe such tribute to the family of their former masters. The tribute may be exacted in the form of labor, as a portion of the crop, or in cash. Wealthy landholders often extend their control in the local community by lending land for cultivation to the landless or those without adequate holdings.

Local notables may have estates of hundreds or even thousands of acres. A study of the Wolof shows that in most villages a minority of households control a major share of the farmland. In the country as a whole more than half of the family farms are between 2½ and ten acres in size. More than 35 percent of the holdings are between ten and twenty-five acres. Nearly 60 percent of the acreage cultivated consists of medium-sized holdings, on which the cultivators rotate groundnuts and food crops, usually sorghum or millet.

Descendants of slave groups traditionally do not have landrights, but the proportion of such former slaves is relatively low among the Wolof and Serer. Moreover, the mobility of the Wolof and the relatively egalitarian social structure of the Serer have tended to erode slave status. Among the Toucouleur of the northeast, on the other hand, landless former slaves are the principal unit of production. The tenure system of the Toucouleur is somewhat more complex than those of the Wolof and Serer because, among other things, it involves distinguishing among the different varieties of arid and riverain land.

As numbers of the Wolof and Serer left the older settled portions of the Groundnut Basin for new lands to the east, they often left their traditional tenure systems behind. The Wolof pioneers in the Terres Neuves were often members of religious communities, and their rights and obligations were those of the collective brotherhood (see ch. 7). A study of Serer migration found that, in the newer, eastern portions of the Groundnut Basin, tenure systems in some settlements became more egalitarian. All the members of the new community derived their landrights exclusively from clearing and no longer owed a portion of the harvest to the noble from whom their rights in the old community had theoretically derived. The new system, however, sometimes resulted in an uneconomic scramble to clear rapidly as much land as possible, without regard to traditional conservation safeguards.

In many of the newer settlements a new inequality based on capital has developed, as large producers with the money to invest in equipment have appropriated large tracts of land by virtue of large-scale clearing operations. The new capitalists, however, are often the same individuals who enjoy status in the old feudal hierarchy. Nobles, chiefs, and marabouts may use their traditional authority to assemble a work force for clearing; and they also tend to be those with the necessary financial resources. The new large producers may also include large traders, government agents, and even war veterans whose pensions can be invested in labor or equipment.

Diola tenure practices in southern Senegal are more typical of the communal usufructuary systems most prevalent among non-Muslim groups of tropical Africa. Rights to use land are usually held by individuals, but disposal rights pertain to the group and are exercised by traditional authorities or community elders in accordance with unwritten customary law, which is in a continual state of modification.

As elsewhere in Senegal, the right to use land is customarily inherited, but the individual may not sell or otherwise dispose of the land.

This traditional principle of inalienability of tribal land, where it is still effectively enforced, protects individuals from being deprived of their land by creditors and other unscrupulous exploiters. It tends, however, to foster security and communal cohesiveness rather than ambition, acquisitiveness, or incentive to invest in improvements. It was therefore regarded by the colonial authorities and often by development planners as suitable for the traditional subsistence economy but as an impediment to efficient commercial agriculture and to rapid rural development. The colonial authorities consequently introduced regulations intended to modify the ancient systems by making possible individual or corporate ownership of farmlands and long-term leasehold of agricultural concessions. They also enacted laws permitting chiefs, in the name of their people, to confirm traditional rights over lands by written title.

In 1970 most of these procedures had been in effect for more than fifty years, but most farmland was still held under customary tenure without benefit of registered civil title. Only a small amount of farmland was held under concession by corporate entities, and most of this was operated with government participation for development or experimental purposes. There were no large plantations privately owned or leased by foreigners.

A law of June 17, 1964, gave the government eminent domain over nearly all rural land and provided that the rights to use land hitherto exercised by landowners and peasant families would henceforth legally derive from the state. The state can expropriate lands that are no longer being exploited personally by the possessor of the rights or that remain idle or insufficiently developed. It also has the general power to expropriate lands in the public interest. The law also provides that "pioneer zones" of planned resettlement (as distinct from areas of earlier spontaneous migration) are to be exploited in conformity with the provisions of the development plans and the agricultural improvement programs.

The 1964 land reform law was thus enacted with a twofold purpose: gradually to reform some of the inequities of traditional tenure systems by eliminating tribute and tenancy; and to permit the orderly evolution of planned resettlement and other development projects. In principle, it is designed to eliminate the feudal rights of domain of the chiefs or religious leaders. According to a study of Serer migrants published in May 1971, however, the law had had little real impact by that date. Its main effect had been to make landowners hesitant to grant temporary use rights to others for fear that the tenant or borrower might be able to take advantage of the new law to appropriate the land permanently. Thus at least in the short term, the law had operated to impede access to farmland by the less privileged. In certain areas of eastern Sine-Saloum Region where land was becoming scarce, loans of land were being limited to one year or were being replaced by rentals.

TRADITIONAL CULTIVATION PRACTICES

Historically, most of the cultivating groups of Senegal followed the combination of shifting cultivation and slash-and-burn agriculture most common in the forest and savanna woodland areas of Africa. Land fertility was preserved by long years of fallow, a feature of shifting cultivation, and by the burning of the soil and the incorporation of wood ash attendant upon clearing by the slash-and-burn technique. Only the Serer people combined stockraising with cultivation and used animal manure on their plots. Although the range of crops was limited by the poor soils and arid climate through most of the country, mixed cropping was the usual practice. These practices were severely modified, however, by the early introduction of groundnut production for export toward the middle of the last century, resulting in the prevalence of single-cropping, the progressive reduction of fallow, and the increasing exhaustion of the soils.

The principal cultivating groups have been the Wolof and Serer (see ch. 4). The Diola farmed in the Casamance River valley of the south, and the Toucouleur in the Sénégal River valley of the northeast. The numerically preponderant Wolof and Serer dominated rain-fed cultivation in the plains, moving gradually eastward from the western Groundnut Basin. The Serer have a long history of cultivation in the regions of Thiès and Sine-Saloum to the south of Dakar, and since independence they have been settling new lands in the eastern portion of Sine-Saloum. In the middle of the nineteenth century the Wolof were concentrated in the northwestern portion of the Groundnut Basin, but they have since migrated in sizable numbers to the eastern and southern areas of the Saloum River basin and to Casamance Region in the South.

The Serer are particularly noted for their economic skill and minute knowledge of the local soils and vegetation. They plant several different varieties of millet or the still more drought-resistant sorghum, in accordance with the requirements and potential of the soil of a given field. Livestock are kept and are turned out to manure one plot or another at specified intervals in the rudimentary rotation of crop and fallow. Even before the introduction of groundnuts as a permanent crop, the Serer practiced both permanent cultivation and the traditional system of bush fallow, in which new fields are cleared in rotation within a given radius of a permanently settled village. The permanent plots are renewed by means of animal manure rather than by fallow.

In the traditional system the permanent plots around the village are usually devoted primarily to quick-ripening varieties of millet. Although cultivated by individual families, they present the appearance of one common millet field, punctuated by plots of cassava or cotton or by the kitchen garden plots of vegetables and condiments. The more distant fields on the outer perimeter are arranged in a checkerboard fashion and are traditionally devoted to late-ripening millet, to groundnuts, and to fallow plots where the livestock are grazed. The Serer systematically organized reserve supplies of millet to tide the village over the period of food scarcity before the harvest. The commercial system introduced by the colonial authorities, with its emphasis on increasing groundnut production, often disrupted this self-reliant traditional food supply system of the Serer villages.

Some observers have recognized an optimum threshold of population density, beyond which the traditional Serer system apparently cannot be maintained intact. When the pressure on the adjacent land becomes too great, not enough land can be kept in fallow to maintain the livestock. The cultivators affected will stop keeping livestock and reduce the length of fallow, and the ecological balance of the system will be disrupted.

Traditional Wolof practices were less carefully adapted to an optimum population balance and had a higher land requirement. During the nineteenth century the Wolof had abundant resources of unused land in proportion to their numbers. Certain other peoples who inhabited areas of low population density practiced highly extensive land use methods similar to those of the Wolof. These included the peoples of eastern Senegal and such of the Manding and Peul peoples as practiced cultivation in Fouladou or Upper Casamance. The Wolof generally followed the classic African system of shifting cultivation; but each group had landrights to its own permanent territory, within which it would move on to clear new fields when the old had been exhausted, returning only after long years of fallow had restored vegetation and soil fertility. The Wolof also practiced slash-and-burn clearing, relying on burning and on fallow to preserve the soils. They did not rotate crops to the same extent as the Serer and did not raise livestock and use manure on their fields. Because of their extensive methods, their productivity was even more strongly dependent on length of fallow and on an abundant supply of new or restored land than was that of the Serer. There is thus a two-way cause-and-effect relationship between the land use methods of the Wolof and their high mobility, as they have fanned out far to the south and east of their early nineteenth-century homeland (see ch. 4).

The traditional methods of the river valley cultivators are more complex than those of dryland cultivating peoples, such as the Wolof and Serer. Planting and cultivation must be timed to take optimum advantage of the flooding seasons of the rivers. The Diola of Casamance Region have long practiced the most highly perfected traditional system of rice cultivation in tropical Africa. They grow rice both under river flood irrigation and by the dryland slash-and-burn method. Two different types of rice are used for these two different methods, but each has a number of subvarieties. The Diola keep livestock in the village stockade and manure their irrigated paddies and the nursery seedbeds near the village from which the rice seedlings are transplanted to the more distant paddy fields. They practice an intricate system of irrigation, using dikes with hollowed logs at strategic points to permit drainage of the saline residue. By the use of nursery seedbeds, manure, and tilling, the Diola are able to maintain permanent ricefields that have been producing uninterruptedly for centuries.

The traditional methods of the Toucouleur in the Sénégal River valley of the northeast are much less intensive. Because the population density of the region was once relatively low, the people have retained attitudes appropriate to extensive cultivation systems, despite the growing population pressure that has developed in recent years. Many of these people have one village near the river where they cultivate during the dry season, leaving at the end of June for another village in the dunes, where land is more plentiful but of very poor quality and where they practice rain-fed cultivation. Despite the practice of two growing seasons and the advantage of the river floods, however, the people have not perfected an effective farming system and have been among the poorest of the country's peoples (see ch. 4).

Many of the Toucouleur have adopted the Peul practice of keeping livestock in an enclosed paddock, but they do not make effective use of manure on their fields. Similarly, they practice slash-and-burn clearing but do not make the most effective use of ash on their soils. The river valley Toucouleur divide their land into two main classes: *dieri* (rain-fed land), on which slash-and-burn cultivation is practiced, and *oualo* (river-flooded land). The flooded land, which is cultivated during the dry season, is the most desirable and the most scarce. It is further classified into subgroups according to its proximity to the river and how often and how regularly it is flooded in consequence. Those fields richest in alluvial sediment are most in demand; some of them may be used for the cultivation of vegetables. Another class consists of clay basins of varying depth within reach of the river floods, which are also considered fairly desirable. A class of land intermediate between *dieri* and *oualo* is reached only when the river is in exceptionally strong flood. It is also cultivated during the dry season, but its yield tends to decline after a year or two.

AGRICULTURAL IMPROVEMENT PROGRAMS

Since independence the government has continued, on a revised and accelerated basis, the efforts initiated by the French authorities to attain increased productivity in agriculture by more widespread dissemination and higher average input of such improvements as better seed, fungicides, fertilizer, and animal traction. With a history of more than 150 years of commercial cultivation in some areas, the farm population had a head start in familiarity with the concept of such inputs. Where the effects of permanent cultivation had been complicated by overcrowding, however, improved methods without adequate soil conservation safeguards had not always resulted in improved yields.

Use of animal traction for farm implements is the most widespread in West Africa. One reason for this success is that light donkey-drawn equipment appropriate for African soils has generally been used. Elsewhere in West Africa, use of European-style equipment has often been attempted; and, although lighter than American-style equipment, it has still proved to be too heavy for local conditions. In some areas of Senegal somewhat heavier ox-drawn equipment has been introduced, but it too is especially designed for Africa and is lighter than the usual European product. The mechanized equipment is generally not used for basic cultivation. The most popular light animal-drawn implements are seeders and weeders. In 1972 it was estimated that 73 percent of all farms in the Groundnut Basin owned animal-drawn seeders, and 60 percent had weeders.

A continuing research program was under way for the development of improved, higher yield seed varieties appropriate to local conditions. In 1972 high-yield varieties of sorghum and millet that would be accepted by the peasants were not yet available for distribution. The quality of the groundnut seed in use had deteriorated during the late 1960s. The government's seed multiplication program for groundnuts was concentrating on increasing stocks of five new varieties adjusted to the length of the average rainy season in different areas of the country, ranging from one that matures in three months (to be distributed in the north) to one with a four-month growing period for Casamance Region in the south.

Like the other improved inputs, seed is distributed by the government marketing agency ONCAD through the local cooperatives. In 1970 the system was still somewhat costly and inefficient, and there was a need for reorganization and for improved seed storage facilities. For each 100 pounds of seed received, the farmer is obliged to reimburse 125 pounds in kind at the time of the harvest. He also retains some seed out of the harvest for his own use. In time of drought and famine, as in 1973 in the Sahel, the farm families were obliged to eat their store of seed, and the following year's crop was expected to suffer.

Agricultural improvement projects under way in 1973 included the Groundnut-Millet Productivity Project, the Terres Neuves Resettlement Pilot Project, the Casamance Agricultural Development Project, the Casamance Rice Projects, the Delta Rice Project, the Cotton Project, the Sine-Saloum Project, and the Louga-Kebemer Agricultural Development Project. Most of these programs were being carried out in the river valleys, but the Terres Neuves resettlement effort was in the western portion of Sénégal Oriental Region, and the Groundnut-Millet Productivity Project was dispersed over much of the Groundnut Basin (see fig. 10).

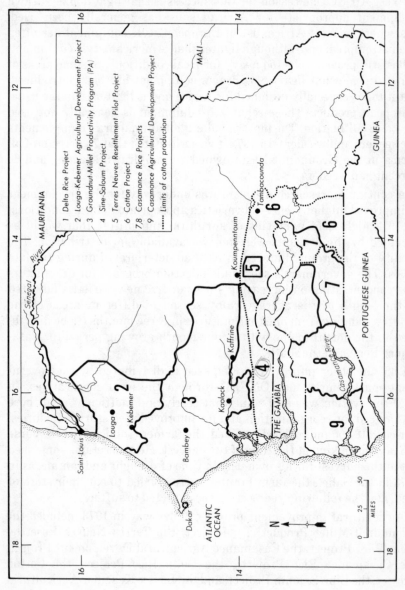

Figure 10. Senegal, Location of Agricultural Development Projects, 1973

The Groundnut-Millet Productivity Project was known simply as the Agricultural Program (Programme Agricole—PA). It was initiated in the early 1960s and, by 1972, had involved more than 80 percent of the country's farmers through the comprehensive government cooperative and marketing system. By distributing improved inputs it hoped to increase average yields, but it was also designed to increase the acreage under cultivation for both groundnuts and food grains. Besides supplying fertilizer, seed, and equipment on credit, it provided extension services and instructions in their use. Besides problems of bureaucratic organization and high operating costs, the program encountered setbacks resulting from drought and from the inadequate producer price policy pursued by the government. It was necessary to cancel debts incurred for supplies under the program in 1971 and again in 1972. Moreover, the utility of fertilizer under conditions prevailing in the Groundnut Basin had not yet been established. Most farmers were not sufficiently convinced by their experience to date to be committed to its consistent use, and fertilizer input fluctuated greatly from one crop year to the next.

In 1969 assistance was obtained from the World Bank Group (see Glossary) for the PA operation, and Senegal applied for renewed assistance in 1972 for a second phase of the program to extend through the 1975/76 season. Because of the setbacks from drought, the first phase of the project could not be considered successful. As the country's third largest source of foreign aid, the World Bank Group had been involved in eleven operations by 1972. Among them were the Casamance Rice Project and the Terres Neuves Resettlement Pilot Project, initiated in 1972, and the Sénégal River Polders Project, begun in 1973. All three were designed to develop new crops and open up new agricultural regions.

The Terres Neuves Resettlement Pilot Project was initiated as a program to develop methods and experience for more large-scale resettlement in the future. Over a period of three years beginning in 1972, it was to resettle some 300 families from the overpopulated area of the Groundnut Basin in the project area of Sénégal Oriental Region. It would also provide extension and credit services to some 240 families already in the project area. The project as a whole was designed to last for ten years. It would involve construction of feeder roads, storage facilities, and wells and would establish a central equipment pool for use of project farmers. A crop rotation pattern was planned to include food grains, groundnuts, and cotton.

The Sénégal River Polders Project, for the 1973–76 period, was to construct a new irrigation system at Dagana and improve existing irrigation systems at Debi and Lampsar, to expand the acreage under irrigated rice cultivation, and to develop a new method of double-cropping for irrigated rice and vegetables. On completion, the project was expected to involve some 10,000 people from a particularly poor

291

stratum of the population, whose per capita incomes could be doubled. It would also permit a saving in import costs equivalent to about US$1.2 million a year for rice and tomato paste.

Another project designed to help achieve the government's goal of self-sufficiency in rice by the end of the 1970s was the Casamance Rice Project. It called for construction of irrigation and drainage facilities for 5,000 acres of swampland and clearing of another 23,000 acres of nonirrigated land for rain-fed cultivation of upland rice and groundnuts by 5,000 farm families. Some twenty-four rice mills and appropriate storage facilities also were to be constructed. Participating farmers would be instructed in improved cultivation of upland rice, which was less commonly grown in Casamance Region than the traditional swamp rice. The upland rice would be rotated or grown in association with subsistence food crops and groundnuts. The project was expected to result in a net foreign exchange saving equivalent to US$1.7 million as a result of increased export of groundnuts and reduced imports of rice.

LIVESTOCK

Such limited progress as had been achieved in the livestock sector during the 1960s was wiped out by the disastrous drought of 1972 in the northern and north-central parts of the country, which by mid-1973 had resulted in drying up of streams and wells, permanent degradation of grazing, and virtual decimation of the cattle population, estimated at about 2.7 million head in 1972. During the preceding five years, nomadic or semisedentary herders had been obliged to move farther and farther south in search of grazing for their herds, and many were obliged to enter areas infested with tsetse fly or other disease vectors.

In May 1973, toward the end of the dry season, it was reported that much of the cattle herd had forsaken the more traditional grazing areas of the north for the region somewhat to the southeast of Saint-Louis. In this area, in the department of Louga alone, 65 percent of the cattle had died, chiefly from trypanosomiasis or other diseases worsened by their starved and weakened condition. Even after the first rains came at the end of June, more livestock were expected to succumb from overeating and overdrinking or from brackish water or disease. It was thought that the livelihood of most herders would be permanently affected by the consequences of the drought.

In the mid-1960s two-thirds of the cattle, sheep, and goats, four-fifths of the horses and donkeys, and all of the small number of camels had been concentrated in the northern third of the country, mainly toward the west and along the Sénégal River valley. Tsetse fly and other disease vectors were most prevalent in the far south, along the Casamance River, where the larger domestic animals were consequently more scarce. By 1972, however, veterinary action in Casamance

Region made it possible to use ox-drawn equipment on the government-sponsored rice project there.

In the country as a whole, one official source estimated that only about 2 percent of the population had derived its livelihood entirely from livestock. Another 8 percent lived from livestock and cultivation combined. The Peul in the north and center of the country were the only people who specialized in herding (see ch. 4). Many of them have become sedentary or semisedentary, but about a fifth were thought to be still nomadic. The nomadic Peul have traditionally moved with their herds through the arid and semiarid areas of the Fouta Toro, the Ferlo, and Sénégal Oriental Region during the brief rainy season, retreating in search of more favorable localities or congregating around the few good wells in the area during the long dry season. They also have traditional grazing areas in Djolof and Saloum. In 1973 the Ferlo area, devastated by sandstorms, had become a desert; and many of the nomadic herders, deprived of their livestock, had sought refuge in the towns. Numbers of the Wolof and Serer peoples, who kept livestock in conjunction with their cultivation of groundnuts and millet, suffered the consequences of the drought. The northern Toucouleur were also herders as well as cultivators.

Even before the drought of 1966 to 1972, livestock productivity had been low. Scarcity of water and grazing was only part of the problem. Parasitic diseases were also a major factor, as was the disinclination of traditional herders to part with their stock. Around 1970 it was estimated that the rate of takeoff for sale or slaughter was only 8 percent for cattle and 25 percent for sheep and goats. The country consequently relied heavily on imports of live animals and meat to cover about one-fourth of aggregate beef consumption and as much as one-half of lamb, mutton, and goat meat consumption. Between 1965 and 1967 there was an appreciable increase in the national herd owing to the success of the government's antirinderpest campaign. Between 1968 and 1971, however, the mortality rate was on the increase as a result of drought.

Several government projects for livestock development were under way in 1972. Emphasis under the second and third development plans had been on improving veterinary control and on establishing watering points. A model ranch had been established at Doli, and a dairy complex entered operation at Saint-Louis in 1968. Other projects in progress included the construction of two new slaughterhouses and cold storage plants and expansion of the government's livestock extension service. Presumably, livestock development plans would have to be revised as a result of the 1972 drought. In June 1973 the World Food Program (WFP) of the United Nations had dispatched a mission to prepare an integrated long-term program for six West African Sahelian countries to combat the effect of drought. Among its proposals was a project, resembling one it had previously carried out successfully in

Turkey, for restoring vegetation cover by revising customary pasture rights and eliminating the goat population, which destroys pasturage, by paying a premium for the slaughter of goats.

FISHING

With some 360 miles of coastline, as well as inland waters, the country has always taken advantage of its abundant fish resources, but since the 1950s systematic attention to the fishing sector has materially increased the catch and improved export earnings. In 1972, for the first time, total turnover from fishing, at CFAF15 billion, surpassed the level of turnover in agriculture. The agricultural harvest had been hard hit by the drought; but the gain in fishing earnings also reflected permanent strides in rationalization of both the traditional and industrial fisheries. At about 248,000 tons, fish landings in 1972 were 11 percent above the previous year, which itself had set a new high. Of the 1972 catch 197,000 tons were landed by the traditional fleet, consisting largely of dugout canoes, and 51,000 by the modern industrial fleet, which is partly foreign owned.

In 1972 sizable inroads by other foreign fishing fleets not based in Dakar depleted the fishery resources near the coast. Senegal had extended its territorial waters to twelve miles and its fishing limits to 110 miles. Only French and Spanish vessels were authorized by special agreement to fish within these limits. To protect the fishery resources for its traditional dugout fleet, Senegal had prohibited all trawling within the twelve-mile territorial limit.

Between 26,000 and 30,000 fishermen were thought to participate in the traditional shallow-water fishing on an artisanal scale, but only about 80 percent of them operated full time. The number engaged in fishing may have increased temporarily in 1972 as a result of the drought and the scarcity of food. The substantial increase in their catch was largely attributed to progress in motorization of the canoes. Between 1948 and 1968 the traditional catch had increased nearly fivefold, but the rate of increase became particularly notable after 1955, when the motorization policy was first introduced. After a few setbacks, motorization was stepped up in the early 1970s with foreign aid from Belgium and Canada. The number of canoes with motors had been reported as 1,995 in 1970 and 2,578 in 1971. In 1972 there were 3,209 canoes with motors and only 2,408 with sails. There were fourteen motorized longline cutters, which had first been introduced in 1962 but accounted for only about 1,500 tons of catch. The government's goal was complete motorization of all canoes by 1975.

Of the industrial fleet operating out of Dakar, only about thirty-three boats belonged to Senegal in 1972. Some eighty-seven were still under the French flag, and twenty-five were under other flags. Senegalese participation in trawler activity and tuna fishing was reportedly growing.

The industrial fleet in 1972 consisted of five sardine boats, ninety-two trawlers, and forty-eight tuna boats. Tuna fishing was carried out by a Senegalese mixed company with government participation and also by several private French firms. The French firms had hitherto predominated, but in 1972 two-thirds of the tuna catch was landed by the Senegalese firm, which was to acquire five new Soviet tuna boats in 1973. The tuna exports enjoyed protection and price support on the French market. In 1972 a portion of the tuna was exported directly, but the larger share was exported by local canneries to France.

Landings by the traditional fleet in 1972 attained the high target set under the third national development plan (1969/70-1972/73). About a dozen different commercial varieties are caught by the traditional shallow-water fisheries, including shrimp, crayfish, oysters, sardinella, mullet, pike, and a number of less familiar species. There were no data on the freshwater catch in 1972. In 1968 it had been estimated at about 35,000 tons, compared to a total maritime catch of 150,000 tons. National consumption of fish is quite high for a tropical country, having been variously estimated at seventy-five pounds per capita or as much as ninety pounds per capita per year. About 80 percent is consumed fresh, the remainder being dried, smoked, fermented, or salted by specialized traditional techniques. Subsistence consumption was thought to account for about 15 percent of total domestic fish consumption in 1964 and about 12 percent in 1968. The remainder was widely distributed. Despite the unsatisfactory state of roads and transport facilities, statistics indicated that fish was consumed in areas some distance from the coast or from rivers.

The catch of the industrial fleet was landed at the three newly equipped commercial wharves at Dakar; but dugout canoes were prohibited in the port at Dakar, and their catch was landed on the beaches along the coast. In the mid-1960s the dugout catch was being transported from the beaches by any available truck, bus, or taxi to the markets of the larger towns. Many of these vehicles and the roads they traveled were in poor condition, resulting in frequent breakdowns and a high rate of loss. Further losses ensued from the lack of equipment and the unsanitary conditions at the town markets. Both fresh and processed fish were sold in the town markets, and the villagers from the surrounding countryside usually came to town to get their supply of fish. Of the fresh fish consumed in Senegal, Dakar was handling an estimated 53.2 percent; Thiès, 18.5 percent; Kaolack, 16.4 percent; Diourbel, 4.5 percent; Saint-Louis, 2 percent; and Louga, 0.4 percent. The remaining 5 percent was distributed through other towns on the Louga-Touba-Thiès circuit or to markets along the Kaolack-Tambacounda-Kidira and Louga-Linguère railroads.

Under the third and fourth national development plans, the

government allocated funds to build ice depots at some of the canoe landing places and to equip the main fish markets with stands possessing adequate facilities. It also provided for central maintenance shops and warehouses for the sale of motors and spare parts at five regional fishing centers. The fishing cooperatives were to be reorganized, but the plans indicated that private enterprise would be preserved in the fishing sector, in view of its success to date.

The industrial sardine catch had also increased greatly and went to local canneries. The sardinella catch had increased most of all, but very little of it was processed, as the price for canned sardinella had declined to the point where one of the canneries had gone out of business. A law prohibited use of sardinella in the manufacture of fish meal, but there were two local plants that produced fish meal from cannery residue. About 60 percent of the trawler catch consisted of shrimp and sole, which were exported frozen to Europe, the United States, and Japan. Total exports from the industrial catch increased from 12,119 tons in 1971 to 14,800 in 1972. Exports from the traditional catch, which go chiefly to West African countries, could not be quantified. The increase in the industrial catch in 1972 was attributed to improved wharf facilities at Dakar and to the acquisition of a new air tunnel, a refrigerating sardine boat, and a refrigerating freighter.

MINING

Mineral extraction in 1973 was largely limited to phosphates, salt, and construction materials such as marble and limestone. Output from two phosphate deposits mined by foreign-owned firms had begun in 1960 and by 1971 was contributing 12 percent of export earnings, up from 7 percent in 1966. A French-owned company had suspended titanium mining in 1965 as prices and reserves declined, but another French company started in 1965 to extract attapulgite (used in oil drilling) around Pout and Nianing.

Exploration for metallic minerals and petroleum was continuing in the 1970s, but such deposits as had been found did not seem remunerative at the world prices prevailing in 1973. Traces reported included gold, copper, tin, graphite, diamonds, and columbite-tantalite (see ch. 3). An offshore petroleum deposit of about 100 million tons had been located off Casamance Region, but the quality was so poor that exploitation would be justified only if the world petroleum shortage should become acute. Offshore exploration was also under way for ilmenite.

The most promising find to date was an extensive iron ore deposit inconveniently located on the Falémé River in the southeastern corner of the country, more than 400 miles inland from Dakar. The grade of ore had not yet been established, and it was clear that commercial exploitation would require costly investments, including extension of a spur from the railroad line from Tambacounda to the border and construction of new port facilities at Mbour. Another alternative might be shipment down the Sénégal River from the river port of Kayes in Mali. The river is navigable four months of the year. A dam already planned for construction at Manatali, at some distance on the Mali side of the border, might provide the needed low-cost energy. In mid-1973 the aid fund of the European Economic Community (EEC, known as the Common Market) had financed a feasibility study by a German consultant group on possible exploitation of the Falémé deposit.

MANUFACTURING

At independence in 1960 the Dakar area represented the most advanced and most concentrated industrial complex of French-speaking Black Africa. With a limited domestic market for manufactures, its industry was strongly oriented toward export, not only to Europe but to the 20 million consumers of the integrated former federation of French West Africa. After the federation broke up, its former members established their own competing industries. Trade was broken off with Mali and reduced with Guinea and Dahomey (see ch. 2). The ensuing process of readjustment for Senegal's industry was thought to have been largely completed by 1971.

In the early 1970s the country had a relatively well-developed industrial sector. In terms of total turnover in industry, it had been overtaken by Ivory Coast; and rate of growth in total industrial output had been somewhat slowed by the groundnut crisis of the late 1960s. The authorities nonetheless continued to place much faith in industry as one of the most dynamic sectors of economic growth. They pointed out that despite its poor physical resources the country enjoyed a relatively well-developed infrastructure and abundant supply of skilled and semi-skilled labor and that its favorable location on the coast of West Africa gave it an advantage in the movement of matériel and in potential trade with other countries of the area.

To promote industrial development, the government encouraged private foreign investment and, where it was inadequate, favored the formation of mixed companies with both government and private participation. Industrial production for the domestic market was accorded strong tariff protection against import competition, which in some branches had permitted relatively high-cost production. In 1969 a semipublic agency had been established to promote greater participation by Senegalese nationals in small- and medium-scale industries by providing credit and technical assistance in leading management and accounting techniques.

Under the fourth national development plan CFAF39 billion was to be allocated for the development of industry, against CFAF24 billion under the preceding plan. This did not include the planned investment of about CFAF25 billion in a new petroleum refinery to have an annual processing capacity of about 20 million tons of crude petroleum. There were also plans for an eventual petrochemical complex to use the by-products of the refinery. The development planners were emphasizing programs for promoting the local processing of crops, livestock products, and fish. There were also plans for new, more labor-intensive industries and the production of semifinished products. In introducing the fourth plan government spokesmen expressed disappointment over the progress of import substitution industries for the domestic consumer market.

Industry was heavily concentrated around Dakar. About 80 percent of the permanent employees, value added, and total turnover of industry was attributed to the Cap Vert Region in 1969 and 1971. In terms of turnover alone, another 8 percent came from Sine-Saloum Region, mostly from oil pressing, and 6 percent from Thiès Region, mostly from phosphate mining. Casamance Region accounted for only 3.4 percent, Diourbel Region for 1.8 percent, Fleuve Region for 1.4 percent, and Sénégal Oriental Region for 0.9 percent. To diversify employment opportunities, the authorities were seeking to promote the establishment of small enterprises in urban centers other than Dakar. Because of the commanding position enjoyed by the seaport, however, such enterprises had been largely limited to local processing facilities, often with government participation.

In the second half of the 1960s the domestic market for manufactured consumer goods suffered from the decline in cash income of the rural population as a result of the recurrent droughts and poor groundnut prices. The fluctuations in groundnut output from one year to the next also had a more direct impact on the rate of growth in industry. Processing activity begins where the farm year ends, with the crushing of the groundnut harvest at the edible oil mills, which account for more than 30 percent of the total turnover of the industrial sector. During the 1960s and early 1970s the odd-numbered years, which saw such poor results in agriculture, were also the years of low or negative growth in industry; 1963, 1965, 1967, 1969, and 1971 all registered a sharp slowdown from the good growth rates of the intervening even-numbered years, and it was generally predicted that 1973 would bring another setback for industry. The influence of the groundnut harvest on these year-to-year fluctuations is illustrated by the industrial production index in 1971, which showed a gain of 0.7 percent including the edible oil mills and a gain of 10.9 percent if the oil mills are excluded.

Assessments of the overall vigor of growth in the industrial sector have consequently been various and sometimes conflicting, depending largely on the years selected for comparison. The official index of industrial production, including phosphate mining and output of electric energy, shows 1959 as the base year. On this basis the adjusted average annual rate of growth, which had been 6.3 percent for the 1959-66 period, had dwindled to 4.5 percent for the 1959-71 period. According to another report, the real rate of growth in industry, at constant prices, had slowed to between 2 and 3 percent a year during the six years 1966 through 1971. The drought year 1972, however, saw a record growth rate in industry of more than 22 percent at current prices, bringing the reported average for the eight-year 1965-72 period up to about 7 percent a year.

Probably the biggest factor in the record 1972 gain had been processing of the bumper groundnut crop of the 1971/72 season, and consequently a new and serious slowdown in industry was expected in 1973 as a result of the drought and the exceptionally poor harvest of the 1972/73 season. Oil mill production had been up by 110 percent in 1972 over 1971 not only because of the harvest but because of the government's decision to process the entire export crop within the country instead of shipping a portion of the crop unprocessed. The country's five edible oil mills, which had a capacity of about 1 million tons, had processed 760,000 tons of groundnuts in 1972 and were expected to receive only about 350,000 to 380,000 tons from the poor 1973 crop. In the first quarter of 1973 the index of industrial production was 14 percent below the corresponding quarter of 1972.

The food and beverage branch was heavily predominant in the industrial sector, not only in permanent wage employment but in value added, which represents its contribution to GDP (see table 11). In the mid-1960s about 72 percent of the turnover in the food and beverage branch was accounted for, in a good crop year, by the edible oil mills. The largest of the five oil mills, a subsidiary of a major French company, Huiles Lesieur, had an annual crushing capacity of 400,000 tons of unshelled nuts and a turnover of CFAF9 billion in 1970. The food and beverage industry also included the production of beer, soft drinks, sugar and biscuits, and canned fish and tomato paste (see table 12). Beer, soft drink, and flour production had all suffered from the closing of outlets in neighboring countries that developed their own production capacity after independence. The brewing industry had also suffered from the loss of the French military establishment in Senegal. The fish canning industry depended mainly upon export markets. Despite the record catch of 1972, cannery earnings had declined because a portion of the tuna catch was exported directly from the freezer ships. Tomato-paste canning was promoted by the government in a move to replace imports, but the Senegalese product was considerably higher priced than the imported product.

Textiles were the second most important branch of manufacturing, after foods and beverages. The textile industry was dominated by three foreign-owned firms and enjoyed a high level of protection against imports. Its production capacity expanded considerably between 1966 and 1973 with the establishment of a number of new enterprises. By 1972 it included capacity for spinning, weaving, dyeing, and printing and production of ready-to-wear clothing and household linens. Production of cotton yarn gained steadily during the late 1960s, but output

Table 11. Senegal, Structure of Industry, 1969

Category	Number of Enterprises	Number of Permanent Employees	Value[1]		
			Total Sales	Value Added (GDP)	Exports
Mining.....................	11	1,344	4,200	1,866	3,514
Food and beverages	62	6,574	34,256	9,080	21,218
Textile manufactures.........	12	3,214	6,931	3,528	2,157
Footwear, clothing, and household textiles..........	5	1,688	2,225	840	930
Wood products..............	14	810	988	429	75
Manufactures of paper........	22	618	1,225	550	110
Chemicals and related products (soap, paint, and other)....................	23	1,295	7,480	2,047	1,073
Construction materials	7	598	1,444	675	239
Mechanical products and repair....................	20	1,562	3,355	1,003	330
Electric power and water supply...................	2	2,369	4,390	3,000	0[4]
TOTAL (1969)	178[2,3]	20,072	66,494	23,018	...[5]
TOTAL (1968)	151	16,500	61,471	21,061	...[5]

[1]In million CFA francs. For value of the CFA franc—see Glossary.
[2]Of the 230 enterprises that received questionnaires, 178 responded.
[3]70 of these enterprises had been created after 1960.
[4]0 means none.
[5]--- mean not applicable.

Source: Adapted from Ediafric-Service, Memento de l'Economie Africaine, Paris, 1972.

of cotton fabrics encountered setbacks. It declined moderately in 1971 but revived strongly in 1972 as domestic demand improved and as exports were increased. In the early 1960s cotton fiber had been imported from Mali, but in the mid-1960s domestic supply had been increased and by 1972 was supplying the entire requirements of domestic spinning mills. In 1972 a plant for the manufacture of polyester-fiber textiles was established.

ELECTRIC POWER

Until 1972 a private French firm controlled the production and generation of electricity in Senegal, but in that year it was taken over by a state-owned company, Electricity of Senegal (Electricité du Sénégal—EDS), which in turn leased its installations to a mixed company, the Senegalese Company for the Distribution of Electric Energy (Société Sénégalaise de Distribution d'Energie Electrique—SENELEC). The government owned half the capital of SENELEC, and the remaining capital was to be ceded to it within a maximum period of fifteen years. The French company was to continue to provide technical and administrative personnel for the power administration.

Electricity consumption had tripled since independence, from 104

Table 12. Senegal, Industrial Production, 1966-71

	Unit	1966	1967	1968	1969	1970	1971
Lime phosphates	thousand metric tons	990.0	1,115.0	1,110.0	1,035.0	998.0	1,454.2
Aluminum phosphates	do	144.8	151.3	160.4	164.4	130.4	185.9
Salt	do	68.7	81.1	80.0	113.0	116.0	116.0
Beer	million gallons	2.2	1.9	2.1	2.4	2.8	3.0
Soft drinks	do	3.5	2.7	2.7	3.3	3.5	n.a.
Sugar (cubes)	thousand metric tons	20.4	20.4	20.7	21.2	21.6	n.a.
Tobacco products	do	1.3	1.3	1.1	1.4	1.6	n.a.
Matches	million boxes	104.8	61.6	68.7	93.7	99.3	n.a.
Groundnut (peanut) oil	thousand metric tons	185.8	179.5	221.1	158.2	177.4	117.0
Tuna (canned)	do	7.5	7.5	10.2	11.0	10.5	17.1
Shoes	million pairs	4.6	5.0	4.5	4.5	5.3	n.a.
Cotton yarn	metric tons	407.0	446.0	548.0	597.0	636.0	324.0
Cotton fabric	do	1,346.0	1,426.0	1,083.0	1,140.0	7,200.0	7,693.0
Cotton blankets	do	243.0	158.0	127.0	110.0	160.0	134.0
Soap	thousand metric tons	13.1	16.2	15.6	18.4	16.5	n.a.
Paints and varnishes	do	2.5	2.5	3.1	3.2	3.2	n.a.
Cement	do	194.5	172.4	202.3	206.9	241.2	241.0
Metal drums	thousands	27.7	36.5	32.8	52.4	61.5	n.a.
Metal cans	millions	25.1	27.2	30.5	33.7	31.7	n.a.
Pasteboard boxes	thousand metric tons	4.9	4.9	5.1	6.4	5.5	n.a.
Electric power	million kilowatt-hours	222.5	239.5	247.7	280.0	283.9	298.0

n.a.—not available.

Source: Adapted from Ediafric-Service, *Memento de l'Economie Africaine*, Paris, 1972; and Senegal, Ministère des Finances et des Affaires Economiques, Direction de la Statistique, *Bulletin Statistique et Economique Mensuel, 1972*, Nos. 7 and 8, Dakar, 1972.

million kilowatt-hours in 1959 to 298 million in 1971 (see table 13). Consumption requirements by 1980 had been projected at between 570 million and 760 million kilowatt-hours, of which 74 percent was expected to be needed for industry, 20 percent for household appliances, and 6 percent for lighting. Total installed capacity was 110 million kilowatts from 1966 through 1971, but investments programmed under the third national development plan and financed by the International Bank for Reconstruction and Development (IBRD—also knows as the World Bank) were to bring it up to 150 million kilowatts by 1974. The entire existing capacity consisted of thermal power installations.

Apart from private installations operated by industrial firms or isolated operations, the power network in 1972 was centered on two lines running from Dakar to Thiès, a thirty-kilovolt line from Thiès to Saint-Louis, and another thirty-kilovolt circuit from Thiès to Mbour, Fatick, Kaolack, Guinguinéo, Diourbel, and back to Thiès. Three regional power centers were at Diourbel, Tambacounda, and Ziguinchor, where industrial consumption had been steadily expanding. The Diourbel and Ziguinchor centers were operated by concessionary companies. In addition, there were nineteen secondary power distribution centers. Until 1967 they had been controlled by the respective municipalities concerned but were then integrated into the national system. Between 1967 and 1971 their consumption had increased by 55 percent.

Investment of about CFAF820 million in power distribution was planned for projects to be completed by 1978. Four new substations were to be constructed to increase the voltage, which in 1971 was only 6.6 kilovolts. A transformer station was also to be built in Hann, and the overhead lines in Cap Vert Region were to be replaced by sixteen miles of underground cable.

Table 13. Senegal, Energy Consumption, 1966–71

	Unit of Quantity	1966	1967	1968	1969	1970	1971
Electric power:							
Lighting..........	million kilowatt hours.	28	28	27	· 28	28	28
Air conditioning and other appliances......	........do	30	30	32	39	39	38
Low voltage.......	........do	13	14	14	17	16	15
High voltage	........do	152	168	175	196	201	217
Total..........	........do	223	240	248	280	284	298
Petroleum products:							
Gasoline..........	million gallons	25	25	26	27	28	30
Gas oil	........do	10	10	12	13	14	16
Diesel oil	thousand metric tons..	37	29	28	27	28	33
Fuel oil..........	........do	140	138	150	165	184	184

Source: Adapted from Senegal, Ministère des Finances et des Affaires Economiques, Direction de la Statistique, *Situation Economique du Sénégal, 1971,* Dakar, 1972.

CHAPTER 15

TRADE AND TRANSPORTATION

After the political bonds of the colonial period had been broken at the end of the 1950s, the 1960s witnessed a gradual loosening of the ties of Senegal's economic interdependence with France; but the country's cash economy remained heavily dependent on foreign trade and aid. During this period, the search for new forms of association with the industrial countries and with the other developing countries to replace the old colonial forms and to cushion the economic shocks of independence had been an important feature of foreign policy (see ch. 11). In mid-1973 this process of transition was just entering a new and untried phase. After two rather unsuccessful attempts to perfect a functioning West African customs union, Senegal and five other French-speaking West African countries were about to embark on a new and more ambitious West African economic community. At the same time the debate touched off by the entrance of the United Kingdom into the European Economic Community (EEC, known as the Common Market) was reaching its height, as French-speaking and English-speaking African nations sought to coordinate a common policy on the terms of their future expanded association with Western Europe. In the broader context of the United Nations Conference on Trade and Development (UNCTAD), Senegal was joining with other developing nations in pressing for new and more generalized forms of import liberalization and commodity price stabilization for their tropical exports.

The development financing and export price support that had previously been provided by France had become major objectives of foreign policy for the 1970s. France continued to provide the largest share of development aid, both on a bilateral basis and through the aid fund of the EEC; but reliance on aid from third countries and from multilateral organizations was increasing, and the prospect was that more aid would be allocated on a regional instead of a country-by-country basis. French price support for Senegal's exports of groundnut (peanut) oil was a thing of the past, and there was a vital interest in proposals in EEC or UNCTAD to end the anarchy of the world commodity market by promoting trade liberalization and compensatory price arrangements.

Throughout the 1960s and into the early 1970s the foreign trade deficit had been growing ominously as import requirements increased and export earnings fluctuated widely around a declining trend. The rate of overall economic growth and per capita income tended to fluctuate in rhythm with export earnings (see ch. 13). Aware that better groundnut oil prices could not provide the whole solution, the authorities were also seeking to improve the foreign exchange position by replacing a share of imports by domestic manufactures; by developing earnings from more dynamic activities, such as tourism, fisheries, and manufacturing; and by introducing reforms on the national and regional levels that would prepare the ground for more effective use of foreign aid.

Regarded as a sector of domestic economic activity, commerce was second only to rural activities (agriculture, forestry, and fishing), contributing 31 percent of gross domestic product (GDP) in 1970. Transport accounted for 8 percent of GDP in that year. Rail and air transport had been nationalized, but except for the marketing of groundnuts and food grains, which was done by a government agency, commercial activity was dominated largely by private French or Lebanese interests. In mid-1973 the government introduced measures to reserve a major share of domestic trade for Senegalese nationals.

Because of the excellent natural port at Dakar and because it could serve as a gateway to neighboring landlocked West African countries, the country's transportation system had been developed early and well by the French. It had helped to determine the pattern of settlement within the country and had given it a strong advantage in the development of industry and trade within the old colonial area of French West Africa. After the closing of the Suez Canal in the 1960s, Dakar benefited more than ever from its position as a hub of maritime traffic and inland trade.

FOREIGN ECONOMIC RELATIONS

Trade and aid were the two keystones of the country's relations with overseas countries. With few exploitable mineral resources and no foreign-owned farms, activity by foreign investors was limited largely to the sectors of commerce and industrial processing. The annual net inflow of foreign private direct investment since independence had been quite limited but, because many French trade and industrial firms were already well established, there was a sizable outflow of dividends and undistributed profits.

Nonmerchandise Transactions

Net movements in the principal components of the country's foreign exchange position were reflected in its balance of payments. Because transactions other than merchandise trade were not statistically recorded before 1968, long-term trends in the balance of payments with foreign countries could not be quantified. The balance of payments consistently had a deficit. The deficit derived mostly from the excess of merchandise import costs over export earnings, which was either partially offset or slightly augmented by a small surplus or deficit on services (invisible transactions). Between 1968 and 1970 the balance for these invisibles, or services, shifted from a deficit equivalent to US$12 million to a surplus of US$7 million.

The main deficit item among the invisibles was salary and investment income (dividends and undistributed profits) remitted abroad by foreign residents or by foreign-owned firms operating in the country. There was little change in the outflow on this item over the 1968–70 period. It was offset to a varying extent by invisible earnings—which consisted largely of earnings from the port of Dakar, remittances from Senegalese working abroad, and local expenditure by foreign personnel. Net earnings from tourism were small but growing.

The balance-of-payments deficit, consisting of the net balance for goods and services, is offset by net receipts from unrequited transfers (foreign grant aid or private charity) and from capital transactions. The resulting overall deficit is then covered by drawing down the country's foreign exchange reserves.

During most of the 1960s domestic interest rates were lower than those prevailing abroad, and there was therefore an outflow of saving abroad, notably to France. A portion of this entered the capital account, but unrecorded capital outflows may have entered the balance of payments as errors and omissions. Receipts from foreign loan aid made up the major share of the surplus on capital account and, along with foreign grant aid (unrequited transfers), they usually covered most or all of the heavy deficit on goods and services.

In the 1966–70 five-year period, foreign aid receipts averaged the equivalent of US$30 million a year, or about US$8.80 per capita. For the three years 1969 to 1971 alone, aid receipts averaged the equivalent of US$13.29 per capita, ranking Senegal as fourteenth among the world's aid-recipient countries. In those years annual aid receipts were equivalent to about 26 percent of the country's imports and 6.6 percent of GDP.

In the 1966–70 period about 40 percent of aid receipts came from the EEC aid fund, 30 percent from France, 13 percent from the World Bank Group (see Glossary), and 10 percent from the Federal Republic of Germany (West Germany). In addition, France provided the equivalent of US$29 million a year in technical assistance (see ch. 11). Aid from the United States, which totaled US$43 million for the entire 1953–72 period, included US$22 million of emergency deliveries under the Food for Peace program and US$7 million for Peace Corps personnel. Between 1954 and 1967 the equivalent of US$7 million had been received from the Soviet Union. Other aid receipts came from a variety of sources, ranging from Saudi Arabia to both the Republic of China (Nationalist China) and the People's Republic of China (PRC).

Because most of its foreign credits had been received at concessionary low rates of interest, the country's foreign debt burden was not excessive in relation to its ability to pay. In 1970 debt-servicing payments amounted to the equivalent of US$5.5 million, about 3.5 percent of export earnings. In 1971, however, the debt reportedly increased significantly.

Because of receipts from these other payments transactions, the growing trade deficit did not cause a serious drain on foreign exchange. During the 1966-71 six-year period the level of export earnings had fluctuated more or less in consonance with the year-to-year variations in the level of rainfall and of groundnut production (see ch. 13). Although they briefly attained a new high in 1970, on the average exports showed a generally declining trend over the period, whereas imports were increasing at an average rate of 6.5 percent a year. Delayed and unreliable statistics made it unclear exactly how the growing trade deficit was being covered; but with the exception of investment earnings, most other categories of the balance of payments were probably showing improved net earnings during the period. Revaluation of the dollar enhanced the CFA franc value of foreign exchange reserves (for value of the CFA franc—see Glossary). Unutilized foreign grant and loan aid probably also swelled official holdings.

In the first nine months of 1972 the trade deficit was substantially lower as a result of the favorable harvests of the 1971/72 season, and exports covered 82 percent of imports as compared to 57 percent in the comparable period of 1971. A sharp reversal was anticipated in 1973, however, as a result of the previous year's drought and the heavy emergency imports of food grains. In February 1973 official foreign exchange reserves were equivalent to about US$33 million, or approximately six months' imports.

Direction of Trade

Sources of Imports

In the early 1970s France had retained a very strong lead both as the main market for the country's major exports and as a source of the entire spectrum of imports (see table 14). Characteristically, Senegal imported most of its raw materials as well as its capital goods and manufactures from the industrial countries (see table 15). The heavy share of crude and intermediate materials for industry imported from France may have been attributable not only to language, currency, and established trade connections but to French ownership of many of the country's manufacturing plants, which were thus vertically integrated with supplier enterprises in France.

After France, the principal suppliers in most commodity groups were West Germany, Italy, and the Netherlands. The Maghreb countries of former French North Africa were important suppliers of crude petroleum, and the refinery at Port Gentil in Gabon probably accounted for most of the imports of petroleum products from other countries of the franc area (see Glossary). The Khmer Republic (Cambodia) and Thailand were grouped together in the statistics as major suppliers of rice; the share of Cambodia may have declined by 1970.

Table 14. Direction of Trade, Senegal, 1966-71
(in millions of U.S. dollars)

	1966	1967	1968	1969	1970	1971
Exports[1]:						
France	110.03	109.85	100.43	74.50	82.60	64.71
Other five EEC countries[2]....	11.59	4.99	14.15	13.09	17.11	9.21
West African Customs Union countries[3]................	3.97	2.56	11.26	11.84	26.12	23.54
Other franc area countries...	4.75	3.33	4.41	6.29	4.21	5.54[4]
United Kingdom............	1.62	2.20	2.22	2.50	3.05	4.40
Japan	1.87	2.45	2.30	2.04	2.16	1.17
United States	0.19	0.17	0.53	0.34	0.62	0.65
Other countries	16.33	13.27	18.04	13.03	16.02	15.76
Total exports...........	150.35	138.82	153.34	123.63	151.89	124.98
Imports:						
France	82.15	75.56	79.65	80.59	99.02	103.33
Other five EEC countries[2] ...	22.24	21.88	27.02	37.22	27.29	28.44
West African Customs Union countries[3]................	7.54	9.12	10.96	11.35	11.41	12.66
Other franc area countries...	6.57	9.90	10.22	11.08	7.45	8.24[4]
Khmer Republic (Cambodia) and Thailand............	10.97	10.00	9.52	10.96	12.08	13.14
United States	7.24	4.87	6.56	12.58	9.20	13.07
Maghreb countries[5]	6.01	6.28	5.99	5.80	6.75	3.91
Republic of China (Nationalist China)	7.13	13.07	5.71	6.43	4.50	6.18
Other countries	9.97	14.49	29.88	19.40	16.20	28.92
Total imports	159.82	165.17	185.51	195.41	193.90	217.89
Trade deficit[6]	9.47	26.35	32.17	71.78	42.01	92.91

[1] Includes reexports.
[2] European Economic Community, including Federal Republic of Germany (West Germany), Italy, the Netherlands, Belgium, and Luxembourg.
[3] Ivory Coast, Mauritania, Mali, Dahomey, Niger, and Upper Volta.
[4] The franc area appears to have been differently defined in the 1971 source.
[5] In 1966-70 includes Algeria, Morocco, Tunisia, and probably Libya; in 1971 only Algeria and Morocco.
[6] The deficit, like trade, is reported according to the customs definition rather than the balance-of-payments definition. Exports include reexports; imports include cost of insurance and freight.

Source: Adapted from Senegal, Ministère des Finances et des Affaires Economiques, Direction de la Statistique, *Bulletin Statistique et Economique Mensuel, 1972,* Nos. 7 and 8, Dakar, 1972; Senegal, Ministère des Finances et des Affaires Economiques, Direction de la Statistique, *Situation Economique du Sénégal, 1971,* Dakar, 1972; and Banque Centrale des Etats de l'Afrique de l'Ouest, *Le Commerce Extérieur du Sénégal en 1970,* Dakar, 1971.

Nationalist China, which had sponsored an important rice-growing aid project in Casamance Region, consequently ranked higher than Japan as a source of total imports, although lower than the United States. In 1973, however, it was announced that the PRC would gradually replace Nationalist China as a source of foreign aid (see ch. 11).

Principal Markets

In the first half of the 1960s France's share of total exports had

Table 15. Foreign Trade by Direction and by Principal Commodity Groups, Senegal, 1970

Imports (in percent of total)	Food, Beverages, and Tobacco	Other Consumer Goods	Capital Goods	Petroleum Products	Raw Materials	Intermediate Materials for Industry
France.	35.1	60.5	59.7	9.5	46.4	61.4
Other five EEC countries[1]	12.5	12.3	19.7	2.7	33.4	17.0
West African Monetary Union countries[2]	10.1	8.0	0.0[3]	0.6	0.0[3]	4.3
Other franc area countries	5.0	1.5	0.0[3]	39.0[4]	0.0[3]	2.4
Khmer Republic (Cambodia) and Thailand	22.3	0.2	0.0[3]	0.0[3]	0.0[3]	0.0[3]
Maghreb countries[5]	2.3	0.9	0.2	44.9	0.5	0.3
United States	1.8	3.6	13.1	0.4	6.5	1.0
Republic of China (Nationalist China)	3.0	0.1	0.1	0.0[3]	2.2	0.2
Other countries	7.9	12.9	7.2	2.9	11.0	13.4
Total	100.0	100.0	100.0	100.0	100.0	100.0

Exports (in millions of CFA francs)[7]	Shelled Groundnuts	Groundnut Oil	Groundnut Feed Cake	Phosphates	Canned Fish	Cotton Fabrics and Blankets
France.	1,670	11,534	2,982	822	1,638	n.s.s.
Netherlands.	548	489	437	699	n.s.s.	n.s.s.
Norway and Sweden	n.s.s.	n.s.s.	780	n.s.s.	n.s.s.	n.s.s.
West African Economic Community . . .	n.s.s.	152	n.s.s.	n.s.s.	n.s.s.	1,592
Japan	n.s.s.	n.s.s.	n.s.s.	512	n.s.s.	n.s.s.
Countries not separately specified[7]. . .	473	801	395	1,267	94	238
Total	2,691	12,976	4,594	3,300	1,732	1,830

n.s.s.—not separately specified in source.

[1] European Economic Community, Federal Republic of Germany (West Germany), Italy, the Netherlands, Belgium, and Luxembourg.

[2] Ivory Coast, Mauritania, Niger, Togo, and Upper Volta.

[3] 0 means none.

[4] Probably mostly from the refinery at Port Gentil, Gabon.

[5] Algeria, Morocco, Tunisia, and probably Libya.

[6] In 1970 CFAF277.7 equaled US$1.

[7] The value reported under countries not separately specified may include small exports to those countries for which n.s.s. is given.

Source: Adapted from Senegal, Ministère des Finances et des Affaires Economiques, Direction de la Statistique, *Situation Economique du Sénégal, 1971*, Dakar, 1972; and Banque Centrale des Etats de l'Afrique de l'Ouest, *Le Commerce Extérieur du Sénégal en 1970*, Dakar, 1971.

averaged around 80 percent. Principally as a result of the decline in exports of groundnut products, its share fell from 79 percent in 1967 to around 52 percent in 1971. This was partly a result of the gradual termination, between 1962 and 1967, of French price support for Senegalese groundnut oil, but more important causes were potentially temporary in nature: the recurrent drought and the crisis of peasant confidence in groundnut production in the late 1960s (see ch. 14).

The apparent concurrent increase in exports to West African customs union markets may have been partly illusory. Export data may include reexports of goods not of Senegalese origin, and there was a considerable volume of such trade through the port of Dakar. Senegal's main trading partner in the union, however, was Ivory Coast, which had its own port facilities. There was also a considerable improvement in statistical reporting of intraunion trade toward the end of the 1960s, so that a portion of the apparent increase in trade may simply reflect better statistical coverage. Nevertheless, much of the improvement was real; manufacturing firms in Senegal reported that a significant share of their increase in output in 1972 was generated by increased demand from West African markets. By 1971 Ivory Coast, Mauritania, and Mali had replaced the Netherlands at the top of the list of markets for Senegal's exports and reexports, after France.

Although with the removal of price supports conditions for entry into the French market became identical with those of the other countries of the EEC, most of Senegal's groundnut products continued to go to France. A major French cooking-oil firm owned an important share of Senegal's oil-pressing capacity. There was thought to be an expanding market in Western Europe for both cooking oil and oil cake for animal feed; but groundnuts had to compete with other oilseeds, including soybeans and those oilseeds produced in increasing volume within the EEC countries, such as sunflower seed, rapeseed, and colza.

Association with the European Economic Community

New terms of association for the African and Caribbean countries with the expanded nine-nation EEC were scheduled for discussion in a top-level meeting in Brussels at the end of July 1973. Full-scale negotiations were to begin in October 1973 and might last for more than a year. Senegal was one of the eighteen African countries associated with the EEC under the Yaoundé Convention, which had been renegotiated twice before and would expire again in 1975. In the intervening negotiations, the association was to be fundamentally revised to provide for entry of the English-speaking African and Caribbean countries. Senegal's President Léopold-Sédar Senghor had visited EEC headquarters in Brussels in March 1973 on behalf of the thirty-nine African associates and "associables," as the prospective new associate countries were called. He was strongly in favor of association for the English-speaking countries, if necessary with special and varying systems to provide for the reservations that certain associables maintained toward the existing Yaoundé association arrangements. He also urged that the EEC aid fund be enlarged in order to give the associable states assistance comparable to that which had been provided to the associates in the past.

In March 1973 the EEC Commission—an administrative body without negotiating authority—had issued for the consideration of the ministers of the nine member countries a document known as the Deniau Memorandum, proposing certain arrangements for the expanded Yaoundé association. It recalled that during the second and third phases of the Yaoundé Convention the commercial advantages of association to the African countries had progressively decreased, although this had been offset to some extent by the provision of aid funds.

Particularly since 1971, the margin of preference accorded by the EEC to its African associates had been narrowed by the accelerated liberalization of imports from nonassociated countries, particularly developing countries. The EEC had continued to accord preference to processed vegetable oils from associated countries, but it was regarded by the eighteen as insufficient. Yaoundé Convention provisions for special aid grants to compensate for the instability of associates' export earnings had been made conditional upon a drop in world prices and had not been applied. Actually, unstable export receipts had been attributable as much to fluctuations in volume as to fluctuations in price. For example, associates' exports of groundnut oil to the EEC market fell by an average of 28 percent in volume from 1965 to 1969, but the variation in price was only 10 percent.

The Deniau Memorandum therefore proposed that the new agreement should contain provisions guaranteeing incomes from exports of certain tropical products from African countries. The proposed list of products included groundnuts and groundnut oil, as well as cotton, cocoa, bananas, sugar, and copper. The measures proposed would not interfere with the liberalization of imports from nonassociated countries or with the free operation of the price mechanism but instead would directly compensate African countries for the instability of export earnings resulting from the loss of preference and price support on EEC markets. It was proposed that the EEC should extend loans to the exporting countries in poor harvest years to be repaid during good crop years. In some cases a portion of these loans might be converted into subsidies not subject to repayment. Thus, although an expanded EEC association would bring competitors such as Nigeria into the EEC market, if part or all of the Deniau proposals should be adopted, the new arrangement might help to compensate Senegal for the loss of price support and also to stabilize severe annual fluctuations in income such as characterized the late 1960s (see ch. 13).

The Deniau Memorandum also dealt with the subject of reverse preferences accorded by the associates to products from the EEC countries—perhaps the most controversial issue scheduled for discussion at the EEC negotiations in August 1973. The memorandum recalled that under the Yaoundé Convention the granting of reverse preferences had always been optional. This total autonomy in the formulation of tariff policy could be an advantage to the associates in the forthcoming Nixon Round of general international negotiations under the General Agreement on Tariffs and Trade (GATT), scheduled for September 1973 in Tokyo. The United States, for example, strongly opposed reverse preferences for EEC exports as constituting unfair competition to its own exports to Africa.

Since 1966 Senegal had extended reciprocity in the form of exemption from customs tariffs (but not import taxes) for goods from EEC countries, giving EEC suppliers a degree of preference somewhat narrower than that accorded to members of the West African customs union. President Senghor had been a leading defender of the principle of reverse preference. Some of the English-speaking associables, led by Nigeria and reportedly inspired by the United Kingdom, were strongly opposed to according these reverse preferences, which they regarded as a form of neocolonialism. There was reportedly also disagreement on the issue among the EEC countries themselves, some favoring unilateral preferences for developing country exports of tropical raw materials and manufactures. In France, which had had a long history of paternalistic state subsidy to industry, some manufacturing enterprises were still in the process of being painfully weaned from dependence on heavily protected markets at home or in the former French colonies.

Until the last moment a hard core of associates grouped around Senegal had maintained their stand in favor of reverse preferences, but in July 1973, on the eve of the opening of negotiations with the EEC, it was reported that the thirty-nine African countries had patched up their disagreements and resolved to negotiate as a single bloc, with possible elimination of reciprocal concessions for EEC goods entering Africa.

Composition of Trade

The commodity composition of merchandise trade in the 1966–71 period reflected two of the country's outstanding economic problems: excessive dependence on exports of groundnut products and excessive dependence on imports of staple foods (see table 16). With the help of development assistance, careful planning, and an enhanced degree of regional and international cooperation, the policymakers were hoping to relieve the most serious of these defects and to alter the commodity structure of foreign trade by the 1980s.

During the six-year period imports of food, beverages, and tobacco had ranged between 28 and 36 percent of total import costs. Major programs to replace food imports were focused on achieving self-sufficiency in rice and sugar during the 1970s (see ch. 14). Imports of wheat during the period had been almost as costly as sugar imports, but they were used as raw material for the flour-milling and bakery industry, which exported to the other West African countries. If yields of sorghum and millet could be improved, however, recurrent emergency imports of other food grains might be reduced. Other sizable categories of food imports during the period included dairy products, fresh fruit and vegetables, canned tomatoes and tomato paste, kola nuts (a popular stimulant), and meat and live animals for slaughter. Projects for increasing domestic production of canned tomato paste and of fresh fruits and vegetables had already been launched by 1973, but programs for improved meat and dairy production were expected to take a long time to mature.

Over the six-year period imports had increased by 36 percent, an average of 6.5 percent a year. More than half of the increase was in imports of capital goods, which rose from about 12 percent of total imports in 1966 to 21 percent in 1971 as industrial capacity and development expenditure expanded. Imports of fuels and of semifinished materials for further processing accounted for most of the rest of the rise in imports. Imports of food, beverages, and tobacco had increased by about 17 percent over the period. There was only a slight increase in imports of other consumer goods, so that their share in total imports declined from 29 percent in 1966 to 23 percent in 1971. This was partly a result of the stagnation of rural incomes, but it was also attributable to restrictive credit policies (see ch. 13). The improved structure of imports had created revenue problems for the government, as capital equipment and intermediate goods for industry were largely tax exempt or subject to lower rates of duty than consumer imports.

A further modification of import structure was anticipated as domestic manufacture of finished consumer goods expanded during the 1970s. Domestic manufacture of unprinted cotton fabric and other textiles was already replacing imports by 1972. The unit cost of petroleum imports would be reduced by 1980 if the projected new refinery were constructed (see ch. 14). The usual trend, however, is for import requirements of machinery and intermediate materials to become heavier as industrialization progresses.

Groundnut products continued to determine the level of export earnings. In a reasonably good crop year such as 1972, they accounted for more than half of the value of total exports. By 1973 the country's groundnut exports were taking place entirely in processed form, either as fats and oils or as animal feed, and a few sources therefore classified them as industrial exports. This would make industrial products more than 90 percent of total exports. In fact, however, the processing component of groundnut-oil export earnings was not very large, and much of it probably accrued to foreign-owned firms and was remitted abroad in the form of dividends, undistributed profits, or managerial salaries.

During the 1960s and early 1970s the odd-numbered years were poor

Table 16. Commodity Composition of Foreign Trade, Senegal, 1966–71
(in millions of U.S. dollars)

	1966	1967	1968	1969	1970	1971
Exports:						
Edible groundnuts	n.a.	0.11	0.04	0.25	0.46	0.20
Other groundnuts	52.22	31.38	33.28	15.67	9.89	6.43
Groundnut Oil:						
Refined	9.66	9.98	8.58	6.14	9.24	7.95
Unrefined	43.83	48.38	45.24	29.41	37.48	18.73
Groundnut feed cake	10.14	16.76	21.86	14.99	16.54	11.30
Subtotal (groundnut products)	115.85	106.61	109.00	66.46	73.61	44.61
Gum arabic	0.30	1.22	1.47	3.21	5.01	5.14
Fruit and vegetables (fresh or canned)	0.58	0.50	0.92	1.20	1.81	1.50
Fish (mostly canned)	6.24	7.14	7.68	8.67	8.03	11.20
Wheat flour and bran	3.70	1.98	2.95	3.66	3.77	1.57
Tobacco (cigarettes)	n.a.	0.04	1.04	0.75	2.11	2.39
Salt	0.10	0.28	0.20	0.74	1.63	1.31
Cement	0.09	0.17	0.40	0.41	1.26	1.28
Phosphates and phosphate fertilizer	10.98	10.88	10.96	11.76	13.21	16.17
Shoes	0.93	0.65	1.32	1.31	2.24	2.23
Textiles and textile products*	1.34	0.44	4.18	5.36	10.45	6.85
Petroleum products*	1.66	1.57	1.98	2.90	4.15	6.93
Containers and other metal products*	1.09	0.91	1.12	2.40	3.39	4.20
Electrical equipment*	0.22	0.46	0.68	0.81	1.40	0.72

Other machinery*	0.69	0.77	1.15	2.04	2.14	2.04
Transport equipment*	0.69	0.73	1.55	3.15	1.99	2.14
Other exports*	5.89	4.47	6.74	8.80	15.69	14.70
TOTAL	150.35	138.82	153.34	123.63	151.89	124.98
Imports:						
Rice	17.54	22.33	28.55	18.11	12.01	16.70
Sugar	9.70	8.76	8.09	7.94	9.39	10.85
Other food, beverages, and tobacco	30.69	28.06	29.41	39.69	32.53	40.17
Petroleum and products	8.82	8.62	10.68	11.39	10.91	13.60
Raw materials	8.64	9.29	9.14	9.74	8.29	9.32
Unprinted cotton fabric	9.32	8.91	6.48	3.49	5.04	5.57
Metals and semimanufactures	4.05	4.35	6.25	16.92	9.79	5.97
Other semimanufactures	4.47	6.87	10.27	14.00	17.94	19.23
Machinery and electrical equipment	12.93	15.50	18.74	23.64	25.03	26.70
Transport equipment	9.85	10.92	12.37	12.22	20.73	24.83
Chemicals and pharmaceuticals	9.88	10.82	14.36	10.67	11.54	11.28
Clothing, household linens, and other textile manufactures	14.38	11.18	10.85	10.04	8.92	} 33.67
Other finished manufactures	19.55	19.56	20.32	17.56	21.78	
TOTAL	159.82	165.17	185.51	195.41	193.90	217.89

n.a.—not available.

*Possibly including a large element of reexports of goods not of Senegalese origin.

Source: Adapted from Senegal, Ministère des Finances et des Affaires Economiques, Direction de la Statistique, *Bulletin Statistique et Economique Mensuel, 1972*, Nos. 7 and 8, Dakar, 1972; and Banque Centrale des Etats de l'Afrique de l'Ouest, *Le Commerce Extérieur du Sénégal en 1970*, Dakar, 1971.

crop years and years of low or negative growth in industry, so that a time-series such as 1966 through 1971 that compares an odd-numbered year with an even-numbered year may be misleading. Export data for 1972 were not yet available in mid-1973; but 1972 had been a year of strong growth in exports of finished manufactures as well as of ground-nut products. In the 1968–71 four-year period there had already been a decided increase averaging 14 percent a year in exports of finished manufactures and semimanufactures such as cotton fabrics.

At independence the country's industry had inherited a high cost structure deriving from the protection accorded to French manufac-turers located in the Dakar area and exporting to its economic hinter-land in French West Africa. Specific factors burdening the price structure included the high salaries offered to attract non-African managerial and technical personnel. After independence, and more particularly after 1968, the authorities had been quite successful in containing price increases, which in turn permitted moderation in wage increases. Between 1968 and 1971 the price and wage level had risen by only about 3 percent a year. This made it possible for domestic indus-tries such as textile and shoe manufacturing to begin competing successfully on the export market, particularly within the West African customs union. Senegal was reportedly also exporting shoes and textile products to the United States. An example of a successful enterprise to replace imports and promote exports was an agricultural equipment factory built in 1964 near Thiès. By 1973 it was exporting 40 percent of its production, principally to Mali, but also to Dahomey, The Gambia, Ivory Coast, and other African countries.

Regional Economic Cooperation

Despite repeated setbacks and disappointments, Senegal under President Senghor has continued to exercise constructive leadership in efforts to improve the effective coordination of development and other economic policies at the regional level. Besides promoting closer cooperation among the French-speaking countries of former French West Africa, President Senghor has also consistently expressed support for the eventual inclusion of both English-speaking and French-speaking countries of West Africa and even central Africa in a common regional organization (see ch. 11). He had even drawn up a draft agreement providing for the progressive economic integration of the countries on or oriented toward the Atlantic coast of Africa from Mauritania to Zaire (formerly, Congo Kinshasa).

Senegal had enjoyed a position of economic advantage in the pre-independence federation of French West Africa and suffered econom-ically from the moves toward increased self-sufficiency made by the other members after 1960. In promoting postindependence cooperation, however, the country has taken a constructive approach toward compensation arrangements designed to help the less favored West

African countries and to allay the fears of economic dependence or loss of tax revenue that have sometimes kept them from cooperating whole-heartedly in the past. This approach was also reflected in Senegal's policies during the drought-relief efforts of 1973. Government relief and emergency aid were extended to those in need without regard to nationality and included large numbers of nomadic herders who had moved south into Senegal from the even more arid regions to the north and east. Within West Africa Senegal has sought especially close cooperation with its immediate neighbors Mauritania, Mali, and The Gambia (see ch. 11).

The West African Economic Community and the West African Customs Unions

By the Bamako Treaty of June 1972, supplemented by ten annexed protocols adopted at the Abidjan conference of April 1973, six countries of French-speaking West Africa established the West African Economic Community (Communauté Economique de l'Afrique de l'Ouest—CEAO). Scheduled to enter into operation in January 1974, the CEAO represented a third stage in the previously rather unsuccessful efforts since independence to restore some measure of the economic integration that had obtained during the colonial era among the eight countries of French West Africa and the trust territory of Togo. The CEAO treaty had been carefully worked out over a period of three or four years and was designed to remedy past mistakes and to benefit by the lessons of experience derived from the largely unsuccessful West African customs unions—the Customs Union of West Africa (Union Douanière de l'Afrique Occidentale—UDAO) of the 1959-66 period and the Customs Union of West African States (Union Douanière des Etats de l'Afrique de l'Ouest—UDEAO) of the 1967-72 period. More ambitious than a mere customs union, the CEAO aimed not simply at raising the level of trade between members but at promoting balanced economic development throughout the region, fueling more rapid growth in the weaker as well as the stronger member countries.

Before independence the nine countries had formed an exceptionally well-integrated region. They had a common central bank and a common currency. They had a common external tariff (except for French goods, which were duty free), but they had no tariffs or other official trade barriers among themselves. Although promoted by the colonial authorities primarily as a market for French goods, the arrangement also provided a potential market of some 20 million consumers for developing infant industry in the member countries. The Dakar area in particular, because of its advantageous situation, had developed industrial and commercial capacity—much of it French-owned—that was based upon trade with other countries of the region. As these other countries established their own infant industry after independence, much of this capacity had been left idle for a period of years (see ch. 14).

Of the nine countries, Guinea and Togo did not become members of the UDAO or UDEAO. Guinea had embarked after independence on a policy of isolationism. When the CEAO treaty was confirmed in 1973, Togo and Dahomey opted for observer status because of their geographic position between the English-speaking countries of Ghana and Nigeria. The remaining six full members of the CEAO are Senegal, Ivory Coast, Mali, Mauritania, Niger, and Upper Volta.

Because the CEAO had not yet begun to operate in mid-1973, its architects were best able to explain its highly complex and detailed provisions in terms of what had gone wrong in practice with the functioning of the two previous attempts, the UDAO and UDEAO. An acquaintance with the most important defects of these earlier customs unions was essential to an understanding of the main plans for the CEAO.

The provisions of the UDAO convention of 1959 to 1966 had proved rather unrealistically ambitious in their attempt to achieve an immediate full customs union without providing adequate consultative machinery. The UDAO failed most notably in harmonizing policies on import taxes, which were often as important in their impact on import prices as were customs tariffs. In the 1964–66 period, for example, they ranged between 35 and 47 percent of import value in five of the seven member countries.

Like most developing countries with low per capita income, all the member countries depend heavily upon import and export taxes as a source of government revenue. The ratio of import taxes to total tax receipts between 1964 and 1966 ranged from 60 percent in Dahomey, Ivory Coast, and Upper Volta, through 40 to 45 percent in Senegal and Mali, to 33 to 34 percent in Niger and Mauritania. Although the UDAO convention prohibited any member from changing its import taxes without the consent of all the other members, it failed to establish any effective machinery or procedure for consultation, and the members in practice proceeded to change their taxes at will in accordance with their rapidly growing fiscal needs. The common external tariff and tax structure thus could not be maintained.

Because the relatively rigid provisions of the UDAO convention had not worked out in practice, the UDEAO convention of 1966 provided for a looser customs association. In realistic recognition of the trend toward independent establishment of competing infant industries in the member countries, the UDEAO convention authorized fiscal duties and other taxes on trade between member countries amounting to 50 percent of those imposed on trade from third countries outside the union. To protect an industry less competitive than its counterpart in another member country, taxes as high as 70 percent of the external rate were permitted. Goods from EEC countries and African countries associated with the EEC were subject to full rates on fiscal duties and other taxes on imports but were exempted from the common external customs tariff, which was levied on all imports from non-EEC countries. Unlike the customs union among the French-speaking countries of central Africa, the much looser UDEAO thus did not attempt to harmonize its external import levies other than customs tariffs.

Moreover, provisions to compensate for the disadvantages of the other five members relative to Ivory Coast and Senegal proved largely ineffective. These two countries have relatively well-developed industrial capacity, ports, and other transport facilities and thus profited not only from higher direct exports to the other member countries but also from the transit trade from overseas to the landlocked countries of the interior, which is far larger in volume and value than direct trade. Efforts to certify the origin of imports in order to distinguish direct trade were not entirely effective, and the most difficult problem of all was that of redistributing vital revenues from import taxes imposed at the port of entry.

Because it was found that the internal tariff reductions benefited the stronger members inequitably at the expense of others, the provisions of the treaty were increasingly disregarded in practice, and several of the member countries concluded bilateral agreements among themselves that in practice were substituted for the operation of the treaty. Thus Senegal and Mauritania, for example, had a bilateral agreement that effectively reallocated customs and import tax receipts collected at the point of entry, the machinery of the union having proved ineffective for this purpose.

The provisions of the CEAO treaty are numerous and complicated. Their effective application will require establishment of a complex regional administrative apparatus and gradual coordination not only of relevant legislation and decrees but of statistical and customs nomenclature, definitions of origin, customs procedures, and forms. The common external tariff and fiscal levies on imports will be erected gradually over a period of years. Among member countries, unprocessed commodities "for which the countries have comparable potential" will move freely (although if neither trading partner possessed any relative advantage, there would be no reason for trade to take place). Industrial goods—that is, processed commodities—moving between member countries will enjoy a tariff advantage that is not simply automatic but differentiated on a case-by-case basis as each industry is established.

These industrial exchanges among member countries will be subject to a single tax, known as the Regional Cooperation Tax (Taxe de Coopération Régionale—TCR), which will take the place of all other taxes (except for that portion equivalent to domestic taxes). Industrial enterprises will be able to submit an application presenting their case for protection against competing industries in other member countries. The application will be forwarded by the member government concerned to the CEAO Council of Ministers for individual decision on the rate of the TCR to be applied to the products of that industry.

As trade among member countries increases, there will be a loss of revenue as a result of the diversion of imports from third countries subject to higher rates. A central feature of the complex CEAO provisions is the effort to compensate for this loss of revenues that are so vital to the participating countries. This is to be done by means of the Community Development Fund, the most significant innovation of the new association. The fund has three important functions: to compensate for loss of revenue; to finance the study and preparation of development projects at the regional level; and to attempt to equalize the economic and fiscal benefits of union as among member countries. Two-thirds of the fund will be used to equalize fiscal disparities by fueling the government budgets of the member countries. The remaining one-third is intended eventually to reduce economic disparities through the financing of development feasibility studies at the regional level. In the context of current trends in world foreign aid allocation, such studies might greatly facilitate the attraction of badly needed foreign aid funds to the region.

The size of the contribution to be made to the Community Development Fund from each member country according to its ability and the redistribution of the proceeds to each according to its need will be determined annually on the basis of careful monthly calculations of the trade taking place. In the past, trade between members of the customs union had been unrecorded. Those members having the largest share of industrial exports to other members will make the largest contribution to the fund. It is expected that most of the fund will be contributed by Ivory Coast and Senegal and that only a minor share will be contributed by Mali, Upper Volta, Niger, and Mauritania— probably in that order. The monthly customs trade statistics will also permit annual calculation of the amount of tax revenue lost by each member country by importing industrial goods from other member countries instead of from third countries. This loss will be compensated for by an allocation to the member country's fiscal budget from the Community Development Fund.

Organizations of Sénégal River Basin States

Plans dating back to colonial times for relieving the crucial problem of water supply in the drainage basin of the Sénégal River have remained unrealized largely because of the failure to achieve effective cooperation among the riverain countries: Senegal, Mali, Mauritania, and Guinea. The old Organization of Sénégal River States (Organisation des Etats Riverains du Sénégal—OERS), formed in 1968, had been disrupted by mounting antagonisms between the government of Guinea and the governments of Mali and Senegal (see ch. 11). The OERS had formulated ambitious goals for industrial planning and unification of laws, but it was unable to function in practice and was finally dissolved in October 1971. The new Organization for Development of the Sénégal River (Organisation pour la Mise en Valeur du Fleuve Sénégal—OMVS) was formed in March 1972 without the participation of Guinea. Its first task was to formulate joint plans to combat the advance of the Sahara Desert into the Sahelian region. The task took on new urgency after the disastrous drought of 1972, which graphically underscored the need for more effective cooperation at the regional level (see ch. 14).

Regulation of the flow of the Sénégal River by jointly constructed dams would improve the groundwater level at considerable distance from the river valley itself. Effective control of drainage from the river would help to provide grazing and watering points for the livestock herds of the region, permit controlled irrigation for crops in the river valley, and help to arrest and eventually reverse the southward progress of the desert. It would have to be supplemented, however, by forestation projects and eventually by controlled grazing to stop the destruction of the vegetation cover by overgrazing in the vicinity of watering points.

TOURISM

The tourist industry was regarded by international consultants as one of the most promising sectors for expansion and diversification of foreign exchange earnings. The country's valuable basic assets—a pleasant, temperate climate from mid-November to mid-June, miles of beautiful unspoiled beaches, and colorful folklore—were being made more accessible by the construction of a number of new hotels and tourist villages suitable for an international clientele. The principal obstacles were the high cost of transport from distant Western Europe or North America, the limited number of hotel rooms, and relatively high domestic prices, particularly in Dakar. In 1973 the price of meals in Dakar restaurants or hotels catering to non-African tastes was often prohibitive, and the cost of living for American transients was reckoned by the United States Department of State as one of the highest in Africa.

By mid-1973 about 1,400 Senegalese were employed in the tourist sector. There were some 1,500 hotel rooms of international class, and by 1974 there were expected to be about 2,300, mostly in or near Dakar. Two large new luxury hotels had been completed in early 1973, one in Dakar and one about six miles outside the city. Both were largely owned by French interests, including Air France. Two modern holiday villages catering to the European popular mass-tourism clientele had been built, one by the large German mail-order house of Neckermann and one by the French Club Mediterranée. Among projects in the planning stage was a new tourist complex on the historic island of Gorée near Dakar, which offered excellent sport fishing. The area around Saint-Louis on the north coast and the game preserve of Niokolo

Koba National Park in southernmost Sénégal Oriental Region were also to be more fully developed as tourist attractions. In 1973 a mission of the International Bank for Reconstruction and Development (IBRD—also known as the World Bank) had returned from a visit to Senegal to study the possibilities for tourist development.

Both the press and the authorities were vigilant and concerned that the development of tourism should not entail any degradation of the dignity, independence, or moral standards of the local population in such matters as the provision of services and entertainment, begging, public nudity on beaches, or racial discrimination, as in the alleged refusal to serve Africans at the Neckermann tourist village. It was evident that, if any decline in public standards in such matters were perceived, there would be opposition from the press and an informed public to the further promotion of tourism.

DOMESTIC TRADE

In the 1960s domestic trade was still largely a subordinate branch of foreign trade, dominated by a few large foreign-owned firms that were also engaged in import and consisting largely of the distribution of imported goods and an increasing volume of domestically processed goods from Dakar to the rest of the country. Because much of the population produced most of its own food and because relatively uniform climatic conditions left only limited scope for diversification of agricultural production, there was little interregional trade except that from Dakar. The level was expected to increase somewhat with the progress of government programs for decentralization of farm production, including eventual self-sufficiency in sugar, rice, and cotton textiles.

After independence, government agencies had taken over the collection and distribution of most domestically grown staple foodstuffs, as well as imported rice (see ch. 14). The government-sponsored cooperatives and marketing agencies also imported farm supplies and implements and distributed them to the peasants. This eliminated some of the most important activity of the smaller scale French and Lebanese merchants, and many of them left the country. An important share of earnings from commerce continued, however, to accrue to foreign merchants and foreign-owned wholesale firms.

In the early 1960s the Ministry of Commerce undertook a census of the commercial sector and learned of a number of weaknesses in the structure of retail trade. There were gaps in the network after the departure of a number of foreign shopkeepers, and some of the rural areas were poorly served; yet the proliferation of small-scale shops in the towns burdened the price structure. The big cities dominated the distribution system, and the inadequacy of many roads in the interior further added to the level of retail prices.

In 1965 the government established the New Supply and Distribution

Company of Senegal (Société Nouvelle pour l'Approvisionnement et la Distribution au Sénégal—SONADIS), jointly owned by the government and two private firms. It was to improve supply to the interior by setting up a network of variety stores throughout the country and undertaking the training of Senegalese shopkeepers. By 1970 the company was operating eighty stores, and the formation of cooperatives grouping Senegalese shopkeepers was making progress.

In early 1973 the government announced a program to promote the participation of Senegalese nationals in domestic wholesale and retail trade. The minister of finance and economic affairs asserted that commercial enterprise within the country should not remain eternally in the hands of foreigners. A specific share of the domestic market in a list of goods most widely consumed would be reserved to Senegalese nationals and nationally owned firms. Of this share in turn, an only slightly narrower share would be reserved to specific Senegalese private businessmen specially selected by the government for their qualifications and dedication, starting with 100 businessmen to be established in business by April 1973. These 100 selected wholesalers were also urged by the minister to engage in retail trade. They would be provided with bank loans and supplier credits.

Heading the list of reserved products was edible groundnut oil, of which some 40,000 tons a year were consumed within the country. About 90 percent of domestic distribution would be reserved for Senegalese nationals and 70 percent for the selected wholesalers. They were to buy directly from the oil mills, eliminating the foreign intermediary. They would also be able to import directly from foreign markets such products as tea and tomato paste, which had hitherto been imported by foreign-owned firms. Among the other reserved products were flour, sugar, condensed milk, soft drinks, cigarettes, matches, soap, razor blades, domestically produced shoes, textile fabrics, and cement.

In the early 1960s two levels of local trade could be observed in the numerous village markets that were essential to the life of the rural population. In these markets, which were largely operated and patronized by women on a direct producer-to-consumer basis, two classes of goods were sold. One consisted of locally grown food products surplus to the needs of the household that grew them; the other included manufactured or lightly processed goods, such as salt, sugar, kerosine, cloth, and shoes. There was an almost total absence of farm products other than those from the immediate vicinity of the village. Only the large, well-organized markets of the urban centers were exceptions to this pattern.

TRANSPORTATION

The country has considerable importance as a crossroads of heavily traveled maritime routes and as a regional transportation axis for the movement of ocean freight and air passenger traffic. Its railroad moves more than two-thirds of the imports and one-third of the exports of neighboring landlocked Mali. The transportation system is relatively well developed, and in the late 1960s transport earnings provided an average of more than 5 percent of GDP.

In 1972 the internal transportation network included 640 miles of rail line, more than 5,600 miles of roads, and some river transport. There were seventeen airfields, handling mainly passenger traffic. Two-thirds of the country's freight traffic moved by rail, including almost all of the groundnut and phosphate production. The transport system was concentrated in the western portion of the country and focused on the port and industrial center of Dakar (see fig. 11). Most areas of the country were linked by road, although much of the road system was in poor repair. Low population density through much of the rural east had retarded costly construction of rural feeder roads needed to assist population resettlement (see ch. 14).

Most of the country's transportation infrastructure, including the rail line and the basic road network, was inherited at independence. After 1960 its extension and maintenance ranked high among the government's investment priorities, absorbing approximately 25 percent of expenditure under the first four-year development plan, 30 percent under the second plan, and 15 percent under the third plan. Under the Fourth Four-Year Plan for Economic and Social Development (1973-77), only about 18 percent of total expenditure was to be earmarked for transportation facilities, about 5 percent being destined for roads. The World Bank Group was heavily engaged in the financing of transportation projects, including a project to strengthen the railroad authority, a loan to improve the finances and administration of the Dakar Port Authority, another project to extend the capacity of the port, a highway project, and an airport project.

Although the transportation system in 1973 was relatively well developed, several important problems remained to be solved. The inadequacy of rural feeder roads was threatening to retard agricultural development and notably the expansion of the frontier of rural settlement eastward into Sénégal Oriental and eastern Casamance regions (see ch. 14). There was also a need to improve main arteries to connect these newer areas of settlement with the rest of the country and notably to evacuate their production to the port and urban market at Dakar. Proposed railroad investment would substantially improve this link.

After the poor groundnut harvest of the 1970/71 season, groundnut freight traffic amounted to only about half its potential level, yet transport capacity was just adequate to carry it. If the government's plans to increase groundnut production were realized, serious transport bottlenecks could arise. There was consequently a need to upgrade capacity and efficiency of both rail and truck transport. The truck fleet

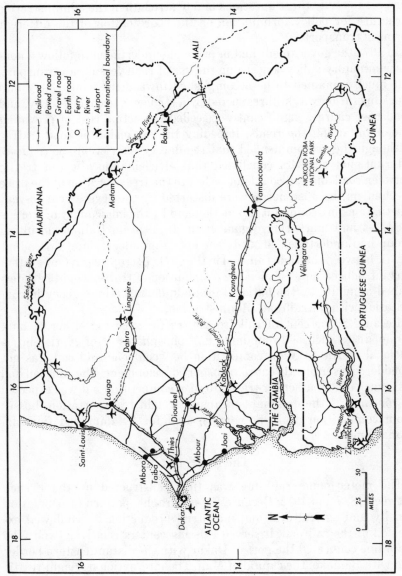

Figure 11. Transportation System, Senegal, 1972

was partly obsolete and in poor condition, and replacement as well as expansion was needed.

Substantial improvement was needed in transport coordination in such matters as pricing, restrictive regulation, and investment planning. The government had agreed to engage international consultant services to study these questions and to strengthen the administrative structure for policy formulation on the coordination of the different forms of transport.

In 1973 the government had in principle undertaken to follow a nondiscriminatory policy concerning the use of road versus rail transport, but much remained to be accomplished toward this end. Entry into truck operation was still restricted by a stringent licensing policy, and road user charges significantly exceeded the actual cost of providing and maintaining the roads, impeding the expansion of road traffic. Although they recommended that regulatory restrictions be reduced, international advisers concluded that efficient allocation of traffic between road and rail could not be left to the free operation of the price mechanism, because needs were distorted by the severe year-to-year fluctuations in groundnut production and by the inadequacy of storage facilities and marketing organization. In 1970 an Italian consulting group had undertaken to study the optimum allocation of groundnut traffic between road and rail, and in the 1971/72 crop year a new system was introduced under which the distribution of traffic would be determined annually by the national groundnut marketing agency in consultation with the railroad administration.

Because 80 percent of rail freight traffic consisted either of bulk commodities such as groundnuts and phosphates or of captive international traffic to Mali, competition between road and rail was not considered a serious threat to transport development. The railroad had lost much of its passenger traffic to road competition but was expected to continue as the dominant means of freight transportation. Losses from competition could be compensated for by improved financial management.

The Railroad

The meter-gauge rail line was first constructed by the French between 1885 and 1912. Because the geographic pattern of population density and agricultural and industrial production has followed extension of the railroad, it served existing centers relatively well. The main line connected the port of Dakar with the distant eastern border and with Bamako, the capital of Mali. The international freight traffic between the port and points in Mali and eastern Mauritania accounted for 43 percent of the railroad's freight traffic and provided more than half of its earnings in 1970. The remainder of the rail network served the western Groundnut Basin, which occupied about one-seventh of the country's land area but contained 60 percent of its population (see ch. 14). From the line from Thiès to Saint-Louis, a short spur served to evacuate phosphate production from Taiba.

Under the first four development plans expenditure on the railroad has been used for track renewal and rehabilitation, for acquisition of rolling stock, and for the improvement of rail safety and operational efficiency. Between 1966 and 1972 about 150 miles of the 400-mile main line from Dakar to the Mali border were rehabilitated. Most of the system was single track, but on the most heavily traveled stretch— from Dakar to Thiès—a second line was added to the existing forty-four-mile track to permit simultaneous two-way traffic. The fourth four-year plan included a program for renewal of another 108 miles of track. The main railroad workshops at Thiès were to be partially rebuilt, and obsolete equipment was to be replaced. Additional diesel locomotives were to be acquired and rolling stock further modernized. There was also a program for extensive training of managerial and technical personnel.

At independence 62 percent of the property and assets of the old Dakar-Niger Railways was taken over by the government-owned autonomous Public Railroad Corporation of Senegal (Régie des Chemins de Fer du Sénégal—commonly called Régie). The remainder was taken over by the Mali Railways. The Régie inherited a relatively high cost structure resulting primarily from overstaffing and a salary level higher than that prevailing in the rest of the economy. A World Bank-sponsored program to reduce personnel costs and to improve financial management had resulted in considerable improvement by 1972, but the Régie was still operating at a loss. It was expected to move into the black during the 1970s.

Roads

The road network generally gave adequate access to most parts of the country, but poor maintenance made road transport slow and unreliable, causing frequent breakdowns and delays. Of the country's 5,650 miles of roads, only 3,500 miles were maintained at all. These included the 1,400 miles of paved roads and 2,100 miles of gravel and dirt roads. The remaining 2,150 miles consisted of sometimes ill-defined and sandy tracks that could be used only seven or eight months of the year.

A survey of the country's road network determined that in 1972 it provided a sound basis for a long-term program of improvement to meet the needs of the heavier truck traffic expected to develop. Most of the paved roads were at least twenty-five years old and were not wide enough or well enough maintained to handle the current volume of traffic. Of the improved gravel and dirt roads, only about 620 miles had been adequately engineered.

Most of the hard-surfaced roads were in the more heavily populated areas of the west, in some cases paralleling the railroad. Paved roads connected Dakar with Thiès, Diourbel, Kaolack, and Saint-Louis and with Mauritania by way of the northern border area along the Sénégal River. Paving was being extended during the early 1970s from Kaolack eastward to the area of Koungheul and northward to Louga. A paved road also reached southward to Ziguinchor on the Casamance River estuary near the border with Portuguese Guinea. This road crossed The Gambia seventy-five miles inland. Transportation across The Gambia was a major problem, and there were plans for a costly bridge to replace the ferries in use in 1970.

Only a skeletal system of improved roads served areas lying more than 100 miles inland. Over 5,000 miles of trails formed a loose network throughout the country. Used by foot travelers, animals, and four-wheel-drive vehicles, they were the only routes between most of the small settlements in the east and northeast.

Many feeder roads in the western and southwestern agricultural areas had been improved since the mid-1960s, and extension of the feeder road system was scheduled for priority attention during the 1970s. They were usually constructed in the context of agricultural development projects, but some were included in the continuing road programs. In February 1973 the World Bank Group approved a US$8 million credit partly for road construction to be completed by 1977 and partly for technical studies of future requirements for highways and feeder roads. The loan was a step in a long-range series of road improvement projects. Among the early projects was rehabilitation and strengthening of paving on four sections of the main highway between Dakar and Casamance Region.

For every 1,000 inhabitants in 1972 there were 2.5 miles of road and 16.25 motor vehicles in use, of which 10.73 were passenger cars. The country possessed 40,779 private passenger cars and taxis and 20,941 trucks, buses, and utility vehicles. Many of the vehicles in use were in poor condition, and the truck fleet was badly in need of replacement. Of the motor vehicles imported in 1971 and 1972, more than three-fourths were French models. Volkswagen and Ford led the list of non-French passenger car imports, and imports of trucks and utility vehicles included Land Rovers, Mercedes, Volkswagens, Fords, and Fruehaufs.

Ports and Waterways

Dakar's potential as a deepwater port was recognized more than a century ago, and it was being visited by sailing captains before the days of steam power. Improvements such as protective jetties were built during the 1860s, and the various facilities required at a major port have been added as required. In 1970 depths in the harbor and in some berths were adequate for ships with drafts of as much as thirty-three feet, and docking facilities to accommodate supertankers were to be constructed. Besides handling cargo, the port had become an important way station for maritime traffic to other destinations. Only about half the ships calling at Dakar during the 1960s were there to discharge or pick up cargo; much of the port's activity consisted of replenishing stores or servicing ships traveling between the Mediterranean or the North Atlantic and ports in the South Atlantic or the Indian Ocean.

Major installations in use in 1973 included berths for forty ships, quiet-water anchorage spaces for sixty ships, various heavy cranes and other cargo-handling equipment, petroleum pipelines and storage, refrigerated and unrefrigerated warehouses, and facilities for transshipment of bulk minerals. There were also important facilities for the service and support of the industrial fishing fleet (see ch. 14).

In 1972 the port of Dakar handled more than 5 million tons of cargo and was used by 11,344 ships. There had been a decline in passenger volume and in the provisioning of ships with fuel and water. Earnings were expected to increase, however, after the completion of ambitious projects for expansion of the fishing port and construction of the largest dry dock in the South Atlantic for repair of supertankers. There were also plans for establishment of an industrial free trade zone at the port of Dakar.

There was a secondary port at Saint-Louis and river ports at Kaolack and Ziguinchor. Historic Saint-Louis had been the principal port for this area of West Africa for two centuries, from the landing of the French in 1659 to the development of Dakar in 1854 (see ch. 2). The entry gradually sanded up, however, and in 1973 it was a mainly regional port accommodating only ships with drafts of less than eleven feet.

Kaolack's location deep in the Groundnut Basin has enabled it to compete with Dakar for shipments of considerable tonnages of groundnuts and other crops. It possessed good rail and road connections to the surrounding farmlands. Sandbars near the entrance of the Sine-Saloum estuary and tight bends in the channel limited the port's use to small ships. As internal transport improved, a larger share of deliveries from Kaolack's hinterland was expected to be shipped overland to the more modern port at Dakar.

Similarly, merchants in Casamance Region were tending to get an increasing portion of their imports via the paved highway from Dakar, bypassing the port at Ziguinchor on the Casamance River estuary. In 1973 Ziguinchor was still handling most of the region's imports and its exports of groundnuts and palm products. Improvements included a 1,100-foot quay and several groundnut warehouses.

The Sénégal River in the north was navigable for about six months of the year. During the late summer high-water season, vessels drawing less than ten feet could travel from Saint-Louis 600 miles upstream to Kayes in Mali, and barge traffic from Kayes might conceivably provide an evacuation route for eventual exploitation of the iron ore deposits in the southeastern corner of Senegal (see ch. 14).

Several lesser coastal ports or landings handled shipments of salt, minerals, or groundnuts from the farm areas along the Sine and Saloum rivers. There were plans for possible expansion of the port of Mbour and for improvement of storage and other facilities at a number of fish landing beaches along the coast.

Air Facilities

In 1972 there were seventeen airports or landing fields, of which Yoff International Airport at Dakar was the only fully equipped modern air facility. Like Dakar's coastal port, it was a crossroads for air routes between sub-Saharan Africa, Western Europe, and the Americas. It served as the link with international air routes for a number of neighboring countries and was an important stop for long-range flights between Europe and South America. In 1971 the country's airport system served 347,000 passengers, of whom 97 percent were traveling on international flights through Dakar.

Runways and other facilities in use at Dakar in 1973 were adequate for long-range jet transports such as the Boeing 707, but improvements were to be effected before the airport could be used on a regular basis by the largest new transports coming into international service, such as the DC-10. Proposals to extend the main runway from the existing 7,270 feet to 11,700 feet were being studied in 1973. There were plans to exploit the anticipated jumbo jet passenger stopovers by developing the country's tourist facilities.

In 1973 seventeen international air carriers were using the Yoff facilities regularly, including Air Afrique, Pan American, and Air France. Senegal was participating in the operation of Air Afrique along with other French-speaking African countries but in mid-1973 had threatened to withdraw because of political disputes regarding the firm's management.

Domestic air service, operated by the government-owned Air Senegal, was not fully developed in 1973. Flights by small passenger aircraft were regularly scheduled to about thirteen of the seventeen airfields, but they carried fewer than 9,000 passengers in 1971. The most active internal routes were from Dakar northward to Saint-Louis, eastward to Tambacounda, and southward to Ziguinchor.

COMMUNICATIONS

In comparison with those in other West African countries, Senegal's communications network was relatively well developed, although very costly. Telecommunications facilities were unevenly distributed, telephones being found mostly in Dakar, with major gaps in service in the rest of the country. The long-distance circuits were congested, entailing long delays; local exchange lines were often very old and in need of replacement. Rates were twice as high as in most developing countries outside of West Africa.

All domestic postal, telephone, and telegraph services were owned and operated by a government entity. International services were provided by TELESENEGAL, a mixed firm in which the Senegalese government held 40 percent ownership. In mid-1973 the government had completed the first portion of a nationwide investment program to expand, modernize, and rehabilitate the telecommunications network. The first phase had concentrated on facilities in the southern areas; the second, financed by the World Bank Group, would concentrate on rehabilitating the Dakar network and on expanding and modernizing the system in the northern part of the country. In April 1972 a satellite communications ground station was inaugurated to improve connections with France and other international areas by way of Intelsat IV.

SECTION IV. NATIONAL SECURITY

CHAPTER 16

NATIONAL SECURITY

In 1973 Senegalese social controls included inherited African family and religious guidelines within the political framework of a national constitution and penal code based almost entirely upon French legal structures. Although most ethnic groups had retained their traditional social controls during more than two centuries of French colonial influence, they also had become accustomed to a centralized authority outside the group. When independence was established in 1960, most of the people accepted the new national government as a proper guardian of peace and order in their communities.

As both ethnic and governmental controls were strict and most people were accustomed to accepting them, such disorders as occurred during the late 1960s and early 1970s were confined to and supported by very small percentages of the total population. The most troublesome disturbances were initiated by groups of students and teachers, who staged demonstrations and strikes to dramatize their demands for curriculum changes and a reduction of French influence in the schools and throughout the society. They were sometimes supported by unemployed or dissatisfied wageworkers. Although government spokesmen had referred to communist influence in student and teacher groups that demonstrated against official policies, such influence—and communist influence in other internal security issues—appeared to be negligible (see ch. 10).

By the mid-1960s most members of the security forces had been reasonably well trained, and they were usually effective, containing sporadic demonstrations or disorders with a minimum of violence. A Senegalese penal code adopted in 1966 and amendments passed during the next several years had provided the executive branch of government with increased emergency powers and greater freedom of action in dealing with riots or acts considered to be threats to the security of the state.

Under these laws a limited but undetermined number of militant students were sentenced to prison. Organizations that opposed government policies could be banned, and several student organizations were officially dissolved. After a number of cases of arson in schools in 1972 and early 1973, the government also dissolved a teachers union that had been critical of government policies. This apparently marked the end of the last legally organized group openly opposing government policy.

The nation's military forces were patterned after those of France and had been trained and equipped through French aid programs. By 1973 most of the senior positions in the military and internal security forces, which had been filled by French officers during the early years of independence, had been taken over by Senegalese. Almost all of the French officers remaining in senior staff positions were scheduled to be replaced by Senegalese by the end of 1974, but French military personnel continued to have considerable influence as advisers in all of the military and other security forces. By agreement French military forces also had the use of facilities for naval, air, and ground forces in Senegal, including docks and repair facilities for large naval units at the port of Dakar. This arrangement enabled France to maintain a military presence in the westernmost area of Africa, a site of considerable strategic importance.

In 1973 Senegal's armed forces consisted of approximately 6,000 men, most of them in the army. Although the strategic offensive or defensive capability of the military was limited, it was reasonably well trained and constituted a backup to the 1,600-man National Gendarmerie and the 3,600-man National Police Force (Sûreté Nationale—SN) in the preservation of public order and internal security. Military personnel also were assigned to a number of civil government positions, especially in the top levels of some regional governments.

Concurrently with other precautionary measures, the military staffing of various positions in Casamance Region was increased after about 1970, as the national government became concerned over incursions upon Senegalese territory by rebels from Portuguese Guinea and by troops of that nation who purportedly attacked these guerrilla forces. In 1971 the Senegalese armed forces held maneuvers in southern Casamance Region, thereby creating a show of force in the area. In 1973 an undetermined number of troops—probably several mixed companies—were stationed in the region.

Although President Léopold-Sédar Senghor was philosophically opposed to the continued control of African territory by Portugal or any other European nation, his primary goal appeared to be the reduction or prevention of border violations or the use of Senegalese territory by either armed guerrillas or government troops from Portuguese Guinea. The situation was not being fully reported in 1973, but available information suggested that the primary mission of the Senegalese troops and other security forces in the border area was to reemphasize Senegalese hegemony in this remote area and to provide security for the local population.

THE ARMED FORCES

From the early years of penetration into West Africa, leading eventually to control of much of this area, the French made a practice of using Africans from occupied areas in their colonial forces. Their abilities as fighters had been demonstrated during a long period of resistance to the French forces. Once West Africa had been penetrated, the French turned these qualities to their own advantage. As early as 1765 young men were enlisted in the army in Senegal, and over the years the practice was extended to all of French West Africa. The Africans soon had reputations as tough and disciplined soldiers of the French colonial army.

In 1838 a company of Senegalese was dispatched to Guinea. Senegalese soldiers fought in the Crimea, under Maximilian in Mexico, and in the Franco-Prussian War of 1870. Senegalese units were used extensively by the French in their eastward penetration south of the Sahara and gained distinction in the Madagascar and Moroccan campaign of 1912.

As part of a plan to raise a large colonial force for service wherever needed, in 1916 France formally adopted military conscription for its West African territories. From that time on, many Africans were called up and incorporated in the French army. They were organized into units designated Senegalese Riflemen (Tirailleurs Sénégalais), although the troops were drawn from all parts of West Africa. The units usually were maintained at a ratio of two-thirds conscripts to one-third regulars. The great majority of officers and noncommissioned officers were French, but Africans could and did advance to noncommissioned officer status, and a limited number gained commissions.

During World War I West African troops fought on several battlefronts, and a large percentage of the 181,000 men involved were from Senegal. Losses were high, and incapacities resulting from unaccustomed climates took a toll that equaled the battle casualties. Known generically as Senegalese, the West African soldiers earned a considerable reputation as fierce and reliable fighters.

Many Africans joined the French forces during the early phase of World War II. After the defeat of metropolitan France's military forces in 1940, French West Africa gave its allegiance to the surviving French government, located in Vichy, until the landings of the Allied armies in North Africa in 1942. Senegalese units then joined the Free French forces and took part in battles in North Africa, France, and Germany.

After World War II ended, the French continued to maintain their West African units at considerable strength to help meet worldwide military commitments. Some 15,000 served in the Indochina conflict; and 30,000, in North Africa and the Suez area. Meanwhile, only about 4,000 were garrisoned in the whole of West Africa.

French control of military forces in Senegal and French influence on organization, training, and tactics continued after World War II ended. When the country became independent in 1960, its leaders retained the

French approach as they developed their national military forces, with some adaptations to Senegal's special needs.

By the mid-1960s most command positions were held by Senegalese, although various units still had French advisers. Many of the Senegalese officers had held commissions in the French overseas forces. All were products of French schooling or training; some had graduated from Saint-Cyr military academy, and others had attended schools for nonregular officers in metropolitan France. Candidates for such schools had been selected from military or civilian volunteers who had successfully completed a course of required preparatory training given at local instruction centers for elementary preparation.

Many noncommissioned officers during the first years after independence were career men who had enlisted originally as regulars in the colonial forces or reenlisted after completion of their required military service. Selected on the basis of performance and demonstrated leadership, they had been seasoned on the job, and some had attended technical schools.

Other noncommissioned officers who had been transferred to inactive status were recalled for further duty in the national army during the first few years of independence. They were in fact the primary source for filling the few vacancies that occurred and became a mainstay of the Senegalese military structure.

Many of the enlisted men in the national forces during the 1960s were also veterans of colonial service. As Senegal moved toward independence, French and Senegalese leaders had arranged for the transfer of African units from the colonial forces to the control of the new national government. Most of the troops transferred under this agreement, a part of the 1960 Accord on Cooperation in Matters of Defense, were men who had had considerable training and experience under French leadership. They formed a nucleus of small but experienced units.

Legislation authorizing increased personnel strength was enacted, but total active military strength remained under 2,700 men for several years. Subsequent increases to about 6,000 men by 1973 consisted almost entirely of volunteers. France continued to provide technical advisers, equipment, assistance with training, and other forms of military aid.

Senegalese-French Military Arrangements

The legal basis for France's continuing use of the naval base and headquarters areas at Dakar is one of several cooperation agreements included in the original Accord on Cooperation in Matters of Defense between the Mali Federation and France. In addition to its provisions for the transfer of African troops from the French forces to the forces of the Senegalese government, the accord and its three detailed annexes set forth the basic policies for French assistance in military training and the conditions for direct aid from France in matters of defense if requested by the government of the federation.

Published accords with Senegal, after the breakup of the short-lived Mali Federation, covered details of aid and cooperation. For example, two agreements formalized in 1966 dealt with French use of Senegalese airfields and French logistic support for Senegalese military and gendarmerie forces. Other military accords were worked out, but details were not made public. Arrangements were probably included whereby France could assist, upon request of the Senegalese government, in case of serious civil disorders. As of 1973 the Senghor government had not had occasion to request active support from French combat units. French forces did, however, protect major military facilities at Dakar during a series of riots in mid-1968.

France continued in 1973 to provide military assistance to Senegal, but the amount of matériel provided since 1970 was very limited. During the years since many of the French-speaking African nations became independent, successive French governments had continued to maintain a capability to intervene with French forces in support of these nations and to show the French flag off West Africa in the central and southern Atlantic Ocean. French interests in offshore waters were monitored from Dakar, where a senior French naval officer commanded the headquarters for France's South Atlantic Naval Zone. This officer usually had no more than a few medium-sized naval units in the Senegal area, but these were adequate to maintain a French naval presence off West Africa. A naval storehouse and dry dock under his command constituted a base of support for a larger naval force if needed. Nearly 1,000 naval men were usually in the area. About half of these men were shore based, and half were serving on French naval vessels that were either based at the Dakar port or on operational visits. Small French ground and air units also were assigned to the South Atlantic Naval Zone. In 1973 the ground troops reportedly included at least 1,200 men, most of them trained for airborne operations or associated combat support activities. An air transport section of several hundred men operating from facilities at Dakar-Ouakam airfield, three miles from the port, provided air support for the other French forces, including the specialized support needs of the airborne troops.

These French forces in the Dakar area could assist the Senegalese government at its request or could be sent elsewhere in Africa to protect French interests or the interests of friendly nations in other African areas. From this strategically located westernmost point in Africa, the French commander looked both seaward and landward, and the relatively limited military forces under his control had considerable importance as symbols of French influence in both African and offshore areas. Moreover, these forces could be augmented quickly by air without overflying other nations or by oceangoing vessels traveling from staging areas in either western or southern France to the deep-water berths and modern port facilities at Dakar.

Strength and Organization

In 1973 the personnel strength of Senegal's armed forces had been increased since the early 1960s, but the total was still slightly under 6,000 men, less than 0.15 percent of the population. The army was the senior service. About 5,000 of these men were in army units, the majority in two infantry battalions and an engineer battalion. There were also two companies of parachute troops, two companies of men who had had commando training, and small support units.

The air force had about 200 men. This service had no combat aircraft but assisted with military and civil transport needs, parachute troop training, and reconnaissance, using about eight light transports, two helicopters, and a few other aircraft.

The nucleus of a navy, with about 150 men, had a few patrol craft of less than 100 tons each and one heavier patrol boat. Its primary mission was coastal surveillance, and it had the additional assignments of enforcing navigation laws and monitoring territorial waters. The headquarters and primary installations used by both the air force and navy were at Dakar.

From the senior headquarters at Dakar, military administration was handled through four military district headquarters: the western district (Dakar), manned by an infantry battalion; the northern district (Saint-Louis), manned by another battalion; the eastern district (Tambacounda), manned by a composite or mixed group of small units; and the southern district (Ziguinchor), manned by another composite group known as the Casamance Group, which had taken on added importance since 1970 because of problems along the border with Portuguese Guinea.

The more important military bases were located at Dakar, Rufisque, Kaolack, Saint-Louis, Tambacounda, Kédougou, and in three locations in Casamance Region—Ziguinchor, Kolda, and Bignona. The primary military supply and ordnance bases for the nation were in the Dakar-Cap Vert area and at Thiès and Kaolack. Lesser support facilities were located in most other areas of the country.

Command Structure

Laws that came into effect as Senegal achieved independence were designed to ensure supremacy of the civil components of government in military matters. The constitution named the president commander in chief of the armed forces and empowered him to appoint all military personnel. He presided over the Supreme Defense Council, which was the senior policymaking body in military matters and was composed of the principal cabinet ministers and ranking military chiefs.

Most of the provisions relating to the military establishment in

338

Senegal's first constitution were retained when the constitution was revised in 1970. Law No. 70-23 of June 1970 updated the legal basis for the general organization of the national defense structure. Law No. 72-42 of June 1972 reaffirmed much of the existing structure but added other provisions. The president of the republic was reaffirmed as supreme commander of the national military and police forces. The Supreme Defense Council was retained by the 1972 law, and the prime minister was given the responsibility for implementation of military policy decided upon by the council. The minister of state for the armed forced was given responsibility for maintaining the services in a state of readiness and for executing decisions on military matters handed down by the president. He was to be assisted by a senior military staff of the army, to which the commanders of the engineer battalion, air force, and navy were subordinated.

Membership of the Supreme Defense Council was to include the president of the republic as chairman; the secretary general of the office of the president; an official known as the secretary general of the government; the prime minister; the minister of state for the armed forces and his military chief of staff; the ministers of foreign affairs, interior, and finance; and the heads of several other cabinet-level agencies. The law provided for specialized working groups to support the needs of the Supreme Defense Council and for a permanent secretary to assist it (see ch. 9).

The June 1972 decree authorized the minister of state for the armed forces to maintain a staff of military and civilian technical advisers and a section to handle organization, budgets, and logistics; a central administrative agency for the armed forces and another for the national police; and an agency to handle the affairs of veterans and war victims.

An office of planning and operations, authorized by the June 1972 decree, included a document and security section that was directed to maintain information on the capabilities and deployment of military forces of neighboring countries that were capable of intervention on Senegalese Territory. This section was also directed to keep informed on groups that were hostile to the government or threatened the unity of the armed forces.

General Alfred Diallo, a close associate of President Senghor and longtime commander of all Senegalese military forces, retired from military service in June 1972. Concurrently, the new law authorizing a reorganization of the armed forces command structure was put into effect. The power that had been centralized in General Diallo was divided among several senior officers and a civilian minister. A civilian leader and longtime political associate of the president, Magatte Lo, was appointed minister of state for the armed forces. During the preceding four years the president had functioned as his own minister of state for the armed forces, depending upon General Diallo as a loyal associate and competent leader to keep effective control of the forces. In 1973 the most powerful military post was that of the inspector general. The incumbent, Colonel Amadou Belal Ly, former governor of Casamance Region, reported directly to President Senghor. The chief of staff of the armed forces and the head of President Senghor's personal military staff also had considerable authority.

The 1972 reorganization divided responsibilities formerly residing in one military commander. Its practical effect was to make the inspector general the senior officer in the military services. The minister of state for the armed forces and the military chief of staff handled routine management problems and executed the decrees of the president, who received much of his support and advice from the inspector general, his personal staff, and a senior French officer assigned as adviser.

As president and commander in chief of the military forces, Senghor retained full authority over military developments, assignments, and promotions. The armed forces ministry was also the president's channel for controlling the National Gendarmerie. Although it was a separate structure with its own commandant, its activities were coordinated by the minister of state for the armed forces.

Recruitment and Training

Almost all recruits entering the service in the 1970-73 period were volunteers. During the early 1970s an estimated 1,000 men per year were allowed to enlist and were sent to a fort near Saint-Louis for basic training.

Of about 950,000 males between fifteen and forty-nine years of age, possibly half could be considered capable of military service in a major emergency, but many would fail peacetime physical examinations. Recruitment officers were able to be highly selective. Most of the men accepted were between eighteen and twenty-two years of age, and about 85 percent were able to read and write. More than half of the new recruits were from the Wolof ethnic group, which had been known for centuries as a source of good soldiers (see ch. 4).

Usual periods of service were set forth in a law revised in June 1970. Active service for volunteers was for five years unless they were shifted to a ready reserve before the end of the tour. This five-year period was to be followed by twenty years in reserve status, during which time the men were subject to recall. The law provided that special regulations could be applied to noncommissioned officers, reserve officers, and fathers of large families.

Young men accepted for military service generally benefited both physically and educationally. These factors contributed to an excess of volunteers throughout the 1960-73 period, which made extensive use of the draft laws unnecessary. Volunteers included many veterans of the French forces in Africa during the preindependence period, men who were in most cases well qualified for further service or for cadre duties and who accepted the less desirable aspects of military service with little complaint.

In line with the French policy followed by Senegal's military leaders, troop training continued to be thorough. Recruits received basic training and comprehensive individual training; units had continuing on-the-job instruction; and selected soldiers received specialist training. Under guidance from French advisers, they received much the same instruction given to French troops, and the quality of the training was generally good.

Noncommissioned officers were trained in a school opened in Kaolack (Sine-Saloum Region) in 1971. The standard course for most entrants was eighteen months in length. Gendarmerie personnel and trainees for certain civil service positions were also sent to this school. Noncommissioned officers received specialized training in France for assignments in the air force or the navy and for support duties in communications, medical, or ordnance units.

The Dakar-Bango Military Preparatory School (Dakar-Bango Ecole Militaire Preparatoire) at Saint-Louis was a highly rated training ground for about 550 young students, of whom only a minority entered military careers. Its curriculum was comparable to that of a French *lycée* (secondary school); military training and discipline were added as a major part of the program.

Entrants were carefully selected and were taught by a competent civilian faculty, mostly Frenchmen and a few Senegalese. In 1973 the school commandant was a French officer. Although some students went on to advanced military schools in France and eventually to a military career, many students—including many non-Senegalese students—were enrolled because the school also provided a good educational background for nonmilitary careers.

In the 1970s many future officers were drawn from the military preparatory school, but others came from other high schools in Senegal, from the University of Dakar, or from the ranks of enlisted men and noncommissioned officers. Officers received much of their advanced training in France at the academies for French officers, such as Saint-Cyr and Saumur. Others were sent to schools in Morocco and in the Malagasy Republic. In some years as many as 100 Senegalese military men, including noncommissioned officers and technical specialists as well as officers, were attending various military training courses in France.

Unit training up to battalion level was enhanced by periodic tactical field exercises. During the 1960s a few sizable unit training exercises had been held in Sine-Saloum Region, which offered good terrain for learning basic tactics and field engineering. A large-scale maneuver was held in Casamance Region in January 1971 involving members of all components and services. The activity was concentrated in southern and southwestern Casamance, an area of forests, swamps, and farmland. It constituted a show of force and a demonstration of Senegal's determination to defend the area against border crossings by the forces of Portuguese Guinea; it was also a useful large-scale training exercise and an opportunity to analyze unit performance.

Civic Action

Military units, particularly the army's engineer battalion, participated in numerous economic construction projects and in other civic work. Projects included the building of roads, bridges, and airfields; the preparation of sites for housing projects; the improvement of ports; and the development of water supplies.

On several occasions government spokesmen had confirmed the importance attached to civic projects carried out by the military forces. In 1972 the minister of state for the armed forces indicated that many civil engineering projects being executed by the government would be turned over to the army, as this approach provided vocational training to recruits and also produced economic improvements. Government leaders referred in speeches to the double mission of the military, giving its civic mission an emphasis rivaling that accorded to its defense mission.

Morale and Conditions of Service

Most military units were at bases originally used by French forces where facilities ranged from fair to very good. Most barracks for unmarried men were adequate, and family housing was available for career officers and noncommissioned officers. In general, housing compared favorably with what equivalent income groups would find in local civilian housing areas. Troops received an adequate diet based on typical Senegalese staple foods (see ch. 6).

Conditions of service remained similar to patterns established by the French in the earlier colonial forces. The daily routine was often arduous, and discipline was strict. On the other hand, service benefits included medical care, annual leave, and travel allowances; recreation programs and facilities were available; and career servicemen could look forward to retirement income.

Lo, the civilian who was appointed minister of state for the armed forces in 1972, reportedly had taken an interest in details of routine military activities and made many of the decisions even on minor matters. Some officers reportedly had reservations concerning this intensive supervision by a civilian official and questioned the need for the reorganization ordered by President Senghor, but there was no evidence that these had become important issues.

Reports of slow deliveries of ammunition and supplies and stories of problems with used or obsolescent equipment received from France were circulated in 1972. Whether or not they were well founded, they reportedly had caused morale problems among officers and noncommissioned officers responsible for using and maintaining this equipment.

Meanwhile, however, President Senghor continued his longtime policy of providing adequate pay, prestige, and rewards for military men. In the past they had, with few exceptions, been loyal to him and had contributed to the government's stability and its generally effective control of the country. Evidence available in mid-1973 did not indicate any critical change in this relationship among the great majority of military men.

Military Costs and Sources of Aid

Defense was allotted the equivalent of about US$4.3 million in fiscal year 1961, or about 3.3 percent of the total national budget. This was increased in succeeding years, exceeding the equivalent of US$13.7 million, or 7.4 percent of the total budget in fiscal year 1964. These figures represented only part of the total defense costs. Indirect aid from France covered much of the cost of the military forces, but data on such aid were not published.

Increases brought Senegal's military budget up to the equivalent of about US$18 million for the 1969 and 1970 fiscal years, or more than 10 percent of the national budget. Military costs for fiscal year 1973 were projected at about US$19 million, less then 9 percent of the government's total budget.

Soon after Senegal gained independence, it was recognized that the military would eventually have to assume greater responsibility for its own logistics, and plans had been outlined for a staff organization to take over supply administration, procurement, and distribution. Medical, quartermaster, ordnance, and construction services were included in the general staff organization, but during the first years of independence their functions consisted for the most part of coordination with counterparts in the French forces still serving in Senegal.

Basic weapons, vehicles, base installations, uniforms, small naval vessels, aircraft, and other matériel used by Senegalese forces were provided by France. During the 1962-72 decade the United States provided about US$2.8 million in aid, mostly in the form of equipment for use in civic construction by the engineer battalion. In 1973 almost all other equipment continued to be of French origin, obtained by grant or purchase. Military aid from France between 1954 and 1973 was valued at the equivalent of nearly US$20 million, but annual aid was reduced considerably after 1969, amounting to less than US$1.5 million from 1970 through 1972.

Approximately thirty French officers and thirty-five noncommissioned officers were serving in either supervisory or advisory positions with the Senegalese armed forces in 1973, about the same number as a year earlier. Army units, except the engineer battalion, were headed by Senegalese officers, with French officers as advisers. President Senghor consulted with a French colonel assigned as his adviser. A

French officer was assigned as head of the engineer battalion, and other French officers were in charge of various support functions, including supply and medical activities.

Plans arranged by mutual consent of the French and Senegalese governments called for an end to the use of French technical assistants and advisers by the end of 1974. Information available in 1973 indicated that some exceptions could be anticipated, such as in the field of military medical care; Senegal had few military or civilian doctors (see ch. 6).

PUBLIC ORDER AND SECURITY

During its first thirteen years as an independent nation, Senegal had not suffered from a widespread degree of internal violence or insurgency. Interethnic conflicts, often a problem to other new nations, had not been a violent issue as of 1973. A 1962 attempt by Prime Minister Mamadou Dia to force President Senghor to relinquish power was a failure, in large part because the great majority of the armed forces remained loyal to the president. Dia was still under detention in mid-1973, but his sentence had been reduced. Other government officials convicted of charges related to the same coup attempt had been released. Since that attempt no other rival political figure has been able to gather together a large revolutionary following or to mount a full-blown coup attempt (see ch. 2; ch. 10).

There had been numerous displays of opposition to government policies, however, particularly by students at the University of Dakar and at high schools in several towns. Militant student and teacher groups were suspected of arson in a number of fires that occurred in schools during 1972 and 1973. Government leaders and the gendarmerie had effectively controlled the activists, in some instances through the use of emergency powers that had been enacted during the late 1960s, enlarging the authority provided in the Senegalese penal code.

The only significant postindependence border security problems were the numerous small-scale incursions across the poorly defined southern border by both African nationalist guerrillas and troops from Portuguese Guinea. As these became more frequent and troublesome during the late 1960s, the Senegalese increased the strength of their military and other security forces in that area. In 1973 Senegalese troops were reportedly reducing the area in which the guerrillas could operate, apparently with the primary purpose of reaffirming national sovereignty and demonstrating the government's ability to protect and control the local population.

Both the internal problem with a critical minority of the academic community and the issue of incursions along the southern border appeared to be under control in mid-1973. On both matters the official attitude toward any possible danger to state security or sovereignty showed restraint along with an increased firmness. Prison sentences had been handed down to militant students in Dakar and to persons alleged to have been aiding the government of Portuguese Guinea by their activities in Casamance Region. The Penal Code and the Code of Penal Procedures of 1966 and emergency powers in subsequent amendments provided the legal basis for strong security measures, permitting arrests and heavy sentences for activities interpreted as inimical to the security of the state.

Criminal Law and Prisons

The penal code of metropolitan France was applied during the colonial period to French citizens in French West Africa and to those Africans who had become familiar with its provisions and who had been accepted into the French-oriented colonial elite. Thus a considerable number of the most influential Senegalese were accustomed to the French code before the nation became independent. The criminal courts and the police continued to function under the French code until 1966, when the Penal Code of 1966 and the Code of Penal Procedures of Senegal were promulgated.

The new code was based almost entirely on the French code and caused little change in established legal norms, police powers, or court procedures. Under its provisions suspects or defendants have most of the same protections that would be available to persons in similar circumstances under the legal systems of France or those of most Western European countries. Following the French system, investigations are made by members of the national police or the gendarmerie who previously have been trained and designated as judicial officers. On the basis of the investigation a magistrate decides whether or not a trial should be held.

Detention of defendants awaiting trial is provided for by the Penal Code but is limited in cases concerning lesser offenses. If, for example, the maximum possible sentence is less than two years' imprisonment, detention awaiting trial is limited to five days. Persons charged with major crimes may be held for much longer periods.

Cases involving minor offenses are heard by local justices of the peace or by courts of first instance. Punishments are fines or short-term jail sentences, usually served at local prisons.

Special laws and legal procedures are provided for juveniles who are charged with violations of the law, and the Penal Code prescribes that there be a children's court at each court of first instance. Nevertheless, sentences similar to those for adult offenders can be meted out to minors over thirteen years old if the court decides that the penalties are justified. On the other hand, minors can simply be released to the control of an official assigned by the court (see ch. 9).

Defendants charged with serious crimes, such as killing or wounding another person or major crimes against property, are tried by juries.

Jurors are required to be able to read and write French and are selected from lists prepared annually for that purpose.

Punishments in such cases may range from two to twenty years in prison and in rare cases to forced labor. The law provides a distinction between minor offenses for which punishment ranges from two to five years' detention and more serious crimes. Those who are sentenced for serious crimes are kept separate from those serving sentences for minor ones.

Whatever the crime or sentence, the prisoner's civil rights, such as the right to vote or to enter any of several professions after his release, may be withdrawn for a specified period. Such a ruling usually accompanies sentences for serious crimes.

Various forms of theft were probably the most common crimes during the early 1970s. Minor thefts often resulted in fines or prison sentences of one month to two years or a combination of the two punishments.

More serious forms of embezzlement or direct theft result in sentences of five to ten years. Armed robbery or robbery through violence or threats can be punished with ten to twenty years of forced labor.

The most severe punishments—the death sentence and long sentences involving forced labor—are relatively rare. Sentences of death by shooting can be handed down by the higher courts for premeditated murder, for the murder of one's parents or child, or for a killing in association with another serious crime such as robbery.

Crimes against the security of the state are also punishable by death or forced labor. Bearing arms against the government, intelligence work for a foreign power, and less specific offenses such as corrupting the loyalty of the army make the offender liable to the death penalty. Conviction of lesser but related crimes may bring long-term prison sentences. Plotting against the authority of the state is subject to punishment by a life sentence at hard labor.

In 1967 the courts handed down the first death sentences since independence, one for a politically motivated murder and another for an unsuccessful attempt to kill President Senghor. A review of official data for the 1967-71 period indicated that a limited number of prisoners had been sentenced to forced labor. Only three men and one woman were given this punishment during 1970 and 1971, in contrast to the several thousand per year who were given terms of one month or more in the less onerous correctional sections of the prisons.

The nation had twenty-six penal centers in 1971 with a designed capacity of 2,750 prisoners. Other prisons were under construction, as these facilities were overcrowded, containing at times more than 3,600 prisoners either serving sentences or awaiting trial. For the years 1967 through 1971 government data reflected an increase in the number of persons entering prison—mostly for short sentences—from about 5,260 in 1967 to a little over 6,000 in each of the four succeeding years.

346

Such an increase appeared small in relation to the total population increase during that five-year period.

Most crimes occur in the urban centers, especially in Dakar and other towns in Cap Vert Region, which accounted for more than half of all prisoners sentenced and jailed in Senegal. Nevertheless, there was a reduction in the number of persons convicted and sentenced in Cap Vert Region between 1969 and 1971. Meanwhile, increases occurred in Fleuve, Sine-Saloum, and Thiès regions for reasons not covered in the limited data available.

The Police System

The 1,600-member National Gendarmerie, which was controlled by the president through the minister of state for the armed forces, maintained units known as legions in each of the country's seven administrative regions. Legions were divided into smaller units called brigades—some consisting of only a few men—stationed at key positions throughout the country. They constituted a rural police force, but they also had other duties and capabilities. Three well-trained and well-equipped rapid reaction companies were available, for example, for use in the control of riots or other forms of violence in urban areas. They also guarded the presidential palace, other government buildings, airports, harbors, and key border points. Many members were veterans of preindependence service in the French security forces and had military as well as police training and experience. Generally neutral in their political views, the gendarmes were considered the most dependable and effective force available for defense of the government against insurgency. They were skilled in the use of infantry weapons as well as modern antiriot techniques and were adequately equipped with weapons, vehicles, and communications gear.

The mission of the National Gendarmerie apparently also included counterintelligence matters. This was an area of overlapping responsibilities, as the civil police also maintained records on security problems.

The National Police Force (Sûreté Nationale—SN) was centrally directed from Dakar by the minister of interior, who controlled police activities nationwide through seven regional centers and numerous smaller stations and guard posts. The force had more than 3,600 members in 1973, up somewhat from an estimate of about 3,300 during the late 1960s. It was primarily an urban law enforcement agency. Protection of people and property was its function. The SN policed the towns, directed traffic, enforced crime and vice laws, guarded the railroads, and provided other general law enforcement services.

During 1970 the SN had absorbed the former Republican Guard (Garde Républicaine) which had been primarily a personal protective force and honor guard for the president. Three mobile companies with special capabilities for riot control were included in the transfers from the former guard organization. One of these mobile companies was usually on duty in Dakar; and another, in Thiès. In 1973 the third company was stationed in Kolda, a town near the most troubled section of the border with Portuguese Guinea.

Although most police units lacked the firepower or the level of discipline and training shown by most of the National Gendarmerie, police personnel were reasonably well trained and equipped adequately for general duties. The SN mobile units and the ordinary police in most communities would be effective in the control of small-scale violence or rioting and could offer considerable support to the National Gendarmerie or the military forces in more serious emergencies.

Internal Security Trends

Dissatisfaction Among Students

Student demonstrations against governmental policies on education and other matters had occurred a number of times before, but they became of increased concern to the government in March 1969. During the next month President Senghor's cabinet authorized several measures, including administrative internment, to strengthen the government's ability to deal with the dissidents. Nevertheless, overt protests continued, and disaffected students called for a general strike. Schools were ordered closed at the end of May, and President Senghor declared a state of emergency after describing the general strike as a failure. Meanwhile, rural dwellers had staged counterdemonstrations to express support for the Senghor government.

Other demonstrations were mounted in mid-June, and at least one person was killed as the demonstrators were being dispersed. Thereafter the situation became relatively calm. Certain reforms at the University of Dakar were announced. On June 2 a total of thirty-six people were sentenced to prison for periods of eighteen to thirty-six months for damaging property or injuring other people during the strikes and demonstrations. The state of emergency was ended on June 23 without any additional serious incidents having been reported. Schools reopened peacefully on October 28, 1969.

Expressions of dissatisfaction continued during the next two or three years but were limited to small groups and involved little or no violence. The government improved its ability to control dissident groups, and the majority of the population continued to accept the authority and policies of the central government. In 1970 a referendum registered approval for a law authorizing the president to issue orders in defense matters and in the exercise of emergency powers awarded by previous legislation without the formal concurrence of cabinet members.

After a year without a major public demonstration, students at the University of Dakar initiated new protests against government and school policies in late January 1973. There were fights between strikers and progovernment students who were members of the Senegalese Progressive Union (Union Progressiste Sénégalaise—UPS). Two units of the National Gendarmerie were dispatched to the campus and remained there for two days. Eleven students were injured during these disturbances. During the following week nine students were expelled permanently, and forty-six were suspended for a year. In early February the minister of information warned students that dissidents would lose their scholarships if they continued to demonstrate. Sporadic problems continued, and some students demanded the discharge of certain professors and the reinstatement of expelled students. As spokesman for the government the minister of national education expressed a firm official attitude, indicating that students must avoid violence and attend to their studies or be expelled from the university.

Tensions and minor clashes continued, apparently instigated by minority groups of students and teachers who continued to oppose government policies. A strike at the University of Dakar and several high schools on March 1 led to short prison sentences and fines for a teacher, a student, and a few other unidentified people. After four schools in Saint-Louis were set afire on March 16, four teachers and a headmaster were arrested.

On March 28 the government officially dissolved the Teachers Union of Senegal (Syndicat des Enseignants du Sénégal—SES) after arresting three of its top leaders for activities endangering state security. Government spokesmen cited a 1965 law empowering the government to act against organizations considered to be seditious. Some observers expressed doubt that SES was responsible for the arson at various schools, but government spokesmen described the organization as a rallying point for opposition to the government's educational policies.

A number of students staged a strike in early May 1973 to protest the detention of students who had been involved in the previous protests. Larger demonstrations were held in mid-May after government officials announced that a former student, sentenced in 1971 for endangering state security, had committed suicide in prison by hanging himself. The student had been in prison for trying to organize the escape of two brothers who had been convicted in January 1971 for attempting to burn the French Cultural Exchange Center in Dakar. The youth's father charged that his son had died as a result of brutality, but President Senghor said that the young man had been held in Senegal's least onerous form of detention and defended the official autopsy findings of suicide. On May 14, 1973, student demonstrators set fire to cars and buses in central Dakar, and mobile intervention units of the National Gendarmerie used tear gas to put an end to the rioting.

In the aftermath of these problems President Senghor denied that military forces and armored vehicles had been used to deal with the students. At the same time, however, he indicated to his cabinet and to the national security forces that they were to ensure public order and protect all citizens. Reports indicated that persons arrested as a result of the antigovernment actions would be tried by the state.

Southern Border Problems

Incidents along the border between Senegal and Portuguese Guinea had flared sporadically during Senegal's first thirteen years of independence. The issue was sometimes active on three levels: in efforts by security forces to monitor or control the activities of guerrillas who attempted to use areas inside Senegal as havens between clashes with Portuguese troops and to prevent forays into Senegal by Portuguese Guinea troops; in direct or indirect diplomatic exchanges between the governments of Senegal and Portugal; and in the United Nations Security Council (see ch. 11).

The basic problems were those of border crossings or use of Senegalese territory by members of the African Party for the Independence of Guinea and the Cape Verde Islands (Parti Africain pour l'Indépendance de la Guinée et des Iles du Cap-Vert—PAIGC) and incursions or light artillery bombardments by Portuguese troops. Surreptitious crossings by small groups were not readily detected or proved, as most of the border had never been thoroughly surveyed or posted. It passed through a complex of swamps, rivers, and forests laced with minor foot trails. In what was usually the most troubled area—where central Casamance Region adjoins Portuguese Guinea—the border cut through territories used for hunting, fishing, gathering, or farming, traditionally held by various family or ethnic groups. The line sometimes bisected villages.

People in the area tended to be loyal to their family or group rather than to the nation in which they happened to live. Except at guard posts on the few important roads across the border, the local population was barely aware of the location of the border until it became an issue as the PAIGC began to flee to Senegalese territory when pressed by the Portuguese forces. Local residents, opponents of the government in Portuguese Guinea—such as members of the PAIGC—or anyone else could cross at will in most areas.

By 1970 PAIGC activity in the border area was apparently increasing slowly. More Portuguese incursions into Senegalese territory occurred, and more artillery attacks by Portuguese Guinea forces were reported during the 1970-72 period. Sporadic reports indicated small PAIGC encampments within Senegal, where the rebels presumably felt safer from Portuguese Guinea counterguerrilla operations than in the forests south of the border. The various attacks initiated by the government of Portuguese Guinea suggested that they hoped to convince Senegalese government leaders that they should renounce aid to, or contact with, the PAIGC and join in declaring the border a neutral area.

Review of a few of the more important incidents of the 1970s illustrates the problem. In 1971, for example, a village in Senegal was attacked, and Senegal charged that the Portuguese armed forces were responsible. The issue eventually was discussed in the United Nations

Security Council, which then sent a mission to investigate. In September spokesmen for the United Nations mission reported that the attack had been very destructive and that witnesses had identified the attackers as Portuguese army troops.

There were few significant incidents along the border during the early months of 1972, but six Senegalese soldiers were killed in early June, when a force consisting of more than 200 Portuguese soldiers crossed the border, according to Senegalese reports. In October a Senegalese officer was killed and another wounded. By that time Senegal was somewhat more openly supporting the PAIGC political struggle without making concessions to the guerrillas concerning the use of Senegalese territory. The Senegalese government was coordinating a limited flow of nonmilitary aid to Portuguese Guinea refugees in Senegal. At the same time President Senghor was apparently continuing to work for an end to incursions upon Senegalese soil by either PAIGC or Portuguese Guinea troops. Incomplete reports suggest that, far from actively supporting the guerrillas at the tactical level, Senegalese forces in Casamance Region were limiting the freedom of movement of the PAIGC, even when they were threatened by Portuguese Guinea forces.

Judicial actions growing out of these incidents included the trials of fourteen people in late 1972 for activities described in formal charges as "acts and maneuvers of a nature to compromise public security." Official reports referred to the deaths of six soldiers as a result of such actions, which were said to have included forbidden contacts with citizens of Portuguese Guinea. The court of first instance in Ziguinchor sentenced one person to five years in prison and the loss of certain rights for ten years. Nine other defendants were given sentences ranging from one to five years' imprisonment, and four were released.

The Senegalese government apparently wanted the issue kept at a low key. At the same time it sought to affirm Senegal's ability as a sovereign nation to maintain security in Casamance Region and to police and defend one of its most remote and difficult border areas.

BIBLIOGRAPHY

Section I. Social

Adamolekun, Ladipo. "The French Tradition of Administrative Training in Africa. The Senegalese Experience," *Administration* [Ibadan], January 1969, 93-102.

Administration et Diplomatie d'Afrique Noire et de Madagascar, 1962. Paris: Europe-Outremer and Ediafric, 1962.

African Music. Paris: United Nations Educational, Scientific and Cultural Organization, 1972.

African Studies Bulletin, V, May 1962.

African Systems of Thought. (Third International African Seminar.) New York: Oxford University Press, 1965.

Africa Report (Special Issue on "African Socialism"), VIII, May 1963.

Africa 69/70. Paris: Société Presse Africaine Associée, 1970.

Afrique Occidentale Française. 2 vols. (Under the direction of Eugène Guernier.) Paris: Encyclopédie Coloniale et Maritime, 1949.

Altbach, Philip G. *Higher Education in Developing Countries: A Select Bibliography.* (Occasional Papers in International Affairs, XXIV.) Cambridge: Harvard University Press, 1970.

Ames, David W. "Belief in 'Witches' Among the Rural Wolof of the Gambia," *Africa* [London], XXIX, July 1959, 263-273.

Angrand, Armand P. *Les Lébous de la Presqu'île du Cap Vert.* Dakar: Gensul, 1950.

Annuario Pontificio per l'Anno 1973. Rome: Tipografia Poliglotta Vaticana, 1973.

Balandier, Georges, and Mercier, Paul. *Particularisme et Evolution: Les Pêcheurs Lébou du Sénégal.* (Etudes Sénégalaises, No. 3.) Saint-Louis: Centre IFAN-Sénégal, 1952.

Bal, M. "l'Homme noire dans la poésie," *Pensée* [Paris], No. 103, 1962, 18-29.

Banque Centrale des Etats de l'Afrique de l'Ouest. *Rapport d'Activité, 1961.* Paris: BCEAO, 1962.

Ba, Oumar. "Trois poèmes populaires," *Cahiers d'Etudes Africaines* [Paris]; VIII, No. 2(30), 1968, 318.

Ba, Ousmane. "Du Nom au Fouta Toro," *Bulletin de l'Institut Fondamental d'Afrique Noire* [Dakar], XXIX, No. 3-4, July-October 1967, 923-962.

―――. "Notes sur la démocratie en pays Toucouleur," *Afrique-Documents* [Dakar], Nos. 81-82, 1965, 223-235.

Ba, Sekou. *L'Emploi des Jeunes au Sénégal.* Dakar: Institut Africain de Développement Economique et de Planification, November 1970.

——. *Structure des Populations Africains.* Dakar: Institut de Développement Economique et de Planification, 1970.

Behrman, Lucy C. *Muslim Brotherhoods and Politics in Senegal.* Cambridge: Harvard University Press, 1970.

——. "The Political Significance of the Wolof Adherence to Muslim Brotherhoods in the Nineteenth Century," *African Historical Studies* [Boston], I, No. 1, 1968, 60–78.

Beier, Ulli. "The Theme of the Ancestors in Senghor's Poetry," *Black Orpheus* [Ibandan], May 5, 1959, 15–17.

Benot, Yves. "Négritude, socialisme Africain et réalisme," *Pensée* [Paris], No. 121, June 1965, 22–53.

Beth, and Bertin. *Le Sénégal, Pays d'Animisme, d'Islam et de Christianisme.* Paris: Centre Militaire d'Information et de Documentation sur l'Outre Mer, February 11, 1966.

Billen M.; le Guerinel, N.; and Moreigne, J.P. "Les Associations des Jeunes à Dakar," *Psychopathologie Africaine* [Dakar], III, No. 3, 1967, 373–400.

Bolibaugh, Jerry B. *Educational Development in Guinea, Mali, Senegal, and Ivory Coast.* Washington: U.S. Department of Health, Education and Welfare, 1972.

Bonvin, Jean. *L'Education Facteur de Croissance et de Développement Economique: Une Etude de Planification à long terme dans le Cadre du Sénégal.* Berne: H. Lang, 1970.

Bourges, Y. "La Formation et l'enseignement dans l'aide française aux pays francophones de l'Afrique Noire et de l'Océan Indien," *Communautés et Continents* [Paris], LXIV, No. 27, July-September 1972, 17–21.

Bourlon, A. "Mourides et Mouridisme 1953." Pages 53–74 in M. Chailley, et al.; *Notes et Etudes sur l'Islam en Afrique Noire,* (Recherches et Documents, I.) Paris: Centre de Hautes Etudes Administratives sur l'Afrique et l'Asie Modernes, 1962.

Boutillier, J.-L., et al. *La Moyenne Vallée du Sénégal: Etude Socio-Economique.* Paris: Presses Universitaries, 1962.

Brasseur, Gerard. "Démographies des Ndout," *Notes Africaines* [Dakar], No. 48, October 1950, 121–123.

——. *Le Problème de l'Eau au Sénégal.* (Etudes Sénégalaises No. 4.). Saint-Louis: Centre IFAN-Sénégal, 1952.

Brench, Anthony C. *The Novelist's Inheritance in French Speaking Africa.* London: Oxford University Press, 1967.

Brigaud, Félix. *Histoire Moderne et Contemporaire du Sénégal.* Dakar: Research and Documentation Center, 1966.

Bulletin de l'Afrique Noire [Paris], VII, March 13, 1963.

Bulletin Général de la Congrégation du Saint-Esprit [Paris], No. 702, 1962.

Campion-Vincent, Véronique. "Systèmes d'enseignement et de la mobilité sociale au Sénégal," *Revue Française de Sociologie* [Paris], II, No. 2, April-June 1970, 164-178.

Cassirer, Henry R. "Audio-visual Media for Adult Education in Africa: The Dakar Pilot Project," *UNESCO Chronicle* [Paris], XII, No. 2, February 1966, 61-66.

————. "Telecommunications and Education," *Telecommunication Journal* [Paris] (UNESCO), XXXVII, No. 7, July 1970, 315-326.

Chabas, J. "Le Droit de Succession chez les Ouolofs," *Annales Africaines* [Dakar], No. 1, 1956, 75-119.

————. "Le Mariage et le divorce dans les coutumes des Ouolofs habitant les grands centres du Sénégal," *Revue Juridique et Politique de l'Union Française* [Paris], VI, October-December 1952, 474-532.

Chailley. *L'Islam au Sénégal.* Paris: Centre Militaire d'Information et de Documentation sur l'Outre-Mer, July 1965.

Chambre de Commerce d'Agriculture et d'Industrie de Dakar. *L'Economie du Sénégal.* Dakar: Chambre de Commerce d'Agriculture et d'Industrie de Dakar, April 1961.

Chataignes, Abel. "Les Populations du cercle de Kédougou," *Bulletins et Mémoires de la Société d'Anthropologie de Paris* [Paris], No. 5, 1963, 87-111.

Church, R.J. Harrison. "Senegal," *Focus*, No. 15, 1964 (entire issue).

————. *West Africa: A Study of the Environment and Man's Use of It.* London: Longmans, Green, 1960.

Cohen, William B. "A Century of Modern Administration: From Faidherbe to Senghor," *Civilisations* [Brussels], XX, No. 1, 1970, 40-49.

Collomb, Henri, and Ayats, Henri. "Les Migrations au Sénégal: Etude Psychopathologique," *Cahiers d'Etudes Africaines* [Paris], II, No. 4, 1962, 570-597.

Colloque sur la Négritude. Paris: Editions Présence Africaine, 1971.

Colloquium on Negro Art: 1st World Festival of Negro Arts. Paris: Présence Africaine, 1968.

Copans, J. "La notion de dynamisme différentiel dans l'analyse sociologique: société traditionnelle, système mouride, société sénégalaise." Pages 19-34 in J. Copans, et al. *Maintenance Sociale et Changement Economique au Sénégal, I: Doctrine économique et pratique du travail chez les Mourides, No. 15. Paris: Travaux et Documents de l'Office de la Recherche Scientifique et Technique Outre-Mer, 1972.

Cornevin, Robert. *Histoire des Peuples de l'Afrique Noire.* Paris: Berger-Levrault, 1960.

Coughlain, Robert, et al. *Tropical Africa.* Life World Library, New York: Time, 1962.

Coutumiers Juridiques de l'Afrique Occidentale Française, I: Sénégal. (Publications du Comité d'Etudes Historiques et Scientifiques de l'Afrique Occidentale Française, Série A, No. 8-10.) Paris: Larose, 1939.

Crowder, Michael. *Senegal: A Study in French Assimilation Policy.* London: Oxford University Press, for Institute of Race Relations, 1962.

———. *Senegal: A Study of French Assimilation Policy.* London: Methuen, 1967.

Cruise O'Brien, Donal B. "Co-Operators and Bureaucrats: Class Formation in a Senegalese Peasant Society," *Africa* [London], XLI, No. 4, October 1971, 263-278.

———. *The Mourides of Senegal: The Political and Economic Organization of an Islamic Brotherhood.* London: Oxford University Press, 1971.

Cruise O'Brien, Rita. *White Society in Black Africa: The French of Senegal.* Evanston: Northwestern University Press, 1972.

Curtin, Philip D. *The Atlantic Slave Trade.* Madison: University of Wisconsin Press. 1969.

Dalby, David. "Distribution and Nomenclature of the Manding People and Their Language." Pages 1-13 in Carleton T. Hodge (ed.), *Papers on the Manding.* Bloomington: Indiana University Research Center, 1971.

———. "Further Indigenous Scripts of West Africa: Manding, Wolof and Fula Alphabets and Yoruba 'Holy Writing'." Pages 161-181 in Malcolm Guthrie (ed.), *African Language Studies,* X. London: School of Oriental and African Studies, 1969.

De Garine, Igor. "Usages Alimentaires dans la Région de Khombole (Sénégal)," *Cahiers d'Etudes Africaines* [Paris], III, No. 2, 1962, 218-265.

Delbard, B. *Les Dynamismes Sociaux au Sénégal: les Processus de Formation de Classes Sociales dans un Etat d'Afrique de l'Ouest.* Dakar: n.pub., 1966.

de Lestrange, Monique. *Les Coniagui et les Bassari.* (Monographies Ethnologiques Africaines, Institut International Africain.) Paris: Presses Universitaires, 1955.

Deloisy, E. "1969-La Crise Universitaire à Dakar," *Projet* [Paris], No. 37, July-August 1969, 864-868.

De Sapir, Olga Linares. "Agriculture and Diola Society." Pages 193-227 in Peter F.M. McLoughlin (ed.), *African Food Production Systems.* Baltimore: Johns Hopkins Press, 1970.

Deschamps, Hubert Jules. *Peuples et Nations d'Outre-mer.* Paris: Dalloz, 1954.

———. *Le Sénégal et la Gambie.* Paris: Presses Universitaires de France, 1964.

Despont, J. *Afrique, Terre Chrétienne?* Paris: Editions St. Paul, 1960.

Diakhate, Lamine. "La Littérature sénégalaise d'expression française," *Afrique* [Dakar] (Quarterly Supplement No. 4), 1966, 50-55.

356

Diarassouba, Valy-Charles. *L'Evolution des Structures Agricoles du Sénégal*. Besancon, France: Imprimerie Moderne de l'Est, 1968.

————. *L'Evolution des Structures Agricoles du Sénégal*. Paris: Editions Cujas, 1969.

Diarra, Souleymane. "La Population du Sénégal," *Bulletin de l'Institut Fondamental d'Afrique Noire* [Dakar] (Series B), XXXIII, No. 3, 1971, 642–657.

Diop, Abdoulaye Bara. "La Culture Wolof: traditions et changements," *Notes Africaines* [Dakar], No. 121, January 1969, 1–7.

————. "Enquête sur la migration Toucouleur à Dakar," *Bulletin de l'Institut Fondamental d'Afrique Noire* [Dakar], Série B, XXII, No. 3–4, 1960, 393–418.

————. "Parente et famille Wolof en milieu rural," *Bulletin de l'Institut Fondamental d'Afrique Noire* [Dakar], XXXII, No. 1, January 1970, 216–229.

————. *Société Toucouleur et Migration*. Dakar: Institut Fondamental d'Afrique Noire, 1965.

Diop, Cheikh Anta. "Etude Comparée des Systèmes Politiques et Sociaux de l'Europe et de l'Afrique, de l'Antiquité à la Formation des Etats Modernes." Ph. D. dissertation, Faculté des Lettres et Sciences Humaines. Paris: University of Paris, May 14, 1959.

Diop, Papa A. "Senegal: The Battle to Create Employment," *ILO Panorama* [Geneva], March-April 1970, 18–27.

Diouf, Bara. "La Littérature sénégalaise d'expression française," *Senegal Carrefour* [Dakar], No. 1, January 1967, 27–30.

Dubie, Paul. "La Vie matérielle des Maures: Les Nomades, l'agriculture, le commerce la sédentarisation des Maures et leurs activités hors de Mauritaine." Pages 116–252 in Institut Français d'Afrique Noire (ed.), *Mélanges Ethnologiques* (Mémoires de l'IFAN, No. 23.), Dakar: Institut Français d'Afrique Noire, 1953.

Dubois, Jean-Paul. *L'Emigration des Serer vers la zone arachidière Orientale*. Office de la Recherche Scientifique et Technique Outre-Mer, May 1971.

Duchemin, Claude. "Les Français à Dakar," *Europe-France Outremer: Une Décolonisation Réussie: Le Sénégal*, XXXVII, No. 376, March 1961, 49.

"L'Ecole Nationale de l'Economie Appliquée de Dakar," *Chronique des Instituts et Ecoles d'Administration* [Tangiers], 2C, December 1967, 41–44.

Educational Planning: A World Survey of Problems and Prospects. Paris: United Nations Educational, Scientific and Cultural Organization, 1970.

"The Education of Women in Rural Senegal," *Foreign Education Digest*, XXVII, July-September 1962, 38–41.

Emmerson, Donald K. *Students and Politics in Developing Nations*. New York: Praeger, 1968.

357

Europe-France Outremer: L'Afrique d'Expression Française [Paris], XXXIX, No. 385, March 1962.

Fage, J.D. *An Introduction to the History of West Africa.* Cambridge: Cambridge University Press, 1959.

"Fermeture des éstablissements scolaires au Sénégal," *Afrique Nouvelle* [Paris], Nos. 20-26, June 1968, 1089.

Fofana, B.S. *Examen du Phénomène de Migration dans les Pays de L'O.E.R.S.* Dakar: Institut Africain de Développement Economique et de Planification, July 1971.

Foltz, William J. "The Political Parties of Senegal." In James S. Coleman and Carl Rosberg (eds.), *Political Groups in Middle Africa.* Berkeley: University of California Press, 1963 (prepublication typescript).

Fougeyrollas, Pierre F., and Valladon, F. "Sénégal." (Monographies Africaines No. 11.) Paris: UNESCO Institut International de Planification de l'Education, 1966.

Froelich, J.C. *Les Musulmans d'Afrique Noire.* Paris: Editions de l'Orante, 1962.

Gamble, David P. *The Wolof of Senegambia, Together with Notes on the Lebu and the Serer.* (Ethnographic Survey of Africa, Western Africa, Pt. XIV.) London: International African Institute, 1957.

Garnier, Christine, and Ermont, Philippe. *Sénégal, Porte de l'Afrique.* Paris: Librairie Hachette, 1962.

Gaskin, L.J.P. *African Art: A Bibliography of.* London: International African Institute, 1965.

————. *Music in Africa: A Select Bibliography of.* London: International African Institute, 1965.

Gavrand, H. "Dynamisme interne de la famille Serer," (Part I) *Afrique-Documents* [Dakar], Nos. 85-86, 1966, 95-122.

————. "Dynamisme interne de la famille Serer," (Part II) *Afrique-Documents* [Dakar], Nos. 81-82, 1965, 223-235.

————. "Dynamisme Serer dans le Sénégal moderne," (Part II) *Afrique-Documents* [Dakar], Nos. 105-106, 1969, 291-318.

Gayet, Georges. "Les Libanais et les Syriens dans l'Ouest Africain." Pages 161-172 in International Institute of Differing Civilizations (ed.), *Ethnic and Cultural Pluralism in Intertropical Communities,* (Report of the Thirtieth Meeting Held in Lisbon, April 15-18, 1957.) Brussels: 1957.

Girard, J. "De la communauté traditionnelle à la collectivité moderne en Casamance. Essai sur le dynamisme du droit traditionnel," *Annales Africaines* [Dakar], XI, 1964, 135-165.

Gonidec, Pierre. *La République du Sénégal.* Paris: Berger-Levrault, 1968.

Gorer, Geoffrey. *Africa Dances.* London: Faber and Faber, 1935.

Gouilly, Alphonse. *L'Islam dans l'Afrique Occidentale Française.* Paris: Editions Larose, 1952.

Greenberg, Joseph H. "The Languages of Africa," *International Journal of American Linguistics*, XXIX, No. 1, Pt. 2, 1963.
———. *The Languages of Africa.* (3d ed.) Bloomington: Indiana University, 1970.
———. *Studies in African Linguistic Classification.* New Haven: Compass, 1955.
Guid'Ouest Africain: L'Afrique Occidentale, 1961-1962. Dakar: Agence Havas, 1961.
Hauser, A. "Quelques Relations des Travailleurs de l'Industrie à Leur Travail en A.O.F. (Sénégal, Soundan, Guinée)," *Bulletin de l'Institut Fondamental d'Afrique Noire* [Dakar], Série B, XVII, No. 1-2, 1955, 129-141.
Heissler, Nina, et al. *Diffusion du Livre: Développement de la Lecture en Afrique, Tchad-Sénégal.* Paris: Culture et Développement, 1971.
Hennebelle, Guy (ed.). "Les Cinémas africains en 1972," *L'Afrique Littéraire et Artistique* [Paris], No. 20, January-March 1972, 1-371.
Herdeck, Donald E. *African Authors: A Bibliographical Companion to Black African Writing 1300-1972.* Esplanade, Maryland: Black Orpheus Press, 1973.
Hopkins, Nicholas S. "Maninka Social Organization." Pages 99-128 in Carleton T. Hodge (ed.), *Papers on the Manding.* Bloomington: Indiana University Research Center, 1971.
Huegel, S. "Una produzione cinemetografica africana è in via di sviluppo: cinema senegalese," *Missioni* [Rome], LIII, No. 2, February 1967, 60-63.
Hunter, Guy. *The New Societies of Tropical Africa.* New York: Oxford University Press, 1962.
Hymans, Jacques L. "French Influences on Léopold Senghor's Theory of Negritude, 1928-1948," *Race*, VII, No. 4, April 1966, 365-370.
———. *Léopold Sédar Senghor: An Intellectual Biography.* Edinburgh: University of Edinburgh Press, 1971.
Idowu, H.O. "Assimilation in 19th Century Senegal." *Bulletin de l'Institut Fondamental d'Afrique Noire* [Dakar] (Series B), XXX, No. 4, 1968, 1422-1477.
———. "The Establishment of Elective Institutions in Senegal, 1869-1880," *Journal of African History* [London], IX, No. 2, May 1968, 261-277.
Ilboudo, Gilbert. "L'Afrique Noire d'Expression Française au Rendez-vous Littéraire," *Afrique Nouvelle* [Dakar], June 7-13, 1963, 8, 9.
International Yearbook of Education, 1968, XXX. Geneva: United Nations Educational, Scientific and Cultural Organization, International Bureau of Education, 1968.
International Yearbook of Education, 1969, XXXI. Geneva: UNESCO, International Bureau of Education, 1969.
Jahn, J., and Dressler, C.P. *Bibliography of Creative African Writing.* Nendeln, Liechtenstein: Kraus-Thomson Organization, 1971.

"Jazz à Dakar," *Bingo* [Dakar], No. 123, April 1963, 12, 13.

Joachim, Paulin. "African Literature: Part III, French-Speaking Africa," *Africa Report*, VIII, March 1963, 11, 12.

Johnson, G. Wesley. *The Emergency of Black Politics in Senegal, 1900–1920*. Stanford: Stanford University Press, 1971.

Johnston, Bruce F. *The Staple Food Economies of Western Tropical Africa*. Stanford: Stanford University Press, 1958.

Kane, Cheik Hamidou. "Comme si nous étions donné rendez-vous," *Esprit* [Paris], XXIX, No. 199 (New Series), October 1961, 375–387.

Kimble, George H.T. *Tropical Africa*. 2 vols. New York: Twentieth Century Fund, 1960.

Klein, Martin A. *Islam and Imperialism in Senegal: Sine-Saloum, 1847–1914*. Stanford: Stanford University Press, for the Hoover Institution, 1968.

————. "Social and Economic Factors in the Muslim Revolution in Senegambia," *Journal of African History* [London], XIII, No. 3, 1972, 419–441.

Koren, Henry J. *The Spiritans: A History of the Congregation of the Holy Ghost*. (Duquesne Studies, Spiritan Series No. 1.) Pittsburgh: Duquesne University, 1958.

Lafont, F. "Le Gandoul et les Niominkas," *Bulletin du Comité d'Etudes Historiques et Scientifiques de l'A.O.F.* [Dakar], XXI, No. 3, 1938, 385–458.

Leary, Frances Anne. "The Role of the Mandinka in the Islamization of the Casamance, 1850–1901." Pages 227–248 in Carleton T. Hodge (ed.), *Papers on the Manding*. Bloomington: Indiana University Research Center, 1971.

Le Blanc, C. "Un village de la vallée du Sénégal: Amadi-Ounaré," *Cahiers d'Outre-Mer* [Bordeaux], XVII, No. 66, April-June 1964, 117–148.

Leeming, Owen. "Africa: TV in Senegalese Adult Education," *School and Society*, XCVI, November 23, 1968, 442–444.

Léger, Jean-Marc. *Afrique Française—Afrique Nouvelle*. Ottawa: Le Cercle du Livre de France, 1958.

Legum, Colin (ed.). *Africa Contemporary Record: Annual Survey and Documents, 1970–1971*. London: Rex Collings, 1971.

————. *Africa Contemporary Record: Annual Survey and Documents, 1971–1972*. London: Rex Collings, 1972.

Legum, Colin, and Drysdale, John (eds.). *Africa Contemporary Record: Annual Survey and Documents, 1968–1969*. London: Africa Research Limited, 1969.

————. *Africa Contemporary Record: Annual Survey and Documents, 1969–1970*. Exeter: Africa Research Limited, 1970.

Leiris, Michel, and Delange, Jacqueline. *African Art*. (Trans., Michael Ross.) (The Arts of Mankind Series.) New York: Golden Press, 1968.

Leuzinger, Elsy. *Africa: The Art of the Negro Peoples*. (2d ed.) (Art of the World Series.) New York: Crown, 1967.

Lewis, I.M. *Islam in Tropical Africa.* London: Oxford University, 1966.

Lorimer, Frank. *Demographic Information on Tropical Africa.* Boston: Boston University Press, 1961.

Ly, Boubakar. "L'honneur dans les sociétés Ouolof et Toucouleur du Sénégal," *Présence Africaine* [Paris], No. 61, 1967, 32-67.

Mandery, Guy, and Dumont, Pierre. "Voies nouvelles de l'enseignement," *Coopération et Développement* [Paris], No. 38, November-December 1971, 3-8.

Marc, Elisabeth. "L'émigration des paysans et ses conséquences sur la vie d'un village sénégalais," *Afrique Littéraire et Artistique* [Paris], IV, No. 16, April 1971, 46-56.

"Le Marché Sénégalais," *Marchés Tropicaux et Méditerranéens* [Paris], XXVI, No. 1283, June 13, 1970, 1925-1933.

Markovitz, Irving L. "A Bibliographic Essay on the Study of Ideology, Political Thought, Development, and Politics in Senegal, Part I," *Current Bibliography on African Affairs* [Westport], III, No. 3, March 1970, 5-29.

————. "A Bibliographic Essay on the Study of Ideology, Political Thought, Development, and Politics in Senegal, Part II," *Current Bibliography on African Affairs* [Westport], III, No. 4, April 1970, 5-35.

————. *Léopold-Sédar Senghor and the Politics of Negritude.* New York: Atheneum Press, 1969.

————. "Traditional Social Structure: The Islamic Brotherhoods and Political Development in Senegal," *Journal of Modern African Studies* [London], VIII, No. 1, April 1970, 73-96.

Marty, Paul. *Etudes sur l'Islam au Sénégal.* 2 vols. (Collection de la Revue du Monde Musulman.) Paris: Ernest Leroux, 1917.

Massé, L. "Contribution à l'étude de la ville de Thiès 1er dépouillement sur la situation matrimoniale," *Bulletin de l'Institut Français d'Afrique Noire* [Dakar], Série B, XVIII, 3-4, 1956, 255-280.

Masson-Diop, Assane. "Le Mouvement coopératif Sénégalais," *Revue Française d'Etudes Politiques Africaines* [Paris], No. 61, January 1971, 49-61.

Mauny, Raymond A. *Glossaire des Expressions et Termes Locaux Employés dans l'Ouest Africain.* Dakar: Institut Français d'Afrique Noire, 1952.

————. "The Question of Ghana." Pages 109-122 in *Africa from Early Times to 1800.* London: Oxford University Press, 1968.

————. *Tableau Géographique de l'Ouest Africain au Moyen Age.* (Mémoires de l'IFAN, No. 61.) Dakar: Institut Français d'Afrique Noire, 1961.

Mazel, J. "Le Festival mondial des arts Nègres: Un magnifique exemple de coopération international," *Communautés et Continents* [Paris], No. 3, July-September 1966, 29-32.

M'Bengue. "Enseignement et journalisme," *Afrique* [Dakar] (Quarterly Supplement), No. 4, 1966, 45-49.

Mercier, Paul. "Aspects de la société Africaine dans l'agglomération Dakaroise: Groupes familiaux et unités de voisinage." Pages 11-14 in Institut Français d'Afrique Noire (ed.), *L'Agglomération Dakaroise: Quelques Aspects Sociologiques et Démographiques* (Etudes Sénégalaises, No. 5.), Saint-Louis: Centre IFAN-Sénégal, 1954.

————. "Aspects de la stratification sociale dans l'Ouest Africain," *Cahiers Internationaux de Sociologie* [Paris], XVII, 1954, 47-65.

————. "Etude du mariage et enquête urbaine," *Cahiers d'Etudes Africaines* [Paris], I, No. 1, 1960, 28-43.

————. "Evolution of Senegalese Elites," *International Social Science Journal: African Elites* [Paris], VIII, No. 3, 1956, 441-452.

Mercier, Roger. "L'Imagination dans la poésie de Léopold-Sédar Senghor," *Literature East and West* [Austin], XII, No. 1, March 1968, 35-55.

————. "La Littérature d'expression Française en Afrique Noire," *Dakar-Matin* [Dakar], April 29, May 8, 14, 1963, 5.

Milcent, Ernest. "Senegal." Pages 87-147 in Gwendolyn Carter (ed.), *African One-Party States*. Ithaca: Cornell University Press, 1962.

Milcent, Ernest, and Sordet, Monique. *Léopold-Sédar Senghor et la Naissance de l'Afrique Moderne*. Paris: Editions Seghers, 1969.

Monteil, Vincent. "Black Islam," *Croissance de Jeunes Nations* [Paris], X, November 1971, 14-15.

————. "Une Confrérie Musulmane: Les Mourides du Sénégal," *Archives de Sociologie des Religions* [Paris], No. 14, July-December 1962, 77-102.

————. *L'Islam Noir*. Paris: Editions du Seuil, 1971.

Moore, Gerald. "Toward Realism in French African Writing," *Journal of Modern African Studies* [London], I, No. 1, 61-73.

Morganthau, Henry. "Guides to African Films," *Africa Report*, XIII, No. 5, May 1968, 52-54.

Morgenthau, Ruth Schachter. *Political Parties in French West-Africa*. New York: Oxford University Press, 1964.

Mpiku, J. Mbelolo Ya. "From One Mystification to Another: 'Négritude' and 'Négraille' in 'le Devoir de Violence'," *Review of National Literature*, II, No. 2, Fall 1971, 124-145.

Murdock, George Peter. *Africa: Its Peoples and Their Culture History*. New York: McGraw-Hill, 1959.

Nasri, Samir. "Conditions of Lebanese in Senegal," *al-Nahar* [Beirut], No. 3, 1971, 47.

Newbury, C.W. "The Formation of the Government General of French West Africa," *Journal of African History* [London], I, No. 1, 1960, 111-128.

Nicol, Davidson. "West African Poetry," *Africa South in Exile* [London], V, April-June 1961, 115-122.

Nikiprowetzky, Tolia. *Trois Aspects de la Musique Africaine: Maurita-nie, Sénégal, Niger.* Paris: Office de Coopération Radiophonique, 1965.

Oliver, Roland, and Fage, J.D. *A Short History of Africa.* (Penguin African Library, AP2.) Baltimore: Penguin Books, 1962.

Oluruntimehim, B. Olatunji. "The Idea of Islamic Revolution and Tukulor Constitutional Evolution," *Bulletin de l'Institut Fonda-mental d'Afrique Noire* [Dakar] (Series B), XXXIII, No. 4, October 1971, 675-692.

————. "Resistance Movements in the Tukulor Empire," *Cahiers d'Etudes Africaines* [Paris], VIII, No.1, 1968, 123-143.

————. *The Segu Tukulor Empire.* London: Longmans, 1966.

"L'Orientation du deuxième plan revoit le développement de l'enseigne-ment secondaire et technique," *Afrique* [Dakar] (Quarterly Supple-ment), No. 4, 1966, 45.

Paques, Viviana. *Les Bambara.* (Monographies Ethnologiques Afri-caines, Institut International Africain.) Paris: Presses Universitaires de France, 1954.

Paricsy, Paul J. "Selected International Bibliography of Negritude, 1960-1968," *Studies in Black Literature,* I, No. 1, September 1970 (entire issue).

Parrinder, Geoffrey. "Islam in West Africa." Pages 220-235 in A.J. Arberry (ed.), *Religion in the Middle East,* II. Cambridge: University Press, 1969.

"Peinture populaire et art moderne," *Afrique* [Dakar] (Quarterly Supplement), No. 4, 1966, 60-64.

Pélissier, Paul. *Les Paysans du Sénégal: Les Civilisations Agraires du Cayor à la Casamance.* St. Yrieix: Imprimerie Fabrègue, 1966.

————. "Les Paysans Sérères: Essai sur la Formation d'un Terroir du Sénégal," *Les Cahiers d'Outre-Mer* [Bordeaux], VI, No. 22, 1953, 105-127.

Pentecôte sur le Monde: Sénégal, "Terre Embrasée" [Paris], No. 13, January-February 1959.

Peterec, Richard J. *The Port of Ziguinchor: The Direct Ocean Outlet for Casamance (Senegal).* New York: Columbia University, Division of Economic Geography, 1962.

————. *The Position of Kaolack (Senegal) and Other Ports of the Sa-loum Estuary in West African Trade.* New York: Columbia Univer-sity, Division of Economic Geography, 1962.

————. *St. Louis de Senegal: The Natural Ocean Outlet for the Senegal River Valley.* New York: Columbia University Press, 1966.

Peterec, R.L. *Dakar and West African Economic Development.* New York: Columbia University Press, 1967.

Phillips, John. *Agriculture and Ecology in Africa.* New York: Praeger, 1960.

Pichl, Walter J. *The Cangin Group: A Language Group in Northern Senegal.* Pittsburgh: Duquesne University Press, 1966.

Quesnot, F. "Les Cadres Maraboutiques de l'Islam Sénégalais." Pages 127-194 in M. Chailley, et al., *Notes et Etudes sur l'Islam en Afrique Noire* (Recherches et Documents, I), Paris: Centre de Hautes Etudes Administratives sur l'Afrique et l'Asie Modernes, 1962.

————. "Influence du Mouridisme sur le Tidjanisme." Pages 115-125 in M. Chailley, et al., *Notes et Etudes sur l'Islam en Afrique Noire* (Recherches et Documents, I), Paris: Centre de Hautes Etudes Administratives sur l'Afrique et l'Asie Modernes, 1962.

Quinn, Charlotte A. *Mandingo Kingdoms of the Senegambia: Traditionalism, Islam, and European Expansion.* Evanston: Northwestern University Press, 1972.

Rajaoson, François. *Enseignement Supérieur et Besoins en Main-d'oeuvre: le Cas du Sénégal.* Dakar: United Nations, African Institute for Economic Development and Planning, 1972.

Ravault, F. "Kanel, l'Exode rural dans un village de la vallée du Sénégal," *Les Cahiers d'Outre-Mer* [Bordeaux], XVII, No. 65, January-March 1964, 58-80.

Republic of Senegal. (Studies on Developing Countries.) Budapest: Center for Afro-Asian Research of the Hungarian Academy of Sciences, 1972.

Reverdy, J.C. *Une Société Rurale au Sénégal: Les Structures Foncières Familiales et Villageoises des Serer.* Aix-en-Provence: Centre Africain des Sciences Humaines Appliquées, 1968.

Richard-Molard, Jacques. *Cartes Ethno-Démographiques de l'Afrique Occidentale.* (Feuilles No. 1.) Dakar: Institute Français d'Afrique Noire, 1952.

Rivkin, Arnold. *Nations by Design: Institution-Building in Africa.* Garden City: Anchor Books, 1968.

Robinson, Kenneth. "Senegal: The Elections to the Territorial Assembly, March 1957." Pages 281-390 in W.J.M. MacKenzie and Kenneth Robinson (eds.), *Five Elections in Africa*, Oxford: Clarendon Press, 1960.

Rouset de Pina, J. "La Nouvelle bibliothèque centrale de l'Université de Dakar," *Bulletin des Bibliothèques de France* [Paris], XI, No. 8, August 1966, 293-304.

Ruth Sloan Associates. *The Educated African: A Country by Country Survey of Educational Development in Africa.* (ed., Helen Kitchen.) New York: Praeger, 1962.

Saint-Martin, Yves. "Les Relations diplomatiques entre la France et l'Empire Toucouleur de 1860 à 1887," *Bulletin de l'Institut Fondamental d'Afrique Noire* [Dakar], XXVI, Nos. 1-2, April 1965, 183-222.

————. "Senegal: Dix Ans d'Indépendance," *Europe-France Outremer* [Paris], March 1970, 6-59.

Samba Ba (ed.). *Who Is Léopold-Sédar Senghor?* Dakar: n. pub. n.d.

Samb, Amar. "L'Influence de l'Islam sur la littérature 'Wolof'," *Bulletin de l'Institut Fondamental d'Afrique Noire* [Dakar] (Series B),

XXX, No. 2, April 1968, 628–641.

Sanaklé, Marc, and Pène, Pierre. *Médecine Sociale au Sénégal.* (Dossiers Africains, I.) Dakar: Afrique-Documents, March 1960.

Sapir, J. David. *A Grammar of Diola-Fogny.* Cambridge: Cambridge University Press, 1965.

Sasnett, Martena, and Sepmeyer, Inez. *Educational Systems of Africa: Interpretations for Use in the Evaluation of Academic Credentials.* Berkeley: University of California Press, 1966.

Seck, Assane. *Dakar, Métropole Ouest-Africaine.* Dakar: Institut Fondamental d'Afrique Noire, 1970.

——. "La Formation d'une Classe Moyenne en Afrique Occidentale Française." Pages 159–163 in International Institute of Differing Civilizations (ed.), *Development of a Middle Class in Tropical and Sub-tropical Countries.* (Record of the XXIXth Session held in London, September 13–16, 1955.) Brussels: Institute of Differing Civilizations, 1956.

——. "l'Université de Dakar," *Afrique Nouvelle* [Paris], No. 1094, July 25–31, 1968, 8.

Selected Economic Data for the Less Developed Countries. (RC–W–136). Washington: Agency for International Development, 1973.

Sembène, Ousmane. "God's Bits of Wood" (Reviewed by James Fernandez), *Africa Report*, VIII, February 1963, 29.

Senegal. Commissariat à l'Information à la Radiodiffusion et au Tourisme. *Faits et Chiffres.* Dakar: 1965.

——. *Sénégal: Les Pays et Les Hommes.* Dakar: 1965.

Senegal. *Enquête Démographique Nationale, 1970–71; Résultats Provisiores du ler Passage.* Dakar: Ministère des Finances et des Affaires Economiques, Direction de la Statistique, 1971.

Senegal. Ministère de l'Education Nationale. *Renseignements Statistiques sur la Situation de l'Enseignement du 1er Degré et de l'Enseignement Secondaire Général au 1er Janvier 1962.* N.pl.: n.d.

Senegal. Ministère des Finances et des Affaires Economiques. Direction de la Statistique. *Situations Economique du Sénégal, 1971.* Dakar, n.pub., 1972.

Senegal. Ministère du Plan et du Développement. *Cartes pour servir à l'améngement du territoire.* Dakar: n.pub., October 1965.

Senegal. Presidence du Conseil. Comité d'Etudes pour les problèmes sociaux. *Etudes des Besoins de l'Enfance au Sénégal.* N.pl.: n.pub., n.d. (mimeo).

Senegal. Presidence du Conseil. Commissariat Général au Plan. *Rapport sur la Première Année de l'Execution du Plan Quadriennal 1961–1964 de la République du Sénégal.* Dakar: June 20, 1962.

Senegal. Service de la Statistique et de la Mécanographie. *Recensement Démographique de Dakar, 1955.* N.pl.: Ministère du Plan, du Développement et de la Coopération Technique, March 1962.

Senghor, Blaise. "Le cinéma sénégalais," *Afrique* [Dakar] (Quarterly

Supplement), No. 4, 1966, 58–60.

Senghor, Léopold-Sédar. *L.S. Senghor, Poéte Sénégalais.* Paris: F. Nathan, 1965.

———. *Nocturnes.* New York: The Third Press, 1972.

———. *Poems.* Paris: Editions du Seuil, 1964.

———. "What is 'Negritude'?" (Extracts from a lecture given at Oxford.) *West Africa* [London], November 4, 1961, 1211.

Senghor, Sonar. "Les Difficultés du Théâtre Africaine," *L'Unité Africaine* [Dakar], April 10, 1963, 13; April 17, 1963, 15.

Shorter Encyclopedia of Islam. (Eds., H.A.R. Gibb and J.H. Kramers.) Ithaca: Cornell University Press, 1953.

Silla, Ousmane. "Langage et techniques thérapeutiques des cultes de possession des Lebou de Sénégal," *Bulletin de l'Institut Fondamental d'Afrique Noire* [Dakar] (Series B), XXXI, No. 1, January 1969, 215–238.

———. "Persistance des castes dans la société Wolof contemporaine," *Bulletin de l'Institut Fondamental d'Afrique Noire* [Dakar] (Series B), XXVIII, No. 3–4, July-October 1966, 731–770.

———. "Structure familiale et mentalité religieuse des Lebou du Sénégal," *Notes Africaines* [Dakar], No. 119, 1968, 79–83.

Smith, Pierre. "Les Diankhanké, histoire d'une dispersion," *Bulletins et Mémoires de la Société d'Anthropologie de Paris* [Paris] (Series XI), VIII, No. 4, 1965, 231–302.

Southall, Aidan (ed.). *Social Change in Modern Africa.* New York: Oxford University Press, for International African Institute, 1961.

Sow, Abdourahmane. "Monographie du village Camberène (Sénégal)," *Notes Africaines* [Dakar], No. 94, April 1962, 51–60.

"Special Festival," *Afrique* [Dakar], LV, May 1966, 35–39.

Stanislaus, Joseph, Brother. "The Growth of African Literature: A Survey of the Works Published by African Writers in English and French." Unpublished Ph.D. dissertation, Faculty of Letters. University of Montreal, 1952.

Statistical Yearbook, 1971. Paris: United Nations Educational, Scientific and Cultural Organization, 1972.

Statistiques Scolaires, 1969–1970. Dakar: Ministère de l'Education Nationale, n.d.

Suret-Canale, Jean. *Afrique Noire Occidentale et Centrale.* Paris: Editions Sociales, 1958.

Tardif, J. "Kedougou-aspects de l'histoire et da la situation socio-économique actuelle," *Bulletins et Mémoires de la Société d'Anthropologie de Paris* [Paris], VIII, No. 3–4, 1965, 167–230.

Terrisse, André. "Aspects du malaise paysan au Sénégal," *Revue Française d'Etudes Politiques Africaines* [Paris], V, No. 55, July 1970, 79–91.

Thaim, N'diaga. "L'Apprentissage du Bijoutier Wolof," *Notes Africaines* [Dakar], No. 42, April 1949, 53–54.

Thiam, Bodiel. "Hiérarchie de la Société Ouolove," *Notes Africaines* [Dakar], No. 41, January 1949, 12.

------. "Le Teugue ou Bijoutier Ouolof," *Notes Africaines* [Dakar], No. 61, January 1954, 22-25.

Thomas, Louis-Vincent. "Les Diola de Bassê Casamance," *Afrique-Documents* [Dakar] (New Series), No. 51, May 1960, 73-90.

------. *Les Diola: Essai d'Analyse Fonctionnelle sur une Population de Basse Casamance*. 2 vols. (Mémoires de l'IFAN, No. 55.) Dakar: Institut Fondamental d'Afrique Noire, 1959.

------. "Les Diola. Points de vue sur le présent et l'avenir d'une ethnie Sénégalaise," *Revue de Psychologie* [Le Havre], XXIII, No. 3, 1968, 244-275.

------. "L'espace social chez les Diola," *Notes Africaines* [Dakar], No. 111, July 1966, 89-97.

------. "Evolution de l'éducation au Sénégal," *Notes Africaines* [Dakar], No. 107, July 1965, 88-91.

------. "La Recherche sociale au Sénégal," *Social Science Information* [Paris], IV, No. 2, June 1965, 21-66.

------. "Les 'rois' Diola, hier, aujourd'hui, demain," *Bulletin de l'Institut Fondamental d'Afrique Noire* [Dakar] (Series B), XXXIV, No. 1, 1972, 151-174.

------. "Tradition et modernité chez les Diola de Casamance; Reflex sur le devenir des valeurs éducatives," *Bulletin de l'Institut Fondamental d'Afrique Noire* [Dakar] (Series B), XXX, No. 4, October 1968, 1488-1532.

------. "La Vie Pulsionelle du Diola," *Bulletin de l'Institut Fondamental d'Afrique Noire* [Dakar] (Series B), XXIV, No. 1-2, 1962, 105-154.

Thompson, Virginia, and Adloff, Richard. *French West Africa*. Stanford: Stanford University Press, 1958.

Thoré, Luc. "Dagoudane-Pikine. Etude Démographique et Sociologique," *Bulletin de l'Institut Fondamental d'Afrique Noire* [Dakar] (Series B), XXIV, No. 1-2, 1962, 155-198.

------. "Mariage et divorce dans la banlieue de Dakar," *Cahiers d'Etudes Africaines* [Paris], IV, No. 16, 1964, 492.

Trimingham, John Spencer. *A History of Islam in West Africa*. London: Oxford University Press, 1962.

"Two Initiatives" (editorial), *Présence Africaine* [Paris], XVI, No. 44, 1962, 5-8.

United Nations Educational, Scientific and Cultural Organization. *World Survey of Education*, III: Secondary Education. New York: International Documents Service, 1961.

U.S. Department of Commerce. Office of Technical Services. Joint Publications Research Service—JPRS (Washington). The following items are from the JPRS series *Translations on Africa*.

"African Student Protest Movement Examined," *Decennie 2*, Paris,

1973. (JPRS: 44,561, Series No. 337, 1973).

"AIPLF Cultural Affairs Resolutions Announced," *France-Eurafrique*, Paris. (JPRS: 58,798, Series No. 1029, 1971).

"Cabinet Adopts Educational Reforms," *Le Soleil*, Dakar, June 7, 1972. (JPRS: 56,344, Series No. 1175, 1972).

"Cabinet Notes Government-GES Endeavors," *Le Soleil*, Dakar, September 16, 1970. (JPRS: 51,508, Series No. 950, 1970).

"Education Minister Assane Seck Gives Views on Education," *Le Soleil*, Dakar, December 13, 1971. (JPRS: 54,988, Series No. 1106, 1972).

"Education Minister Speaks on Education Reform," *Dakar-Matin*, Dakar, October 18, 1969. (JPRS: 49,436, Series No. 842, 1969).

"French Assistance to University of Dakar Explained," *Le Soleil*, Dakar, April 9, 1971. (JPRS: 53,035, Series No. 1029, 1971).

"Higher Education Committee," *Dakar-Matin*, Dakar, April 7, 1970. (JPRS: 50,303, Series No. 893, 1970).

"Minister of Education Reports on University Reform," *Dakar-Matin*, Dakar, April 24, 1970. (JPRS: 50,541, Series No. 899, 1970).

"New Rector of University of Dakar Explains Changes," *Le Soleil*, Dakar, November 15, 1971. (JPRS: 54,652, Series No. 1090, 1971).

"Number of Registered School Children Increasing," *Europe-France Outremer*, Paris, January-February 1970. (JPRS: 50,463, Series No. 896, 1970).

"Senegal, Gambia to Cooperate in Education," *Le Soleil*, Dakar, November 3, 1972. (JPRS: 57,657, Series No. 1240, 1971).

"Spoken French Taught by Radio," *Coopération et Développement*, Paris, November-December 1971. (JPRS: 55,171, No. 116, 1972).

"Students Studying Abroad," *Le Soleil*, Dakar, September 7, 1971. (JPRS: 54,179, Series No. 1070, 1971).

"University Policy Changes Being Effected," *Le Soleil*, Dakar, July 28, 1971. (JPRS: 53,974, Series No. 1065, 1971).

"University Rector Comments on Student Orientation," *Le Soleil*, Dakar, November 24, 1971. (JPRS: 54,773, Series No. 1095, 1971).

"University Rector Discusses Enrollment, Programs," *Le Soleil*, Dakar, December 7, 1971. (JPRS: 54,923, Series No. 1101, 1972).

University of Dakar. Bureau Universitaire de Statistique et de Documentation. *Livret de l'Etudiant, 1961–1962.* N.pl.: 1961.

————. *Statistiques des Effectifs des Etudiants. Année Universitaire, 1961–1962.* Dakar: Bureau Universitaire de Statistique et de Documentation, December 1961.

Van Niekerk, Barend van Dyk. *The African Image (Negritude) in the work of Léopold-Sédar Senghor.* Cape Town: Balkema, 1970.

Vieyra, Pantin. "Le Cinéma et l'Afrique," *Topic*, No. 70, December 1972, 30–33.

Wane, Yaya. "Besoins sociaux et mobilité des Toucouleurs," *Notes Africaines* [Dakar], No. 101, January 1964, 16–23.

————. "Le Célibat en pays Toucouleur," *Bulletin de l'Institut Fondamental d'Afrique Noire* [Dakar] (Series B), XXXI, No. 3, July 1969, 717–770.

————. *Les Toucouleur de Fouta Toro: Stratification Sociale et Structures Familiales*. Dakar: Institute Fondamental d'Afrique Noire, 1969.

Willet, Frank. *African Art*. (Praeger World of Art Paperbacks.) New York: Praeger, 1971.

Winder, R. Bayly. "The Lebanese in West Africa," *Comparative Studies in Society and History*, IV, No. 3, 1962, 296–333.

Wioland, François, and Calvet, Maurice. "L'Expansion du Wolof au Sénégal," *Bulletin de l'Institut Fondamental d'Afrique Noire* [Dakar] (Series B), XXIX, No. 3–4, 1967, 604.

World Christian Handbook 1962. (Eds., H. Wakelin Coxill and Kenneth G. Grubb.) London: World Dominion Press, 1962.

World Christian Handbook 1968. (Eds., H. Wakelin Coxill and Kenneth G. Grubb.) London: Butterworth Press, 1967.

The World of Learning, 1972–73, II; Laos-Zambia. (23d ed.) London: Europa Publications, 1972.

(Various issues of the following periodicals were also used in the preparation of this section: *Africa Research Bulletin* [London], January 1973–June 1973; *Christian Science Monitor*, June 1972–July 1973; *Le Monde* [Paris], January 1973–June 1973; *New York Times*, January 1972–June 1973; and *Washington Post*, January 1973–June 1973.)

Section II. Political

Abraham, W.E. *The Mind of Africa*. (The Nature of Human Society Series.) London: Weidenfeld and Nicolson, 1962.

Adamolekun, Ladipo. "Bureaucrats and the Senegalese Political Process," *Journal of Modern African Studies* [London], IX, No. 4, December 1971, 543–559.

American Society of African Culture (ed.). *Pan-Africanism Reconsidered*. Berkeley: University of California Press, 1962.

Ansprenger, Franz. *Politik in Schwarzen Afrika*. Cologne: Westdeutscher Verlag, 1961.

Audat, Paul Louis. "Decentralization and Development: Experience of Some French-Speaking West African States," *African Administrative Studies* [Tangier], IV, B, December 1968, 1–5.

Behrman, Lucy C. *Muslim Brotherhoods and Politics in Senegal*. Cambridge: Harvard University Press, 1970.

Berg, Elliot J. "The Economic Basis of Political Choice in French West Africa," *American Political Science Review*, LIV, No. 2, 1960, 391–405.

Blanchet, André. *L'Itinéraire des Partis Africains Depuis Bamako*. (Tribune Livre, No. 31.) Paris: Plon, 1958.

Carter, Gwendolyn. *African One-Party States*. Ithaca: Cornell University Press, 1962.

Coulon, Christian. "Political Elites in Senegal," *Mawazo* [Kampala, Uganda], II, No. 2, June 1970, 21–35 and II, No. 4, December 1970, 29–37.

Cowan, L. Gray. *Local Government in West Africa*. New York: Columbia University Press, 1958.

Crowder, Michael. *Senegal: A Study in French Assimilation Policy*. London: Oxford University Press, for Institute of Race Relations, 1962.

Cruise O'Brien, Donal B. *The Mourides of Senegal: The Political and Economic Organization of an Islamic Brotherhood*. London: Oxford University Press, 1971.

Cruise O'Brien, Rita. "Senegal-The Gambia: Political Union Later," *Africa—An International Business, Economic and Political Monthly*, No. 23, July 1973, 38–39.

————. *White Society in Black Africa: The French of Senegal*. Evanston: Northwestern University Press, 1972.

Davis, Edward Braxton, III. "Relations Between France and Senegal, 1960-69." Unpublished doctoral dissertation, Woodrow Wilson Department of Government and Foreign Affairs, University of Virginia, 1970.

Delavignette, Robert. *Freedom and Authority in French West Africa.* London: Oxford University Press, for International African Institute, 1950.

Dia, Mamadou. *The African Nations and World Solidarity.* New York: Praeger, 1961.

Diop, Abdoulaye. "La Culture Wolof: traditions et changements," *Notes Africaines* [Dakar], No. 121, January 1969, 1-7.

———. "Les Migrations modernes en Afrique Occidentale," *Seminaire International Africain*, XI. Dakar: United Nations African Institute for Economic Planning and Development, 1972.

Diop, O.S. "Communication in Senegal," *American Scholar*, XXXV, No. 2, September 1966, 220-222.

Doob, Leonard W. *Communication in Africa: A Search for Boundaries.* New Haven: Yale University Press, 1961.

Dugué, Gil. *Vers les Etats-Unis d'Afrique.* (Preface by Modibo Keita.) Dakar: Editions "Lettres Africains," 1960.

Easton, Stewart C. *The Twilight of European Colonialism.* New York: Holt, Rinehart and Winston, 1960.

Foltz, William J. "The Political Parties of Senegal." In James S. Coleman and Carl Rosberg (eds.), *Political Parties and National Integration in Tropical Africa.* Berkeley: University of California Press, 1964.

———. "Social Structure and Political Behavior of Senegalese Elites," *Behavior Science Notes*, IV, No. 1, 1969, 145-163.

Fougeyrollas, Pièrre. *Pilot Project at Dakar.* (Reports and Papers on Mass Communications No. 50.) Paris: United Nations Educational, Scientific and Cultural Organization, 1967.

———. *Television and the Social Education of Women.* Paris: United Nations Educational, Scientific and Cultural Organization, 1967.

Gautron, Jean Claude. *L'Administration Sénégalaise.* Paris: Berger-Levrault, 1971.

Gonidec, P.R. *Constitutions des Etats de la Communauté.* Paris: Sirey, 1959.

Hachten, William A. *Mass Communication in Africa: An Annotated Bibliography.* Madison: University of Wisconsin, Center for International Communication Studies, 1971.

———. *Muffled Drums: The News Media in Africa.* Ames: Iowa State University, 1971.

Hare, A.P., et al. (eds.) *Small Groups: Studies in Social Interaction.* New York: Alfred Knopf, 1965.

Hazard, John N. "Negritude, Socialism, and the Law," *Columbia Law Review*, LXV, No. 4, May 1965, 778-809.

Heissler, Nina, et al. *Diffusion du Livre: Développement de la Lecture en Afrique, Tchad-Senegal.* Paris: Culture et Développement, 1971.

Hennebelle, Guy (ed.). "Les Cinémas africains en 1972," *L'Afrique Litteraire et Artistique* [Paris], No. 20, January-March 1972, 1-371.

Henry, Paul-Marc. "Pan-Africanism: A Dream Come True," *Foreign Affairs*, XXXVII, April 1959, 443-452.

Hodgkin, Thomas L. *African Political Parties*. (African Series, WA12.) London: Penguin, 1961.

Hodgkin, Thomas L., and Schachter, Ruth. "French-Speaking West Africa in Transition," *International Conciliation*, No. 528, May 1960, 375-436.

Hoffmann, Michel. "Research on Opinions and Attitudes in West Africa," *International Social Science Journal: Opinion Surveys in Developing Countries* [Paris], XV, No. 1, 1963, 59-69.

Hyman, Herbert H., and Singer, Eleanor (eds.) *Reading in Reference Group Theory and Research*. New York: Macmillan, 1968.

Kachama-Nkoy, Stéphane. "From Karl Marx to Pierre Teilhard de Chardin in the Thought of L.S. Senghor and Mamadou Dia," *Civilisations* [Brussels], XIII, Nos. 1-2, 1963, 98-121.

Kelman, Herbert C. (ed.) *International Behavior: A Socio-Psychological Analysis*. New York: Holt, Rinehart and Winston, 1965.

Kiba, Simon. "La Liberté de la presse dans les Etats d'Afrique," *Relations* [Montreal], No. 295, July 1965, 202-204.

Lavroff, Dmitri-Georges. *La République du Sénégal*. Paris: R. Pichon et Duran Auzias, 1967.

Lawrence, Robert de T. "In Rural Africa: New Frontiers for Journalism," *Quill*, LVII, No. 10, October 1970, 20-22.

Legum, Colin. "The Mass Media—Institutions of the African Political Systems." Pages 27-38 in Olav Stokke (ed.), *Reporting Africa*. New York: African Publishing Corporation, 1971.

————. *Pan-Africanism: A Short Political Guide*. New York: Praeger, 1962.

Maddison, John. *Radio and Television in Literacy: A Survey on the Use of Reports and Papers on Mass Communication*. No. 62, Paris: United Nations Educational, Scientific and Cultural Organization, 1971.

Markovitz, Irving L. "A Bibliographic Essay on the Study of Ideology, Political Thought, Development, and Politics in Senegal, Part I," *Current Bibliography on African Affairs* [Westport], III, No. 3, March 1970, 5-29.

————. "A Bibliographic Essay on the Study of Ideology, Political Thought, Development, and Politics in Senegal, Part II," *Current Bibliography on African Affairs* [Westport], III, No. 4, April 1970, 5-35.

————. *Léopold-Sédar Senghor and the Politics of Negritude*. New York: Atheneum Press, 1969.

————. "Traditional Social Structure: The Islamic Brotherhoods and Political Development in Senegal," *Journal of Modern African Studies* [London], VIII, No. 1, April 1970, 73-96.

Mercier, Paul. "Evolution of Senegalese Elites," *International Social Science Journal: African Elites* [Paris], VIII, No. 3, 1956, 441-452.

Morgenthau, Ruth Schachter. "African Socialism: Declaration of Ideological Independence," *Africa Report*, VIII, May 1963, 3-6.

Mortimer, Robert A. "From Federalism to Francophonia," *African Studies Review*, XV, No. 2, September 1972, 283-306.

Neres, Philip. *French-Speaking West Africa*. London: Oxford University Press, for Institute of Race Relations, 1962.

Pélissier, Paul. *Les Paysans du Sénégal: Les Civilisations Agraires du Cayor à la Casamance*. St. Yrieix: Imprimerie Fabrègue, 1966.

Pickles, Dorothy. *The Fifth French Republic*. New York: Praeger, 1960.

Robinson, Kenneth. "Political Development in French West Africa." Pages 140-181 in Calvin W. Stillman (ed.), *Africa in the Modern World*. Chicago: University of Chicago Press, 1955.

Saint-Martin, Yves. "Sénégal: Dix Ans d'Indépendance," *Europe-France Outremer* [Paris], March 1970, 6-59.

Schachter, Ruth. "Single-Party Systems in West Africa," *American Political Science Review*, LV, June 1961, 294-307.

Senegal. Assemblée Nationale. *Plan Quadriennal de Développement, 1961-1964*. (Loi Sénégalaise No. 61-32.) N.pl.: n. pub., n.d.

Senegal. Laws, Statutes, etc.

  Code du Travail. (Loi No. 61-34, June 15, 1961.) Rufisque: Imprimerie Officielle, 1961.

  Relatif aux Pouvoirs des Gouverneurs et de Leurs Adjoints. Décret No. 61-482, December 20, 1961.

  Sur l'Organisation de la Haute Cour de Justice et la Procédure Suivie Devant Elle. Loi Organique, No. 61-65, December 22, 1961.

Senegal. *Rapport Général sur les Perspectives de Développement du Sénégal*. (2d ed.) 2 vols. (Prepared by Compagnie d'Etudes Industrielles et d'Amenagement du Territoire and Société d'Etudes et de Réalisations Economiques et Sociales dans l'Agriculture.) Dakar: n.pub., July 1960.

Senegalese Target Groups: Media Habits and Exposure to USIS Programs. (R-26-70.) U.S. Information Agency, Office of Research and Assessment, 1970.

"Senegal," *Revue Française d'Etudes Politiques Africaines* [Paris], No. 8, March 1973, 19ff.

Senghor, Léopold-Sédar. "African Road to Socialism," *African Forum*, I, No. 3 (winter), 1966, 18-33.

―――. "Africans, Arabs, Israelis: A Triad of Suffering Peoples," *Africa Report*, XVII, No. 7, July 1972, 11-13.

―――. *On African Socialism*. New York: Praeger, 1964.

―――. "West Africa in Evolution," *Foreign Affairs*, XXXIX, No. 2, January 1961, 240-246.

―――. "What is 'Negritude'?" (Extracts from a lecture given at Oxford.) *West Africa* [London], November 4, 1961, 1211.

374

Skurnik, Walter A.E. *The Foreign Policy of Senegal.* Evanston: North-western University Press, 1972.

——. "Léopold-Sédar Senghor and African Socialism," *Journal of Modern African Studies* [London], III, No. 1, March 1965, 49–69.

Smith, Pierre. "Les Diankhanké, histoire d'un dispersion," *Bulletins et Mémoires de la Société d'Anthropologie de Paris* [Paris] (Series XI), VIII, No. 4, 1965, 231–302.

Spiro, Herbert J. *Politics in Africa: Prospects South of the Sahara.* Englewood Cliffs: Prentice-Hall, 1962.

Staar, Richard F. (ed.). *Yearbook on International Communist Affairs—1972.* Stanford: Hoover Institution Press, 1972.

Stokke, Olav (ed.). *Reporting Africa.* New York: Africana Publishing Corporation, 1971.

Strausz-Hupé, Robert, and Hazard, Harry W. (eds.). *The Idea of Colonialism.* (Foreign Policy Research Institute Series, University of Pennsylvania, No. 5.) New York: Praeger, 1958.

"10 Years of Senegalese Politics," *Moniteur Africaine* [Dakar], April 4, 1970, 15–24.

Thibaud, Paul. "Dia, Senghor, et le socialisme Africain." *Esprit* [Paris], XXXI, No. 9, September 1963, 332–348.

Union Progressiste Sénégalaise. Secrétariat Politique. *Le Militant U.P.S.* Dakar: UPS, n.d.

United Nations Educational, Scientific and Cultural Organization. *World Communications: Press, Radio, Television, Film.* Paris: UNESCO, 1964.

U.S. Department of Commerce. Office of Technical Services. Joint Publications Research Service—JPRS (Washington). The following items are from the JPRS series *Translations on Africa.*

"Decree Concerning Organization of the Presidency," *Journal Officiel de la République du Sénégal,* Dakar, March 7, 1970. (JPRS: 50,202, Series No. 883, 1970).

"Foreign Radio Advertising," *Agence France Presse,* Paris, May 19, 1971. (JPRS: 43,809, Series No. 250, 1971).

"Gambia's Readiness to Federate," *Le Soleil,* Dakar, February 11, 1972. (JPRS: 55,404, Series No. 1128, March 9, 1972).

"Major Marabouts Approved New Family Code," by A. N'Diay-Baudin. *Le Soleil,* Dakar, June 21, 1972. (JPRS: 56,614, Series No. 1191, July 26, 1972).

"Municipal Reforms Reported," by A.K. N'Daw. *Le Soleil,* Dakar, March 22, 1972. (JPRS: 55,723, Series No. 1144, April 17, 1972).

"Publication Suspended," *Afrique Nouvelle,* Paris, June 15, 1972. (JPRS: 56,344, Series No. 1175, 1972).

"Radio Broadcasting in Africa," by Michael Dircks. *Afrika Heute,* Bonn, October 1, 1971. (JPRS: 54,749, Series No. 1094, December 20, 1971).

"Results of Decentralization Authority Noted," by A.K. N'Daw.

Le Soleil, Dakar, March 29-31, 1973. (JPRS: 58,798, Series No. 1298, April 19, 1973).

"Senegal Adopts Constitutional Revisions," *Journal Officiel de la République du Sénégal,* Dakar, February 28, 1970. (JPRS: 50,205, Series No. 884, 1970).

"Senegalese—Malian Cooperation Expanded," by Bara Diouf, *Le Soleil,* Dakar, December 6, 1971. (JPRS: 54,923, Series No. 1101, February 11-12, 1972).

"Significance of Diouf's Visit to Mauretania," by Bara Diouf, *Le Soleil,* Dakar, October 7-8, 1972. (JPRS: 57,415, Series No. 1231, November 2, 1972).

"Spoken French Taught by Radio," by Guy Mandery and Pierre Dumont. *Coopération et Développement,* Paris, November-December 1971. (JPRS: 55,171, Series No. 1116, 1972).

"Text of President's State of the Nation Message," *Le Soleil,* Dakar, January 3, 1972. (JPRS: 55,071, Series No. 1111, February 1, 1972).

"12th URTNA Meeting Opens with Fraternal Message for Africa," *Le Soleil,* Dakar, December 17, 1971. (JPRS: 54,988, Series No. 1106, 1972).

U.S. Department of State. *World Strength of the Communist Party Organization, 1970.* Washington: Department of State, 1971.

Vieyra, Pantin. "Le Cinéma et l'Afrique," *Topic,* No. 70, December 1972, 30-33.

Witherell, Julian Wood. *The Response of the Peoples Cayor to French Penetration, 1850-1900.* Madison: University of Wisconsin, 1964.

World Peace Through Law Center. *Law and Judicial Systems of Nations.* Washington: World Peace Through Law Center, 1968.

World Radio-TV Handbook, 1973. (Ed., J.M. Frost.) Hvidovre: World Radio-TV Handbook, 1973.

Zuccarelli, François. *Un Parti Politique Africain: L'Union Progressiste Sénégalaise.* Paris: R. Pichon et R. Durand-Auzias, 1970.

(Various issues of the following periodicals were also used in the preparation of this section: *Africa Research Bulletin* [London], 1970-1973; *Christian Science Monitor,* January 1973-June 1973; *Washington Post,* January 1973-June 1973; and *West Africa* [London], January 1973-June 1973.)

Section III. Economic

Africa South of the Sahara. London: Europa Publications, 1973.

"Au Sénégal, les paysans disposent sans le savoir des remèdes contre la sécheresse," *Le Monde* [Paris], June 26, 1973, 19.

Banque Centrale des Etats de l'Afrique de l'Ouest. *Le Commerce Extérieur du Sénégal en 1970*. Dakar: n.pub., 1971.

Bentin, Lutz A. *Senegal als Wirtschaftspartner*. Cologne: Bundesstelle für Aussenhandels-Information, 1968.

Betz, Fritz H. *Entwicklungshilfe an Afrika*. Munich: IFO-Institut für Wirtschaftsforschung, 1970.

Bloom, Bridget. "An Enviable Stability," *Financial Times* [London], October 7, 1971, 32.

————. "Full-Scale Association Talks in Autumn," *Financial Times* [London], July 27, 1973, 6.

Brochier, J. *La Diffusion du Progrès Technique en Milieu Rural Sénégalais*. Paris: Presses Universitaires de France, 1968.

Brown, Godfrey. "Too Dependent on Groundnuts," *Financial Times* [London], October 7, 1971, 32.

"Les Comptes Economiques du Sénégal, 1969-1970," *Marchés Tropicaux et Méditerranéens* [Paris], XXVIII, No. 1424, February 23, 1973, 605-606.

Cruise O'Brien, Donal B. "Co-operators and Bureaucrats: Class Formation in a Senegalese Peasant Society," *Africa* [London], XLI, No. 4, October 1971, 263-278.

David, Jacques E. "La Communauté économique de l'Afrique de l'Ouest: Communauté de développement et espace de solidarité," *Marchés Tropicaux et Méditerranéens* [Paris], XXIX, No. 1444, July 13, 1973, 2185-2194.

Diarassouba, Valy-Charles. *L'Evolution des Structures Agricoles du Sénégal*. Paris: Editions Cujas, 1969.

Diop, Papa A. "Senegal: The Battle to Create Employment," *ILO Panorama* [Geneva], March-April 1970, 18-27.

Dubois, Jean-Paul. *L'Emigration des Serer vers la zone arachidière orientale*. Dakar: Office de la Recherche Scientifique et Technique Outre-Mer, 1971.

Ediafric-Service. *L'Economie Sénégalaise*. Paris: Ediafric, 1970.

————. *Memento de l'Economie Africaine*. Paris: Ediafric, 1972.

Food and Agriculture Organization. *Approaches to International Action on World Trade in Oilseeds, Oils and Fats*. Rome: FAO, 1971.

Heuss, George. *Senegal: Voraussetzungen und Möglichkeiten der In-*

dustriellen Entwicklung. Series Afrika Industrieberichte no 15. Hamburg: Afrika-Verein, 1971.

Institut de Science Economique Appliquée. *Les Aspects du Problème Vivrier Sénégalaise.* Dakar: Ministère de l'Economie Rurale de Sénégal, 1965.

International Monetary Fund. *International Financial Statistics.* Washington: IMF, June 1973.

————. *Surveys of African Economies,* III: Dahomey, Ivory Coast, Mauritania, Niger, Senegal, Togo, and Upper Volta. Washington: IMF, 1970.

Lewis, Paul. "Economy Must Diversify to Solve Present Crisis," *Financial Times* [London], October 7, 1971, 31.

Le Marché Sénégalais. (Special issue of *Marchés Tropicaux et Méditerranéens.*) [Paris], XXVI, No. 1283, June 13, 1970, entire issue.

May, Jacques M., and McLellan, Donna L. *The Ecology of Malnutrition in the French Speaking Countries of West Africa and Madagascar.* New York: Hafner, 1968.

Organization for Economic Cooperation and Development. *Development Assistance: 1972 Review.* Paris: OECD, 1972.

————. *Resources for the Developing World: The Flow of Financial Resources to Less-Developed Countries, 1962–1968.* Paris: OECD, n.d.

Pélissier, Paul. *Les Paysans du Sénégal: Les Civilisations Agraires du Cayor à la Casamance.* St. Yrieix: Imprimerie Fabrègue, 1966.

Peterec, Richard J. *Dakar and West African Economic Development.* New York: Columbia University Press, 1967.

Pfeffermann, Guy. *Industrial Labor in the Republic of Senegal.* New York: Praeger, 1968.

Plessz, Nicolas G. *Problems and Prospects of Economic Integration in West Africa.* Montreal: McGill University Press, 1968.

Reverdy, J.C. *Une Société Rurale au Sénégal—les Structures Foncières, Familiales, et Villageoises des Serer.* Aix-en-Provence: Centre Africain des Sciences Humaines Appliquées, 1967.

Rocheteau, G. *Pionniers Mourides au Sénégal: Changement Technique et Transformations d'une Economie Paysanne.* Dakar: Office de la Recherche Scientifique et Technique Outre-Mer, 1970.

Sampaio, Mario. "Senegal's Groundnut Crop Makes Dramatic Recovery," *African Development* [London], July 1972, 12–13.

Sampson, Henry (ed.). *Jane's World Railways, 1971–72.* New York: McGraw-Hill, 1972.

Seck, Assane. *Dakar, Métropole Ouest-Africaine.* Dakar: Institut Fondamental d'Afrique Noire, 1970.

Seck, Mansour. "Etude des Principaux Facteurs Agrométéorologiques au Sénégal," *L'Agronomie Tropicale* [Paris], XXV, No. 3, March 1970, 241–276.

Senegal. Commissariat à l'Information. *Sénégal, Faits et Chiffres.* Dakar: n.pub., 1965.

Senegal. Ministère des Finances et des Affaires Economiques. Direction de la Statistique. *Bulletin Statistique et Economique Mensuel, 1972,* Nos. 7 and 8. Dakar: n.pub., 1972.

———. *Comptes Economiques: Année, 1969-70.* Dakar: n.pub., December 1972.

———. *Situation Economique du Sénégal, 1971.* Dakar: n.pub., 1972.

Senegal. Ministère du Développement Rural. Direction des Services Agricoles. *Rapport Annuel: Campagne 1971/72.* Dakar: n.pub., 1972.

U.S. Department of Agriculture. *World Supply and Demand Prospects for Oilseeds and Oilseed Products in 1980.* (Foreign Agriculture Economic Report No. 71.) Washington: GPO, 1971.

Vanhaeverbeke, André. *Rémunération du Travail et Commerce Extérieur.* Louvain: Centre de Recherches des Pays en Développement, 1970.

(Various issues of the following periodicals were also used in the preparation of this section: *Africa: An International Business, Economic and Political Monthly* [London], January 1972-June 1973; *Africa Research Bulletin* [London], January 1971-June 1973; IMF *International Financial Statistics* [Washington], January 1960-June 1973; *Jeune Afrique* [Paris], January 1971-June 1973; *Marchés Tropicaux et Méditerranéens* [Paris], January 1971-June 1973; FAO *Monthly Bulletin of Agricultural Economics and Statistics* [Rome], January 1969-June 1973; *West Africa* [London], January 1972-June 1973; *World Agricultural Economics and Rural Sociology Abstracts* [Oxford], No. 1, 1970-No. 2, 1973; and *World Agricultural Production and Trade* [Washington], January 1972-May 1973.)

Section IV. National Security

Afrique Occidentale Française. 2 vols. (Under the direction of Eugène Guernier.) Paris: Encyclopédie Coloniale et Maritime, 1949.

Ball, M.J.V. *Army and Nation in Subsaharan Africa.* (Adelphi Papers, No. 21.) London: Institute for Strategic Studies, 1965.

Booth, Richard. *The Armed Forces of African States, 1970.* (Adelphi Papers, No. 67.) London: Institute for Strategic Studies, 1970.

Chailley, M., et al. *Notes et Etudes sur l'Islam en Afrique Noire.* (Recherches et Documents, I.) Paris: Centre de Hautes Etudes Administratives sur l'Afrique et l'Asie Modernes, 1962.

Coleman, James S., and Brice, Belmont, Jr. "The Role of the Military in Sub-Saharan Africa." Pages 359-405 in John J. Johnson (ed.), *The Role of the Military in Underdeveloped Countries.* Princeton: Princeton University Press, 1962.

Cornevin, Robert. *Histoire des Peuples de l'Afrique Noire.* Paris: Berger-Levrault, 1960.

Crowder, Michael. *Senegal: A Study in French Assimilation Policy.* London: Oxford University Press, for Institute of Race Relations, 1962.

Davis, Edward Braxton, III. "Relations Between France and Senegal, 1960-69." Unpublished doctoral dissertation, Woodrow Wilson Department of Government and Foreign Affairs, University of Virginia, 1970.

France. Laws, Statutes, etc. *Codes de Justice Militaire.* Paris: Jurisprudence Générale Dalloz, 1961.

French West Africa. Gouvernement Général. *Procédure Criminelle en Afrique Occidentale Française. Code d'Instruction Criminelle et Annexes.* Rufisque: Imprimerie du Gouvernement Général, 1956.

French West Africa. Haut Commissariat. Direction Générale des Affaires Politiques. *Relevé des Textes Relatifs à la Protection de l'Ordre Publique.* Rufisque: Imprimerie du Gouvernement Général, 1957.

Garnier, Christine, and Ermont, Philippe. *Sénégal, Porte de l'Afrique.* Paris: Librairie Hachette, 1962.

Great Britain. Naval Intelligence Division. *French West Africa.* 2 vols. Oxford: University Press, under the authority of HMSO, 1943, 1944.

Guid'Ouest Africain: L'Afrique Occidentale, 1961-1962. Dakar: Agence Havas, 1961.

Guillot, E.J. *Code Pénal Analytique.* Paris: Libraires Techniques, Librairie de la Cour de Cassation, 1959.

Gutteridge, William. *Armed Forces in New States*. London: Oxford University Press, 1962.

Histoire et Epopée des Troupes Coloniales. Paris: Presse Moderne, 1956.

Ingold, Commandant François. *Les Troupes Noires au Combat*. Paris: Berger-Levrault, 1940.

Lubrano-Lavadera, Capitaine. *Législation et Administration Militaires*. Paris: Berger-Levrault, 1954.

Mangin, Gilbert. *L'Organisation Judiciaire des Etats d'Afrique et de Madagascar*. Paris: Librairie Générale de Droit et de Jurisprudence, 1962.

Marchand, Général Jean. *Vérités sur l'Afrique Noire*. Paris: Peyronnet, 1959.

The Military Balance, 1972–73. London: Institute for Strategic Studies, 1972.

Robert, André-P. *L'Evolution des Coutumes de l'Ouest Africain et la Législation Française*. (Bibliothèque Juridique de l'Union Française.) Paris: Encyclopédie d'Outre-mer, 1955.

Salacuse, Jeswald. *An Introduction to Law in French-Speaking Africa*, I: Africa South of the Sahara. Charlottesville: Michie, 1969.

Senegal. *La Justice au Sénégal*. Rufisque: Imprimerie Nationale, 1962.

Senegal. Laws, Statutes, etc.

　Code de Justice Militaire pour l'Armée de Terre. Paris: Charles-Lavauzelle, 1950.

　Code de Procédure Pénal. Dakar: 1966.

　Code Pénal et Code des Contraventions. Dakar: 1966.

　Code Pénal. Paris: Jurisprudence Générale Dalloz, 1958.

Senegal. Service de Presse. *Sénégal Faits et Chiffres*. Dakar: Service de Presse, 1962.

"Senegal-New Government," *Africa Research Bulletin* [London], X, No. 4, April 1-30, 1973, 2819.

"Senegal—School Protests," *Africa* [London], No. 21, May 1973, 44–45.

"Senegal: Senghor on Diop's Death," *West Africa* [London], No. 2922, June 11, 1973, 792.

Thompson, Virginia, and Adloff, Richard. *French West Africa*. Stanford: Stanford University Press, 1958.

U.S. Department of Commerce. Office of Technical Services. Joint Publications Research Service—JPRS (Washington). The following items are from the JPRS series *Translations on Africa*.

　"Army to Handle 50 Percent of Civil Engineering Tasks," *Le Soleil*, Dakar, September 29, 1972. (JPRS: 57,442, Series No. 1232, 1972).

　"Decree on Organization of Defense," *Journal Officiel de la République du Sénégal*, Dakar, December 2, 1972, (JPRS: 57,936, Series No. 1250, 1973).

　"French Role in Army Engineer Corps Development Reported," *L'Armée*, Paris, April 1971. (JPRS: 53,237, Series No. 1039, 1971).

　"National Defense Direction Decrees Promulgated," *Journal Offi-*

ciel de la République du Sénégal, Dakar, June 27, 1970. (JPRS: 51,126, Series No. 930, 1970).

"Reorganization of Armed Forces, National Police Decreed," *Journal Officiel de la République du Sénégal*, Dakar, June 24, 1972. (JPRS: 56,817, Series No. 1110, 1972).

"Retiring Chief of Staff's Career, Succession Appraised," by Pierre Biarnes, *Revue Française d'Etudes Politiques Africaines*, Paris, July 1972. (JPRS: 56,914, Series No. 1208, 1972).

"Senegalese Army Defends Boundary Against Portuguese Invasions," by Abdon Salam Kane, *Le Soleil*, Dakar, July 22, 1970. (JPRS: 51,210, Series No. 935, 1970).

"Two Plotters Pardoned," *Le Soleil*, Dakar, April 5, 1973. (JPRS: 58,888, Series No. 1303, May 1, 1973).

U.S. Department of State. *World Strength of the Communist Party Organization.* Washington: Department of State, 1971.

Weygand, Général Maxime. *Histoire de l'Armée Française.* Paris: Flammarion, 1953.

GLOSSARY

AOF—Afrique Occidentale Française (French West Africa). Federation of French West African territories established in 1904; replaced by membership in French Community (*q.v.*) beginning in 1958.

assimilation—The French policy aimed at political and cultural integration of colonial peoples into the French nation.

caliph—A title given to heads of Islamic brotherhoods in Senegal, especially to the head of the Muridiya order.

caste—Traditionally, one of several groups each of which is marked by an inherited occupation. Membership in such a group is fixed by birth. Its members are ranked above slaves but below nobles and ordinary freemen.

CFA franc—Currency of the Communauté Financière Africaine (African Financial Community), which is linked to the French franc (CFAF50 equal 1 French franc). From 1958 through 1968 the rate of exchange was CFAF246.8 per US$1. From August 10, 1969, through November 1971 the rate was CFAF277.8 per US$1. From December 1971, when the United States dollar was first devalued, through January 1973 the rate was CFAF255.79 per US$1. After the second devaluation in February 1973, the general exchange rate became CFAF230.2 per US$1.

clan—Senegalese term for a group organized around a person of standing and dependent on him. Such a group competes or coalesces with others in the quest for social and political status and power.

commune—Self-governing municipality; historically, the four urban communes of Saint-Louis, Gorée, Rufisque, and Dakar.

endogamy—Marriage within a group; in Senegal usually the practice of taking a spouse from the traditional social stratum to which one belongs, but sometimes the term refers to marriage within an ethnic group.

exogamy—Marriage outside a group; in Senegal usually the practice of taking a spouse from a lineage or clan other than one's own.

extended family—A group consisting of two or more related nuclear families; for example, a man, his wife or wives, his married sons, their wives and children.

franc area—The monetary area formed by the states of the former French Community (*q.v.*) with the exception of French Somaliland but with the addition of Tunisia, Togo, and Cameroon. The currencies of these countries are tied to the French franc and are freely transferable. Also known as the franc zone.

French Community—A politicoeconomic association of France and its former overseas possessions. Formed in 1958, it replaced the French Union, which was the successor of the French colonial empire. Although technically the association continues to exist, all of its institutions have ceased to function.

GDP—Gross domestic product. The total value of productive activity occurring within the national borders, theoretically obtained by adding up the estimated value added by each productive sector of the economy. The value added by each producer is equivalent to actual or imputed wages, profits, and other incomes payable for factor services. GDP differs from gross national product (GNP), which excludes the value net factor payments to nonresidents (interest, profits, and salary remittances). Monetary GDP excludes the imputed value of subsistence production.

griot—A member of a traditional caste (found in most ethnic groups) of musicians, genealogists, and praise singers; the term may be applied in the modern context to anyone who regularly sings another's praises.

harmattan—Warm, dry northeast wind from the Sahara Desert that prevails over most of Senegal and other West African countries during the dry season.

IFAN—Institut Fondamental d'Afrique Noire (Basic Institute of Black Africa). Established in 1938 by the French for research in the physical sciences, ethnology, history, and economics of former French Africa. Originally known as Institut Français d'Afrique Noire (French Institute of Black Africa), it was reconstituted and renamed in 1959. In 1963 it was attached to the University of Dakar.

indigénat—System of French colonial disciplinary law; abolished in 1945.

lineage (patrilineage, matrilineage)—A group of people who can trace their descent from a known common ancestor; a patrilineage if descent is traced through males only, a matrilineage if descent is traced only through females.

loi-cadre—Legislation passed by French Parliament in 1956, setting up a new structural framework for governing the overseas territories. It granted universal suffrage and gave broad legislative powers to the territorial assemblies.

lycée—Classical French secondary school providing an almost exclusively academic education.

marabout—Term applied in Senegalese Islam to a variety of persons ranging from those who prepare protective amulets containing a verse from the Koran to teachers of the Koran and leaders of Islamic brotherhoods.

métis—Descendants of European-African unions, they formed a special group in nineteenth- and twentieth-century Senegalese towns. Term is sometimes applied to descendants of Portuguese-African unions from the Cape Verde Islands who are settled in Senegal.

Muride—A member of the Muridiya, an Islamic brotherhood.

nuclear family—A group consisting of a man, his wife, and their unmarried children.

originaires—assimilated Africans born in one of the four self-governing urban communes (*q.v.*) of Senegal. During the time of federation of French West Africa, they possessed the legal rights of French citizens but were allowed to retain their own private or customary law in certain categories, such as civil disputes, inheritance, marriage, and divorce.

petit blanc—A European wageworker or small shopkeeper; may be used in a derogatory sense.

polygyny—Practice of having two or more wives simultaneously; a man, his wives, and their children constitute a polygynous family.

serigne—Title applied to marabouts, particularly of Muridiya brotherhood; sometimes given to any pious, learned Muslim. May be used as a given name.

UPS—Union Progressiste Sénégalaise (Senegalese Progressive Union). President Senghor's governing political party.

World Bank Group—Consists of the International Bank for Reconstruction and Development (IBRD) and its two financial affiliates, the International Finance Corporation (IFC), which became operational in 1956, and the International Development Association (IDA), which became operational in 1960. IFC works specifically with the private sector in developing countries, and IDA operates in the same sectors and with the same policies as the IBRD but provides credits only to the poorer developing countries and on easier terms than conventional IBRD loans.

INDEX

Abidjan conference: 317
Accord on Cooperation in Matters of Defense: 336
Addis Ababa: 240
Adrar: 68
adult education: 160, 165–166
Africa: 1, 17, 22, 24, 33, 216; and peacekeeping, 221
African and Malagasy Associates (Etats Africains et Malgaches Associés— EAMA): x
African Democratic Assembly (Rassemblement Démocratique Africain—RDA): 31, 32, 34
African Filmmakers Association (Fédération Panafricaine des Cinéastes— FEPACI): 149
African Financial Community (Communauté Financière Africaine—CFA): 261, 262
African Financial Community franc (Communauté Financière Africaine franc— CFAF): viii, ix
African Liberation Committee: ix, 222
African, Malagasy, and Mauritius Common Organization (Organisation Commune Africaine, Malgache, et Mauricienne— OCAM): ix, 5, 221
African National Radio-Television Union (Union des Radio-Television Nationales Africaines—URTNA): 231
African Party for the Independence of Guinea and the Cape Verde Islands (Parti Africain pour l'Indépendance de la Guinea et des Iles du Cap-Vert—PAIGC): 222, 223, 350, 351
African Party of Independence (Parti Africain d'Indépendance—PAI): 32, 36, 189, 193, 196
African Publishing Company: (Société Africaine d'Editions et de Publication): 240
African Realignment Party of Senegal (Parti du Regroupement Africain-Sénégal—PRA-Sénégal): 36, 190, 193, 195
African School of Medicine: 157
African Socialist Movement (Mouvement Socialiste Africain—MSA): 32

africanization: 79, 191, 209
Afrique Medicale: 237, 238
Afrique Noire: 236
Afrique Nouvelle: 236
L'Afrique Occidentale Française: 236
Afro-Asian Dance Festival: 148
age-groups: 89, 95, 97, 102
Agency for International Development: 120
agricultural cooperative: 37, 228
Agricultural Development Agency: 275
Agricultural Marketing Board: 274
Agricultural Program (Programme Agricole—PA): 291
agriculture (see also cattle, crops, farms and farming, food supply, grains, livestock): 6, 7, 20, 27, 44, 56, 57, 62, 70, 75, 84, 87, 90, 97, 101, 103, 176, 204, 265–294; and credit, 263, 264; and economy, 244, 245, 247, 255, 304; expenditures, 260; and labor, 202; planning, 37; and religion, 133, 135; and research, 155; settlements, 2, 54–55, 57, 63; training, 160, 164, 165, 167, 224; and transportation, 324, 326; and wildlife, 54
Aid and Cooperation Fund (Fonds d'Aide et Coopération—FAC): 37
Air Afrique: 330
air force: x, 334, 338, 339, 341; and France, 337
Air France: 321, 330
Air Senegal: 330
air transportation: ix, 304, 324, 325, 330
Albania: 216
Algiers: 28
Alliance Française: 149, 156
almany: 13
Almoravids: 12, 69, 75
alms: 99, 127
America (see also North America): 16; and air transportation, 330
American Cultural Center: 156
Amina: 240
amulets: 75, 102, 117, 118, 130, 140
Angel Gabriel: 126
animal traction: 289
animals, domestic. See cattle, livestock
Applied Linguistics Center of Dakar (Cen-

389

69, 70, 71, 74, 75, 81, 90, 91, 94, 199, 298; and agriculture, 266, 269, 270, 278, 282, 283, 286; and security, 341; and transportation, 329
Sisters of Saint-Joseph of Cluny: 18
slash-and-burn technique: 286, 287, 288
slaves: 12, 14, 15, 16, 18, 79, 83, 84, 85, 87, 88, 89, 90, 93, 94, 96, 98, 99, 126, 131, 132, 136, 140, 283, 284; and civil liberties, 173, and employment, 251
Socé, Ousmane: 151, 152
Socé people: 72
social change: 2, 3, 98–103
social classes (*see also* caste, chiefs, elite, middle class, nobles, slaves, social stratification, warriors): 77, 83–103; and Marxism, 203–204
social reform: 28, 98–103
social security: 121, 179; rural, 122
social stratification (*see also* social classes): 66, 71, 74, 75, 83–103
socialists and socialism: 28, 32, 36, 192, 193, 196, 202; African socialism, 203–204, 208
soil: 44, 45, 46, 50–51, 55, 58, 106, 115, 118, 243, 265, 266, 269, 278, 286, 287
Le Soleil du Senegal: 195, 237, 238
Songhai empire: 12
Songrougrou River: 47, 52
Soninké. *See* Sarakolé people
soottiBe: 85, 88
sorghum: 115, 116, 265, 268, 272, 275, 277, 278, 279, 280, 284, 286, 289, 313
Sosse. *See* Socé people
soudure: 107, 115
South Africa: 6
Soviet Union: 31, 53, 196, 216, 235, 241, 305; and fishing, 295; and press, 240
Spain: 241, 294
spirit worship: 102, 125, 138–140, 145
statut personnel: 24, 29
stockraising. *See* livestock
strikes: 4, 183, 190, 333, 348
students: 2, 3, 4, 36, 38, 86, 88, 100, 142, 162, 163, 164, 168, 169; and disorders, 333, 344, 345, 348–349; and films, 150; and media, 232–233; in politics, 194, 202, 211; and protests, 166, 169, 190, 191, 224
subalBe: 85, 86
sub-Saharan area: 21
Sudan: 7
Suez Canal: 304; area, 335
suffrage (*see also* franchise): viii, 23, 26, 30, 33, 172, 174, 177, 185, 186
Sufism: 130
sugar: 114, 277, 281, 301, 311, 312, 313, 315, 322

Sunna: 126
Supreme Council of the Public Service: 183
Supreme Court: viii, 179, 180, 181, 182
Supreme Defense Council: 174, 338, 339
suudu: 101–102
Swahili language: 80
Sweden: 309, and socialism, 203
Switzerland: 161, 216
Syrians: 77
Sy, Al Haj Malik: 129, 132
taboos: 61, 116
Taiba: 53, 327
talibé: 91, 133, 134
tamal: 147
Tambacounda: 56, 63, 75, 137, 296, 302; and airways, 330; and media, 234; and security, 338
Taoué: 47
tariffs (*see also* customs, duties): 247, 259, 297, 312, 317, 318, 319
TASS: 240
taxes: 24, 255, 256, 257, 260: export, 273; local, 186, 187; structure of, 259; and trade, 318
teachers: vii, 156, 160, 161, 162, 184, 210; and disorders, 333; and France, 217, 218; and media, 234; training, 157, 165
Teachers Union of Senegal (Syndicat des Enseignants du Sénégal—SES): 197, 349
technical education and vocational training: vii, 158, 159, 160, 162, 163, 164–165, 253; and armed forces, 342; and France, 217
Teilhard de Chardin, Pierre: 153, 203
Tekrur: 13, 18, 71, 126
telecommunications satellite: ix, 173, 330, 331
telephones: 113, 114, 330
television: 165, 166, 227, 231, 235
tenants: 92
Terres Neuves (New Lands): 27, 63, 78, 91, 92, 94, 102; agriculture, 269, 282, 284
Terres Neuves Resettlement Pilot Project: 289, 290, 291
textbooks: 160, 161, 167
textiles: 249, 282, 299–300, 314, 315, 316, 322
Thailand: 306, 307
The Gambia: 1, 5, 22, 39, 40, 41, 46, 47, 50, 51, 62, 66, 72, 114; and agriculture, 273, 274, 282, 283; and foreign relations, 213, 214, 216, 218–219; and trade, 316, 317; and transportation, 328
Thiès Region: 40, 42, 53, 55, 59, 69, 74, 81, 99, 120, 298; and agriculture, 266, 270, 272, 280, 282, 286; and economy, 256; and electric power, 302; and fishing, 295; and poli-

PUBLISHED AREA HANDBOOKS

550-65	Afghanistan		550-30	Japan
550-98	Albania		550-34	Jordan
550-44	Algeria		550-56	Kenya
550-59	Angola		550-50	Khmer Republic (Cambodia)
550-73	Argentina		550-81	Korea, North
550-66	Bolivia		550-41	Korea, Republic of
550-20	Brazil		550-58	Laos
550-168	Bulgaria		550-24	Lebanon
550-61	Burma		550-38	Liberia
550-83	Burundi		550-85	Libya
550-166	Cameroon		550-163	Malagasy Republic
550-96	Ceylon		550-45	Malaysia
550-159	Chad		550-161	Mauritania
550-77	Chile		550-79	Mexico
550-60	China, People's Rep. of		550-76	Mongolia
550-63	China, Rep. of		550-49	Morocco
550-26	Colombia		550-64	Mozambique
550-67	Congo, Democratic Rep. of (Zaire)		550-35	Nepal, Bhutan and Sikkim
550-91	Congo, People's Rep. of		550-88	Nicaragua
550-90	Costa Rica		550-157	Nigeria
550-152	Cuba		550-94	Oceania
550-22	Cyprus		550-48	Pakistan
550-158	Czechoslovakia		550-46	Panama
550-54	Dominican Republic		550-156	Paraguay
550-155	East Germany		550-92	Peripheral States of the Arabian Peninsula
550-52	Ecuador		550-42	Peru
550-150	El Salvador		550-72	Philippines
550-28	Ethiopia		550-162	Poland
550-167	Finland		550-160	Romania
550-29	Germany		550-84	Rwanda
550-153	Ghana		550-51	Saudi Arabia
550-87	Greece		550-70	Senegal
550-78	Guatemala		550-86	Somalia
550-82	Guyana		550-93	South Africa, Republic of
550-164	Haiti		550-95	Soviet Union
550-151	Honduras		550-27	Sudan, Democratic Republic of
550-165	Hungary		550-47	Syria
550-21	India		550-62	Tanzania
550-154	Indian Ocean Territories		550-53	Thailand
550-39	Indonesia		550-89	Tunisia
550-68	Iran		550-80	Turkey
550-31	Iraq		550-74	Uganda
550-25	Israel		550-43	United Arab Republic (Egypt)
550-69	Ivory Coast			

550-97	Uruguay	550-55	Vietnam, South
550-71	Venezuela	550-99	Yugoslavia
550-57	Vietnam, North	550-75	Zambia

*U.S. Government Printing Office: 1974 0—585–917) (2)